"J. Blake Fichera has delve~ ~~~p.y ....
finding that rear lobe of the brain where terror connects with
sound. Some of these composers are well known to horror
aficionados, others will be surprising discoveries, but all of
them have something unique to say about this least
understood aspect of genre filmmaking."
— Joe Bob Briggs, movie critic and author of
Profoundly Disturbing: Shocking Movies that Changed History!

"Horror is a genre that has generated many of the film
world's most original and influential scores. In *Scored to Death*,
J. Blake Fichera has assembled an impressive international cast of
scary-music masters—and he knows what to ask, when to listen,
and how to follow up on their behind-the-terror insights."
— Michael Schelle, author of *The Score*

"This was music to my eyes! About time someone
shined a light on the unsung heroes who compose many
of the soundtracks of our nightmares. Great insight
into their varied approaches to the craft."
— Jeff Lieberman, director of *Squirm, Blue Sunshine,* and *Just Before Dawn*

"The men in this book create music that
makes our adrenaline pump and our fists clench.
Reading it is a mini course in mastering horror."
— Rob Schmidt, director of *Wrong Turn* and *The Alphabet Killer*

"Too rarely do we hear from the maestros of film music,
so preoccupied are we with the auteurs behind the camera
and the actors that fill the frame.... J. Blake Fichera goes a long
way towards correcting that. The musicians in this generous
volume are given the time to reveal themselves and their
processes. What emerges is a better understanding of the
demands of the craft and the essential influence that
the film score has on the audience's experience."
— Larry Fessenden, director of *Habit, Wendigo,* and *The Last Winter*

SCORED TO DEATH

CONVERSATIONS
WITH SOME OF
HORROR'S
GREATEST
COMPOSERS

J. BLAKE FICHERA

SILMAN-JAMES PRESS   LOS ANGELES

First Edition
10 9 8 7 6 5 4 3 2 1

Photo credits:
Nathan Barr: Photo by Remy Boudet
Charles Bernstein: Still from a video shot by Georgianne Cowan
Joseph Bishara: Photo by Shem Andre Byron
Simon Boswell: Photo by LG White
John Carpenter: Photo by Sophie Gransard. © Storm King Productions
Jay Chattaway: Photo provided by Jay Chattaway
Fabio Frizzi: Photo provided by Fabio Frizzi
Jeff Grace: Photo by Adriana Grace
Maurizio Guarini: Photo provided by Maurizio Guarini
Tom Hajdu: Photo provided by Tom Hajdu
Alan Howarth: Photo by Jason "Jaypoc" Bauman
Harry Manfredini: Photo by Katrina Zemrak
Claudio Simonetti: Photo by Fabio Capuzzo
Christopher Young: Photo by Joaquin Montalvan

Library of Congress Cataloging-in-Publication Data

Names: Fichera, J. Blake, interviewer.
Title: Scored to death : conversations with some of horror's greatest
composers / [interviews] by J. Blake Fichera.
Description: First edition. | Los Angeles : Silman-James Press, [2016]
Identifiers: LCCN 2016015520 (print) | LCCN 2016015875 (ebook) | ISBN
9781935247142 (alk. paper) | ISBN 9781935247142
Subjects: LCSH: Film composers--Interviews. | Motion picture music--History
and criticism. | Horror films--History and criticism.
Classification: LCC ML2075 .S45 2016 (print) | LCC ML2075 (ebook) | DDC
781.5/420922--dc23

Cover design by Wade Lageose

Printed and bound in the United States of America

Silman-James Press

www.silmanjamespress.com

Dedicated to

Wes Craven
(1939–2015)

His work continues to inspire generations of dreamers . . .
and dream warriors.

CONTENTS

FOREWORD

BY LARRY FESSENDEN

SOME OF THE MOST ICONIC films in the history of cinema are distinguished by their soundtracks. Who can think of Hitchcock without hearing the theme to *Psycho* or *North by Northwest* (Bernard Herrmann scores) in their head? Or *Jaws* without John Williams's shark theme? *Taxi Driver* (Bernard Hermann again, his last score), *Chinatown* (Jerry Goldsmith), *The Godfather* (Nino Rota), *To Kill a Mockingbird* (Elmer Bernstein), and *Charade* (Henry Mancini) are all classic films with indelible themes. Then there is *Star Wars* and *Harry Potter* (Williams again) and Christopher Nolan's *Batman* trilogy (Hans Zimmer/James Newton Howard). Where would Tim Burton be without composer Danny Elfman so perfectly capturing the dark and whimsical melancholy of his better films?

May I mention a few of my favorite scores? Check out the soundtracks to *Ravenous* (Damon Albarn and Michael Nyman) and Coppola's *Dracula* (Wojciech Kilar) and del Toro's *Pan's Labyrinth* (Javier Navarrete) and Polanski's *The Tenant* (Philippe Sarde) and *Dead Man Walking* (David Robbins, Nusrat Fateh Ali Khan) and *The Cook, the Thief, His Wife & Her Lover* (Nyman) and the largely unused soundtrack by Ennio Morricone for John Carpenters's *The Thing* (Tarantino recycled an essential track from this for *The Hateful Eight*). I will always remember an evening when *The Shining* (score by Wendy Carlos) was playing on the TV in another room, and that the music alone, without the visuals, was terrifying.

Too rarely do we hear from the maestros of film music, so preoccupied are we with the auteurs behind the camera and the actors that fill the frame. In this collection of interviews, J. Blake Fichera goes a long way towards correcting that. The musicians in this generous volume are given the time to reveal themselves and their processes. What emerges is a better understanding of the demands of the craft and the essential influence that the film score has on the audience's experience.

There's a lot to chew on in this book, but some comments struck a nerve with me, and I already feel like I have benefited from the insights herein, so let me share a few of them, as a way of whetting your appetite.

I was struck but Alan Howarth's observation that sound effects are music. This is a tremendously valuable perspective, acknowledging that the overall film mix is a combination of score, sound effects, and ambiences, not to mention dialogue. It is the very special alchemy of a film soundtrack that forces music to be accompanied by the percussion of footsteps or gunfire or stabbing or a scream, the underlying drone of a steady wind or cricket ambience, the insistent chatter of dialogue, or even the lone hoot of an owl: It is the marriage of effects and score that creates the music of film.

Simon Boswell says that repetition is such an essential part of music, and while he might well be speaking about the rudiments of a pop song, the fact is there needs to be a certain simplicity to a movie score for it to establish itself and achieve an emotional resonance in two hours.

The great John Carpenter, who of course created one of the most memorable film scores of all time with *Halloween*, discusses the difference between "Mickey Mousing" and "underscoring." He makes the essential distinction between commenting on and synching up with the action on screen versus laying an atmospheric bed. Scores still do both, and which way to go becomes a conversation between composer and director.

A shout-out to Christopher Young, who confesses that the only way he was able to really listen to film scores before VHS rentals existed was to sneak into theaters and record a movie's audio onto cassette tape. That's how I myself gained an appreciation for sound and music in film; the only way a kid in the Seventies could revisit a picture over and over was through this benign form of pirating.

Finally, I want to highlight my own collaborator who appears in these pages, Mr. Jeff Grace. He makes the observation that I have always found invaluable in our work together that the composer, often confronted with a near-complete film, has the obligation to unify the movie and themes with the score, bring disparate scenes together, and make connections musically that will then provide a roadmap for the audience: The composer has responsibilities to the narrative as well as emotion and mood.

I write this with the enthusiasm of a film buff excited to see an essential aspect of the craft highlighted. What I have downplayed in this foreword is the genre we are speaking of in this book—horror. Let's be honest here: Music for horror movies is particularly exciting, immersive, effective, and scary when done right.

Now let's hear from some guys who know how to do it right.

Larry Fessenden
April 2016

PREFACE

I<small>T'S A BRISK</small> O<small>CTOBER NIGHT</small> in 2013, and I'm standing in a crowd of strangers in a dark and dank club in Brooklyn, New York. The room is humid, and the stench of pot smoke and stale beer wafts through the air. The lights fade to total darkness, and we all stand in silent anticipation as a powerful PA system bounces the sounds of heavy breathing, a woman screaming, and eerie whispering voices saying things like *Help me!*, *I'm watching you!*, and *Go away!* around the room. Though it is like something out of a surreal nightmare, I am not afraid. Instead, nervous excitement—like a thousand fluttering butterflies—fills my stomach.

Suddenly the stage lights ignite, and the audience erupts with unbridled cheer as the Italian progressive rock band Goblin launches into a furious track titled "Magic Thriller." For this cinephile, music lover, and musician, it is truly a dream come true.

It is the first time the group has toured America, and though the original lineup is not completely intact, they sound amazing. For more than ninety minutes, the band tears through a set that includes all the iconic themes that they produced for Italian horror maestro Dario Argento's legendary films, while aesthetically gorgeous film clips infused with spaghetti-flavored gore play on an enormous screen behind them. In some ways, I feel as if I am the protagonist of my own Argento film and Goblin is scoring my narrative. At any moment I could witness a horrific murder or worse—the crowd around me could turn into demons and try to eat me.

During a particularly rocking version of keyboardist Claudio Simonetti's theme for the film *Phenomena* (1985), I look around the room and realize that I am not the only one living out a bizarre Italian-horror-fueled fantasy. This obscure prog-rock band from the 1970s is absolutely blowing the minds of an audience that ranges in age from twenty-one to sixty. I have been to countless packed retrospective film screenings and have attended fan conventions from Comic-Con and Wizard World to New Jersey's Chiller Theatre Expo, but I have never felt more at home than I do at this moment, standing among a sold-out crowd of peers who, like me, are totally entranced by a brand of music that was so innovative and influential, yet so underappreciated.

It is at that moment that the inspiration for this book is born.

I grew up in the 1980s and 1990s, during a time when the music of John Williams was shining a spotlight on the artistry of film scoring, Danny Elfman was shifting gears from pop star to film music royalty, and composers like Vangelis, Giorgio Moroder, John Carpenter, and the band Tangerine Dream were providing an electronic alternative to the traditional symphonic score. So film music has been a part of my life for as long as I can remember. My father had a cassette tape of the soundtrack to *Superman: The Movie* (1978) that, at an extremely young age, I deemed mandatory listening every time we got into the car. The score to *Chariots of Fire* (1981) is forever emblazoned in my memory, due to an extended period of time when it was the musical accompaniment to our dinner, and I still own the scratch-covered vinyl LP of the *Star Wars* (1977) score that I've personally carried to every place I've ever called home. As I flip and cherry pick through my parents' old LP collections today, I find that composers like John Barry, Ennio Morricone, Bernard Herrmann, Henry Mancini, Bill Conti, Maurice Jarre, Vangelis, and John Williams not only scored some of the most iconic films of the twentieth century, but also my youth.

Horror films also played a significant role in my upbringing. For those of us who grew up as part of the video-store generation, easy access to hundreds of movies allowed genre icons like Freddy Krueger, Jason Voorhees, and Pinhead to become cinematic rock stars. At that time, horror could also be seen regularly on television, with Sunday Night Movie adaptations of classic horror fiction and weekly programming that included *Tales from the Darkside*, *Tales from the Crypt*, *Friday the 13th: The Series*, *Freddy's Nightmares*, *Werewolf*, and updated versions of *The Twilight Zone*, *The Outer Limits*, and *Alfred Hitchcock Presents*.

My parents were not ones to regulate my viewing, at least not in any overt way that I can remember, and being left alone in front of the boob tube for much of my youth, I was exposed to things that probably wouldn't be considered "appropriate" for a child today. My real obsession with the genre, though, began while I was in high school, when renting horror movies with my friends became a regular occurrence. Coincidentally, it was also around this time that I began playing the guitar and discovered the music of heavy metal pioneers Black Sabbath. All these things converging on my impressionable teenage brain at the same time made my falling in love with horror film music inevitable.

Looking back on it, I'm not surprised that the first horror film score that really piqued my curiosity was John Carpenter's *In the Mouth of Madness* (1994). Its opening title track was a guitar-driven rock masterpiece that encompassed everything that interested the budding musician in me, and the remainder of the score's beautifully horrific (and sometimes just plain beautiful) tone helped to expand my musical horizons. It was the first horror film soundtrack that I ever purchased, and it turned out to be my gateway into the wonderful world of horror film music, birthing the long-term fascination and obsession that, two decades later, led me to that Brooklyn venue to see Goblin and ultimately to create this book. So, thank you, John . . .

INTRODUCTION

THE HORROR GENRE HAS ALWAYS been an interesting animal. It has a large and extremely loyal fan base and has been popular since the early twentieth century. It consistently makes money: The success of its films have saved studios from financial ruin. It has been the training ground for many of cinema's most celebrated filmmakers. And it often pushes the cinema envelope when it comes to style and social commentary. Countless books have been written about it and numerous college courses have examined it, but due to its countercultural sensibilities it is seldom acknowledged or rewarded for its artistry, innovation, and cultural significance. As composer Christopher Young puts it, "Horror films are the idiot bastard sons of Hollywood."

It is commonly believed that film music plays a similarly overlooked or slighted role in the minds of music lovers and the music industry at large. A film's score will never trump the three-minute pop song in popularity, but that is not its primary concern. By its nature, film music is created specifically to support a greater, collaborative work and thereby isn't written to be heard and appreciated on its own.

However, the soundtrack album, featuring a film's score and/or songs from within a film, has been a brilliant stroke of movie marketing since the release of Miklós Rózsa's score for *The Jungle Book* in 1942. Before the innovation of "home video," soundtrack albums provided film lovers with a way to relive the magic of their favorite movies after they'd left the theater. And as soon as people could listen to a film's music without picture accompaniment, an appreciation for the art form began to grow among a modest yet passionate community of music lovers.

Soundtracks containing hit singles by popular artists and the scores for Hollywood blockbusters have dominated film-related album sales, but in recent years horror movie music has been experiencing a boom. Beginning in the late 1990s, older films that had previously been hard to find were becoming readily available due to a broad growth in home video distribution. Horror fans were, for the first time, given access to remastered and restored "deluxe editions" of classic genre fare.

And a few years later, due to the growing power of the Internet and the advent of blogs, message boards, and other social media, these fans had a way to share, communicate, and "congregate" online. A worldwide horror community, now invigorated and unified, was growing and, as it turns out, willing to spend money on its passions. This led to an increase in horror-related conventions, merchandise, magazines, television programming, and interest in the music created for horror films.

At the time that I began writing this book, CD and vinyl reissues of horror's most beloved scores were becoming commonplace, and boutique record labels such as Death Waltz Records, Mondo, and Waxwork Records (to name only a few) were gaining notoriety for the effort, time, and craftsmanship they were putting into preserving horror film music primarily from the 1970s and 1980s. Seeing Goblin perform live may have provided the spark of inspiration for this book, but it was the birth of a new and invigorated audience for this music, an audience that allowed a previously forgotten band from Italy to re-form and sell out venues all over the world, that gave me the drive to actually pursue writing it.

And during the two years that this book took to complete, the audience for this unique breed of music and for the people who create it continued to grow. Both Goblin and John Carpenter released well-received albums of all-new material in 2015, and, like Goblin, horror film–based composers such as Alan Howarth, Simon Boswell, and Fabio Frizzi have all found that audiences are eager to hear them perform their music live.

The sounds of horror are clearly alive and well and playing to a substantial and loyal audience. For that very reason, before I began writing this book, I looked to see if there was already one like it. To my surprise, none existed: There were interview-based books about film music, and there were essay-based books about horror film music, but there were no interview-based books about horror film music. Which I found both encouraging and discouraging at the same time: I knew I wanted to read a book like this one, and I assumed that others would too, but was I the right guy for the job?

That question weighed heavily on my mind. I am a musician but not a formally educated one, and I knew that most of the people I wanted to interview were. Was there going to be a language barrier due to my rudimentary understanding of music theory?

After careful deliberations with trusted friends and advisers, I realized that I was not interested in writing a book full of jargon and musical theory anyway, nor would I want to read one. I wanted to write a book for fans like myself. Yes, I wanted it to be interesting and useful for people looking to pursue film music composing as a career, but ultimately I knew that I wanted to write a book that could be understood and enjoyed by the average horror film lover as well as the music conservatory student.

With *Scored to Death*, the intention is to provide readers with a series of in-depth interviews with an array of composers who represent a broad spectrum of age, style, experience, approach, background, and culture. Because of the growing popularity of the films and music of recent decades, my book focuses on modern horror film music through interviews that primarily pertain to works of the 1970s through the present.

The composers who were interviewed for *Scored to Death* are responsible for the music in many of horror's most iconic films and have worked with many of the genre's most noteworthy filmmakers. Providing behind-the-scenes insight regarding specific films and director-composer collaborations was among my top priorities as interviewer, but as my work progressed, I began to find that what interested me most about these artists was their influences, backgrounds, processes, and general outlook on music and the craft of filmmaking. The result is a collection of interviews that incorporate both general questions posed to everyone and specific questions about each individual composer's work.

These are not puff pieces, but at the same time they are not particularly critical, either. The goal was to present each composer in an objective manner through a wide-ranging conversation about his artistic passions and work. My hope is that readers of *Scored to Death* will gain a deeper understanding of and appreciation for the people and talent that it takes to create an interesting, effective, and memorable horror film score. The next time a movie puts you on the edge of your seat, makes your date grip your arm a little bit tighter, makes you jump and spill your popcorn, makes you too afraid to look, or makes you yell at an on-screen character who is going up the stairs when he or she should be going out the front door, remember that a music composer—maybe even one featured in this book—helped make that happen.

The following interviews were conducted between February 2014 and December 2015.

NATHAN BARR

*"Composing is improvisation that becomes
something concrete the further you take it."*

I F I WERE TO TELL YOU that right now there is a man in a garage creating music using instruments made out of human bones and animal
carcasses, you'd think I was either kidding or describing the plot of a
horror film. But it is absolutely true. That garage is a home recording
studio, and that man is Nathan Barr.

Barr first popped up on horror fans' radar as the composer for Eli
Roth's early breakout hits, *Cabin Fever* (2002) and *Hostel* (2005), but
he has since expanded his résumé to include big-budget comedies and
acclaimed television series—for which he has received two Emmy nominations (for *The Americans* and *Hemlock Grove*).

His first job in the film music industry was as an assistant to composer
Hans Zimmer, but his eclectic sensibilities, talent as a multi-instrumen-
talist, and passion for unusual instruments have helped him establish
a distinctive style and a reputation as a "one-man band," making him
one of his generation's most sought-after composers. His résumé

includes collaborations with the acclaimed director Jean-Pierre Jeunet, the Broken Lizard comedy troupe, and rock icons Billy Gibbons and Pete Townshend.

As with all the wonderful artists who participated in this book project, Barr's generosity was overwhelming. I contacted him and explained what I was doing, and within a week I was on the phone with him and his interview was underway. So, purely from an organizational standpoint, contacting and interviewing Barr was a bit of a breath of fresh air. What's more, our similarities in age and our shared loves for both the horror genre and film music made talking to him as easy as it was to get him on the phone.

As a composer who is still fairly early in his career and open to exploring all aspects of the industry, Nathan Barr is able to provide interesting and valuable insight into, not only feature film scoring, but also writing for episodic television and creating original content for digital streaming services like Netflix and Amazon Prime.

SELECTED FILMOGRAPHY

1999	*From Dusk Till Dawn 3: The Hangman's Daughter*
2000	*Red Dirt*
2002	*Cabin Fever*
2003	*Open Water* (additional music)
2004	*Club Dread*
2005	*2001 Maniacs*
	The Dukes of Hazzard
	Hostel
2006	*Beerfest*
2007	*Grindhouse* (Segment: *Thanksgiving*)
	Hostel: Part II
	Rise: Blood Hunter
2008	*Shutter*
	Lost Boys: The Tribe
2008–2014	*True Blood* (TV series)
2009	*The Slammin' Salmon*
2010	*The Last Exorcism*
2011	*The Ledge*
2013	*The Big Wedding*
2013–2015	*Hemlock Grove* (TV series)
2013–present	*The Americans* (TV series)

I know your parents were very musical. Can you talk about how that influenced you and your music?

They had all sorts of interesting instruments around the house when I was growing up. My mother played koto [a Japanese string instrument] when we lived in Japan, so playing around with that at an early age was fun. Then we also had a piano, and my dad had a banjo and a guitar and he played a little bit of shakuhachi [a Japanese flute, typically made from bamboo]. And so I think, for a kid, it was just really interesting to look at these instruments that were each, in their own way, unique and see what kind of sounds they were able to create. That was really inspiring for me, and that has followed me all the way to today. That's still kind of what I do, try and acquire as many instruments as I can, that I know nothing about, and then create wholly unique sounds that way.

So, I would say that hearing my mother play those instruments as a kid was a big part of the influence for me, and then she started me on Suzuki [a music teaching method] violin when I was about four years old. But I was by no means a prodigy or anything. I went to a bunch of Suzuki camps, and that started my interest in classical music. So that was sort of my earliest life. That's what it was.

What kind of music did you listen to during your teenage years?

I was a big fan of Led Zeppelin and Yo-Yo Ma [*laughs*]. Those were two big musical influences growing up, so I loved learning about the cello through Yo-Yo Ma's playing, also through Jacqueline du Pré's playing. There's also a woman named Zara Nelsova who was a teacher at Juilliard for many years, and I fell in love with her recording of the Dvořák Cello Concerto. Then Bach was always a huge influence on me. My mother taught piano at the house, so every day I'd come home from school there'd be someone learning Bach in the living room, and so those all became really familiar sounds and really inspiring sounds for me.

When did the idea of writing music for films come to you?

Well, I always loved film music and I always noticed it in films, and I noticed *that* I noticed it, and my *parents* noticed that I noticed it, so I think the interest in film music came from a very young age. And I think my earliest memory of a piece of film music is actually Max Steiner's score for *Gone with the Wind* [1939]. WWOR-TV used that before and after a commercial break, when they're coming back to a movie, and I remember hearing that and thinking, "Wow, this is an amazing sound." So, that was sort of the earliest example of me noticing film music, and I loved that, the sound of the orchestra and the really thematically driven music. That is my earliest memory of film music.

At what age did you decide that you were going to pursue it as a career?

I really don't think that happened until I got out here and met Hans [Zimmer] in 1997. I'd say as soon as I got to LA it was on my radar as something I could probably do. I got here in January of '96 and, sure, I was interested in the idea of maybe pursuing that career and it literally just sort of happened.

It was one of those weird life instances: I was running packages around town and it had nothing to do with music, and a friend said, "Hey, you like film music, don't you?" And there was an advertisement in the UTA [United Talent Agency] Joblist that said, "Prominent Hollywood film composer seeking driver/assistant." So I sent my résumé in and got a call back. And even when I went there, they were being very secretive as to who it was. And then I found out it was Hans. It was then narrowed down to me and two other guys. We each went in individually and met with Hans, and then I found out I got the job.

What exactly was the job? What kinds of things did you do for him?

I was just an all-around assistant. I don't know if he drives today, but he didn't drive at the time. So I'd pick him up in the morning. I'd drive my car to his house up in Malibu, swap cars, get in his Aston Martin. He'd get in the passenger seat [*laughs*], we'd drive down PCH [Pacific Coast Highway], I'd take him to the studio, get him coffee all day, pick up meals, and sit behind him while he was writing.

I asked him if I could be in on meetings where appropriate, and that turned out to be a really great thing, because I got to sit in on a lot of amazing meetings. I think our first meeting was with Jeffrey Katzenberg—that was a really valuable experience.

Toward the end of my time there, I worked on some short films, and he [Zimmer] was nice enough to let me write demos in his studio when he wasn't in there. So, as you can imagine, I was like a kid in the candy shop in that studio. It's not the one he's in today, it was his previous one.

But that really lit the fire, and I was kind of on my way out of there as soon as I got there.

I didn't relate to the particular way he and his team worked over there because it was very based in computers. And I remember one time wanting to plug in a guitar to record a thing for a short film, and it was this huge process, at that time, to get a mic in there, and then once you had a mic in there the noise of the synths and the fans were so loud that you couldn't really get a good recording. He offered me a room there and I turned him down. In my defense, I'm not trying to sound arrogant or anything, but I turned him down; I said, "I really just want to do this on my own." That was in '98, and I haven't looked back.

Was making that decision scary?

It was scary, but I knew I didn't want to work there. I knew I didn't want to be one of the guys who had to write like him and sort of be under his thumb, because I saw the stress those guys dealt with—and it wasn't even for their own careers. It was really about supporting Hans's career, and I really wanted it to be about me, setting out on my own. And I know he appreciated that spirit from the beginning—he got it, he understood. It was scary, absolutely, but I had a movie. I got my first feature while I still worked for him, and then I said, "I just want to go do this on my own."

Then he called me a week later, because I was, like, freaking out. One of our friends told him I was freaking out, and he said, "Why don't you bring me some music?" So I brought in a scene to show him, and he listened to it and he was, like, "Okay. You know, go do your thing." He gave me some feedback and I left, and as I was walking out he goes, "Hey." And I said, "Yeah?" "So, now that you've got all this shit out of your system, go write some music [*laughs*]." So, tough love! Tough love!

Yes, tough, but at the same time totally generous.

Absolutely—oh, for sure! And the turning point for me was when . . . I was working in there one weekend and he wasn't supposed to be in. Generally, if he was in I knew he was, because I had to go pick him up. But his wife dropped him off, and he just walked in while I was in the middle of writing a piece in his studio. And I kind of like freaked out, and he shoved me out of the way [*laughs*] and hit the space bar to play it, and it was, like, this three-minute demo piece and he just sat there and played it. When it ended, there was silence. I was, like, "Oh, God!" And he turned to me and was, like, "It's really good."

So that made me feel really good, and he told a couple of other composers there that he felt like I could have a really successful career if I wanted to do this. And with that information I sort of thought, "Okay, now I really want to just go do this on my own terms."

You saw how Zimmer worked and sat in on some of his meetings. Did you learn a lot during that time that you've found valuable?

Oh, so I guess I'm selling it short. I didn't know what MIDI [Musical Instrument Digital Interface] stood for when I walked in there to work for him. So I got a major crash course in the technical aspects that go into being a film composer these days: I learned about why music starts where it starts, why it ends where it ends. I learned about why certain sounds can work in a score and why they can't. I learned how to handle people in a meeting when you're playing back music for them for the first time.

I mean, it was invaluable. It was like being dropped into the deep end of the pool and being told to swim. I think it's . . . like when kids go to college: They come out thinking they know everything, and then they get dropped in the real world scenario and realize they know nothing. They have just the shabbiest of maps that they learned [*laughs*], and so that's the way it was for me, too. When I got out of there, I thought I had a really good handle—and then, all of a sudden I was the guy in the middle of the room talking about stuff, and I was terrified. So that first movie or two [on my own] were really, really tough. I didn't know if I wanted to do it or not.

I took away two things from my time there [with Zimmer], which were ultimately not going to work for me. . . . I was working in a way that wasn't conducive to the way I wanted to work, and the first thing was, as I've discovered over the years, that my time away from the studio is as important as my time in the studio on any given project. When I first started, I saw a lot of those guys immediately chaining themselves to their desks, like flogging themselves like they were slaves. I let go of that and I thought, "You know, I'm going to let myself go to the beach today or go to the movies today . . ." And that was, like, one of those epiphany moments: "Oh, it's okay to go away from the studio and take a day or two off." That day or two off is what gave me fuel to keep going.

The other thing was, I wanted to do a lot more recording and hands-on-instruments kind of composing. For me, personally, I found it very difficult to be inspired sitting in front of the same eighty-eight-key controller, writing for orchestra, for flute, for guitar, for bass. I just didn't like it. So that's very much developed into my process. I'm sitting in a room full of instruments with a bunch of mics and literally playing stuff and writing.

You're known for having a collection of unique and interesting instruments from around the world. Can you tell me about a few of them?

Well, let's see. I have a human bone trumpet. People think that is pretty interesting. It is made out of a human femur. Basically, some monks, when they die, they have their bones turned into instruments. I have a *zokra*, which is a Libyan instrument that is very similar to the Tunisian *mizwad*; it is like a bagpipe made out of animal skin and bones. I have a glass harmonica [an instrument consisting of an array of spinning glass bowls that are played with the fingertips, producing the sound one gets when rubbing a dampened finger around the rim of a wine glass] that gets a lot of use. I have an Array *mbira*, which I have used before on scores. It's an instrument that has these metal spokes that you pluck, and the length of the spoke determines the pitch. I have a lot of very cool instruments, and they all have their own sound.

If I Google your name, the two things that frequently come up are (1) you collect weird instruments, and (2) you generally play all of the instruments for your scores. Is it safe to say that you're not a one-man band out of necessity? This is a creative choice, correct?

Oh, yeah, absolutely. It's just the way I wanted to work. It's literally what I was doing as a kid, playing around with all these instruments in my home. It feels very organic and natural, because I'll write a melody differently on a guitar than I will on a piano, than I will on the bagpipes, than I will on the cello. I think about melody differently on each of those instruments.

How do you choose which instrument you're going to use when you're working?

That's one of those things I think you learn over time. I think any good film composer can look at a film with no music in it and go,

"Yeah, that's orchestral," or, "No, that's not orchestral." It's this weird thing, and I think it has to do with the look of the film, the choices the cinematographer makes, the choices the director makes, the pacing, the performances. All of those things add up to some sort of sense of what kind of instruments do and don't work in the story and in the film. So it's kind of weird.

Have you found that being a one-man band has become a real asset when trying to get jobs? Is that appealing to producers and directors?

Yes, absolutely. Hugely appealing. It's not always that way, though; I definitely have done my share of orchestral scores. But it's a huge asset, because people walk into my studio and they see all my instruments and they're, like, "Oh my God, what's that?" And I play it for them and they're, like, "Oh my God, that would be great for this character!"

So, yes, it's a huge asset, because all of my experience and diversity as a player goes into the show. For instance, *True Blood* [2008–2014] has a very interesting organic sound, and that was a show that could've gone orchestral because it's so beautifully shot. Yet there I used the prepared piano [a piano with objects, i.e., "preparations," placed on and/or between its strings to alter its sound] instead. That gave us the bigness of an orchestral sound without being an orchestra in those moments where the show needed it.

Do you find that doing it yourself is economical timewise, or does it take more time?

It took more time in the beginning and now it's quicker. I write really fast. I think as composers we all find our little shortcuts. Which is not to say we're phoning it in—it's just to say we find things that work really well that we can lean on. So now I work very quickly, and that is a huge asset too. Early on, that was a problem, but I've become a much, much better player at all of these things, and I've become much more plugged into when something can stay as-is and has kind of a cool vibe to it, even though it sounds a little off. As opposed to when something needs to be perfect (and there's also software today that can help in a pinch with a bit of quantization [the digital recording process that rhythmically straightens out or aligns where notes fall relative to the music's primary beats]).

Walk me through your scoring process from when you start writing.

I just finished an amazing pilot on Amazon called *Casanova* [2015]. It was directed by Jean-Pierre Jeunet, who also directed *Amélie* [2001] and *The City of Lost Children* [1995]. It's extraordinary, it's an amazing thing. I finished writing the score to that today, actually. So, I can use that one as an example.

It was down to me and one other composer who they were interested in working with, and I recently got an instrument, after a four-year wait, from Sweden called a *nyckelharpa*. (Arguably one of the greatest living makers of the nyckelharpa is a guy named Esbjörn Hogmark from Sweden. I signed up for that instrument about four years ago and he finally made his way through the others he had to make and made me one.) When I got that instrument, I didn't know if I was going to use it or not, but when I saw this show and I saw the way Jean-Pierre Jeunet created the visuals, I thought, "Oh my God, I bet that nyckelharpa would be really a good sound for *Casanova*."

So I literally just picked up the nyckelharpa, and the first thing I played became *Casanova*'s theme. I sent that to the guys, and they were, like, "This is amazing—you're it." Then I used a glass harmonica. The creator of the show came up to the studio and really liked the sound of that, and he said, "That could be the inside of Casanova's thoughts. That's his interior dilemmas that he's going through." So, sure enough, glass harmonica and nyckelharpa became a very important part of the texture of the show, and then, thematically, his theme is also on those instruments.

At that point it's really like experimenting. It's just writing music for that world. It's a lot of just me trying different things on those instruments. For instance, I played the glass harmonica with field drum mallets, which sounded amazing. So we used that quite a bit. And then I brought in Lisbeth Scott, who's a vocalist who I've worked with a number of times, and just slowly by, you know, woodshedding here, the score begins to find itself and the themes begin to find themselves.

This one piece I wrote . . . there's this really sort of sexy montage at the top and the piece is a little bit downbeat. So I never would've put it there, but the music editor cut it in there and everyone was, like, "Wow, this really works here." So even though it's a more melancholic, downbeat piece, that music ended up working really well over these scenes that, when they were going for temp [temp score, the use of existing music tracks as a temporary score for a picture while it is being edited], were just this very traditional upbeat orchestral stuff.

So that's kind of it, and as film composers we deal with a lot of fixes and rewrites. It's all about rewriting and rewriting and rewriting and getting every moment exactly right for the filmmakers.

So would it be safe to say that your composing style is improvisational until you find "it"?

Absolutely, and I think that's what composing is. Composing is improvisation that becomes something concrete the further you take it.

A lot of the composers I have spoken to, especially the ones who are formally educated in music, talk a lot about how, when they watch footage, they hear music in their heads and it's, in a sense, just a matter of dictating it.

Yes, that's certainly a part of it. I think, as composers, we watch a scene and we hear something. We hear a tempo, we hear a key, we hear a melody. That's for sure. That's seamless with what I'm talking about. I have to hear something in order to play it.

I'd like to talk a bit about your work in the horror genre.

Sure.

Were you a fan of the genre, or did you just fall into it as a composer? Were those just the jobs you were offered?

Oh, no. I love horror films; it's my favorite genre [*laughs*]. My whole life, I've just loved horror films. I've adored them, ever since I was a kid. So it was a joy to fall into that, and it's also a joy to be moving into some other stuff lately. My career has really been expanding a bit. Like this *Casanova* show, it's a period drama.

The Americans [2013–present], same thing, it's a period drama. But horror is such a great place to cut one's teeth as a composer, because there's so much experimentation that can go on with all of the requirements of a horror film, to make things scary. Right? Just that orchestral language that [György] Ligeti and all those people came up with, which was never intended to be for horror films, but it becomes that. With horror films you can throw a hell of a lot of stuff up at the screen and it can work, and that's what's exciting about it.

You've worked on many types of films and television shows. Do you find that music in horror has a different function than in other genres?

I think, emotionally, a drama can take you to many different places and it can still be called a drama. A horror film has to terrify you or it can't be called a horror film—or it *should* terrify you. So I think the sort of band-width you're going for in a horror film can be a bit narrower. It has got to scare the shit out of the audience, or freak them out. That's the goal.

So, basically, what you're saying is that with horror you're working on two ends of the spectrum. Your palette is huge because the genre allows you to experiment, but the function of the music within the genre is very narrow.

There you go. That's a great way to put it.

How did you meet writer-director-producer Eli Roth?

I met him before *Cabin Fever* [2002] through my agent and a producer, and he walked into my studio and saw my horror DVD collection and was, like, "Oh my God, this guy's music would really have to suck for me not to want to work with him [*laughs*]." So I played him some stuff that I had written and he really liked it, and that started our collaboration.

He's a super-passionate guy about horror films. We did *Cabin Fever*, *Hostel* [2005], *Hostel: Part II* [2007], and then I did a couple of things he produced, too. I did *Hemlock Grove* [2013–2015]; we're just wrapping up the third and final season of that right now on Netflix. I did *The Last Exorcism* [2010] with him, which he produced but was very involved with. So, it's been a fun ride working with Eli.

You scored his first feature film. What was it like working with him as a first-time director, and how did he communicate to you what he wanted?

With Eli, it's just like bigger, BIGGER, LOUDER, BIGGER! It's, like, Throw in the kitchen sink! He's deliberately throwing as much raw gore and sound and everything else as he can at the audience, and it's always done with this wink and tongue-in-cheek vibe to it, which is what's great. For instance, I remember playing a scene in *Hostel: Part II* where this woman slices this girl and the girl bleeds onto her, and the woman is masturbating [*laughs*]. It is just, like, so over-the-top. I showed it to some friends and I wasn't watching them. I was standing in front of them and I was just laughing my ass off. Then I turned around and they were all horrified [*laughs*]. They were, like, "You need to start spending more time away from your studio."

So what I appreciate so much about Eli's storytelling is that he is very aware of everything that he's showing to the audience. I think it is horrifying, but it is also so funny in the craziness of it all. So musically that's what it was really about. It was like the scene [in *Cabin* Fever] when one of the characters falls in the lake and falls onto the body. (I can't remember which one it was. It may have been Rider Strong's character.) Eli wanted it bigger, bigger, louder, crazier, and so that was really fun to do that.

With the both of you being such big horror fans, did you use references to other horror films to help communicate ideas to each other?

Yes, absolutely, there was a ton of referencing going on. There are references to everything from *The Shining* [1980] to obscure Italian zombie films—all sorts of stuff. I think it's fun to share that reference with a director, because all I have to do is name that movie and he'd go, "Oh, yeah, I get it [*laughs*]."

How did you decide what sound palette you were going to use on *Cabin Fever*?

That was an earlier film for me, so I listen to that score now and it sounds pretty jarring to my ears. I was just multitracking cellos. The vision Eli had and what ended up on the screen has a really unique voice to it, which is why it did so well and why he's had the career he's had. So, musically, it was really about trying to also create a super-unique voice, and so it's a pretty rough-sounding score—but in a way that really complements what was happening on the screen. It was also a smaller-budget film, so financially there wasn't room for an orchestra.

In a way, that can be the best-case scenario, because it really forces the composer to rethink how they're going to approach that. I think that orchestral samples are getting better and better and better. It's kind of amazing, but it's still fun to think outside of that box: "Is there something else that can work that wouldn't be as obvious?" And it was also just about finding something really weird. I mean, it has a kid doing karate chops and screaming "Pancakes!" [*laughs*], so, musically, that kind of points to a lot.

When was the first time you used a full orchestra for a score?

The second film I ever did was this film that no one has ever heard of called *Red Dirt* [2000], and that was a twenty-five-piece orchestra. That was such a pleasure.

Was it intimidating?

No, it wasn't. I grew up playing in an orchestra, so I knew what an orchestra was supposed to sound like. So, no, it wasn't intimidating; it was just an absolute joy, and it's something I hope to get back to more often . . . than I have lately. To this day, it's one of my favorite scores. It's obscure, but thematically it has some really nice moments and orchestrationwise it has some really nice moments too. I'm proud of that one.

You also used an orchestra on *Hostel*.

Yes. With *Hostel* there was a budget there for an orchestra, and I think we used a ninety- or ninety-five-piece orchestra. I went to Prague to record it and, again, it was just sort of like, "Let's get really big and raucus with the orchestra." So there's a lot of almost heavy metal riffs played in the lower end of the strings. And then there's a lot of fun contrabassoon stuff, and then there's glass harmonica, which I played for some of the more magical moments.

And then there is the very deliberate tip of the hat to Bernard Herrmann with the main *Hostel* theme: It has this four-note motif, with sixteenth-note strings bouncing up and down octaves. It sounds a lot like Bernard Herrmann, which I really liked. [*Laughs*] Not that I would compare myself to him, but that was my nod to him.

Herrmann is a name that has come up often during the interviews for this book. Specifically, what do you think it is about his music that is so influential?

A lot of the old guys—like Dimitri Tiomkin, Franz Waxman, Max Steiner, Alex North, Lionel Newman, all those guys—wrote in a style that was very steeped in nineteenth- and twentieth-century classical music, and it sounded like nineteenth/twentieth-century classical music.

There are a lot of scores, and they all draw on [Richard] Strauss and [Gustav] Mahler. I've heard a couple of scores from some of these guys, and it's like you can literally rip the page out of a score of Strauss and there it is.

I think Bernard Herrmann, for me at least, had an unbelievably unique voice with the orchestra. He was working with the same trappings of those guys, but he took it to a place that was so unique, that you hear it and you go, "Yep, that's Bernard Herrmann." I think it's the way he wrote for the instruments. It's the structure of the pieces that he wrote and, more than anything, it's the fact that he was working with one of the most interesting filmmakers of all time [Alfred Hitchcock]. That is something that cannot be stressed enough. If you look at the top guys today, most of them can point to one director who made them.

Danny Elfman is doing this huge tour right now . . . it's all Tim Burton music. Danny Elfman is a great composer, but I think composers win the lottery when they find that one filmmaker that is one of the few in a generation that are here to stay, that have such a unique voice that people love to see. Who's to say maybe Alex North or Dimitri Tiomkin or any of those guys would've done something completely out of their comfort zone that would've given them as unique a voice as Bernard Herrmann had they worked with Hitchcock? Who knows?

Some of the other composers I have spoken to point to Herrmann's use of simplicity as being what was very influential. Do you find simplicity is important in horror?

I guess it depends on what you mean by simplicity. There can be simple melodies, there can be simple orchestration. I think horror music can be, and the genre can handle extremely complex music. So I don't know; it's an interesting thought. I've never thought about it that way.

Well, for example, consider the music from *Psycho* [1960] and *Jaws* [1975] and *Halloween* [1978]. At their core they are very simple musical ideas, but those are the ones that are most memorable.

That's true. Yep. Absolutely—I agree with that completely. The theme from *Jaws* is two notes [*laughs*] over and over again, and *Psycho* is only, like, one note over and over again with screeching. It's true. I like that, certainly in terms of what is the most recognizable or iconic about those scores, for sure. And the theme from *Halloween* is the same thing.

Maybe it is just a matter of being a "snappy" tune, like pop music, and being easily accessible to the layman's ear.

Yeah. I think that's a part of it. And also, again, all those movies you just mentioned have really amazing directors with incredible vision, whether it's Alfred Hitchcock or Steven Spielberg or John Carpenter. I also think it's about having directors who want music to be a character in their movies. They don't want it to disappear into the background. And in those cases, because it's going to be so front-and-center, what you put before an audience is going to be devoured by them if it is good and if it is recognizable and simple.

You did the music for both *Hostel* and *Hostel: Part II*. Is your approach different when working on a sequel?

Well, I guess you can ask, "Was Eli's approach that different with the second story?" It was kind of *Hostel* with women, right? So I think that's why maybe it didn't do as well as the first *Hostel*. I think Eli had some brilliant ideas about what *Hostel: Part II* should have been, and it didn't end up going that way because of studio intervention.

I think with sequels it is similar to a TV series, where you're exploring the same characters or the same idea over a bigger arc. It's kind of like, "Okay, we did that, so let's take a step further and expand it a little bit." Although, honestly, with *Hostel: Part II*, the criteria were kind of the same, just to be as big and horrible as possible [*laughs*]—but that's the fun thing, too.

The thing I love about writing music in this golden age of television we're in is that the storytelling is so expansive and the characters are so interesting. I had seven seasons in which to explore *True Blood*. That is really exciting as a composer.

Aside from being able to explore a certain musical language over an extended period of time, are there other key differences between working on episodic television and feature films?

I think at the core of this thing is what we're talking about, which is, in a feature film, unless there's going to be a sequel, you have ninety to one hundred twenty minutes to say musically what you're ever going to say about that film, and then it's done.

With TV, the exciting thing is the tiniest little germ of an idea, like a little motif in Season One, Episode One, that is literally just off the top of my head. I love when, four seasons later, I'm going, "Oh my God, that blew up into this much bigger melody with these different chords behind it. It became this incredible sound." So I feel like that's a big difference between TV and film. But otherwise it's really about character and story and all that stuff.

One interesting thing is this whole notion of "binge watching," which is something that composers who are working with services like Netflix and Amazon have been running into. I think we [composers] have all noticed that studios have become very sensitive to things like overplaying a theme. That has been an interesting development in this new way in which we view television, and that's certainly different from a film.

Budgets and scheduling are typically much tighter in the television industry compared to feature films. How does that affect your job?

It depends on what part of the TV world you're working in. If you're working on network television, the deadlines are appallingly small, but the money can be quite good. If you're working in cable, the deadlines ease up a bit, but the money is not quite as good as network in terms of fee, and it's appallingly lower than network in terms of royalties. That is still being sorted out.

I think there is something really exciting about working in TV, though, because when you're doing a film it's really like doing an album. It's the same kind of idea. You're really going to take your time to explore a sound. Hopefully, you've got, like, six to eight weeks; you really have time to explore and just stretch out and throw a bunch of stuff at the story and see what sticks with the director. With TV you hit the ground running and nail it and move on to the next.

With episodic television there are typically several different directors. Who do you work with? Do you work primarily with the producer?

With television, the strange thing is, we as composers rarely work with the person who directs the episode. We work with the creator or the lead producer of the show. So on *True Blood* it was Alan Ball; Alan Ball was at the top of the pyramid. And the nice thing about that is, in a medium like television, where there are a lot of people who want to chime in, if it's someone who's had a degree of success, like Alan Ball, he's the endgame. A lot of people can have a lot of different thoughts, but if he's okay with it then it's okay. So it's the creator or the lead producer—and occasionally the director.

There's a really wonderful director named Dan Sackheim who did a bunch of episodes of *The Americans*. He was very involved with the score on his episodes . . . because his sensibilities were so good. But that's the exception.

You spoke about how one of television's strengths is being able to explore a musical palette or set of ideas over an extended period of time, and how it can be exciting to have something in Episode One come back in later seasons, etc. I think it is easy to understand why that aspect of it is very appealing to a composer, but does that also become restrictive after a while? Does it become more difficult to come up with new ideas, when you are forced to work with an established musical palette?

If the characters are good and the story is engaging, that's our bread and butter as composers. We've got to keep being inspired. I think there's nothing harder than working on a show or a movie that didn't get it right, whatever "it" is. That's when it becomes really restrictive and difficult, because everyone's looking to the score to "save the movie." That's a really difficult position to be in, because people are relying on the music to a point which is sometimes unrealistic.

While music can fix and help a performance, while it can help with pacing, while it can help with the scope of a story, at the end of the day there is only so much we can do. But, sure, seven seasons into *True Blood* you're working on your seventy-fifth episode [*laughs*], it can become, like, "Oh God, if I have to play Bill and Sookie's love theme ever again, I'm going to shoot myself."

Can't they just use the take from Season Three?

And they do, and I would say that's the great thing with television, given deadlines and given the nature of these long story arcs: You amass a huge library with each season. The picture editors are often cutting with your library [of cues from previous episodes], and as long it's thematically appropriate, I think it's okay to use cues from previous episodes.

How did you get the job scoring *True Blood*?

My score for *Hostel* ended up in the *True Blood* cutting room, I have no idea how or why. They ended up cutting it into the pilot as temp, and so I was on the shortlist of composers they called in to meet. I watched the pilot, and I thought my score in there was terrible. I didn't think it worked at all, and I just said to myself, "Fuck it."

And I told them that. I said, "I'm really flattered that you used my score, but I don't think it works at all [*laughs*]." And they were kind of taken aback, and they were, like, "Well, what would you do?" And I pitched them my idea and they hired me. Well, actually, Alan Ball went away on vacation with a stack of my CDs and a stack of another composer's CDs. Then he listened through it all and, thank God, he heard what he wanted to hear in my stuff.

What were the ideas that you pitched to them?

My pitch was, "Let's let the source music, which is so rich in the South, define the location, and that will free up the score to become whatever it wants to become. Maybe instead of just using a banjo"—and this is where it's great to have all these different instruments at my disposal— "let's use a *cümbüş*, which is like a Turkish version of a banjo, and it'll sound like a banjo but it won't quite sound like a banjo, and that could be really interesting."

So the score, while at times leaning on harmonica and guitar, I think could have been a much more obvious and much less effective approach to *True Blood* had the wrong composer come aboard.

You said that *True Blood* "was a show that could've gone orchestral." Why did you decide not to use an orchestra for it?"

True Blood is this enormous world that got bigger and bigger and bigger as far as the story goes, but at its core are these really interesting, complex characters like Sookie and Bill. I know this is going to sound pretentious, but I wanted the score to be about that interior intimacy among the characters, and . . . I thought that if I used a small ensemble instead of a giant orchestra, it would maybe draw the audience into the characters' world a bit better. And I think it worked.

In 2013 your themes for both *The Americans* and *Hemlock Grove* were nominated for Emmy Awards [Outstanding Original Main Title Theme Music]. As fantastic as that is, is there a part of you

that wishes your work on *True Blood* got recognized with a win?

I would feel bad about it if the entire show hadn't been shafted. I think you can count almost on one hand the number of Emmy nominations *True Blood* got in seven seasons, across all the categories. Given the amount of people who were, like, "Oh man, what you're doing is so different and it's so interesting," I would think that should lead to something when the award season comes. But I think when it comes to an award ceremony, people just have a problem with vampires and fairies and werewolves. So I don't feel bad about it.

Was it shocking when you found out that you were nominated for two Emmys in the same category?

Oh, it was totally shocking [*laughs*]. Yeah, I was totally shocked—I couldn't believe it. It's the first time that ever happened in that category, that a composer was nominated twice in one year. And the theme for *The Americans* was such a short thing; it's only, like, forty seconds long. I was, like, "They're never going to even blink at this." And *Hemlock Grove* was a bit longer, but still. So, yes, I was thrilled, I was totally thrilled. It was fun.

Careerwise, does that change anything?

No, other than it puts the phrase "Emmy-nominated" before your name [*laughs*]. You know what? I take that back. I think when composers' résumés are crossing the desks of producers and they see "Emmy-nominated" and the show that it's associated with, that can be helpful. It definitely can, but otherwise it doesn't mean a thing. It's about the fun. It's the icing on the cake of going and being a part of the ceremony and having your peers recognize your work.

What makes a good television theme, and how does it differ from the rest of the score?

That's a really good question. I don't remember who it was, but someone described it as "that piece of music you hear in the other room when you're up getting popcorn, and it makes you want to rush back into the room to sit down in front of the TV." And I really like that.

So, I think it's really about calling in the audience to the show, and it's going to tell us a bit about the world and a bit about the story, and it's going to do it really quickly and it's going to become recognizable and associated with the show. It may or may not have anything to do with the score in the show, but I think you want it to be memorable. The melody for *The Americans'* theme is something that I hear a lot of people saying they really like. It's catchy, and I think that's helpful.

You worked with Pete Townshend on *The Americans*.

I did!

What was that like?

Oh, it was amazing. What was funny was, I didn't meet Pete until after we were done working together. I was sitting in Topanga Canyon one morning, and my phone rang and I picked it up. It was Pete Townshend from England and it was just lovely—who am I to him? And he happened to know my work on *The Americans* and happened to really like it. So that was a nice surprise.

So, you just get a call from Pete Townshend . . .

Yeah. I get a call from Pete Townshend. He was a fan of the show and knew my work and liked it. It was incredibly flattering to hear. I said, "I know you're busy, so let me just put together two tracks that are cut from the cloth of the sound of the score for *The Americans*, but that could be worked into some sort of song format for a scene to come this season and send those to you."

So I sent them to him, and one of them I never heard about again [*laughs*], and the other one he flipped out over. He sent me back lyrics. He's, like, "I'm hearing all this stuff and this and this, etc."

Then about a week later I got a notice that a Dropbox link was available, and I went on Dropbox, and not only had he written lyrics and sung parts, but he also did rhythm guitar parts and lead guitar parts. It was really cool, but the challenge was that he was so busy, and so that was kind of it. So when we did find the scene it was about a five-minute-long scene, and I had to work with a limited amount of material and to try and turn it into something that felt like a song but served the scene. I think it ended up working really well in the episode. Stand-alone it's a bit repetitive, but within the scene it really works.

So he called you to work specifically on that show?

Yes, that is correct. Before Season Two started, the producers were trying to up the profile of the show. It was getting a lot of amazing reviews, but they just wanted to get it out there more. So they talked about how could they do this? And they thought, "Well, let's pair Nate up with a well-known musician." There was a long list of people we all threw at our music supervisor, P. J. Bloom, and Pete Townshend was on that list and he was the guy that responded right away.

It was just a pleasure. We finished it up. He signed off on it because it sounds quite different from what he sent me (we had to do that to make it work for the show), and then we met in London and had lunch last September.

What is having lunch with Pete Townshend like?

[*Laughs*] It was great! He just couldn't be nicer. He's totally humble. You're sitting talking to the guy, and you're looking at this rock icon who's probably seen things none of us can even imagine and has been through experiences none of us can imagine, and he was absolutely lovely. We talked instruments. I'm putting this huge Wurlitzer organ in my new studio, and he was very fascinated to learn all about that. So we just kind of talked shop. And no pretense, no ego, nothing—lovely, lovely guy.

Was it through Eli Roth that you came to work on *Hemlock Grove*?

Yes. Again, I was one of a couple composers. Eli has to, obviously, honor the fact that there are other producers on board. So I was brought in and, again, I pitched them an idea which they really loved, and then I got it.

What was the idea?

My idea was to use these small antique barrel pianos and automatic musical instruments from a previous century [nineteenth] as part of the sound of the show. And they just loved that.

When you go in for these meetings, do you see what they have so far and develop your ideas from that?

No. In that case I hadn't seen anything yet; I think I'd read the script of the pilot and that was it. I think they asked me to write a demo, which I did.

(Just a note about demos: I think there are a fair amount of composers who have reached a point in their career—or who *think* they've reached a point in their career—where they don't need to do demos anymore. And it works out really great for the composers who are willing to do demos, because . . . *we* get those shows then.)

So I have never been shy about doing demos. For example, *Casanova*: When I heard it was [directed by] Jean-Pierre Jeunet, I was, like, "Shit, this guy's amazing, I'm not worthy." So, writing a demo, honestly, as much as it was about convincing them, it was convincing myself, too. If I can go into a show and get on board, having already written something they like, I go in with a degree of comfort that I wouldn't otherwise have. That's what it's about, just going in there and pitching, and they may or may not ask for a demo. *True Blood* I got without writing a demo. It just depends on who they are and who they're considering and how many people they have to answer to.

When you are working for a show on Netflix or Amazon Prime, is the schedule more like a feature film, because the entire season is premiering at the same time?

Yes, it can be. Let's say, with *True Blood*, an HBO show, maybe at the start of the series you're getting two to three weeks an episode, which is like heaven. It's, like, ridiculous, and then by the end you're getting just under a week for the episode. With Netflix and Amazon it is kind of the same thing: At the front, there's quite a bit of time and cushion, and at the back it gets really tight. I guess it's comparable in that sense to a movie, where you might have a lot of time upfront, but not toward the end.

With the film *Club Dread* [2004], what was it like working with the Broken Lizard guys?

[*Laughs, followed by a long pause*] It was working with the Broken Lizard guys.

Is that a good thing or a bad thing?

I really like Paul Soter a lot. He's one of the guys. He's the very first guy I met with before *Club Dread*, and he's kind of the one that then told Jay Chandrasekhar he should meet me, and we all hit it off. So it was fun. It's, like, deliberately silly material, a lot of it, and so I guess with *Club Dread* the idea was to play it [the score] straight, as straight as possible, and that was funny. I think if they had wanted to play it as funny, come dic music it would've been much more challenging.

So you just approached it, stylistically, completely seriously?

Yeah, exactly. I would say more or less. I mean, there's a woman screaming in the score at the top [*laughs*], but yes. I think with the violence they
were pretty serious. It's pretty violent in a couple of moments.

**Obviously, comedies and horror films are very different. But they
are alike in that timing is crucial. And just like with a suspense
scene in a horror film, a joke is very much reliant on building tension and providing a release. *Club Dread* is probably not the best
example to cite for this question, but since we're talking about
comedy and you have worked on other comedies, do you find
that there are similarities with the way music functions in both
comedies and horror films?**

I think it depends. With comedy, sometimes they want you to play the
comedy and sometimes they don't want you to play the comedy, which
I think comes up less in horror. Usually they want you to play the horror, though not always.

   With comedy, I have an aversion to that "oompah" comedy music, so
I try to avoid it. If the humor is playing really well, the music is just sort
of there to give it a flavor or a lens to look at it through. It's not really
there to go and try and be funny in itself, though I guess there are also
examples in horror where you're not "playing the horror." Take Dario
Argento, for example: He's playing straight blues music when there's a
guy searching through the house in *Deep Red* [1975, score by Goblin].
That is certainly playing against expectation, and there is something
about that that works. It's really weird.

**You also worked on *Shutter* [2008], which was a remake; it actually
has been remade several times. Had you watched the previous versions of the film before you started working on it?**

I had not, and I have not to this day, although I should probably check
them out [*laughs*].

**How did you find the musical language that you wanted to use
for that film?**

That was a pretty straightforward studio horror film. It was pretty pol-
ished and it looked like a studio horror film. The head of the studio at
the time, his one note was, "I really want a strong, recognizable theme."
So I came up with what I came up with, and at the dub he stood

up after and said, "I think you've done a really wonderful job, Nate." So, mission accomplished. But that was an example of a score that was smaller-budget, and honestly it could've used an orchestra. I think it worked out, but the score is a little bit wonky-sounding at times. I think it would've been really well served by an orchestra.

You mentioned the studio head. Did you work with the director at all on this film?

No. It was a very interesting scenario, it's happened a couple of times. The director was Japanese and had a different vision for what the music should be than the studio, and the director was virtually cut out of the process. So I was actually working with a studio executive. She was spearheading the scoring process. I felt bad for the director at that point, but again, if it's that one person that you have to answer to, it makes things so much easier.

Executives are notoriously thought of as being noncreative and closed-minded. Generally speaking, have you found that to be the case?

It differs from project to project. There are certain executives who are very well known to be very involved in the process at every level—and that could be a good thing or it could be a bad thing. I think the hardest situation for a composer to be in is when there are warring factions between the studio and the creative team, as to what the score should be. At that point it does become really difficult, and in general the studio tends to lean towards the safer choice, whatever that is.

Sometimes the director will really want to try something incredibly interesting and unique and it terrifies the studio. And, you know, it's their money so . . . [*laughs*] I get it on some level, but how amazing is it then when you do see a film which really pushes the boundaries and it does well? It's, like, a marvel to figure out— "How the hell did they get there?"

With *The Last Exorcism*, did the fact that it was a faux documentary alter how you approached writing the music?

Yes, a little bit; we had discussions about that. Obviously, there are similar films that don't use a lot of music at all, like *Paranormal Activity* [2009], for example. That takes it to an extreme, where it's like, "We're not even going to have a score in here." So *The Last Exorcism* was a bit of both, it was blurring the line a bit. They knew a score could really help with the story, and so they were willing to look the other way in terms of it needing to be sold as something absolutely "real." It did affect it a bit, but ultimately not that much.

How often do you read the script before you start working on a film?

Probably half to three quarters of the time. If they're already approaching a director's cut or a locked picture [a film for which the editing has been finalized], then I'll forgo the script and just see it. But oftentimes they're not at that place and they don't want to show you the footage yet, because maybe it's not ready or they're worried about it leaking. Then you read the script. It can be helpful.

Did you read the script for *The Last Exorcism*, or did you watch a cut of it before you started working on it?

I read it and then I saw it, and I thought they did a really good job.

It has a pretty wacky ending, which I personally love.

[*Laughs*] Right, it's pretty out there. That was a fun one, because that was the same approach as *Cabin Fever*, in the sense that I did it completely alone. But it was sort of more abstract: It was, like, tuning my cello down super-low and guitars down super-low. I've actually received quite a few emails about that score, and that was a score I thought would go wholly unnoticed, because it's so much in the background. But I don't know, people seem to like it.

Well, I think it is definitely an interesting score, especially when you listen to it isolated.

Good.

Because you've tuned your cello down so low, it ends up having this oddly Asian feel to it.

Yes, I can totally see that.

You've mentioned a few times that a project's choice of composer came down to you or one other composer. Would you say that it is a competitive industry to be in?

Yes. I'd say it's an extremely competitive industry that gets slightly less competitive once one person with authority endorses you. So when

Alan Ball pointed to me and said, "You're my guy," that was the game changer for me as far as television goes. I actually turn down work now. It's really wonderful as far as television goes. Movies, I've done thirty-one films and I don't have that guy yet, really. So, that's a bit of the luck of the draw.

I'm building a studio, and I bought this Wurlitzer theater organ that was built for the Fox scoring stage in 1928 [and resided there through 1994]. So everyone from the likes of Bernard Herrmann, John Williams, everyone you can imagine, played it over the years. It was also used in *The Sound of Music* [1965]. Part of the reason I'm doing that, other than my love of that instrument and my fascination with using it as a composer, is just to help get work. I think that there will be some filmmakers who are interested in working with that kind of thing.

It's an instrument that is associated with the horror genre, but I want to work that into a hell of a lot more genres than just horror, and I don't want to use it in the way they used it in *Dracula* [1931] or *The Phantom of the Opera* [1925]. It's an instrument that has a universe of sounds that have never been explored beyond what it's traditionally known for. So I'm really excited to do that with horror and many other genres.

Do you think you will continue to work in the horror genre, or do you think there will come a point when you start shying away from it?

I think if it's a good film, I don't care what genre it is. I'm doing a kid show on Amazon right now [*laughs*]. So, I think if it's good, absolutely. I'd love to do more horror films, but I just feel like I have a lot more in me musically than just horror, and that's why it's been nice to stretch out a bit on some of these other genres and shows.

Horror film music seems to attract a large and loyal fan base. There are companies bumping out special edition CDs and vinyl LPs of classic scores. What is it about horror film music that captures the imaginations of so many fans?

Well, I think it's more about the genre. It's just the genre that people really get behind and really love. And it's definitely not for everyone: In my circle of friends, I know a hell of a lot more people who don't like horror films than do. So I think people are just super-passionate about it, and when I think about wanting to watch a horror film, I think, "Oh, it'd be fun to be scared tonight [*laughs*]," you know?

There's just some gravitation towards that that is cool. And so much of that experience, when we watch a horror film, is the music. I think that's why. And the genre allows for really interesting and unique music, just as a genre in general. Drama is so broad. I don't know if you can say that about drama, "Drama allows for really interesting music." Sure, some dramas do, but I think horror really does have that musical identity that people can listen to and go, "Oh my God, I love that movie."

You mentioned that you began recognizing and liking film scores from a fairly young age. Are there any horror film scores that really stood out for you in your youth?

The Shining had a score that I just *really* noticed. As we know, most of that music was not written for that movie, but that was one that really stood out. I could say that about all the big ones. *Psycho* stood out too.

When I first heard it, I thought "Carol Anne's Theme" from *Poltergeist* [1982, music by Jerry Goldsmith] was the most beautiful thing I'd ever heard. Robert Wise's *The Haunting* [1963], that has a great score by Humphrey Searle—it's a great score! It's a brilliant straight orchestral score with just incredibly inventive orchestration and melodies. Also, of course, *Halloween* by John Carpenter. I love that and *The Thing* [1982]! Ennio Morricone's score for *The Thing* is great. And even the score for *The Terminator* [1984, music by Brad Fiedel] has a vibe.

Is there any advice you can give to aspiring film music composers?

I think as composers we're much more approachable than you think. We're so happy to talk to anyone about what we do, because so few people care about what we do [*laughs*]. So, my advice, rather than going to film scoring school, is to just cold-email composers and be really passionate about it. Just beg for an internship. And that can happen. I think it's about just sitting shotgun with a composer as they do their thing. For me it was Hans [Zimmer]. I literally sat shotgun with him, and I saw every angle of the business, from the deals that happen on the movie to the wars to the friendships, everything. I got to see it all and go, "I can do that." And then, once I found out that he also thought I could do that, I was, like, "All right, I'm out of here!"

CHARLES BERNSTEIN

*"I think the best film scores . . . bring something
to the film that is either latent in the film or that isn't
obvious. It doesn't do what the film is already doing."*

C HARLES BERNSTEIN MAY BE BEST KNOWN by horror fans as the man
who gave a musical identity to Freddy Krueger, but he's also an
industry veteran who has scored more than 100 films over the past five
decades. And in recent years his work has experienced a bit of a renaissance, being sampled in countless hip-hop tracks and recycled for many
of indie-film-darling Quentin Tarantino's latest works.

As I researched this book, I discovered that Bernstein is also an
accomplished professor (having taught at USC and UCLA) and author
(*Film Music and Everything Else!* and *Movie Music: An Insider's View*). His
books on the subject of film scoring are fascinating glimpses into the
art form. In them he manages to make complicated musical ideas and
theory accessible to the layman through the creative use of comparison
and metaphor.

His writings have, in many ways, influenced the way I have approached interviewing composers for this book. So when I was granted a short interview with "Professor" Bernstein, I grabbed my notebook and pen and leapt at the chance for a private master class with one of the best teachers on campus.

SELECTED FILMOGRAPHY

1972	*Pigs* (aka *Daddy's Deadly Darling*)
1973	*Invasion of the Bee Girls*
	White Lightning
	That Man Bolt
1974	*Mr. Majestyk*
1976	*Gator*
	Look What's Happened to Rosemary's Baby (TV movie)
1979	*Love at First Bite*
1982	*The Entity*
1983	*Cujo*
1984	*A Nightmare on Elm Street*
1986	*April Fool's Day*
	Deadly Friend
1995	*Rumpelstiltskin*
2003	*Kill Bill: Vol. 1* (additional music)
2007	*Sybil* (TV movie)
2009	*Inglourious Basterds* (additional music)
2015	*Sharktopus vs. Whalewolf* (TV movie)

L et's talk a bit about your musical background. I understand that both of your parents were musical.

Yes. My mom has a bit of a story. When she was a girl, I think around seventeen or eighteen, she had an opportunity to learn the Wurlitzer theater organ, and she played for the last year that there were silent films. . . . She was in Minneapolis, Minnesota. . . . She accompanied them on the organ and also on the piano. So she was scoring films before there was actually a real profession of film composing. My mom lived to be a 101 and still played the piano.

Do you know if they would provide her with sheet music, or would she improvise?

Both. She would improvise the connective tissue, and there was a certain amount of prescribed music from classics and existing music that would be used for romance or for suspense, etc. So the actual music in most of the scenes was existing music, but she would supply the mood, the tempo, and the transitions, you know, that kind of thing. I didn't actually know that when I got into this business. . . . I knew she was a pianist, and she did occasionally mention that she had learned the organ, but I never really got the significance of it until just a few years ago, when she was much older.

Is this where your early love for music came from?

It probably did. She would always be playing the piano in the house, and as a little kid I would hang out under the piano sometimes. It was a baby grand and I would hear the music from that perspective. So, yes, I would say she was largely responsible for my having the sound in my ear as a young guy, hearing Bach and Mozart and also Gershwin—all of that.

My dad was also an interesting guy. He was an older dad, and he was there at the dawn of sound recordings and got into the record business in the 1920s. He actually produced records of jazz, African-American bands, and what he called "hillbilly music." It was early folk, country-folk, country-and-western kind of stuff. By the time I was born he had gotten out of that business and went into the furniture business, but he had written songs and was a producer and had that acquaintance with early recording technique. Pretty honestly, I'd say I come by this genetically.

When did you decide that you were going to pursue music as a career?

Well, that's a very incremental thing. At some point it became apparent that I could do it and earn a living at it. I was playing in bands, doing that kind of stuff, and simultaneously writing and studying. I hadn't really premeditated it to a great degree, but as I realized I had a certain affinity for it, I just started to do it. The more I did it, the more I realized I could sustain myself that way.

But there was a moment when you decided that you were going to pursue an education in it.

That's true. Come to think of it, I had written and conducted a piece when I was sixteen, so I was still in high school at that point. I hadn't thought about it as a career yet, but I seemed to be able to write orchestral music. I had a huge love of Beethoven and other classical composers when I was thirteen and fourteen. I just taught myself some degree of composition at that point. The roots of it go back pretty early, but the actual profession manifested later.

I heard that you worked on something with Phil Spector when you guys were fairly young.

Oh yeah, definitely: I did Phil's first demo. Just Phil and I went into Gold Star Recording in Hollywood. He was a little older than me, and I was in middle school. I grabbed a snare drum and some stuff from the middle school band room and got together with him at Gold Star. He sang and played guitar. We overdubbed; in those days I think it was only three tracks, for some reason. I was playing drums, and I think we overdubbed a little effect on the drum. That was before his first hit. I think this was actually the B-side of his first hit. I did stay in touch with Phil in those days, but as time went on we grew more distant.

How did you become interested in composing music for films?

I was in New York. It was a musical theater town and I have a certain affinity for musical theater. I was writing musical theater . . . in a kind of Off-Off-Off-Broadway revue. I was just in that world, and at some point it became clear to me that you couldn't really earn a living doing it. Very few guys do. It is not impossible, but it just looked like it would be a really rough road. So films looked like a more attractive way of utilizing that affinity that I seemed to have for giving musical sound to dramatic situations. So it had its roots in musical theater.

I know that you also have an affinity for the music of Ennio Morricone.

Oh yeah, I love him.

When did you hear his music for the first time, and what about it excited you?

There was a music store named DeKeyser Music up on Hollywood Boulevard, where you could go and peruse scores. I really hung out there a lot. It was a very tiny little storefront run by an immigrant guy, DeKeyser; I don't know where he was from. Across the street was the Vogue Theater, and if I'm not mistaken it was at the Vogue Theater where I first heard the score to *The Good, the Bad and the Ugly* [1966]. I remember going to that movie, I think it was a matinee. I was already interested in film music. I would carry a notebook in my pocket and write down the names of the composers, because it was all very new to me.

I had heard a lot of Westerns, obviously we all had, and here was a Western that just knocked me out of my chair. I remember the gun-fight—that three-way duel at the end—and just the sound of the music, the fact that it was so fresh. It didn't sound like all of the Westerns I had heard, and that music was so humorous and imaginative and elevating. It just did so many things that the film was not doing. It was actually bringing so much to the movie that wasn't already there that I was elec-trified. There have been a few moments in my life where I knew I was a different human being when I walked out of a theater, and that was one of them. I was absolutely enthralled with what had just happened.

Is that your favorite score of his?

I wouldn't say it is my favorite of his scores, but it is a perfect example of an absolutely brilliant, novel, exciting, imaginative score, and I think it still sounds as fresh to me now as it did then. It hasn't dated. His use of the human voice and all those odd instruments and solos, and the way he recorded the guitar, the EQ—it was just everything he did.

Years later I had a chance to meet Ennio and talk to him, I think it was in the 1980s. I've met him many times since, but that first time I really had a chance to talk to him. Through an interpreter, I asked him about a lot of the things in that score. There was a trumpet player that played this incredibly fast double-, triple-timing figure in the main cue. Ennio spoke about how that guy was probably the only guy in the world that could play that part, and he wrote it specifically for him. Just the way he approaches film music in such a highly specialized way, like casting the trumpet player so carefully and all that. His music still sounds very fresh and wonderful to me.

What exactly is the job of the film music composer?

That's a pretty good question. I think we all take for granted that we all know what that is, and it probably deserves more scrutiny. It is not just one job. There are what the French would call a "medley" of things that we bring to the job. We set moods. We do a lot of obvious things—create atmosphere, lead the audience this way and that.

But I think the best film scores, like we were talking about with Morricone, bring something to the film that is either latent in the film or that isn't obvious. It doesn't do what the film is already doing. In the case of the spaghetti Westerns, it brings a little bit of a "wink." The material might be violent, it might be historical—the Mexican Revolution, what have you—but the music brings something extra.

I'd say that is one of the underrated parts of film scoring, the *job* of the film score. It can also give the movie a musical identity, so that when you hear that music away from the film, it evokes the film. It is something that lives parallel to the film, but outside of it. So it also has that job of giving a certain kind of identity. We hear the theme to *Gone with the Wind* [1939] all these years later and it still carries the identity of the film.

The job of the music is multifaceted, but I always say, "First do no harm." It is so easy to do destructive things with the music. Its first job is to not harm the film and, from that point, to, hopefully, elevate it.

At what point during the making of a film do you become involved?

I've done probably as many as 120 feature-length films, somewhere around there, definitely over 100, and I would say that in most of them I am brought on too late. They are already out of money, out of time, they're out of patience, they have a release date, etc.; they are just up against the clock. So generally we come in too late with too little. That is part of the dilemma of the film music community.

Having said that, there have been instances where I've been brought in very early. Joe Sargent, a director I've worked with a lot, on the remake of *Sybil* [2007] . . . brought me in before he had cast the role of Sybil and he was just starting to do location scouting. He and I had worked together for many years, so he decided to bring me on very early. It was just wonderful. There have been other occasions with Joe where I've come on very early, and we could talk about the style and I could be thinking and gestating the musical ideas. But generally we don't have that luxury.

Can you talk a little bit about your process?

I'd say the process is, once I have the gig and a deal has been made, then the first thing I do is start exploring, in the most general sense, the territory of whatever the film is—whether it is horror, romance, or whatever it is. I try to get a handle on it, and my method is to be as absolutely initially undisciplined and unfocused as possible. I want to leave every single possibility open: Maybe there's a way to do this thing with neoclassical music, bluegrass, or Indonesian monkey chants. I rule out nothing, and then I work from that to narrow it down.

That is generally my process. [I start with] what's the most imaginative and outlandish thing I might think of, and then, obviously, I end up having to reel it in—particularly if it is a television product where they are very conservative. Also, a lot of it depends on the director's taste and all of that. Then we generally go through the film. I won't even talk about temp tracks; that's a whole other issue that comes up. Hopefully, I'm not tethered to the temp music. If I am, as I am right now, luckily they've temped with Morricone and Nino Rota, so I couldn't be happier.

Let's talk about the temp track briefly. Do you find that it is helpful or stifling?

It can be either. The problem is more the attitude of the people you are working for vis-à-vis the temp score. If they love it, you're in a difficult spot, because the chances of doing anything original are pretty slim, especially if they've already marketed it with the temp music and played it for the studio with the temp music. The more they are married to the temp music, the less one will be able to bring a fresh insight. I try not to hear the temp music on my first viewing of a film. It is very handy to know what that temp is, but I like to have the freedom, on the very first viewing, to imagine anything that comes into my mind. Once you hear the temp, you will never ever be able to view the film in that same "virginistic" manner. So that is generally an important factor.

Do you read the script before you watch the rough cut of a film?

I try not to. I find that the information that I get from a movie, that tells me what the music should be, is rarely available in the printed word. What helps me is usually the lighting, the rhythm of the editing, the look of the acting, the flavor of the cinematography, etc. Film is such a visual language. On many occasions they send me a script and I try not to read it, or I explain to them, unless they really want me to, I'd prefer to have my first experience with the picture be visual rather than literary.

Okay. Now you've watched the film. You've thought about what you want to do and you've gone through all of your initial prep. When you sit down to actually begin the process of writing, do you work from the beginning of the film, chronologically, to the end, or do you choose specific scenes from throughout the film and work out of order?

That's a subject that comes up. I was curious about other composers on that count, and I asked John Williams on one occasion, Jerry Goldsmith on another occasion, and I've asked that of several of my other heroes.

Jerry initially said to me that he liked to start at the beginning and go through the picture in chronological order. And John, and Bill Conti as well, mentioned to me that they preferred the notion of overviewing the film and then zeroing in on something near the end that was very crucial musically—climactic, even—and then working outward and backward from that complex moment.

I lean more toward what Jerry originally said. I like experiencing the movie so that my music develops along with my forward motion, where I can feel the thematic material deepening as I'm going more and more into the film. I like that process.

On the other hand, I do often try to do an overview and have certain things in my pocket, so to speak. In *A Nightmare on Elm Street* [1984] and also with *Cujo* [1983] I was in Reel Three before either picture came to me thematically. I was just writing moods, and I probably could've done the whole picture without themes in either of those cases. But then the theme sort of suggested itself, and I went back and wove it into the first few reels and developed it from Reel Three forward. So I guess I am probably a combination [of those approaches].

When you're writing, do you physically write down notation, or do you record it?

Well, obviously, for many, many years I did have to write everything down, and there was a certain point when the themes needed to be written down and the timings needed to be written down and worked out musically. But the more home studio work I did, the less necessary notation became, because either I was playing it myself or I'd just be printing out a part for an individual singer or musician. So the whole way of notating just got turned on its head during the course of my career. Initially it was more like 100 percent writing and zero percent recording, but that equation has slowly shifted year after year, until now I would say that it's ten or twenty percent notation on a score, and the rest just lives in the computer as MIDI data and stuff like that.

In your first book, *Film Music and Everything Else!*, you have many interesting things to say about inspiration. Can you talk a little bit about that?

I'm glad you like that chapter, because it alludes to *Being There*, which is that Jerzy Kosinski book and [1979] movie with Peter Sellers— which, by the way, has a lovely score by Johnny Mandel, a guy that I love and respect. The notion is one of being in a constant gardening state, so that you can always be harvesting. You don't need to plant the seeds and harvest on the same day. I think that is where people get into trouble with writer's block, when they haven't been tending the garden all along.

A day doesn't go by that I'm not "harvesting." If I'm driving the car and listening to the radio, I'm looking out the window of the car and thinking about how that music works with the visuals and lighting. There's a constant "How would this music work in a film?" If I'm listening to a concert somewhere, that's what I'm thinking about. There's a constant process going on. So I'm not always starting from a standing stop, but I hit the ground running, so to speak. I think that is really important when you're writing for a living.

How do you know when a score is finished?

I liken it to cooking or baking. It is like when you put something in the oven: There's a perfect moment to take it out. If you take it out too soon, it is half-baked. If you take it out too late, it is overcooked. It is like knowing when a chicken is perfectly tender but still has a crispy skin. Do you know what I mean?

Knowing that exact instant to take something out of the oven or the exact quantities to put into a recipe, and so forth—that's a skill, and you develop it in a number of ways. When you're making a broth or a soup, you tend to put the spoon in and taste it while you're seasoning. I think, with writing music, we're doing the same thing. We taste it as we go along, and you think, "Okay, this has the right flavor. I don't need to add any more of this or that." I think you always want to taste as you cook. You want to be constantly taking the temperature as you go, when you're writing.

Is it something that you can learn, or is it something that, as an artist, you know instinctually and you just need to recognize it?

I have to relearn it every day. I always overdo; I'm almost always trying to subtract stuff that I've overwritten. I think many composers write more than is necessary to tell the tale, and our job is to pare it back down to the very minimum that will make it work. It is the notion of making things as simple as necessary, but no simpler. I make a distinction between nudity and nakedness in art, and music should be like a nude where it is not all covered up, but not to the degree where it is overexposed. As to how you judge that moment, I don't know. I guess that is what makes each artist unique.

One thing I don't think many people know about your job is that sometimes you work with a team of people. How do the jobs of the composer and the orchestrator differ?

The job of the orchestrator covers a wide range of things. What the composer does is give a multi-staff sketch to the orchestrator. It is usually six staffs and divided into three sections: strings, winds, and then keyboard/harp/percussion on the third. So we reduce everything down to its essence, because it is very laborious to have a huge sheet of scoring paper where you have one staff for the flute, another staff for the second flute, another staff for the third flute, another staff for the oboe, etc.

Instead, on one grand staff [a "grand staff" is a joined double staff, usually covering both treble and bass ranges] we'll put all the wind instruments, and we will write "WW," meaning woodwind, or "FL," meaning flute.

There's a shorthand, so that we don't have to redundantly spell out if three flutes are playing the same part together. The abbreviation is the letter "A" and the number "3." So we just the write the melody and we write "FL A3," and then we only have to write the melody once.

But then the orchestrator does that laborious work of writing it onto the orchestration paper, the score paper. I've seen Jerry Goldsmith's sketches, I've seen John Williams's, and generally these sketches are so complete that even a music student could orchestrate from them. They are really immaculate and very complete. However, I've also seen some sketches from early Hollywood composers, Dimitri Tiomkin and some others from the golden age (they are in libraries and different studios, and so forth), and they are pretty vague. The music is all there, but the orchestration aspect is very vague. There's a lot of leeway for the orchestrator to be creative, and there were certain orchestrators: Alexander "Sandy" Courage, Arthur Morton, the great Irwin Kostal, Leo Shuken, and Jack Hayes. These are famous orchestrators; these guys could turn a piano part into the most gorgeous orchestral writing you've ever heard.

So in the case of great composers like John Williams and Jerry Goldsmith, the orchestrator's job is minimal; they just translate and do their job. But there are many stories of great Hollywood orchestrators who have been responsible for the great beauty of many early Hollywood scores, and later ones, too.

Do you prefer to work with directors who are hands-off, or ones who like to be more involved in the score?

I pray for intelligent directors that are also sensitive. It is really good when you work with smart people. They tend to know how to work with a composer, how to work with actors, etc. They get good results. . . . I don't think any composer likes to be micromanaged. You want broad instructions, a broad idea of what style they like, a broad idea of what they want to accomplish at different points in the film.

What you *don't* want is a director saying, "I hate oboes," or, "Don't use any plucked instruments." I get this a lot, personal taste prejudices of the director. Sometimes they have a little musical knowledge and ask, "Do you think a clarinet will be better than an oboe here?" That kind of micromanagement is very unwelcome to actors as well as composers. Actors don't like to be told specific things to do; they like to be given a range of what the director is going for, and then they like to find a way of doing it. Composers are similar in that regard. Certainly I am.

Do you find it difficult to create in order to fulfill somebody else's vision?

No, that's our job. We're part of a storytelling team; it is not an opportunity to show off our musical abilities. Last night I saw *Grand Budapest Hotel* [2014]. I didn't know who had scored it, but it was my friend Alexandre Desplat. I love his music. Wes Anderson [the director] has a very specific style in the movie, and I could see how Alexandre was able to help Anderson's vision, rather than showing what he can do. In so doing, I can hear the beautiful work of Alexandre, but it is clear that all of the stylistic choices are very much like the stylistic choices of all the other aspects of the film: the scenery, the costuming, the acting.

So, our job is to be part of that team and do the musical part of bringing the director's vision to the screen. If we do that well, we deserve praise, but not if we make ourselves look good at the expense of the film or the director's vision.

Let's talk a little bit about *Cujo*. It is an interesting film because much of it plays more like a family drama than a horror film, and your score reflects that. Can you talk a bit about what it was like seeing that film for the first time and then sitting down and working on it?

I did a Web series with Lewis Teague [director of *Cujo*] a few years ago called *Charlotta* [-TS, 2010], about a transgendered woman. It was kind of comedic, almost slapstick at times, but in so doing, I had a chance to visit a lot with Lewis and we talked a lot about *Cujo*. It was our first picture together. I had known him before that, but it was an important picture for both of us and he was fond of the score.

When I first saw the film, Dan Blatt [the producer] had brought me in, and I was a little worried about the very things you brought up. It takes the movie a long time to get dark, and its conflicts are almost like two movies: There's the dog and then there's the whole family thing, and the two come together very late in the film, to very dark results.

So I was very worried about how to open the movie. It originally opened with a fade-in on the grass where the rabbit comes out of the rabbit hole, and there was no title graphic. I requested that they consider doing something really dark, something that would tell the audience right away that this is going to be a dark movie, and let me score a graphic of the *Cujo* title that lets the audience know what they're in for, and then let's back up and let the rabbit come in.

Dan Blatt was very open to that idea, but I never did see that graphic completed when I recorded the music. It was just a black slug [a strip of blank film used to stand in for missing or forthcoming footage] in the film. Anyway, that was helpful, and I approached *Cujo* in a very thematic fashion. There was a theme for the dog (a low French horn theme), and there was a theme for the family drama and for the boy. Those themes were musically able to then be dark and combined in ways that I think helped unify the film. It was challenging.

Why did you choose the French horn to represent the dog?

The quality of the hunting horn and that quality of dogs that is associated with the nobility of the outdoors . . . taking that and doing it in a very low register for the big, lumbering dog, and being able to darken it with textures and so forth.

You've worked with Wes Craven on a few occasions, and I hope you will talk about your relationship with him. How does he work with a composer?

Wes, as was Lewis Teague, is very smart. He was an academic, I think, before he became a film director. He's a very bright guy, very literarily conscious and very insightful. I found working with Wes to be a really great experience. He also gave me a lot of leeway to bring stuff to him that I thought might be good, and he was very accepting and very encouraging. So he was an ideal director to work with, really.

The process was that you would write stuff, you'd run it by him, and he would either say yes or no or ask for alterations?

Well, they are all a bit like that. But in the case of Wes I just remember wanting to do a thematic approach to [*A Nightmare on*] *Elm Street*, and most of those—what were then called "slasher films"—weren't terribly thematic. I had a lyrical theme that took some weird turns [*hums the theme*]. That theme came to me rather late in the process. I said, "Look, Wes, you may not go for this, but I'd like to have a lyrical theme like this that I can transform through the film, and I think it will be a good thing." I was actually a bit worried that he'd think it would be edgier to just do mood music and stay edgy, but he was very open to it. I think it really helped the film to have a thematic unifying theme in it.

If you came up with that lyrical theme fairly late in the process, what were you writing before that?

If you listen to the opening of *Elm Street*, you realize that that cue could exist with or without the theme. The theme is just sprinkled in like parsley on top of a soup, but the soup was basically consisting of mood elements, dark things, percussion hits. And the actual notes that are present could be part of a theme or they could be just random, and it probably would have had a very similar effect.

There was already that little jump-rope thing, because that was in the movie. That was filmed with the girls saying, "One, two, Freddy's coming for you." I didn't write that *per se*, but I could allude to it [*hums a few notes*] in a way that makes you remember the jump-rope activity. The thematic element, I then went back and sprinkled it into that opening thing which I had already written.

Do you find that that happens a lot? You come up with something toward the end of the process, and then you have to go back and work it into the beginning to make it uniform?

Well it did happen in *Elm Street* and in *Cujo*, but I wasn't near the end; I was only about three reels in, I was maybe about a third of the way into the picture. Then I was working backward and forward at the same time. Once I had it in hand and I could feel how it influenced the film, it was really helpful to have it. It was very comforting to know that I had something that I could do permutations of and work with and it would serve the film. So, yes, it does happen. It has happened in other films, but certainly in those two.

You've done so many different kinds of scores during your career. Do you like scoring horror films?

Yes, I do, because there is a lot of opportunity to be original and to deal with emotions. I think horror is preferable, in that sense, to romantic comedy, which is often less open to experimentation. Usually you're stuck with a light pop feel in a lot of romantic comedies. So certainly I prefer it to having to do generic things. However, horror can get pretty generic too, because people start imitating each other. I never really listen to other horror scores or try and imitate them. My approach is usually to just try and find music that is evocative of the emotion that is needed, rather than worry about what the temp track is doing or where the music has to imitate something else.

So many horror films are made with a limited budget; *A Nightmare on Elm Street* **is a perfect example. Do you sometimes find that working with financial limitations can be liberating?**

I don't think so. I like to have money to work with; you get better people for longer times and better ensembles. But in the case of *Elm Street* it did force me into a kind of style that I probably could not have gotten with the traditional methods, like having a recording session and all that. That was a very early home-studio thing where I played all the parts. I think, in that case, it was good for the movie that I was forced to do all that weird stuff alone rather than writing for an ensemble, where I probably would have gone a little more conventional in some areas.

Do you find the advancements in technology to be just awesome [*Bernstein laughs*], **or do you sometimes feel like you're losing some of the romantic aspects of what the job used to be?**

Well, I think both, but it is unquestionably awesome! The technology is so fantastic that in my wildest dreams, when I started in this business, if I were to make a science-fiction wish list of the future, I could not have imagined how wonderful it could be. The technology is just phenomenal, and I really love it.

I've embraced technology from the very beginning: I was mocking up scores as early as *Mr. Majestyk* [1974] and even before. So I love the technology, but on the other hand there is nothing like being in a room and simultaneously hearing all the musicians playing at once and getting the chemistry of the orchestra just right, like in *Cujo*. That is just so wonderful too.

So the degree to which the orchestral sessions have been squeezed out for budget and technological reasons, I think that is a real loss, but the technology is a real gain. And it is possible to have a win–win here, where you do all the magic with the technology as long as the budgets still allow for orchestras, which is unfortunately not always the case.

Do you find that music in horror films serves a different purpose than music in other types of films?

Yes. There are things that happen in horror movies that don't happen in other movies. Wes [Craven] was very good at this—we call them *stings*. You need to jolt the audience in a horror movie in ways that you don't in other kinds of movies. You need to prepare them for the jolt in a way that the other movies don't do. You need to create a mindset of apprehension and tension. Horror movies have their own set of demands that are different from a romance or a historical epic or something. But each film has its own demands, and each genre has its own peculiar demands as well.

After you've completed work on a film, do you go see it with an audience, and is that a gratifying experience?

Yes. Things change drastically when there is an audience there, and it is a wonderful experience to see a movie with an audience and to feel their reactions. I saw *Elm Street* a few months ago with an audience for the first time in a very long time, a big audience in a beautiful theater. It was at the ArcLight in Hollywood, and I was then interviewed after the movie. Sitting there and experiencing that particular movie after many years (I don't think I had seen it in a theater since the initial release) and feeling how it worked on the audience and being in the audience, I just loved that. To me, that is one of the lovely experiences.

Do you have a favorite session? It doesn't necessarily have to be your favorite score, but is there a specific session that you look back at fondly?

Sure. I can name a few sessions that I just loved. *Love at First Bite* [1979] was absolutely terrific, and the miniseries *Sadat* [1983]—that was a wonderful session with a mixture of Egyptian and American musical elements. There was a movie called *Foolin' Around* [1980], we had a nice healthy budget, I wrote some songs with Seals and Croft. We had a lovely orchestra and we had some disco sessions. Actually we had disco sessions for *Love at First Bite*, where it was more record industry–type stuff, and then there were some very orchestral sessions for that as well. Most of my favorites are from a little more back in the day when orchestras were more prevalent.

Horror films have always had a strong fan base, but in recent years it has become very clear that the music for those films also attracts a large and loyal group of fans. Do you think there is something specific about that type of film music that transcends the picture for its listeners?

There is commonality between all film music genres, and that is, when you hear the music you re-experience the emotions of the film or it brings back the ambience of a film. Horror movies are very atmospheric, they are all very special. They each create an intriguing world, and to be able to re-create that world without the movie is a fun and miraculous thing. And I would guess that a lot of fans enjoy being able to re-experience those emotions by the magic of having the music almost holographically create the world of the movie just through sound. That would be one guess, but it is hard to say.

JOSEPH BISHARA

"[Horror] has always been the genre that I am drawn to
naturally. It is the one that had the most energy for me.
There always just seemed to be something a little bit more
compelling about being on the edge of everything going away."

J OSEPH BISHARA WAS THE THIRD PERSON I contacted when I began
working on this book, but because of his rigorous schedule, it was
more than a year later before our interview finally took place. During
that time, though, he continued to be enthusiastic and supportive about
the project, and in many ways I found that comforting and motivational
as I traveled into the uncharted territory of interview-based horror film
music analysis.

Bishara's journey into the world of film scoring has been an interesting and varied one, and along the way he has worked with many noteworthy people, including filmmakers John Carpenter, Joseph Zito, and James Wan and musicians Ray Manzarek and Diamanda Galás. As one of horror's leading contemporary composers, he has helped some of today's leading horror directors reinvigorate the genre by providing the musical voices for some of this generation's premier paranormal films and franchises.

Unlike many composers who work within the horror genre, even many of the ones interviewed for this book, Bishara is first and foremost a horror fan. Some could call his musical style avant-garde, but his is a unique voice that has found the medium perfectly suited to it, in the genre that he loves. There is something inspiring about a person who is living out his dream, and even though it took a long time for us to sit down for this interview, without his initial enthusiasm and continued support this book may never have been finished. Thanks, Joseph.

SELECTED FILMOGRAPHY

2000	*The Convent*
2001	*Ghosts of Mars* (sound designer)
2002	*Masters of Horror* (TV documentary)
2003	*Power Play*
2006	"Pro-Life" (*Master of Horror* TV series; score mixer)
	The Gravedancers
2008	*Autopsy*
2009	*Night of the Demons*
2010	*Insidious*
2013	*Dark Skies*
	The Conjuring
	Insidious: Chapter 2
2014	*V/H/S: Viral* (segment: *Gorgeous Vortex*)
	Annabelle
2015	*Insidious: Chapter 3*
	The Vatican Tapes
	Tales of Halloween (segments: *Trick, Friday the 31st*)

Tell me about your early musical influences.

Music grabbed me pretty early on. I remember being very young and always going to sleep listening to classical music. It just became a thing. There was a period there when I was very little where it was just how I would sleep. It just became normal, and then I started having music on nearly all the time. I was just really drawn to listening.

I remember finding an old Moog synth at a little electronics store, and I would go in there and play around with the oscillators and listen with headphones. It was just, like, "Wow! This is amazing." So then I got drawn into that kind of sound. Tangerine Dream was a huge thing for me at that time. Some of their sounds and the way they were approaching things were just very compelling.

Since music was always such a big thing in your life, when did you decide that you were going to make it your profession?

I don't think that it was really as much a conscious decision as it was a direction. It was the path that I was on. Around that time, I was also very into jazz. I was listening to a lot of Miles Davis. I played trumpet as a kid. That was actually my first instrument; I played it in school and I learned to read music that way.

Did you pursue music as a college education?

There was some college. I never completed it, but I did find the program I was in to be very useful. At that time I had been playing in a band, and we got a record deal. We went on tour, and then I never made it back to finish my education.

What was the name of the band?

The band was called Drown. It was kind of a heavy industrial band.

And what year was that?

That was around 1994.

Being such a big fan of Tangerine Dream, was scoring films something you always thought about, or did you fall into it?

That is definitely something that I always thought about. I also came across the film *The Cabinet of Dr. Caligari* [1920]. I was able to watch that on Super 8 film and the imagery just grabbed me. So making music for movies was always on my mind, and it grew more and more. As things went on, it was always just something that I wanted to do. It always seemed that the time would come, if I kept on the path.

How does a kid just happen to stumble on to a Super 8 print of *The Cabinet of Dr. Caligari*?

My parents had an old projector, and I came across the print at the local library. I was pretty little at this point, maybe I was six, but seeing it, particularly in that form, just had an effect on me.

I have always felt that around that age is the perfect time to be exposed to silent films. Kids that young haven't had much experience yet; they don't have that many other things to compare such films to. So they don't just dismiss it as being old or outdated, and the acting style is often so over-the-top that it is kind of cartoonish. It is amazing that you got to experience that film at that age, because if you had seen it later, it may not have had as much of an impact on you.

Perhaps. There is something about it that is just so removed from whatever your current era happens to look like that it gives it even more of an otherworldly quality. And there's just so much compelling energy attached to it.

Claudio Simonetti has written original music for *Nosferatu* [1922] and has even performed it live during screenings of the film. Seeing how *The Cabinet of Dr. Caligari* was such an important film for you, have you ever considered writing an original score for it?

I have. I have considered a lot of things, but it is impossible to do everything. Maybe I will do it someday. It's hard to say.

Oddly enough, out of all of the composers I've spoken to, you're one of the few who is actually a horror film fan. What is it about the genre and the music that captured your imagination and made it important to you?

It has always been the genre that I am drawn to naturally. It is the one that had the most energy for me. There always just seemed to be something a little bit more compelling about being on the edge of everything going away. There is something about that that is appealing. It is like walking into a room and something just has more light on it and so that is what you're drawn to—and that's what horror was like for me. That imagery has been what has pulled me from one thing to the next.

Similarly, on the musical side, it has always seemed to explore things that you have not necessarily heard before. Sounds are coming through in a way that just don't seem like another arrangement of the same thing, but it is more, like, "Wow, what's this?"

When you started composing music for film, did you actively seek out horror films, or did you just get lucky and fall into it?

Oh, no! That was absolutely a direction that I wanted to go in. That wasn't even a question. It was definitely horror that I always wanted to do. It is not by accident that I work on a lot of horror movies [*laughs*]—it is definitely a choice.

I ask because many composers do a horror film and they get type-cast, and then that is the only work that they get offered.

It just so happens to work out very well that those are the things that seem to come my way, and I am very glad that is the case. That is what I like, so that is what I want to do.

Is it true that your introduction to film scoring was through composing music for movie trailers?

That is correct.

Can you talk a little bit about that process, and how it differs from working on feature films?

It is much more hyperfocused on moments; it is a completely different mindset. At the time it was just what was happening for me. I was working with a band called Prong on a song for the *Strange Days* [1995] movie soundtrack, a cover of the Doors song [of the same name]. Ray Manzarek [an original member of the Doors] played with us on that, which was pretty cool. From there I was asked to score the teaser trailer for the film, and I just ended up doing some of that for a while. It was cool to just get to play around with some film imagery. I got thrown some footage from interesting films, and it was just a cool thing to do for a while.

Were you scoring to rough cuts of the trailers, or were you supplying music cues and then the editor would edit to them?

It went both ways. I haven't really been too active doing that in a while, but . . . for a while it was just a place where I could make a bunch of music and there'd be a place to put it. Since I was drawn to making horror music, and it was what I was making anyways, it just seemed to be a really natural flow. I feel that I have been pretty fortunate to be able to professionally explore the voice that I would naturally want to anyway.

How did you meet John Carpenter and come to work on *Ghosts of Mars* [2001]?

That was through his music producer, Bruce Robb. He and his brothers owned a studio in Hollywood called Cherokee Studios. It was a really great, legendary room that is no longer there; I believe there are townhomes there now. That is where they were doing the *Ghosts of Mars* score. He contacted me through a producer that I had worked with a lot at that time named Bob Ezrin. Bob worked at Cherokee a lot and recommended me to Bruce. I went in and met Carpenter, Bruce, and the other guys down there at the studio. The next day I moved my setup in and got to work.

What did you do on that film? When I spoke to Carpenter, he seemed incredibly impressed with what you were doing, but he really had a tough time explaining exactly what it was. He did say that it was "amazing to watch," though.

[*Laughs*] That is funny. They already had a lot of stuff recorded, but a lot of it was just sketches. Carpenter played some tracks, and he would layer and play some other parts, and they'd take those tracks and feed them to me into Pro Tools [a digital music recording, editing, and processing program], and I would just play around with them, in a way remixing them to picture.

Also, with the way sync was running in that room, there were a lot of machines talking to other machines. So it was a little tricky, but it was pretty cool being able to sit there and take these tracks from John. He would sit behind me and I would try things, look back at him, and ask, "What do you think?" He would just say, "It's great! I just love watching you work. Keep going." It was a blast. Being such a fan of his work and being able to sit there and work with him . . . I can't tell you how awesome that was.

Did you get a glimpse of his process, or were you working on things after they were recorded?

No, there was still a lot happening. He was still recording a lot of stuff, and it was cool to see his process, how he would just be there with the movie and watch long chunks of the film back with whatever he had been working on. It is not like it was done and I came in and twisted it all up; he was still recording and playing and bringing in musicians and tracking other things. He did a whole chunk of the score with Anthrax. He brought in some metal guys and Buckethead came in and played guitar. It was just a really interesting assortment of players that came in to play on it. It was fun to watch John play around with it. He seemed to be having a good time.

I'd love to get into your process. For example, at what point during a film do you generally come aboard?

In general, it seems that most projects have at least been mentioned to me fairly early on. I've probably had more time than a lot of situations usually tend to permit. I've certainly been thrown some fast curveballs, but I can say that there have been things that have been talked about early enough that they've had a pretty healthy amount of time to ferment before having to come out.

How long do you typically get to do a score?

It really can vary anywhere from a few weeks to a few months to a year-plus [*laughs*], depending on what it is. Sometimes something will start and go for five or six weeks and will just come to a halt and then start back up again sometime later. If you add up the actual work time, it's not necessarily that long, but the projects can be open and around for a long time.

How long did you have for *Insidious* [2010]?

Insidious was one of those films where there was a period of time when I was working on it and there was some mixing and playing around, then we came back to it. That's the thing: There's the earlier period where we're talking about it and just sketching stuff and playing around and there's no ticking clock. We're just working and we're talking, and then, all of the sudden, "Here's an edit. We have this mix date, and now you have three weeks to finish." So that happened with *Insidious*. Then we got to come back and open it up, play around some more, and go mix it again after it got sold at the Toronto Film Festival.

A lot of the composers I have talked to don't really care about the script. Do you like to read the script? Do you find it to be a useful tool?

I will take anything I can get. I will take any information. I love using the script to work off of. It is a really helpful tool for me. It's all great, it is all information, it all feeds into it.

I start getting ideas as soon as we even start talking about something, often right away. Sometimes something will arise out of that and then, a little later on, maybe something totally unexpected will happen, another piece will arise and connect and so on. And it keeps going until, "Oh, there it is." It is all part of it, including the script. It is all about getting into the energies behind it all.

When you meet with a director for the first time to start discussing the music, is there specific information that you're looking for?

Not necessarily. It's more about seeing what the project is and seeing where everybody's head is at. I really just try to be open. I don't have checklist.

When you actually sit down to begin writing, what is your process like?

Keep in mind that with anything I say here, there have probably been times that the exact opposite has also happened. But generally I like to let things just sit and be there for a while. There's a lot of pre-work that I tend to do, which is often just letting things breathe, sketching and grabbing the vaguest ideas and letting them sit there until they naturally grow together. I try to take as much time as I can to just let things sit.

When you say "sketch," what do you mean? Are you physically writing notes on paper, or are you sitting at a keyboard and recording ideas?

Both. I do a lot of pencil-to-paper writing as well as playing and recording. By the time I approach making something, I am usually already hearing it. And sometimes it is immediate. With James [Wan], sometimes he will be describing a scene to me and I am literally hearing it immediately. From then on it is a matter of translating it. It is almost a dictation process: It is like I hear it and then it is just a matter of figuring out how to translate it as clearly as I can.

That's the initial stage, anyway. Later on there's the whole craft part of putting that all together and assembling it to picture, but the initial part is more the hearing it—getting everything out of the way, becoming quiet, and being able to just hear it and translate it clearly.

With several of the composers I have spoken to, particularly the ones who have had formal music training, they describe that they are always hearing music, almost like a radio in their heads, and it is just a matter of getting it down on paper or tape. It sounds like that is what is going on with you.

Yeah, there's definitely that side to it, that is a big part of it. I hear it and then I try to translate it. Then there is taking that translation and figuring out how to build that into the film.

Do you ever deal with writer's block?

Fortunately, I can't say I've had too many issues these days. It's been a steady flow. I don't want to make it sound like it is not a lot of work, because it is a ton of work. There are definitely times when you're butting your head against things, but [when that happens] you have to turn your energy elsewhere and work on something else. Sometimes when the clock is ticking, you're looking at it and it is like a city on fire—you just run around and try to put out the biggest fires first.

It seems like you frequently enter a project fairly early. Is a temp score something you typically have to deal with, and do you have feelings about them one way or the other?

Temp scores are what they are. They are a part of the process now, for a lot of people anyways. I see them as things that should be turned off as quickly as possible. Once we've talked through the film, it becomes something that I try to never look back at, because it is totally irrelevant. It's a tool. I think it is important to keep in mind that "temp" stands for temporary, not template.

What would you say is your goal as the composer?

Ultimately the goal is to do your part to help the film communicate what it is trying to communicate. It is about trying to open up to whatever the world of the film is and helping to create the sound of whatever this energy is that is opening up. And, of course, that is coming from everyone. It is coming from the director, it is coming from the performers. It is coming from everyone in there, but it is certainly driven by the director's intention.

How did you meet Mike Mendez and end up working on *The Convent* [2000]?

I met Mike through a mutual friend, a special effects artist named Screaming Mad George. George does this really incredible, surreal work, and he also had a band at the time. He's in Japan now, but I met Mike through him. Mike was working on *The Convent* and George introduced us.

What is Mendez's process with the music?

Working with Mike is usually pretty loose and fun. We hit it off right away and have been friends ever since. It was a pretty smooth process. We talk about it, he lets me do my thing, then he comes over and addresses it. It's usually more a matter of addressing story points than direct musical notes.

Have you ever had a director play you music, maybe not as a guide, but to show you an example of the kind of feel they're going for?

Of course. People definitely get ideas and get inspired by things, and then you look at it and listen to it. It is more about trying to understand where they are coming from, what the energy is that they are keying into. It usually isn't necessarily about what the actual piece they are playing for you is, but it is about the energy it is drawing out of them. It is kind of like a martial arts move, where you don't look directly at it, but instead you look at what is driving it. Then you interpret it into the language of the score you're actually working on.

What was it like working with Joseph Zito on *Power Play* [2003]? It is not a horror film, but he certainly has a reputation as a horror director.

He was cool, and his horror filmography was a big part of why I did it. It was, like, "Really, the director of *The Prowler* [1981]? I'm in!" It was cool to just hang with him. He's the director of *Friday the 13th* Part Four [*The Final Chapter,* 1984]! It was great!

He's known for being a bit of a character. What were discussions with him like, regarding what he was looking for from the music?

It was interesting. He is looking at his action movies almost like they are horror movies. As he talks through a scene, he describes things as if it was a horror movie, but instead of the villain being Jason or the Prowler, here it's an agent . . . or whoever. He will describe it the same way: "This is your fear object," "That's your fear object." He's looking at things in horror movie terms, at least in the way that he's describing it, for sure.

You worked with Adam Gierasch on a few films, including the remake of *Night of the Demons* [2009], for which you didn't just write the score, you were also the music supervisor. Being a horror fan, were you excited to be working on that one?

Yeah, I definitely knew the original and enjoyed it very much. I enjoyed the music in it, the songs, all of it. Adam did, as well, and [the director of the original] Kevin Tenney was on board. So everybody that was involved creatively was a fan of the original for sure.

Of course, there was a score, but there was also this thing of finding a bunch of songs for Adam, as well. A big chunk of the movie takes place at a Halloween party. That was always his idea, to make a Halloween-party movie and a Halloween-party soundtrack. We brought in [the band] 45 Grave to do the title song for the film and some other cool bands to contribute. That was really enjoyable, getting to dig around into a genre of music that I have always loved. It was the same with Adam. It was definitely made out of, "Hey, let's have fun making this."

With the score, I just got to look into this place and this world and open up to it. I got to see what it sounded like, and I did my best to get it out there.

You're a composer who has worked with many different directors. I'm very curious about how they communicate their ideas and needs to you. I'm sure they all have different ways of doing it. Can you shed a little bit of light on some of the things they do that you find helpful?

Of course everyone approaches things a little bit differently. Adam [Gierasch] really likes to hear music, he likes to come over and listen to stuff. Because of schedules and other duties, he sometimes doesn't get to come over as much as he'd like, but he is very much about coming to the studio, being a part of the process, and hearing as much as he can. He is very story-driven. He is a writer, so he thinks in terms of these things. So that is very much how he approaches music as well.

Mike [Mendez] likes energy. He really enjoys what he does. He just loves making movies, particularly horror movies—like a lot of people do, but perhaps even more than a lot of people. So he just likes to come over and have fun. We listen to music. He really enjoys and loves the process.

James [Wan] is extremely involved in the process, but there are stages. There are times where it is just, like, "Do your thing and let's make this." And then, after I've worked on it for a while, he will come in and want to hear it, because we've talked about it for so long. He also likes to hear some of the early ideas as they develop, to help get inspired while shooting.

How did you meet James Wan and come to work on *Insidious*?

We met through a group of people involved in horror filmmaking around LA. It was this group of friends that would get together and go see each other's films. Mike Mendez was a part of it, [along with] Dave Parker, Adam Gierasch, Joe Lynch, and Adam Green, etc. A whole bunch of people would all get together and go see films. We'd go to horror events around LA. I met James through this group of people.

For your *Insidious* score you take an interesting approach and use the piano in a nontraditional way. You play it more like percussion instrument, hitting and scraping things across the strings, etc. It reminds me a little bit of Carl Zittrer's score for *Black Christmas* [1974]. How did you make that decision?

It was actually a pretty organic decision. My friend found this piano shell behind his studio, abandoned in an alley in Hollywood. They dragged it into their place. He had it there and it was just something that I always wanted to get in there and use. I started calling it the "rust piano," because all the strings had these thick crusty layers of gunk all over them.

Before the film was even cut, I went down and did a session recording on this instrument. It had such a unique character to it. I started assembling some recordings and I sent them to James [Wan]. He loved them, and at that point he actually mentioned *Black Christmas*, and I went back and re-watched it as well as *Deathdream* [aka *Dead of Night*, 1972]. I had already done the sessions on the piano, and it was, like, "Wow! Yeah, we're in tune. We're on the same page." [*Laughs*] James gives me a lot of freedom. We talk a lot and he lets me do my thing. It's a very clear line of communication.

Seeing how you're actually in the film, I'm assuming you entered that project fairly early.

I did come to that one pretty early. We talked some about the music and we started talking about the character. He mentioned being a demon in the film, and then he sent me the script. The way he first talked about it, I didn't realize it was as major a character in the film as it was. I thought it might be a character in passing, somewhere in a scene, and then I read the script and I was, like, "Oh, this is, like, a real character in the script. Okay." Then we got busy with getting the shoot together, and music became the second conversation.

Before you agreed to act in the film, you knew you were going do the music.

Yes, definitely, and I had already started doing some work with it, just sketching on paper.

Did the two things affect each other at all?

Definitely.

Does knowing what the music will be affect your performance? In postproduction do you work extra-hard to score those scenes that you're in?

It's not even that; it is just more information for both things to grow out of. A kind of motion or energy can grow out of what a posture or a movement might feel like. Sometimes being literally in a scene and just feeling the energy of it and hearing the direction and knowing what the intention is can cause a response and cause me to begin to hear something. Then later it becomes a matter of going back and translating it.

You also worked on several films with directors where directing wasn't necessarily their first job in the business. For instance, Scott Stewart, who you worked with on *Dark Skies* [2013], is a special effects guy who became a director. With *Annabelle* [2014], John Leonetti was a cinematographer who became a director. Do you find that these directors who come to projects with more technical and visual backgrounds have a different way of approaching sound than directors who started out being directors?

That is an interesting question. But I think, particularly with Scott and Leonetti, it always comes back to story. . . . It comes down to what it is communicating. That is certainly how Scott looked at *Dark Skies*. He was almost talking as if it was a drama, but there happened to be aliens. It is about the story. It is about what is happening and about communicating what is happening as clearly as possible. It was the same with John Leonetti. He knows what he is trying to communicate and sets out to best tell the story he is trying to tell.

With *Dark Skies* there are aliens, but there is also this concept of "alien tones." When you see that in a rough cut of the film or read that in the script, how do you go about translating that into the score?

That one was actually a pretty quick process. I didn't have too much time to overthink things, which was kind of nice. It came up right before everyone was shutting down for the end-of-the-year holidays and New Year's, etc., and we were coming back in the beginning of the next year to mix it.

I talked to Scott about what he wanted the score to be. It was important to him that we weren't too on-the-nose. In a lot of ways the film is almost an indie family drama. There are a lot of layers; he's almost approaching it like a play. But I started hearing these tones and how these alien tones would work with these other pieces, and how that would work with a very small ensemble and mixing the elements together into this thing. It was almost like the pattern of an oscillator would be a character, where part of the language of it would be a *whoosh* that stops suddenly, or something to that effect.

Would you say that one of the jobs of that score was to keep the alien presence as a character within the movie?

Yes, definitely.

I find that that is a recurring aspect of music in horror films, and it is something that I'm not sure happens all that much in other films. Harry Manfredini used the "ki ki ki, ma ma ma" sounds to keep the killer present throughout *Friday the 13th* [1980]. Goblin used the eerie whispers in its *Suspiria* [1977] score to make it feel like the witch was always there, even when it wasn't. And, of course, the ascending half-step motif in the *Jaws* [1974] theme is another perfect example.

Well, that is definitely a big part of it, to be a presence within the film. I am speaking only for my own way of looking at things at that moment in the process. A lot of it is about looking into what is driving the story, and oftentimes I'm looking at what color the driving force is underneath. What's pushing things? What are we looking at? And it is not all one thing. It might be, but there are a million shades to everything. So it is just a matter of what is driving it and what color it is. It might be similar energy, but it is a very different color. It is always just a matter of creating that presence.

Growing up a fan of horror films, are you also a fan of Goblin and the film *Suspiria*?

Absolutely. *Suspiria* is an incredible and unique piece of work. It is truly exceptional.

I ask because I feel that a lot of the music you did for *The Conjuring* [2013] has a very similar feel to the music in *Suspiria*, not necessarily *Suspiria*'s main theme, but the other music in the film . . . the use of the voice and its overall vibe. It may just be subconscious, but do you sometimes approach doing a score with other scores in mind?

No, not consciously at least. I grew up steeped in Italian horror movies, so it would be part of the language that I was listening to and certainly what I responded to creatively and as a viewer, it was just what I was drawn to. I love the genre and the composers, such as Ennio Morricone. There is so much great work out there, and that is what I spent a lot of time watching and listening to.

I get the sense that *The Conjuring* had a bigger budget than some of the other films you were doing around that time.

It was definitely a bigger palette to play with.

How does a bigger budget affect the creative process?

More time, more musicians, bigger sessions. James and I would talk about the supernatural elements, and we would spend a lot more time talking about the actual ideas in the film than we did the music. Most of our conversations, at least early on, would be about the haunting and the case and what do the ghosts do and what happens—it was about looking at all of that. Then, from there, I'd start hearing it. I was hearing this brass pattern in my head and figuring out how to get that out.

So I was able to put this brass session together and go record it at Capitol [Studios]. Then later on I was able to assemble a bigger recording session with brass, strings, winds, piano, and harp at the Eastwood Scoring Stage at Warner Bros. On a smaller film, there is just no way that could happen. It's just not possible.

Do you find that with the smaller films, restriction can fuel creativity, or for you is it all just the same process?

Well, of course it gives you a set of limitations, but limitations are all you ever really have, no matter what is. It's the combination of time and resources and what you can do with that circumstance.

How do you know when a score is done? Of course that can be dictated by the deadline, but creatively how do you know? It is always tempting with art to just keep on working on it.

I don't feel like I encounter that too much. Sometimes the things will go on way after they feel like they're done [*laughs*], but it seems to mostly be dictated by the calendar. If you have time to keep something open, it is not like it is going to sit dormant. Somebody is likely to come back with a different point of view and want to alter something, even if they say to you, "It's just a small edit." That can still mean a fair amount of work to accommodate.

Mark Isham contributed a track to *The Conjuring* score. Did you work with him on it, or was it done totally separately?

No, I didn't work with him on it. They had a very specific idea of how they wanted this end piece of the film to sound. I did some versions, but they just had a clear idea of what they wanted, so they did that.

You've now worked on *Insidious: Chapter 2* [2013] and *Insidious: Chapter 3* [2015]. When you score a sequel, do you feel like a lot of the work is done already, or is it a more difficult job?

I am really enjoying getting to revisit the language, but translating it for a new film. It always has a bit of a different feel. I hear it differently every time, and a new angle will just speak to me. I'm finding it creatively satisfying to reopen this language.

Is it limiting or is it freeing, in that there are parts of the process that you don't have to think about and you just get to expand on what's already there?

Everything is going to have a certain set of limitations. Everything is going to give you a different circumstance, but in this particular circumstance, how I hear it is like it's a different dialect of an already existing language.

Insidious: Chapter 3 is Leigh Whannell's directorial debut. Do you find working with a first-time director to be different? Easier? Harder?

It's just different. I wouldn't say it was easier or harder because he's a first-time director, because he really did an incredible job with it. It was a very comfortable process, and it seemed to be that way across the board. And that filtered down from how he handled things: He knows what he wants and what he wants to communicate. He's written all these films.

Is seeing the films you've worked on with a crowd nerve-wracking or gratifying or both?

Seeing things with an audience is definitely a different experience. It is always different when there is a new energy added to something that you're viewing. Everything always feels different with an audience. That's why people like to show things to people and just see what it feels like in the room, because sometimes something that is uncertain, like, "Is this sequence too long, is it too short?," can become very apparent once you show it in a room full of people, just by how it feels.

It's always interesting, because you're just seeing things with a very different mindset occupying that space. Sometimes details you didn't even notice will make people jump and scare them, and you'll get a big gasp where you thought it might just pass as another moment. You just never know how any particular audience is going to react to something.

Do you have a favorite session or project? Not necessarily your favorite score, but an experience working on a film that you remember fondly?

I've been fortunate to have a lot of really great sessions. I've got to work with some really incredible players and have really been fortunate to just stand in the same room with some of these musical things happening. It's really humbling. On _The Conjuring_, it was really great to get to work with Diamanda Galás. I've always been a fan of her work. I've seen her perform live many times over the years, and then to get to connect with her and bring her onto the project and to go down to San Diego and record a vocal session with her and just be standing in the room with her, it was incredible.

In that instance, was there a collaboration, or did she just give you what you asked for?

I had my notes as to what it was we had to do. I had a list of pieces we needed to work on, "We need to do something here, and here is this figure for this section, and let's work on that. Let's do this figure and let's take this here." And I stood at the mic with her. Some of her parts were recorded completely wild, and some would be recorded to some of the music that was already recorded with the brass. I remember bringing back the recordings and putting them together—it was just perfect.

One of the main reasons I decided to write this book is that horror film music tends to connect with an audience in the way that other types of film music often don't. Yes, there are people who listen to all types of film music, but horror fans seem to be a little more hard-core about it. Horror scores are constantly being reissued; composers like Goblin, Fabio Frizzi, Alan Howarth, and Simon Boswell can play live to sold-out crowds. Do you have any thoughts as to why horror film music has such a big fan base?

It seems that the people that are fans of the music are also fans of the films and that kind of energy in general. Some people are just drawn to it, drawn to darker things. There is something about being closer to whatever energy that is that captures their attention somehow.

I hope this doesn't offend you, but I would say that you're pretty adventurous, even experimental, as a composer. It seems that horror is the perfect place for musical experimentation.

It seems that there is a lot of room to do that. It is a great place to explore those colors. That presence—that energy that is being generated—that's the fabric of what it is, so it can be any color.

Do you have advice for anyone that wants to pursue composing music for films?

If that's the language that you want to speak, just speak it. Just make music for whatever you can. All you can do is just head in a direction and look for what's out there. And one thing will lead to the next, and that will be your path. That is all you can really do. If that's what you want to do, just do it.

SIMON BOSWELL

"Let's not underestimate repetition. It is absolutely the key to film music, as it is to pop music. Not only is it within a pop song, but it is also within the number of times you hear a pop song, or used to hear a pop song on the radio. Repetition is absolutely everything."

O UT OF ALL OF THE COMPOSERS interviewed for this project, British composer Simon Boswell's path to film scoring stands alone. He spent a decade in the music business as a solo artist, band member, and successful producer before a chance encounter with Italian horror film royalty—Dario Argento—changed his life forever and led him to a successful career as a film music composer.

A bit of an outsider looking in, Boswell began his scoring career working in the eccentric Italian horror film industry with genre masters Argento, Lamberto Bava, and Michele Soavi. The unorthodox methods of Italian cinema provided great training that eventually led Boswell to successful collaborations with noteworthy directors outside of Italy as well, including Alejandro Jodorowsky, Richard Stanley, Danny Boyle, and Clive Barker.

I found Boswell's ability to talk about his life and work with objectivity and candor completely refreshing. As one of the few composers interviewed for this book who is without a "proper" collegiate music education (something he seems to wear as a badge of honor), he provides distinctly interesting perspectives on the art form, the film industry around the world, and the process of creating music for film—particularly the Italian way of doing things.

SELECTED FILMOGRAPHY

1985	*Phenomena* (aka *Creepers*)
1986	*Demons 2*
1987	*Stage Fright* (aka *Deliria* aka *StageFright: Aquarius* aka *Bloody Bird*)
	Delirium
	Graveyard Disturbance (from the *Brivido giallo* series of TV movies)
	Until Death (from the *Brivido giallo* series)
1988	*The Last American Soldier* (aka *Commander*)
	The Ogre (from the *Brivido giallo* series)
	Dinner with a Vampire (from the *Brivido giallo* series)
1989	*Santa Sangre*
1990	*Hardware*
1992	*Dust Devil*
	The Turn of the Screw
1994	*Shallow Grave*
1995	*Lord of Illusions*
	Hackers
1999	*A Midsummer Night's Dream*
2005	*Next Door*
2006	*Incubus*
2007	*Tin Man* (TV miniseries)
2008	*Manhunt* (aka *Rovdyr*)
2011	*The Theatre Bizarre* (segments: *The Mother of Toads, Vision Stains*)
2012	*The ABCs of Death* (segment: *S Is for Speed*)
2014	*Alter*
2015	*Bound to Vengeance*

How old were you when you began playing music?

I started taking piano lessons when I was five. I had an enthusiastic grandfather who was musical and was very keen for me to learn a musical instrument. Really, he encouraged me to learn the piano, as did my parents. So I had some classical piano going on from about the age of five until fifteen. And when I was about twelve, I saw Jimi Hendrix on TV.

[*Laughs*] Along with many people in the world, he kind of blew my mind. I think he started out playing "Hey Joe," and then he said something like, "That's enough of this shit," and then he started playing a version of Cream's "Sunshine of Your Love." I thought, "My God. This is so much better than playing piano!" [*Laughs*] Also around that time, my older brother was playing the guitar and was influenced by a lot of blues guitarists and English singer-songwriters like Bert Jansch. He taught me some bits on guitar, and I carried on then and taught myself. So I had a sort of dual-input music thing of classical piano and rock guitar.

But when I was a teenager, I ended up playing a lot of finger-picking acoustic guitar numbers. That is actually how I got into the whole music world. I was signed by a label called Transatlantic Records, a UK label that specialized in folk music. They heard my guitar picking and signed me up quite young to do some tracks and then to do a solo album, which I did. It was called *The Mind Parasites* [1975]. At this point I was in college at Cambridge, studying English literature—which is something we should touch on in terms of what's useful for writing film music. (I will come back to that.) I was at college studying English literature, not music. I really think the worst thing you can study, if you want to write film music, is music.

Why is that?

[*Laughs*] Well, let me put it this way: Most of the people that I know that had a higher education with music—with learning about music theory, etc.—really ended up as copyists, and quite a few of them also ended up as orchestral players. There's nothing wrong with that, but I think they often feel too intimidated by their knowledge of music to write music. I think I was very fortunate, and I know a lot of people in this respect that have a modicum of classical training, or just enough knowledge of the theory of music and the practice of music, but also come from a rock or pop background and are not intimidated by the level or detail of their knowledge to write their own music.

pop background and are not intimidated by the level or detail of their knowledge to write their own music.

I look at people like Hans Zimmer and Danny Elfman—these people have come from more of a self-taught world. I think it is those kinds of people, and I am one of them ... we know what we're doing and we know our way around an orchestra, but we are not so intimidated by the theory of knowing how difficult it was to be Stravinsky, to have a go at it. At least, that is my feeling on that subject. Not having that kind of formal education makes you ignorant and brave enough to try the impossible.

How did you go from being primarily a performer and producer of pop and rock to being a composer of film music?

It was entirely accidental, really. I always quote John Lennon: "Life is what happens to you whilst you're busy making other plans." I was in bands. I was trying to make it as a singer-songwriter first, and then in various bands, none of which were successful, and I kind of fell into producing other artists—actually very successfully, especially in Italy. I sort of became the person to go to for a whole number of different songwriters and pop stars.

So I was involved in producing other people's music in Italy during the early 1980s, and it was purely by luck, coincidence—good fortune, really—that socially I met the director Dario Argento, who I had not heard of at the time. But he had seen my band play, a band called Live Wire. We performed in Rome and he is very much into rock. He's actually more into heavy metal than the kind of rock we were doing, but he liked my band, and at this point he was working on the film *Phenomena* [aka *Creepers*, 1985]. . . .

Because I think they were really up against it timewise, he asked if I would go and work with two members of the band Goblin, Claudio Simonetti and Fabio Pignatelli. He asked if I would help write some cues and try and basically get this thing done.

[*Laughs*] He suggested that to them, and I arrived in the studio with these two guys I didn't know. It was all very awkward, actually. Not least because I had never written anything for a movie before in my life and I had no idea about it—which I think has definitely worked to my advantage in the long run. I felt a slight tension in this, in that these guys from Goblin had obviously had a lot of success already, working with Argento, and I think they slightly resented [*laughs*] this English guy being forced upon them.

In the end, though, we decided, "Okay, you do those cues and I will do these." And I went off and found another studio in Rome and did my bit, and that is how it happened to me.

It was really an accident. It was a real trial by fire [*laughs*] to have your first working experience be writing film music for Dario. He is quite an extreme character, but I really enjoyed it for that reason and also for the reason, as I said, I didn't know I wasn't a fan of film music, I wasn't a fan of horror films. In fact, I am one of the saps who believed all the publicity about *The Exorcist* [1973]. I didn't go to see it, because I thought I would be too scared [*laughs*]! So I grew up in a kind of vacuum, in the sense of knowing what I was supposed to do, knowing what might be required of me.

I am also very lucky, because Dario is a very experimental guy. He had already really pioneered the use of rock music as part of the soundtrack, with all kinds of bands, actually. What was great for me was, I was just coming out of the whole punk/post-punk/goth scene in London, where I had produced quite a few goth bands, and I felt this was a better kind of scenario . . . if you were going to use songs. I'm not talking about my music here, but songs in movies. I think goth music actually had a better affinity for horror than heavy metal at that time. I can see how they both adopted, certainly, the visual imagery.

So I was, in a sense, thrown into the deep end. I really did not know what to do, and I've said this before, the first piece I was asked to write for *Phenomena* was for a scene, sort of the climax to the movie, really, where this very young Jennifer Connelly is being chased down this underground tunnel by a psychopath and falls backwards into this big tank of rotting body parts [*laughs*]. I had no idea what to do! I was in the studio, on my own, working in the very old style of film composing. This is just pre-video. and they had this scene on a loop with a 35mm projector attached to the recording studio. It was real old-school. It was just going around, around, and around and I thought, "What should I do?"

And I just concocted this sort of unlistenable mixture of harmonics. I actually borrowed a violin. I can't play the violin [*laughs*], but I played some very strange scraping sounds. I would run things down the strings of my electric guitar, and there was a synth lying there in the corner, and I just found some strange sounds.

I was a bit like a kid in a candy store, too, because this was also my return to being creative myself. I had spent seven or eight years producing other people's music, and I think you will find a common thing amongst record producers: If they are creative too, they get an incredible frustration from making other people's shit smell good [*laughs*]. So I was really ready. I was in this great place where I could do quite avant-garde, weird stuff, which was totally liberating.

Was that the reason you said yes? For someone who wasn't a fan of horror films and didn't know who Dario Argento was, it seems like a weird job to accept without any previous experience. Was it simply that longing to be creative that interested you?

I think it was. I think it was just this period of time where I was frustrated by not doing my own music. It was, like, "Oh my God, you want me to write some music? Fantastic!" I didn't really stop to think about it until I was in the studio [*laughs*] having to come up with it. What I then did, of course, was invite the lead singer from a band I had produced back in London (a very early goth band called the Sex Gang Children), Andi [Sex Gang], to come out to Rome, because I thought it would be great to have some really strange vocals and moaning sounds for the soundtrack. Which is what we did. We wrote a couple of songs for the soundtrack, too, one track called "You Don't Know Me Now" and another called "The Naked and the Dead."

That was an interesting time, creatively, for Argento, because starting with that film and then continuing with *Demons* [1985] and *Demons 2* [1986], he began using more of a music compilation approach, as opposed to a more conventional score, where one person or band wrote all the music.

Exactly! Previously, he had composers writing a score for his films. And yes, I think with *Phenomena* and *Demons*, you are quite right: Suddenly it was this mixture of songs and score, which, let's face it, that's what everyone was doing in Hollywood, too. I think that everyone had a bit of an eye on potential record sales, by making a compilation album that they could attach to the movie. So I do think that Argento was quick on the uptake with that.

When Argento gave you this scene to score, did he give you any indication of what he wanted, or did he just give it to you and let you go?

No, I had no indication at all. He just said to Claudio, Fabio, and me, "You guys sort it out." Which we did. I said, "I'll do this bit," Claudio said he'd do that bit, Fabio said he'd do that bit, blahblahblah. And, let's be fair, I didn't do that much of the score in that film. I don't know, maybe it was five or six cues or something like that.

He [Argento] came along to listen. [*Laughs*] I remember being nervous, actually, having made this sort of completely unlistenable sound. He came along and sat at the mixing desk and listened to it, and when it was finished, he looked at me and said, "It's beautiful [*laughs*]." They were wonderful words to use to describe what I had just played him. It was great. He's very amenable to giving people the freedom to come up with something different. And there aren't many directors like that. There're only a handful that I have worked with in my career that are like that. Richard Stanley is one. [Alejandro] Jodorowsky is another. . . . A lot of directors are in sort of a terrible, insecure place where they . . . well, let me put it this way: If they are secure in themselves, they will allow you the freedom. If they are not secure in themselves, they will try and control the thing and destroy it.

Shortly after *Phenomena*, you were asked to work on *Demons 2*. Was that a no-brainer, or did you have to give it some careful thought before accepting?

No, that was a no-brainer, because this was going to be my first score where I did the whole thing. And not only that, they asked me if I could put together a soundtrack with various bands, because I was based in London and I had been working a lot, producing a lot of these acts in London. I did a deal with the Beggars Banquet label—who were an independent label with a lot of very interesting acts—to do the soundtrack. So I put together the whole thing. That was the only time I ever did that, where I had control over the songs too.

I do remember one of the scenes in *Demons 2* where there's a party going on and the demons are beginning to take over the upstairs. All this blood starts dripping down from the ceiling while there is a party going on, and I thought it would be great to have a song by the Smiths in there called "Panic." . . . I knew that Morrissey [the Smiths' lead singer] was a very, kind of, difficult person, especially when it came to this sort of "trash culture"—he liked to think of himself as quite intellectual. So I wrote Morrissey a letter explaining to him that *Demons 2* was this extended metaphor for the media taking over people's minds. [*Laughs*] I was neatly avoiding the fact that there was actually a demon coming out of the TV set and ripping people's heads off. He got the letter and said, "Yeah, great." So I was able to put a Smiths song in there too.

When you sit down to begin work on what is essentially your first full score, is there a moment where the thought crosses your mind that, "Hey, maybe I should go look at other horror scores to see what they're like?" Or are you just flying by the seat of your pants?

[*Laughs*] There should've been. Maybe it's a flaw in my character or maybe it's also a plus, I am not sure. It's not for me to judge, really. I just don't want to do it—I don't want to sit through the other films. I don't want to listen to what other people have done. I really tried to keep myself in this kind of a vacuum, and it may have worked against me in many cases, because maybe I'm not following the zeitgeist or locking into what it is that horror composers are doing.

But I think that's fifty percent of the time. The other fifty, I may be coming up with something different, which I think I've done with *Hardware* [1990] and *Dust Devil* [1993] and those kinds of things. But you're right. Maybe I should check this stuff out. But do I want to? No! [*Laughs*]

Can you run me through your process? What's your first step after you watch the film?

Here's the thing: I have always been very driven by sounds. Sounds inspire me, but I am really not a synth programmer—I am a synth-preset user [*laughs*]. So this is the era, you have to remember, where synths are beginning to get really quite good, really quite cool. Samplers are beginning to come along, and I had access to a fantastic library of quite distinctive sounds. I literally watch a scene like the pianist of a silent movie, and it just kind of goes through my eyes and out through my fingers.

And this is getting back to the thing about studying English literature rather than music. In any kind of film scoring, not just horror film scoring, it is more important to understand what a movie is about than it is to know the complexity of certain kinds of musical arrangements.

I also find with a lot of this horror scoring, simplicity is far more effective. So I will just sit in front of a screen, watching a scene, and I will switch between different sounds, going, "Oh yeah, that sounds good." I will just start playing something, and I'm improvising to the picture. I really do trust my first response, really, generally, and I still do that. I trust my first response usually in terms of the pace of what I am watching. That's the first thing.

And, of course, now with MIDI, you can be recording every pass that you make with this stuff. But I will watch it through, and I will take something from the pace of the editing first. Then, literally in the film, when there's some guy who is standing behind a door, waiting for somebody to come though it . . . then . . . my God! Yeah! Yeah! We don't want to know what is going to happen next!

I am like a punter doing it, I think. There's no great intellectual plan to it, at least initially. But I do think that it is in the grand sweep of going through a movie. Not so much what it is about, but how much you want to reveal to people, how much you want to provide them with a red herring, emotionally or in terms of the music you are writing. It's just a way of being in tune with the storytelling, in a way.

Can you tell me a little more about how the sound of the instrument—the actual tone of the preset or sample you're using on the keyboard—fuels your creativity?

Hugely, especially in this early horror stuff. The tone of the synth sounds does everything to me; even the speed of an oscillator sweep in the sound—if it is too fast, I am not going to use that sound. That's how I work; I am not going to sit there and program it to be slower. I will go through until I find something that really works for at least the fifteen to twenty seconds of what I am watching. Then I can imagine how I am going to layer something over the top. Then I begin to think thematically about if a tune can be reused, if it can be repeated.

Let's not underestimate repetition. It is absolutely the key to film music, as it is to pop music. Not only is it within a pop song, but it is also within the number of times you hear a pop song, or used to hear a pop song on the radio. Repetition is absolutely everything. So there is a point at which you begin to understand the structure of how you're going to make it work through a film: how it is going to develop, how once you have heard a theme two or three times, how the simple act of bringing it back in, however subtly, however few notes of it you use, how that is triggering people in a kind of Pavlovian way.

This may differ from film to film, but do you find that you typically compose from the beginning of the film to the end, or do you find certain scenes that initially speak to you and then start with those and work out of order?

Generally speaking, I work from the beginning to the end, but that kind of theory, in a lot of ways, went out the window once digital editing came along. It used to be that I wasn't even given a call until the film was pretty much "locked" [i.e., the editing was finalized], whereas the idea of a locked film simply doesn't even exist anymore. So that theory kind of goes out the window, and you are forced to work on the bits that you can work on.

The same goes for special effects. *Lord of Illusions* [1995], for example, the Clive Barker movie: I scored so much of the film with blue screen [a blue or green background that stands in for a computer-generated or animated background or environment that is developed and superimposed on it in postproduction, apart from the actors' foreground action] that I actually really didn't know what was going on for a lot of it. As a result, I wrote building blocks of music, which we did in Seattle with the Seattle Symphony Orchestra.

We made cues that weren't written to anything in particular. They were written as sort of tone poems, really—moods, strange atonal flurries—and they were then all put together afterwards in the editing. There were obviously a few things that I wrote and we recorded to the film. Every film is different in this respect. But I like to sit at the beginning and write the music for the opening titles and go from there.

Music budgets, especially with the kinds of films you were working on in the beginning of your career, are often rather tight. Do you

find that financial restrictions can fuel creativity and perhaps cause you to be more experimental?

Absolutely! Completely. I think that I was extremely lucky. About the first twenty movies I did were Italian films, from which I earned practically nothing, and they trusted me after *Demons 2*, which was only my second film. *Phenomena* was the only film soundtrack that I actually did in Italy; all of the others were done in this little bedroom of mine, back in Clapham in South London.

So I was able to sort of escape. I had no input whatsoever, really, from most of these people—and there were quite a few projects where I never met anyone involved. So I was given the fantastic freedom to go home and just send them back music. No one interfered really at all, not that I can remember, not for a very, very long time in my career.

The other thing that was interesting to me was that sometimes people would ring me up, and they wouldn't even send me a video of the film. They would describe what the film was and they would say, "Can you do an action theme and make it five minutes long? And can you do a tension theme? Just give us five minutes. And also a love theme? Just give us five minutes." [*Laughs*] But even when I had done it to picture, when I would sometimes take the music back to the cutting room in Rome . . . again, remember, these were the days of 35mm magnetic tape and editing on a Moviola [a film-based linear editing machine]. They would transfer the music onto 35mm magnetic tape, put it up against the picture, and they would say, "Where does it start?" I would say, "It starts here."

They would put it up, and then you'd sit and watch it, and you could hardly hear it through these tiny little speakers, let alone see it either. But they'd get to some point and they'd look at each other and they'd go, "Well let's stop it here. It doesn't work from here." Then they would literally cut that into another piece of music. No fading, nothing.

It is literally like the broad strokes of a painter. It was like these cuts propelled you through the movie. When it stopped working [*makes a snipping sound*], just put another piece of music on. And I thought that was absolutely genius. At the time, I actually thought, "Jesus, how can they do that?" But in retrospect, you can kind of see the whole style, the "spaghetti" style of making these films, and I think it is something that somebody like [Quentin] Tarantino has taken and run with, this kind of really broad, crude editing style.

Going back to *Demons 2*, is it safe to assume that you worked primarily with Dario Argento and not the film's director, Lamberto Bava?

That was mainly Dario. Yes, that's true. My recollections of that were that I didn't really get any feedback at all. I gave them the stuff. We'd sit there and we'd put it on where we thought it should go, and that was it.

Do you recall if you had any specific creative inspirations for the main theme?

I'm not sure if I had any inspiration for it other than, "Oh, that choir sound would be great. And let's put in this thrashy guitar, with the bending, the tremolo arm." It becomes this sort of kitsch hybrid. I have been listening to all of this stuff a lot, because I am now beginning to perform all this stuff live. But I don't think there was any specific inspiration. I mean, choirs figure into a lot in my—and an awful lot of other people's—horror work. They can sound demonic, they can sound holy. Especially in the Italian horror films, they can sound like this weird subversion of Catholicism, which I think a lot of the films are, especially visually.

I've always thought that a lot of Argento's work, especially, shares an awful lot of that medieval religious imagery. It's beautiful-looking gore. It's lit like it's a fourteenth- or fifteenth-century painting, and I think I have taken some inspiration from that in making the music almost, I guess, choral. That's the best I can say, really.

After *Demons 2*, you did several more films with Lamberto Bava. Did your working relationship change with him at all during that time, or did you continue to just do the music, hand it to him, and then that was it?

Pretty much, I'd just do my music and hand it to him. It became at that point a little bit like a factory—almost like a Roger Corman style of filmmaking. And I don't think that many of those films were very good. They were churning them out, and I'm not even sure if they were for TV or for the cinema [*laughs*]—I didn't even really know. I was just experimenting, myself, with what to do. I'm not terribly proud of a lot of the music in some of that stuff either, but I didn't have a very close relationship with Lamberto at all.

You mentioned the word "factory." Since you weren't educated in film scoring, was that period of your career your schooling?

Kind of. Except, when I listen back to that stuff now, I don't really like it. I think a lot of what I was doing at that time was overusing the sequencer. This stuff usually goes round and around and around, and it has all this repetition, which I guess dance music had and Philip Glass had and Mike Oldfield's *Tubular Bells* especially had. I think that was a huge influence on an awful lot of people, Goblin included, that kind of repetitious, electronic "tinkly" sound that goes around and around. It is very effective for a horror film, because instead of you having a sustained note, it performs the same function with a little more movement in it.

But I listen back to a lot of it now, and I think that it's not very good. So that wasn't my real schooling; my real schooling was not with the Bava things. My real school was working with Michele Soavi, on *Stage Fright* [aka *Deliria*, 1987] for example . . . or Jodorowsky with *Santa Sangre* [1989]. Those were the people who really inspired me.

Let's talk about *Stage Fright*. How did you meet Soavi, and how did you come to work on that project?

I met Soavi because he was Dario Argento's first AD [assistant director]. *Stage Fright* was maybe the fourth or fifth film I did, something like that. I think I was the natural choice for Michele because I worked with Dario and I had been working with Bava, and everyone was going, "Oh, you should use this guy." So it was that simple. I think I was the natural choice.

With this film you're often listed as sharing the credit with another composer, Stefano Manetti.

Yes, that's very interesting. I actually had no idea. I had actually met and worked with Stefano recently, on other things. Basically, he was hired to write the music that appears on stage, in the actual show within the film—that's the only stuff that is his. The actual score is all mine.

You've mentioned in other interviews that you lifted a little something from James Brown's "Funky Drummer," and used it, in a sense, like a sample. Can you talk a little bit about that?

Yes, absolutely. I am just releasing this album again on vinyl and CD, etc., so I've been listening to it a lot. That came about because, at that point, I was able to test out different samplers and synths and stuff. One of the ones that came my way came with a few disks, you know, diskettes [the now-archaic floppy disks used to store computer data in the 1970s through 1990s], and one of them had this James Brown "Funky Drummer" sample on it. And I just thought, "Wow, I should stick this in there." I think I had already written this piece of sustained strings and a horror-type string arrangement, and I just thought that if I would put this beat underneath it, it would make it more interesting. [*Laughs*] It was as simple as that, really. I will probably get sued now; I think he did sue a lot of people for using it.

Compared to most directors, Soavi hasn't made that many films. But the ones he did make, especially during the late Eighties and early Nineties, are all very interesting and creative. He really did manage to carve out a niche for himself as an auteur very quickly. Judging from his films, I would assume that he would've been more hands-on when working with you, but that really doesn't seem to be the "Italian way."

I did it [*Stage Fright*] back in London, and Michele didn't really say anything. He seemed to be pleased with it. There was no to-ing or fro-ing on the stuff at all. I had no idea that Stefano Manetti was even writing the stuff for on the stage. I guess I didn't even really think about whether there was music on it or not.

But Michele was very polite and very thankful. Nobody criticized it, it was all fine. I actually just spoke to him recently, about writing liner notes for the soundtrack, which I am releasing. He kind of retired from the film industry at a certain point, but he had contacted me about doing the music for *Dellamorte Dellamore* [aka *Cemetery Man*, 1994], and I would've loved to have done that, but I had literally just been offered the biggest thing that I could've up to that point, which was *A Midsummer Night's Dream* [1999], So I had to tell Michele I couldn't work on that one.

I assume that with all of those Italian horror scores, you were not working with any temp tracks at that point in your career.

No, none at all. In fact, apart from the lack of a temp score, what was actually quite funny with all of these Italian films was the fact that at that point they were trying to sell all of these films all around the world, and they would dub them all into English. But their way of trying to make them more marketable internationally was to hire an American actor and a German actor, etc., with all of the Italian actors. So I would be watching these movies before they were dubbed into whatever language they were going to be dubbed into, and somebody would be speaking German, somebody would be speaking French, somebody would have an American accent.

It was just hilarious. I really had no idea what the dialogue was. It was just a complete mishmash, and in the end I think that type of dubbing is what has given all these films their style. I think that started with Sergio Leone. That disjointed, that distinct style of dubbing is what people love. It is stylized. It has become a style unto its own.

Did you find not being able to follow the dialogue a hindrance?

Not at all [*laughs*]. It is never a hindrance in any horror film—let's be honest. The language barrier was neither here nor there. I think you can tell where you need to spice up the tension, where you can do the false hope, the red herrings, etc. You can manipulate people simply by being sensible about it. It's not a fine art.

How did you come to work with Alejandro Jodorowsky on *Santa Sangre*?

Well, very interestingly, and I am ever-so-thankful for it, because I still consider it, probably not the greatest film score that I have done, but the greatest movie I have worked on. It came about because Dario Argento's brother, Claudio Argento, was producing this film, *Santa Sangre*. It was an Italian-Mexican coproduction. It was shot in Mexico, and they did postproduction in Rome. I think I was just suggested to Jodorowsky. Somebody said, "Why don't you try this guy? He might come up with something sort of different."

So I went and met with Jodorowsky, and at this point they were editing the film back in Rome, and he was extremely sweet and nice to me. He's the only person to have offered me some seriously good advice at the time. (I will get on to that in a minute.) He is also a musician, and he had scored bits of *Holy Mountain* [1973]. So it was a fantastically generous act of him.

But when you meet him and get to know him, you understand that he has a very good philosophy of life, which is based on the accidents of different creative people and letting them put their own stamp onto something to create a totally new thing that is a collaboration. He's not one of these people who thinks of himself as some sort of auteur. In fact, when you describe him to himself as a filmmaker, he says, "I am not a filmmaker. When I am making a film, I am a filmmaker, but I've only made five films in my life. When I am making comic books, then I am a comic book maker."

So he is a very freethinking individual, and totally he allowed me to do what I wanted. And, I think, fortuitously, that film is not a horror film, even though it has some nasty bits in it. It is poetry and it is a work of art, and I was so lucky that I was able to bring my acoustic guitar stuff and use it in that film for the first time, because there is a lot of Mexican content, and I was able to write some Spanish guitar pieces for the little boy character in it. Then when it gets quite trippy and psychedelic, I was able to use my sequencers with some really out-there sounds, to give it a whole almost-electronic feel. I am really delighted that I was allowed to combine those things, because I think it still really works.

You said he gave you advice?

Yes, and it has proven to be so helpful. There's a scene in *Santa Sangre* . . . where the mother in the film has her arms cut off by her knife-throwing husband. That scene in that film is really quite gory. She has her arms sliced off, and the blood spurts out of the sockets where her arms were.

I watched this when we were going through the film, and I said to Alejandro, "Do you want me to make this really nasty and horrible?" And he looked at me, just shocked, and he said, "No. No. No. No. This is *heaven* for her!" Because this is the moment where she becomes like the saint that she worships in the film. She worships a saint with no arms. She has her own arms cut off, and he said, "This is a moment that must be transcendent for her. This is a beautiful experience for her, a heavenly experience."

Which is why I called that music cue "Heavenly Arms" on the soundtrack album. That taught me so completely that you can write music from a completely different perspective in a film, from a different perspective of any of the characters or no characters. You can write something that, because it is different to what your eyes are taking in, makes you question all the more what it is you're experiencing, what you are watching, and serves to kind of drag you into the movie.

I think it was a real lesson for me that I then began to use in Richard Stanley's films, doing slide guitar and things on what were essentially horror sequences. It taught me that you can make the audience feel a little uncomfortable due to the difference between what they are hearing and what they're watching.

You mentioned Richard Stanley. It seems to me that he and Jodorowsky are probably cut from the same cloth. How did you meet him and start working on *Hardware* [1990]?

Richard is also an Argento fan. So many people I have met, obviously, have been Argento fans. . . . Danny Boyle is another one—that is how I got to do *Shallow Grave* [1994]. But Richard had especially liked *Stage Fright*, Michele Soavi's film. He was aware of me, because he's a big fan of Italian horror films. He thought I was Italian, and he was making *Hardware* in London, where I live, but he called up Argento's office to ask if they could put him in touch with me, if they could give him my number in Rome. They said, "Oh, no, he lives in London."

It was just that fortuitous, really. They gave him my number in London, he called me. I went down to the set where they were shooting, a place called the Roundhouse, in Camden Town in North London. I met with him and that was that, really. Richard was another of these people that gave me fantastic images to write to—and with absolutely no guidance whatsoever about what kind of music to do.

I think that all of this stuff has created my best work. My worst work was from either movies that are uninspiring to actually look at or by people that have tried to be prescriptive in their descriptions of what they want. If they can be that prescriptive, somebody else has probably already done it and the work feels derivative.

Can you talk a bit about where the inspiration to use slide guitar in *Hardware* came from?

Yes, absolutely. I guess, in some senses, I am a very simple soul when it comes to inspiration. I'm not particularly intellectual about these things. Watching the beginning of *Hardware*, which begins with this nomad-type figure (very much inspired by "the man with no name") traipsing through the desert, looking for bits of old robots. Just all that sand made me think, "Oh, that reminds me of *Paris, Texas* [1984]."

[*Laughs*] It was that simple. I had always been a Ry Cooder fan anyway, from my very early years. I played acoustic guitar, I played a bit of slide guitar. I thought, "Wow, I can do something very different here." Not only that, but this film is about the apocalypse and an apocalyptic future in which civilization has very much broken down. I thought, "Hey, there's not very much electricity around." Slide guitar, it kind of fits the bill; it seemed to just work.

With the doomy synthy strings that I put underneath it, it was this weird combination of a synthetic world that is the end of the world and a kind of reluctant blues refrain. [*Laughs*] Playing like blues men do, sitting on a porch, bemoaning their fate, really.

There is a cue in *Hardware* called "Jill Burning" that you have stated was inspired by Jimi Hendrix.

Absolutely. I am a huge Hendrix fan, and I do it in my live show. I love to do that feedback psychedelic stuff. I always take any opportunity I can to do some of that wildness, but I also try to keep the lyricism in it. I think that is where people get Hendrix wrong: He is a very lyrical guitar player, apart from setting his guitar on fire and all that stuff [*laughs*]. What appealed to me was "Little Wing," just as much as "All Along the Watchtower" and "Crosstown Traffic" and stuff like that. "Jill Burning" is that kind of thing. It is kind of wild and it is psychedelic and it is rock-based. It is not film-based. If I have anything that I am proud of, it is that my music is not based on other film music—apart from Morricone, maybe.

Speaking of Morricone, you did a second film with Stanley called *Dust Devil* [1992], and with the opening sequence, the theme is very . . .

It's very spaghetti western.

Yes, very much so.

That is what it is. One of the things I am interested in is mixing up the genres, as is Richard [Stanley] too. So you have a guy dressed like Clint Eastwood who is the Dust Devil, the demonic creature in question. But this is all set in Africa, not America. And, actually, I think this is one of my more successful pieces of music. I made this demonic creature heroic. I mean, that was what I was trying to do in terms of fucking with people's expectations. It's melancholy, but it's quite uplifting and it's heroic. . . .

I think it works really well, because you're really not quite sure, "Are we watching a cowboy film or a horror film or what?" And I like that people are confused by this stuff. You don't get away with it in Hollywood. They will say that people will walk out if they don't understand what the film is about. That's nonsense, really, but I am really pleased with all of these films that you're talking about, in the sense that I think I have done something that I can live with now.

Is it true that you started scoring *Dust Devil* before it was edited?

Yes, I wrote all that whilst they were still shooting it in Africa. They would send me rushes [unedited prints made of each day's work during the actual shooting process.]. I actually wrote the main theme to rushes. I was going off of shots of the desert, of this character walking along a road. Of course, they came back and they edited the thing, and then I was able to make stuff fit. I then wrote a lot of the other stuff, but that main theme was written to rushes.

A few years later, you worked with Clive Barker on *Lord of Illusions* [1995], which you mentioned briefly earlier. You've described that score as being "orchestral chaos." Can you talk a little bit about that, and also what it was like working with Barker?

He's another thoroughly nice person who's very generous in letting one do one's own thing.

In terms of "orchestral chaos," I have always been really impressed with the end of "A Day in the Life," the Beatles track from *Sgt. Pepper's Lonely Hearts Club Band* [album, 1967]—the idea of this orchestra going out of control. It's been something I've liked the idea of and I've liked the sound of. Then people introduced me to the music of Stravinsky and that kind of organized chaotic, atonal music. It is perfect for films, and it is appropriated by all kinds of people, all kinds of great filmmakers—Bernard Herrmann, for starters. I loved the idea of it.

Also, because of the circumstances with *Lord of Illusions*—it was all blue screen—we really didn't have edited scenes to work from. They were kind of edited together, but they were going to change a lot. So, together with an orchestrator named William Kidd in LA, we sat down and decided to write all these atonal clusters, trying to get the orchestra as close as one can to improvising.

The trouble is that, in most cases, orchestral players simply can't improvise. They are too used to being told what to play. So that even if you want chaos from them, you have to tell them in an orderly way, "Okay play those two strings for four bars, and then slide to these notes." It is kind of like you have to write it and then rely on some organized chaos in there, by telling different players within the same group of instruments to do different things. It's really like organizing the painting of a house or something [*laughs*]. Or organizing a team of decorators. It is very strange, but that is what we set about doing. I just wanted the idea of an orchestra going out of control, and that's what a lot of it is.

Up until that point, you had done most of your film work completely by yourself. Was it intimidating to now be leading so many people?

It was terribly intimidating. I think the first orchestral score I had done was for a movie called *Second Best* [1994]. That was a William Hurt film, an English film. That was the first one that I had actually been in with an orchestra and written stuff for them. I was just so nervous, because it is one thing to just come up with stuff on your own and then play it for someone, but it is another thing entirely to have a room full of people that are expectantly waiting for you to come up with a great piece of music for them to play.

So I was very nervous with that. It took me quite a while to get to know a few of the players and to realize that they're up for a bit of a laugh too, they are up for having a bit of fun as well, and that the best thing you can do is not to pretend like you know everything, but to take them into your confidence and say, "I haven't done this very much, but please, will you bear with me? But what I am trying to do is this—I'm trying to get this effect."

Most of them will like you for it, and I have gotten along very well with orchestras because of that. It took me four or five movies to have the confidence to say that. I think, up until that point, I was trying to bluster my way through, pretending I was some sort of Mozart. Which is just not the case.

I love working with orchestras. In some respect it is a much easier job than doing the whole thing on your own. It doesn't really matter what sounds you pick to write the thing on, because it is going to get performed by the real instruments. If you're doing it on your own, you're not only writing it, you have to record-produce it, engineer it, and record it and deliver the whole thing. It's a much harder job, though you do have more control over it. With orchestras, they kind of are what they are.

When you write for an orchestra, is your process still pretty much the same? You sit down at an instrument, watch the film, and let it flow?

Yes, it absolutely is. There is then a huge technical exercise in terms of writing out the parts, making parts work, making scenes fit, and doing what you want to do. But the more the technology has evolved, the more kind of neurotic everyone has gotten about making it more detailed, making it fit here, making it cross-fade nicely from this into that, etc. It has not necessarily improved things. It has given us all more control, but then to what end? I'm not entirely sure.

So you work out these parts on your own and you make recordings. Is that when you sit down with the orchestrator and it starts getting written out into parts for the players?

Yes, using MIDI and using samples, I pretty much write all the parts that I want. And then I mock it all up the way I want. I will use orchestrators to take what I've done, which is pretty detailed. . . . They say to me, using their expertise, "Well you can't have that many cello players, so why don't you give that particular line to a bass clarinet?" I want them to make really sensible suggestions about tone, about color in the thing, and to do a lot of the work, literally transposing the stuff I have done on MIDI into parts that can be played by the orchestra. That is a huge skill in and of itself.

Orchestrators are brilliantly talented at doing their thing. They really are, and I couldn't possibly do an orchestral score without one. I'm not going to pretend that I write it all out by hand, because I don't.

What was working with Clive Barker like? Was he more of a hands-on director?

I would say no, he wasn't really hands-on. He really couldn't be, because he was so struggling, I think, with the process of all the special effects and stuff. I don't think he really enjoys making films. Compared to being a novelist, it is hard work for him, and there's a lot more interference going on on his end. He came along to Seattle, where we recorded it, but he didn't sit there saying, "Can you try this? Can you try that?" We all agreed that I was going to make a kind of library of weird and strange sounds and then we were going to cut them together when the film was cut together. So he was very nice and very polite to me. Nearly everyone has been in my career. [*Laughs*] I can think of a couple of exceptions, but most people are just very generous and positive about the experience, which makes it positive for you.

In essence that film is about a detective, and that character is very much in the mold of classic film noir tradition . . .

Which is how I got the job, by the way.

Could you go into that a bit?

I think Chris Young, who did Barker's other films, had pulled out. I went and met Clive in LA because JoAnne Sellar, who had produced *Hardware*, was producing *Lord of Illusions*—there's always some sort of connection somewhere. She introduced me to him [Barker], but he sent me back to London, saying, "Look, there's this character that is a private investigator, like in a film noir. Can you write me a theme for him? I don't want to hear any horror music; I know you can do horror music. Can you write me a theme?"

So I wrote the "noirish" sax thing, which is in the film first, and then sent that out to him. And he goes, "Yeah, great! Fantastic." So that is how that happened. It is an interesting combination of genres, that movie.

You are now rereleasing some of your scores, and you've put together a band and are playing them live. I don't think that could happen or be profitable without a sizable fan base. I have noticed

in recent years that there seems to be a very strong fan base for horror film music. Do you have any thoughts as to why this might be? Also, please talk about how the decision to play your film music live came about.

First of all, you are right: I think the horror fans are, in a lot of ways, the most dedicated fans in the world. Personally, I think it is maybe something sort of hormonal. People tend to get into horror films at a certain age, and probably younger than they are allowed to. So I think there is some sense of a mutual bonding that goes on amongst horror fans. They are dealing with something that is taboo, or something that they're not really supposed to do.

I know this now from my ten-year-old son, who is wanting to play eighteen-plus videogames. They want to do what they're not supposed to do. I think there is something that bonds these people together, and it is at a formative time in their lives, where it actually meant a lot to them. Also, this rebelliousness is about the forming of their own personalities.

I am forever thankful, but I ignored the horror scene for decades. I never got invited to film festivals, ever, until about four or five years ago, so I had no idea. I never met any fans, I didn't know anyone ever listened to this music. The only time it ever even occurred to me was quite later on, with the film *From Dusk Till Dawn* [1996]. I got some phone call from Robert Rodriguez's office and Tarantino's office, when they were making that film, asking for my availability for it. That conversation made me realize that these people had been watching Argento's films.

I had no idea about the fans. I really had nothing to do with them. I didn't know how many there were, I didn't know what was going on. It is only recently that I have come to realize how loyal they are and how much they did actually like the stuff I was doing on these films, which were a huge part of their growing up, in a way.

I am really thankful for it, and I have now reached the point where I can do something live that really combines my rock stuff with my film stuff. Even with *Lord of Illusions*, I am putting rock drums behind bits and playing along with the orchestral cues, which we have cut up. And I have a live sax player, flute, and vocals, and me playing guitar and keyboards and stuff.

So it sits very nicely in this world that is between rock music and film music. And I am not going to respect the old way that I have done it to such a degree that it is, in a sense, worshiping the things—it is not enshrined in any way. Plus, I have a really, really intricate video show, using a video artist that has taken not clips but just scenes and iconic images from the films, and he loops and combines them with hieroglyphs and bits of art that he has done. It is quite arty to watch, but it is a bit like the territory that Pink Floyd used to inhabit.

I am really pleased. We've done our first gig in the West End of London, and it was amazing! There were 250 people. I know it doesn't sound like a lot, but for a first gig it is pretty good, and it went so well! We are now getting inundated. I am really, really excited, because it is a way for me to kind of reclaim my music as *me*. As a film composer, it is not my movie; I am just one of the guys working on that film. So it is really exciting for me to turn it into something that is an expression of my creativity. And, of course, I am so pleased that a lot of the films have had some longevity themselves. I am very thankful for that, but now I am going to go out and be my own star [*laughs*].

You have already imparted a great deal of knowledge here, but are there any other useful bits of advice you might like to pass along to somebody who is thinking about scoring films or is at the beginning of their career in the music business?

I feel very sorry for anybody starting out and trying to do it now, because it is difficult, as music has been totally debased and has become something that is almost free now. Film is kind of headed in that direction, in the sense that digital technology has made it so much more available to make it cheaper, which means the budgets for doing the music have gotten really cheap. It is hard to make a living at it, I think.

I don't know what to say to people. For the sheer fun of doing it, just score anything. But to actually make a living? I don't know. It has become difficult for me to make a living. I am not one of these Hollywood guys. The whole medium of film and music together has changed, and with the Internet we will have to wait and see how it is all going to work.

I don't really have advice for people, because I meet lots of kids that ask, "How do I become a film composer?" Well, I didn't set out to become a film composer—that's the trouble. It just happened to me. So I can't advise people of a particular route to go, because I don't think there is just one route. I think you need to get lucky, or hang out with filmmakers and say, "Hey I can do that. I can write you some music." I think it is as much a social phenomenon as it is anything else.

JOHN CARPENTER

"I just have no memory, it just came out. That is the wonderful thing, though, about the way I used to compose music. I would work like a fool, like a crazy man possessed, and then it was over. I never had to think about it again. I'd just go on and do something else. I'd go home and get stoned."

JOHN CARPENTER HAS BEEN ONE of my favorite directors for as long as I can remember—since before I even knew what a director was. His films were a huge part of my upbringing and, at age sixteen, when I finally discovered that he was responsible for many of the films I held dear, my life changed forever.

During my teens and early twenties, I was on a mission to learn everything I could about Mr. Carpenter. I devoured his films and soundtracks and every article, interview, and documentary about him that I could find. I was, for lack of a better term, obsessed. And in recent years, with the release of countless deluxe reissues of his works, two successful solo albums (*Lost Themes* and *Lost Themes II*), and a series of sold-out live concert dates, it is clear that I am not the only one.

Despite my efforts to educate myself about all things Carpenter, he has always remained a bit of an enigma to me. Though he seems willing to answer any question that one might ask, his answers are often short. He has never been one to go into great detail about his own work—especially about his music, which, for him, was quite literally an afterthought. He's quick to point out which projects were "just a job," and when asked questions like, "Why did you choose to do your own musical scores?" he always replies with stock answers, such as, "I was the cheapest and fastest guy to do the job."

As an accomplished writer, director, producer, editor, and composer, he is a filmmaker who embodies the auteur theory, and he takes ownership of his films by putting his name above the title. Yet he doesn't like the common credit "A Film by," because he feels that film is a collaborative medium. His tendency to downplay his achievements and contributions has often made me wonder if he is simply modest or is a throwback to an older Hollywood, considering himself more a businessman and craftsman than an artist.

Speaking to him was an absolute thrill and, for me, one of the highlights of this project. I knew that getting to the bottom of the enigma that is John Carpenter was not going to be an easy feat, especially with an interview focused entirely on his music, so I set out to find a crack or two in his calm, cool, and collected veneer.

He is John Carpenter and, for better or worse, that is what you get when you interview him. What I wasn't anticipating, though, was the amount of laughter we would share. I think the quote at the top of this chapter sums up this interview perfectly.

SELECTED FILMOGRAPHY AS COMPOSER

1974	*Dark Star*
1976	*Assault on Precinct 13*
1978	*Halloween*
1980	*The Fog*
1981	*Escape from New York* (with Alan Howarth)
	Halloween II (with Alan Howarth)
1982	*The Thing* (additional music)
	Halloween III: Season of the Witch (with Alan Howarth)
1983	*Christine* (with Alan Howarth)
1986	*Big Trouble in Little China* (with Alan Howarth)
1987	*Prince of Darkness* (with Alan Howarth)
1988	*They Live* (with Alan Howarth)
1993	*Body Bags* (TV movie, with Jim Lang)
1994	*In the Mouth of Madness* (with Jim Lang)
1995	*Village of the Damned* (with Dave Davies)
1998	*Vampires*
2001	*Ghosts of Mars*

Can you tell me a bit about your musical background?

I grew up in a household filled with music, because my father had a PhD in music and he was a music teacher at a university. So I was surrounded by music, and I listened to it all the time when I was very young. It was part of my life and, unfortunately, when I was about eight years old my father decided that it was time for me to learn the violin. I had no talent at the violin—that's a very, very difficult instrument to play. So I struggled along, and then I moved to keyboards and piano, and then I moved to guitar and rock 'n' roll. I just kept playing, and the secret of it, for me, was that it was just a huge part of growing up. It was second nature.

Is it true that your father was also a session musician?

That's correct!

Did he play with anyone of note?

Oh, lots of people. He was one of the original founders of the Nashville Strings. They played with a lot of country stars—Roy Orbison, Brenda Lee—and also Ray Charles and Frank Sinatra, and on and on and on during the 1950s and '60s and '70s. The Nashville Strings were made up of players from the Nashville Symphony Orchestra, which my father played in. He played viola.

Did you get to visit the studio while he was recording?

Sure I did. I saw Roy Orbison, who is one of my all-time favorites. He was unbelievable.

Was that something that helped fuel your love of music?

All of it fueled my love of music. My first love, of course, was cinema; I wanted to get into the movies. I wanted to be a movie director, but I soaked up everything I could with the music. Everything.

Did you play in rock bands when you were a teenager?

I played in a few. Sure.

Did you play covers or originals?

Both, but mostly covers.

Do you remember any of your big closers?

I don't remember a closer. We would play for an hour straight. We would lap one song into another so there was never a break, which was our claim to fame. We just kept playing. Then we'd take a break and then come back and play another hour. It was a lot of fun.

For someone with the musical background that you had, did the music in movies make a significant impression on you?

It made a huge impression. The soundtrack music, the music composed for movies, was enormous and enormously influential to me. I just vividly remember some soundtrack scores. One that pops into mind immediately is a movie called *Forbidden Planet*. It was made in 1956, and it had an electronic music score. There was no actual music, it was just all electronics, and it was stunning to me. I had never heard anything like it, and I thought, "Wow! What is this? This is absolutely awesome." So that was big.

Bernard Herrmann's music was big for me too—and all the Hitchcock movies. Also *The Day the Earth Stood Still* [1951], *The Thing* [*from Another World*, 1951]. So, yeah, soundtrack music was a big fucking deal.

I find it interesting that some of the scores that you gravitated toward were groundbreaking in the world of electronic music, and then you became a bit of a pioneer in the use of electronic music in film for your generation.

I don't know about that. That's very kind of you to say, but I found that by the time I came along to electronic music, you could sound big with just one player. In other words, you didn't have to hire an orchestra. You could sound mammoth, tracking over and over and over again. That is the reason I was drawn to it—the sounds were just so compelling.

You've often said that there are two types of film scores. Can you explain that?

One is "Mickey Mousing." Mickey Mousing was made famous by Max Steiner. For example, in *King Kong* [1933], every step that King Kong takes is scored, *bum-bum-bum-bum*. Every emotion is scored, *everything* is scored. It's wonderful and grandiose, but it tells you exactly what to feel all of the time. It's right on the nose.

The other way of scoring is to *underscore* it, where the music is more unobtrusive. It sets a general mood but doesn't get in the way. It's just providing a foundation. One of the most famous users of underscoring was Bernard Herrmann. His scores were sometimes grand, but they just sit there. Underneath the surface, there's something strange about them. The score he did for *Vertigo* [1958] is a perfect example of underscoring.

Bernard Herrmann's name has been popping up a lot in many of the interviews I've done. Why is he so significant to cinema and the horror genre? Did he influence your music?

He influenced me enormously. I love Bernard Herrmann's work; he is one of my favorite composers. I don't know if it is just the horror genre. I think it is because he did so much work with Alfred Hitchcock and did some amazing scores. The scores for *North by Northwest* [1959] and *Vertigo* are just astonishing scores, but he also did the score for *The Day the Earth Stood Still*, which was an early use of the Theremin [an early electronic music instrument known for its eerie vocal-like quality]. He is enormously influential.

Can you think of anything about his style that directly affected the way you compose?

I know one thing, for instance: His score for *Psycho* [1960]—he only used strings. He was able to achieve a maximum effect with minimal means. In other words, he didn't always use enormous orchestras. Sometimes he used very simple things and was still able to achieve great emotional heights. And that, of course, inspired me [*laughs*], because that is all I can do.

Would you talk a bit about James Bernard? I understand that you are an admirer of his work and knew him personally.

Yes! Oh, yes. James Bernard was a lovely, wonderful, warm man. I met him in the mid-1990s, but I grew up listening to his scores—the first being the score for *The Quatermass Xperiment* [1955], then *Quatermass II* [*Enemy from Space*, 1957], and then [*The Curse of*] *Frankenstein* [1957] and [*Horror of*] *Dracula* [1958]. There is nothing like his music, nothing like it for dread. He came over and visited me in Los Angeles and he told me his secret. He used seconds [the musical intervals] . . . and he would sing the *title* of the film. . . . It was like . . . [*sings*] *Dracula*! It went [*sings Bernard's* Dracula *theme*] . . . *Quatermass II* [*sings the film's title to the film's theme*] . . . The astonishing breadth of his scores! I loved his music.

Did you ever apply that technique to some of your own titles?

No, no, no. But I did learn how to play [Bernard's theme from] *Dracula* on the keyboard. That was fun.

What is the job of the film score composer?

Well, simply put, it is to provide music for the movie, and that goes in various directions. Of course, you think immediately of a main theme or a musical theme that is associated with the movie: The *Jaws* [1975] theme, the *Star Wars* [1977] theme, those are all scores that you associate with the movies. They are inseparable—you can't imagine the movie without that score.

Music also functions as a secondary narrative. It's used to support the scenes that need support. Some scenes don't need it. The most important meeting between composer and director is the spotting session. That is when the movie is cut together, and the director sits down with the composer and they go through the film and watch it together. They talk about where the music should be and where it shouldn't be. That is enormously important, and that is where a lot of the decisions get made. It is crucial.

Then, of course, composers will often put together ideas on piano or do sketches, and sit with a director and say, "This is what I had in mind for this, what do you think?" and then discuss it. It is a collaboration that is essential to the making of a movie. But it's also a weird one, because it is very difficult to talk about music unless you are a musician. A director doesn't say, "I want more sustains and sevenths in your score"; he usually says something that comes from a visual point of view.

There is a behind-the-scenes look at Ridley Scott working with Hans Zimmer on *Black Hawk Down* [2001], and Ridley Scott says, "Let's make this more heroic here." Which just seems like a pretty obvious statement, but there are other ways to go with that. There are other ways to score that movie. That is what the director wanted; that doesn't necessarily mean that is what the composer had in mind. Everyone serves the director. That is the important thing.

It seems that, typically, a film music composer comes into a project pretty late in the postproduction process. Seeing how you're

also the director and often with a film from its inception, when do you start to think about the score?

After the movie is shot and cut together, then I sit down with it and begin to score. For the most part, for ninety-five percent of the time, I don't have anything planned ahead of time—I just don't know what is going to come. It is a lot of improvisation. As I'm watching the movie, the scene dictates what kind of music it is going to be. What does the scene require of me? What do I have to do to support the scene audibly and dramatically?

In that sense I am a journeyman. I do what is necessary for the movie. I don't really think of it as music, other than to support the image. . . . A lot of people discount my scores as being very simple, and they are very simple. I am a musician of only moderate chops, I am not a virtuoso in any respect whatsoever. But within that area I just kind of gouged out my own little area of expertise.

***Assault on Precinct 13* [1976] seems to be your first score that fans really embraced. Could you tell me a bit about what influenced that score?**

Assault was influenced by two musical pieces. The first was "Immigrant Song," by Led Zeppelin [*sings the song's guitar riff*], and the other was the *Dirty Harry* [1971] score, by Lalo Schifrin. . . .

It was very simple, repetitive, and I did it in one day . . . with a synthesizer. It was an old tube synthesizer. I hooked up with Dan Wyman from the USC electronic music department. He taught a course in it. He owned his own synths. They were all tube synths, you had to tune them. So I'd say, "Let's have a string sound." He'd go over and tune away, and we'd have it and then I'd play it. Then we'd move over to the next track. So it was that kind of a thing.

In the past you've talked a lot about your father teaching you 5/4 time. Why did you choose that time signature for the *Halloween* [1978] theme?

That's a really good question [*laughs*], and I don't know that I have a satisfactory answer. It was instinctual, it just seemed like the right thing to do. That's a lot of it. A lot of what I've done is all out of instinct, it is not out of anything particularly thought out. It was something that I was noodling around with on the piano, playing out the 5/4 time and, I don't know, it just felt right. It is always about that—it just feels right.

Were you influenced at all by William Friedkin's use of Mike Oldfield's *Tubular Bells* in *The Exorcist* [1973]?

That and *Sorcerer* [1977]. I love the *Sorcerer* score, by Tangerine Dream. That's a fabulous score, just incredible. I love that score—probably as much as *Tubular Bells*.

With *Halloween* you were on a limited budget and limited schedule. You've said you had three days to do that score.

Yes, I think I had three days.

You've often said, especially regarding the early scores, that you were the fastest and the cheapest guy to do it, so you did it.

That's it! You got the secret.

If you had more money and more time, do you think you would've rather had somebody else do it?

I don't know. That's a good question, but I don't know. Maybe. It would've depended on who the guy was. Maybe.

Two years after your *Halloween* came out, Sean Cunningham's *Friday the 13th* [1980] was released. Harry Manfredini's score for *Friday the 13th* is not huge in scope, but it is more orchestral and more in tune with the work of composers like Bernard Herrmann. Looking back, does any part of you wish that you could have had something more like that for *Halloween*?

Well, I wouldn't have been able to do it. I can't really orchestrate. I wouldn't have done it. That doesn't mean that it wouldn't have been great, but it just didn't work out that way. I've always wanted bigger scores. I wish I could've resurrected Dimitri Tiomkin, who I just love; I just love his music.

By the time you did *Halloween*, were you familiar with the work of Dario Argento and what he was doing with Ennio Morricone and Goblin?

I saw *Suspiria* [1977]. That was probably the first inclination I had that something really cool was happening over there in Italy. I love that soundtrack.

I wouldn't say that your music sounds like Goblin's, but there are some similarities. After you heard the score for _Suspiria_, did it change your perspective on how to approach film music at all?

I saw _Suspiria_ before I made _Halloween_, and the thing that stuck with me—with all these scores by all these musicians, from all the way back to Max Steiner and _King Kong_, all the way up through [Claudio] Simonetti and _Suspiria_—is that they are so memorable. They burn into your head and you cannot forget them. That [_Suspiria_] score starts to play and it is just unbelievable, it is just relentless [_hums the theme from_ Suspiria]. It is just incredible, an incredibly memorable score. That is the big thing, and it brings up images of the movie in your head, because you first heard it when you watched the images on the screen.

These days it is clear that horror film music has a specific and loyal fan base. Many of your scores have recently been reissued. Do you think there is something about horror movie music that transcends the cinematic image in a way that perhaps other genres don't?

I don't know. You'd have to ask the audience for it, not necessarily for me, because I fell in love with all sorts of scores. I can still remember some of them in my fading memory. . . . But I will admit that there are a lot of fans for horror movie music. Which I think is great. I think that is awesome.

Is it true that one of the reasons you were given the job of direct-ing the TV movie _Elvis_ [1979] was because you scored your previous films?

[_Laughs_] Yeah, that was one of the things that they thought was a plus, which I found hilarious.

Did you find that skill at all helpful in directing that film?

Not for directing. [_Laughs_] It's a whole different job, but that was a jus-tification for them, for the people that hired me. Which is fine. I went right along with it, but when you're standing outside in the middle of the night, putting together a movie, none of that matters.

Your score for _The Fog_ [1980] is in a lot of ways similar to _Halloween_'s score in that it is piano-based and repetitive. Repetition, especially in those early films, is definitely a part of your musical

style. Can you talk about the function of repetition in horror film music—especially in your own music?

I don't know that there are any rules to this. That's the thing—I tell people that there are no rules to any of this. I wouldn't say that a horror film needs repetition, but you take a score for a movie like *Jaws*. It is simple and everybody knows it. It's two notes repeated [*sings the theme*] over and over again, and it is really effective for the thing beneath the surface that is coming to get you.

But then there are other, lusher, more developed scores for horror films. It all depends. It depends on the composer and the director, but there are no rules for it. In my case—you're going to laugh about this— but repetition is something that I can do, because I am not a particularly accomplished musician. I can do repetitive really well [*laughs*]. You do what you can do well. I can do repetitive, I can do repetitive all day long. I have minimal chops as a musician, and recognizing that early was one of my strengths. So I play to that. I have always done that.

Do you find that repetition can be a useful device when building tension?

Yeah, it can be. Or silence can be too. In the case of something like *Halloween*, it works because the audience is waiting for something to change and it doesn't. It puts them in a little bit of discomfort emotionally, because they expect it to evolve and change, but it just keeps repeating.

But there's no hard, fast rule about any of this; that is what you have to keep in mind. There are rules for both music and movies, in terms of making them, but not necessarily for what works the best. That's all up to the talent and the taste of the director and the composer.

I understand that on your early films, like *The Fog*, you weren't scoring directly to the picture. It was more like you were scoring to a stopwatch. Can you talk a little bit about that process?

That, in essence, is true. I had a certain amount of time to go and record the music, and it wasn't to picture (the first movie that I scored to picture was *Escape from New York* [1981]). I would do four or five pieces and then put them in, you know, cut it and use various tricks to make it work. It wasn't until *Escape* that I started to compose right to the image, which changed my whole technique. But *The Fog* had a great deal of fix-it stuff too. We went back and worked on the movie after we had completed it once, and that included redoing some music. I'm not sure which *Fog* recording sessions produced which music. I really can't remember now.

More so than any of your other films, except possibly *Christine* [1983], diegetic music [music coming from a visible or implied onscreen source, such as a car radio], licensed music, plays a significant part in the soundtrack of *The Fog*, because one of your main characters is a disc jockey. Can you talk a little bit about your use of the diegetic music versus the nondiegetic music?

Well, first and foremost, I've never heard the word "diegetic" before you, which I am now loving! I want to use that word all the time. "Diegetic"—I think it is fabulous!

I actually didn't have much to do with putting in the source music. That was all done by Tommy Lee Wallace and the assistant editor. They did all that, and it was in contrast with the score, which was more suspenseful, tension-filled, and frightening. The "diegetic" music—wow, I love this, I am loving this, I learned something here—the diegetic music was more soothing. It was 1940s greatest hits. It was like soft jazz, which was a great contrast. It just seemed appropriate for what she would be playing up there in that lighthouse.

It's a style of popular jazz that, by its nature, is sentimental. But in the context of the film it becomes like wallpaper.

Yep, yep.

So the jazz that was done with an emotional response in mind in essence becomes emotionless, and yet the electronic score that *you* created, which is repetitious and, due to its electronic elements, could be viewed as void of emotion . . .

[*Laughs*] That's me—void of emotion!

. . . that is what actually drives the emotion and drama of the film.

I accept what you say. "Carpenter is unemotional." Write that down!

In 1981 you made *Escape from New York*, and that is when you began working with Alan Howarth. How did the two of you meet? Can you talk a bit about the nature of that collaboration?

Alan owned this equipment [synthesizers, etc.], which is a big plus—huge, giant plus. We were introduced to each other by my editor Todd

Ramsey. He said, "This guy does sound effects mainly. He's not really known for scores, but he has a lot of equipment and you guys might be a good fit."

Lo and behold, we were. Alan's personality was such that it was easy to work with him. He was a great engineer, that's what he did. He did a very similar thing that Dan Wyman had done. I would say, "Let me have something that has more bass," and Alan would come up with it. I was just not a technical guy at that point. I'm still not, really. I need a library of sounds that I can go through and pick one. He was a great engineer, and we just worked our way through the score.

The Thing [1982] was a studio picture. You had a lot more money to play with, and you didn't have to do the score yourself.

[*Sigh of relief*] Oh, that was so wonderful. I loved it.

How did Ennio Morricone come to work on the film? What was it like working with him?

It was fabulous. It was a suggestion. Morricone was suggested by, I believe, the associate producer, Stuart Cohen. Stuart was a friend of mine from film school.

Morricone is just a master. His score for *Once Upon a Time in the West* [1968] is one of the great movie scores of all time. But working with him was, like, "Oh wow!" There were a couple of problems: He didn't speak English, and he lived in Italy. So I had to fly over there and get a translator.

Also, I had forgotten the musical education that I got from my father—or maybe it was self-imposed amnesia because I hated playing violin. I didn't want to know any music, really. He [Morricone] had some things worked out, but they didn't sound like our movie, they didn't sound like *The Thing*. So I said, "Do something with less notes. Just simple." And that is what the opening music is. But he did some beautiful orchestral compositions—sad, mournful stuff, oh man, just gorgeous stuff.

It is my understanding that he didn't score to the edited film, but instead just supplied you with prerecorded cues.

That's right. He wrote cues. He said he could do it two different ways. One was to have the movie and the other was to do cues, and he did cues.

Being a young filmmaker at the time, was it intimidating working with Morricone?

Oh God, yes. Oh God, yes! Are you kidding? I mean, this guy was a hero of mine. So, yeah, it was very difficult to ask him to do anything different than what he was doing. He is brilliant, but a very passionate man too. I really, really enjoyed working with him.

It is no secret that while you were editing *The Thing* you discovered that there were some holes that needed to be filled scorewise, and you went into the studio with Howarth and recorded a few additional cues.

Yep.

In my personal opinion, you downplay their significance.

Well, yeah, I do. It was really nothing. It was just carpet; shag carpeting was what it was. It was nothing.

But for those scenes, the music you recorded is really perfect.

They are just tones, drones, just little electronic bridges. It was nothing that I had to really worry about. I just did it and I did it in a few days. I just realized once we had everything going that there were spots where I needed stuff. That's all it was. And rather than call him [Morricone] up in Italy and try to have somebody try to speak Italian and go through the rigmarole of trying to get something else out of him, I just said, "I can do this real quickly."

After *The Thing*, you made *Christine*. Can you talk a little bit about that score?

There's not really much to say, but I am very proud of one piece of music, and that's when the two boys, the two friends [Arnie and Dennis], are driving and they are having a big, long dialogue scene. It is an important scene. This is at night, in the car, and Arnie is already possessed by this thing.

I just did this piece of music that was constantly descending. There was hardly anything to it, it is just tones descending. It had sort of a melody to it, but not one that you'd notice, particularly. The mixer, when we were putting it in, said, "I could put this under dialogue scenes in other movies [*laughs*] and make them work." I'm very proud of that, because it makes you listen to the dialogue, but it doesn't do anything really, it just descends. I'm proud of that.

The licensed rock 'n' roll music in *Christine* plays a really significant role in the film's storytelling. Are you the one who chose those songs?

There was a list. We came up with a list of songs and, yeah, I chose them. They are all from the time period.

The songs you chose act as Christine's voice in the film.

Oh, yeah, big time!

You did the score for *Halloween III: Season of the Witch* [1982]. You were also the film's producer. Was the scoring process different considering that Tommy Lee Wallace was the film's director?

No, I just went off and recorded it with Alan [Howarth], and once again it was the same process. I just banged it out and tried to give the movie as much as we could.

Was there an effort to make it *Halloween*-esque without just copying your *Halloween* music?

Not that I remember. I don't really remember that much about the experience, I honestly don't. I just remember that it is all the same: You sit down with a keyboard in front of you and the movie, and you just start improvising.

I'd like to talk a little bit about the score for *Starman* [1984].

Oh, yeah. Jack Nitzsche was a great genius.

You are once again working with a composer. How does this collaboration work? Does he bring you things to listen to?

He does that, yeah. In terms of Jack, he just did it. He discovered the Synclavier [an early digital synthesizer-sampler music workstation], which was a new instrument at that point, and he sampled his wife at the time, Buffy Sainte-Marie's voice, and he played her voice in the main title. [*Hums the theme*] That's her voice, and it is just beautiful stuff and really inventive stuff. That was [executive producer] Michael Douglas's suggestion: He said, "Jack Nitzsche is a stone genius." So he did it and I'm really happy.

Did working with Ennio Morricone and Jack Nitzsche change how you approached scoring at all?

No. Hell, no. I can't really change what I do; I'm locked into this mediocrity that I can't get out of [*laughs*]. I just don't have the chops to do it, to go any further, so I just do what I do. Luckily, people don't jump on my ass and make me change it, because I don't know what I'd do then. Oh God, it's like in that behind-the-scenes thing for *Black Hawk Down*: Hans Zimmer plays the music for Ridley Scott, and Ridley Scott then comments on it and says, "I want it more heroic," in a very kind of rough way. If I was the composer, I'd say [*laughs*], "Well, fucking do it yourself!" Are you kidding me? I would have no skills in delivering what people wanted. I just don't have that in me. I really don't. I'm a limited character.

I've heard both you and Alan Howarth refer to your *Big Trouble in Little China* [1986] score as being larger and more ambitious in scope than your previous work.

Yeah, we had a lot of equipment by then, and that was a really good one. I just really enjoyed doing that score.

Was it bigger in terms of number of players or just the amount of equipment you had to work with?

No, it was still just Alan and I, essentially, but he kept adding equipment and perfecting equipment. Generally around this time—*Big Trouble*, *Prince of Darkness* [1987], and *They Live* [1988]—I was introduced to the wonderful and the fabulous Oberheim, which is a piece of equipment. [Starting in the 1970s, Tom Oberheim created a line of popular synthesizers and drum machines that bore his name.] Oh, God, I love the sound of that thing. It is so powerful. I love it.

There seems to be a very specific sound to the Asian-influenced film scores of the mid-1980s and before. Did you make a conscious effort to steer away from that sound with your score for *Big Trouble in Little China*?

Yeah, we didn't want to put "chop-socky" music on it. I just wanted to give it a more modern feel. But again, all of this stuff is instinctual. With the kind of movie that *Big Trouble* is, there wasn't an intellectual decision, oh we're not going to do this or we are going to do that—it wasn't like that. It was, "This is the movie. It is a crazy adventure comedy. Let's score it and score it uniquely."

Tell me about the Coupe de Villes and the album *Waiting Out the Eighties* [1985].

It was an album I worked on with the Coupe de Villes in the 1980s, and . . . oh, what can I say about it? Well, the Coupe de Villes, we are three friends: Tommy Lee Wallace and I met in grade school back in Kentucky. Nick Castle was in my class at USC. And we were all together at film school, and we have been friends for years and years and years.

What the Coupe de Villes was about was playing acoustic guitars and singing, mostly at wrap parties [parties thrown after the last day of shooting on a film, i.e., once the production has "wrapped"]. It was an amateur band. It was friends getting together because we all love music. Our big claim to fame was the end title music for *Big Trouble in Little China*, the title song, and we actually had a music video! It was shown on MTV at the time. If you get the special edition of *Big Trouble in Little China*, you can see the video on there. [*Laughs*] It is unbelievable now. It is hilarious, but that was our big moment in the sun.

Did *Waiting Out the Eighties* ever actually get released?

Oh, hell, no. It was just something to do. I just wanted to do it, just write a bunch of songs. It was a lot of work! All of this shit is a lot of work [*laughs*]! Jesus! I can't believe I did so much work.

With your score for *Prince of Darkness*, there is an emphasis on choral effects.

The film was about an evil in religion, and when you think of religion, you think of choral effects. I sang in a choir; my dad played an organ for a church in my hometown, and I had to sing in the choir. It was forced labor. So I think that is where it all came from.

That is a classic Carpenter score. Can you talk a little bit more about it?

I love that score. I love the opening. The main title sequence is almost a reel long, and the music plays throughout the whole thing. It just sets the mood for this weird-ass movie. It is all about setting mood. . . . I couldn't tell you what I did now, I just have no memory. It just came out. That is the wonderful thing, though, about the way I used to compose music. I would work like a fool, like a crazy man possessed, and then it was over. I never had to think about it again. I'd just go on and do something else. I'd go home and get stoned.

Other than the opening, is there anything specific about the score that you love?

I just like the way it sounds [*laughs*]. I just like it. I don't know. It is one of the great things and the curses of music—a lot of it is just beyond words. Anything can be analyzed, but a lot of this is beyond words. It just strikes you directly.

In your early career, I'm sure that selling yourself as a writer-director-composer package was extremely helpful with getting jobs. But by the mid-1980s you were working with budgets where you could've hired someone else to do the scoring. Did you keep doing it because you liked doing it, or . . .

I hear you, I know what you are getting at. Do I like doing it? No! It is too much work, it is too much stress. It is just too much, but it gives me another creative voice, so I can add this other thing. Nobody does music like me, as bad or good, however you want to look at it. It just sounds unique. That doesn't mean it is great. It could be shit, but it is mine. So that is part of it, it is part of the authorship. But then, after so many years I had to stop. I just said, "This is not worth it anymore. I have to stop. I'm dying here."

In the 1990s you started collaborating on the music with more people, and it appears to me that you were attempting to have more fun with it through the kinds of people you began working with.

Sure.

Was your collaboration with Jim Lang on *In the Mouth of Madness* [1994] similar to the way you worked with Alan Howarth, or different?

It was different. It started the same way, but Jim provided more musical input than Alan did. He had a similar setup, but it was just a different location. He was extremely knowledgeable about music.

I just love that score.

Oh, thank you. I do too, I like that score. And I love the main title—Dave Davies' lead guitar song. That really worked out well.

I heard that that cue was inspired by a piece of temp music you used when you were editing the film.

Yeah. It came from Metallica, the song "Enter Sandman." We had that on there [the temp track] and it was, like, "Let me do something like that." I can't do that. I can't do Metallica. Nobody can, but I can do something with that feel.

Can you think of any other times when a temp track influenced how you eventually scored the film?

In *Big Trouble*, when Jack Burton is driving into town. The temp music for that was "Just Got Paid" by ZZ Top. I love those guys.

When did you start using a temp track in editing?

Always. Everybody has used it. Always. You put your favorite records on something and try it out and see how it works.

Even with *Halloween* and *The Fog*?

Sure, although I don't remember *Halloween*. With that, I don't think we had enough time to put any temp tracks on. That's my recollection.

How did Dave Davies become involved with *In the Mouth of Madness*?

I met Dave in the early 1990s. He and I worked on *Village of the Damned* [1995] together, but that was after *In the Mouth of Madness*. I wanted to work with him, I admired his work. He was a friend, still is. So that just seemed like a perfect beginning for a musical relationship.

There is a really mellow guitar thing on the soundtrack for *In the Mouth of Madness* called "Robby's Office." Did you play it?

Yes, I did.

It's an interesting piece for its placement in the film. Do you recall why you chose it for that scene?

The scene was about Sam Neill's character being this smooth operator and uncovering the corruption of the character Peter Jason played. I don't remember the character's name, but he [Neill] smoothly exposed his corruption. So I thought this little blues riff would be appropriate. I don't know . . . again . . . here you are asking all these questions, and I don't have any good answers for you! It's all just instinctual.

With the opening theme for *Village of the Damned* there is an almost classic Hollywood Western tone to it.

That's Dave, that's him. It had a little bit of a heroic feel to it that he put in. I liked it.

What do you mean by "that's him"?

Well, he went off by himself and composed it and recorded it and presented it to me. I thought, "Wow! Listen to this. This is great."

So your collaboration with him on that score was much more musical in nature than some of your other collaborations?

Yes. He did several really terrific things on that score, just amazing things.

On *Vampires* (1998), you went even further into the realm of the Western musically. And worked with some amazing musicians.

Yeah. I used [Donald] "Duck" Dunn, Steve Cropper, and . . . God, I can't remember who else.

Jeff "Skunk" Baxter?

That's it—Skunk! He played pedal steel for me.

Did you seek out those guys specifically?

I was working with Bruce Robb at that point. He was producing, and I thought, well, this is a kind of Western, it takes place in the West. It is a vampire movie, but let's get a little "feel" in there. So it was a choice between ZZ Top and Cropper, Dunn, and Baxter, and we just went with this pickup band that was just unbelievable. They were great. They had quite some personalities.

Let's talk about them a little bit. I interviewed Cropper a few years ago for something else, and he was tickled pink by the fact that I brought up the *Vampires* score.

He loved playing on it. He had a great time. You know, he's a force to deal with, though. You have to deal with him [*laughs*]. I wanted to do a shuffle for one of the songs, and he just would not do it. He hated shuffles—he hated them! So we did something else. "Duck" Dunn turned to me and said, "Do you know 'Hey Joe'?" And I said, "Well, of course." And he said, "Let's do that." So we did "Hey Joe" instead and Cropper was happy.

But you know, it was just amazing, it was amazing to hang with them. And then I added a synthesizer score in addition, and then Baxter came in and added some pedal steel and some guitar work. God, he is amazing too.

When you're sitting in the studio with those guys, is the teenage John Carpenter inside of you exclaiming, "Holy shit!"?

Fuck, yeah! Oh yes [*laughs*]. You know, playing with them was unbelievable. Are you kidding me? It was great. It made me feel like I was hot shit for two minutes [*laughs*]. But there is also a director working there inside me, saying, "We have to get this."

Does working with a band change the way you compose?

No, it doesn't change it, but what it does, is make me have to communicate to the musicians what I want. Because I don't write music, a lot of it is just improvised on the spot. So with Steve Cropper and "Duck" Dunn, we just got together and started playing. "This is what I want." And they just brought a lot of their rock 'n' roll blues to it. Playing with them was a lot of fun.

You were billed as the "Texas Toad Lickers" on the soundtrack.

[*Laughs*] Yeah, I know. That was Cropper's idea.

There is a piece of music in there at the top of a track called "New Mexico" on the soundtrack that seems like a little nod to *Suspiria*.

Oh, really?

Judging from that response, I'm guessing it wasn't a conscious decision.

[*Laughs*] I don't remember. I just don't remember. But I will rip off *Suspiria* anytime I can. It is just such a great score.

You worked with some guys who were a little "harder" on the score for *Ghosts of Mars* [2001]. Guys like Steve Vai and Buckethead and the band Anthrax.

Yeah, I worked with all these great guitarists and bands. We just had a great time, but doing that score was the moment that I realized, "I just can't do this anymore." It is just too hard, it just takes so long and is such a grind. On the *Ghost of Mars* DVD there's a making-of/

behind-the-scenes of doing the music, and it shows me on the first day and then it shows me after we've done all these segments, and you're just seeing a destroyed man. I just can't do it. If I kept at that pace, I'd be dead. I just had to stop. I was burned out, I was completely burned out.

It is my understanding that Joseph Bishara, the composer of *Dark Skies*, the *Insidious* films, and *The Conjuring*, also worked with you on that score.

Oh, he did amazing stuff. He just did a whole different thing I'd never seen before. It was almost visual: He calls up these sounds and he chops them up on a computer. Oh, it is amazing.

What exactly did he do?

Well, he did everything. With every synth score that I did, he did a layer of it, and he took various tracks and various things and created new tracks by calling up his own synth sounds that he had, but then altering them visually, chopping them up, changing the waveforms, making all sorts of bizarre shit. It was really amazing to watch—I wouldn't know how to begin to do that crap. He is really accomplished at it. He does a lot of his own scores now, but he did a lot of trailers too, just a lot of great stuff. He's amazing.

Would you consider scoring for somebody else?

Absolutely! I've had a couple of near-misses, but mostly because I looked at the movie and thought, "God, that's awful. I can't do anything for this [*laughs*]. I can't help." There are video games too. . . . Robert Rodriguez wanted me to do a score for him, but then we didn't. So I was sort of left at the altar.

So you're up for it; you're just waiting for the right project.

I would do it. Sure. I would do it.

You chose not to do the score for your film *The Ward* [2010].

[*Laughs*] Oh God, I would've died.

After doing so many of your own scores, what kind of role did you take as director when you worked with composer Mark Kilian on that film?

Mark Kilian is a fabulous, talented guy. He loved collaboration, and he was really open to anything I said. So it was really easy. We'd just talk through it. I played one simple line on a piece, but even that was too hard [*laughs*]. I had to drive over to his studio, and I began to have the old feelings I used to have, and I was like, "Oh God, no, I don't want to get involved in this. Let somebody else do it." I loved his score.

Going into the film, were you at all tempted to do it yourself?

No. I was not tempted.

So there was no worry that it would not sound like a John Carpenter movie?

I didn't care [*laughs*]! I didn't care. I made so many movies—1970s, '80s, and '90s. My God!

You just released your first solo album, *Lost Themes* [2015]. Can you talk a bit about its concept?

Well, the "concept" is only after the fact. That isn't how everything got started. It got started about two years ago, with my son and I sitting in the house. We would play video games for a couple of hours, and then we would go downstairs to my Logic Pro computer-music setup and improvise music for a couple hours. This went on for quite a while. I had about sixty minutes of music done. Then he went off to teach in Japan and I just sat on it, did nothing. I got a new music attorney, and she asked me, "Do you have anything new?" And I thought, "Well, I have this stuff that Cody and I did. I guess it wouldn't hurt to send it to her." So I sent it, and a couple months later I had a record deal! Just like that.

Why did you get a music attorney? Was it to handle the reissues of all your old scores?

Just everything—to handle everything to do with music.

I would imagine that you are surprised by the fact that companies keep re-releasing your film music.

I love it. Yes, I am surprised. That was never the intention, so it is just an extra, added wonderful thing.

Who named the new album?

The record label came up with "Lost Themes." That was their idea, and I thought, "Oh, well, that's pretty good." They are implying that this is all music from movies I didn't make, but it isn't—it's all new. I like to say that the album *Lost Themes* is for the movies in your mind. We all have movies playing, and this is the score for them. I am trying to take you to just another place, to transport you.

Some of the tracks on the album, like "Vortex" for instance, are very reminiscent of mid-1980s John Carpenter. Would you say that sound and feel are just you, or was there a decision to produce tracks that sound like they might be from that period?

That's just me. There are other tracks, like "Night," that don't sound like mid-Eighties to me, but that's just me. No, I don't think in terms of Eighties or whatever. It's just me fucking around with my son and godson.

Who is your godson, and when did he start participating?

Daniel Davies. That's Dave Davies' son. He's my godson, we raised him. He joined [the project] when Cody was in Japan teaching English. He came over and we added a few tracks and mixed the tracks and things like that, but he really composed as well as mixed.

Can you talk a little bit about the liberation of not being tied to a picture in the studio?

Unbelievable joy. Absolute joy. Yeah, for the first time there was no schedule . . . well, there was a little bit of a schedule, but it was nothing compared to movies. It was fantastic—fantastic! It is the only way I can describe it.

Is there anything about *Lost Themes* that you want the fans to know?

Well, you just have to listen to it. One of the things I am most proud of, besides just the collaboration with my son and godson, is the fact that I think that my music has grown since the old days. It is a lot more complex now. I think that comes with age.

Quite a few of the horror film score composers of your generation, like Goblin, Fabio Frizzi, Simon Boswell, and even Alan Howarth, are taking their acts on the road now. Is playing live something that appeals to you?

It might if they pay us enough money. You can't play the kind of music that I perform cheaply, unless you just reinvent it as a rock 'n' roll band. That can be cheap, but this stuff ain't cheap, man. And to sound like that live? That would be tough. Not impossible, just complex.

Note: Several months after this interview took place, a slew of John Carpenter concert dates were announced.

Jay Chattaway

*"Maniac . . . was pretty grisly! I worked at home on the score, and
I had to hide my notes and stuff, because I had a little daughter. I'd
tell her, 'I have to go work tonight, honey.' And she'd ask, 'Well, what
are you doing?' And I'd have to say, 'I have to go and kill Rita.'"*

WHEN I FIRST CONTACTED JAY Chattaway to ask him to be a part
of this project, he was in the middle of a several-month voyage,
sailing down the coast of California into Mexico. Our interview had to
wait, but that ocean excursion explained a lot about him.

Since the early 1990s his work for nature documentaries, *National
Geographic* specials, and, most notably, the various *Star Trek* TV series
has given a musical voice to the art of exploration. But for horror fans,
Chattaway will always be best known for his role in exploring the
psyche of a street-trolling serial killer in the 1980 film *Maniac*.

As with most composers interviewed for this book, his work is not restricted to horror. But what I've found interesting about his work within the horror genre is that it often—and brilliantly—straddles the line between scary and sentimental. His use of sweet melodies juxtaposed with the more familiar suspense and fear-driven elements of horror scoring is what gives his music a distinctive depth and beauty.

In my interview with him I found him to be, among many other things, extremely personable and outgoing. In some ways I almost felt like I was talking to an old friend, and we spent quite a bit of time, both before and after the interview, chatting about an array of topics ranging from New York City and sailing, to jazz and even the popularity of blues music in Mexico (of all things).

I have often said that I like Chattaway's music because it tells us that he's "all heart." And after interviewing him, I can confirm that that is true.

SELECTED FILMOGRAPHY

1980	*Maniac*
1983	*Vigilante*
1984	*Missing in Action*
1985	*Invasion U.S.A.*
	Silver Bullet
1988	*Braddock: Missing in Action III*
	Maniac Cop
	Red Scorpion
1989	*Relentless*
1990	*The Ambulance*
	Maniac Cop 2
1990–1992	*National Geographic Specials* (TV series, 2 episodes)
1990–1994	*Star Trek: The Next Generation* (TV series, 42 episodes)
1992	*Space Age* (TV series, 2 episodes)
1993–1999	*Star Trek: Deep Space Nine* (TV series, 59 episodes)
2000	*Delta Force One: The Lost Patrol*
2001–2005	*Star Trek: Enterprise* (TV series, 28 episodes)
2006	"Pick Me Up" (*Masters of Horror* TV series)
2015	*Poltergeist* (additional music)

Let's begin by talking about your early passion for music.

My background is in jazz, actually. I'm a jazz guy, and I guess what turned my light bulb on was, I went to a concert when I was in high school. It was with the Pittsburgh Symphony, and Henry Mancini was the guest conductor and performer, and that was when a big light bulb went off and I said, "I'd like to do that."

So I started following that path and figuring out what he did and how he did it. It was kind of cool, because I got to meet him in his later years, when I went out to California. I thanked him for being such an inspiration. He was quite ill at the time, but we became friends. We conversed quite a bit about it, and he lived in the same general area that I did. We are also both from Pittsburgh, PA, and we kidded about how there must be something in the water, etc. He was really a warm gentleman.

A lot of people don't know about his earlier film career, but he wrote a lot of science fiction and horror music as part of Universal [Studios]. The score for *The Creature from Black Lagoon* [1954] was actually written by, like, five different composers, and he was one of them. So he was very well schooled in that style, but he seemed to gravitate more towards the pop and the songwriting thing and scoring those kinds of pictures, or doing whatever Blake Edwards was doing.

Do you remember what it was about hearing Mancini's music live that excited you?

I think it was how he was able to get the Pittsburgh Symphony, which was usually used to playing very classical music, to play this lush, Hollywood-sounding jazzy music that he wrote. And actually, his personality was one that just got the audience completely involved in the communication between composer and audience. It was instant. It wasn't like there was a warming up period. . . . He came out and he played the piano and he played the piccolo.

He just communicated, and I think that is what music is about: If there is no communication, there is really no music happening. He was able to do that in an instant. I guess that's the main thing. It wasn't anything technical about the way he conducted or the types of chords he was using. It wasn't about music theory. It was more of an emotional thing. He is so warm and he's got "it" and he's got the audience right there, so they are going to absorb what it is he is trying to say and play.

It is kind of fascinating how those things work, but that's what got me started. So I went to school and studied, and I was even writing music when I was in junior high school for the band. I don't know how I was able to do that, but somehow I did it.

Were you actually physically writing it out?

Oh yeah! We were writing it out. I used to borrow all the other kids' parts, because a lot of the arrangements from back then, for jazz stuff, didn't have scores and I wanted to see how it all worked. So I would borrow all the other guys in the band's music, and I'd put it in order and try and figure out why it worked the way it did. And then I said, "Oh well, I can do that."

Then my band director gave me a couple books to read, and I started writing charts when I was in eighth grade. They weren't very good; well, maybe they were okay for an eighth-grader. The band director actually kept the first chart that I wrote for the band. Thirty years later I was getting an award at West Virginia University and he showed up—and he laminated that music and kept it for thirty years—and gave it to me! It was really amazing! I still have it, but I am afraid to get it out and have it played. It might not sound so great.

But, yeah, it was an interesting start. I ended up in New York writing for Maynard Ferguson, the jazz trumpet player, and I joined CBS. I lucked out, because I didn't know what record producers did and I was hired by CBS to write and produce, etc. So my first album was Maynard's album called *Conquistador* [1977]. At the very last minute, this movie called *Rocky* [1976] came out, and we decided that its theme [Bill Conti's "Gonna Fly Now"] could be a good vehicle for him, and I wrote a much faster, more jazzy dance arrangement of it and it became a hit record. That was the hit record from the movie, and so my first record as a record producer was a gold record. And now I was this young guy doing big-time records for CBS and doing concerts, etc. It was like, "Wow, how did this happen?" It was amazing.

The way the movie thing happened was a result of that. I had an office at the CBS building at 51 West 52nd (it was called the "Black Rock"), and this guy comes in who was a concert promoter. He wanted to use some of our artists, and I hooked him up with some artists. That worked out well, and he came back one day and he said,

"My friend is directing this movie—do you think any of your artists might be interested in helping find music for it or do the score?" I told him that I didn't know, and that I'd like to see the movie and meet the filmmaker.

The concert promoter was Andrew Garroni, and his friend was William Lustig. I went into this editing room down on 48th Street, and there's Bill [Lustig], and we're watching this movie on a Moviola [a film-based linear editing machine]. They're all excited about it. . . . They were in the middle of shooting and editing it, and they were just so on-fire about the whole thing. I don't know if it still exists in New York, but that "young Turk" filmmaker thing was very infectious. I thought, "Man, these guys are amazing!" But I still had my other music thing to do, and they weren't quite ready to do the music yet. I told them, "I'll think about it and maybe I can find somebody."

Before they finished, I was working with Gato Barbieri, who had done the score to *Last Tango in Paris* [1972] for Bernardo Bertolucci. But he is a sax player and basically a theme writer. (If you've seen *Last Tango*, it is kind of the same theme over and over again.) Gato wasn't really equipped to score films, and he was asked to score a film for Michael Winner, who had done films like *The Mechanic* [1972] and *Death Wish* [1974] and *The Big Sleep* [1978].

Anyway, it was a film called *Firepower* [1979], with Sophia Loren and James Coburn. In this case the film was already cut. With *Last Tango*, Bertolucci would cut the film to Gato's music, so Gato didn't need to figure out any of the mechanics and the math and all that [of composing to picture].

Now, I had done, like, four albums for Gato at that point, and he asked me if I could basically orchestrate the film. Which really meant that Gato would give me the themes and I then I had to make the score—like, eighty minutes of music—from this. The orchestration is when the composer just gives you a very rough sketch or, as in this case, a tune to use in a certain scene in a film. Then you, as the orchestrator, have to be able to take that and finesse it. Pure orchestration isn't really like composing or recomposing. It is like taking the composer's bare essentials and expanding it so that a full orchestra can play it and it can be conducted and made into a performance vehicle.

In this case it was more like, "Here is a theme that I wrote. You think it could go here?" Then I would have to work that theme into a score that was based entirely on his music, except for the parts that I wrote, which were background scoring–types of things that interwove his themes into a score that would work with an orchestra.

The cool part was that it was the London Philharmonic. So my first film was with the London Philharmonic, with eighty pieces and Gato playing sax and scoring in London. It was a trip!

So I did that, and I got really turned on by the process. I came back, and Bill and Andy were still working on their movie, and I said, "I just had this really good experience. I will do the movie." They didn't have much money, but I said, "I will figure out how to do this." So began a long-term working relationship and friendship.

That was *Maniac* [1980], and it was pretty grisly! I worked at home on the score, and I had to hide my notes and stuff, because I had a little daughter. I'd tell her, "I have to go work tonight, honey." And she'd ask, "Well, what are you doing?" And I'd have to say, "I have to go and kill Rita [*laughs*]." That's not something you want to tell your five-year-old, but in those days we didn't have videotaped copies of the film to work with, so I would have to go into the city, watch a scene on the Moviola, check my timings, and then go home and write like that. There weren't any mockups or anything like that, the way it is done now—you had to remember what you saw and then just create.

How would you describe the job of the film score composer?

I think it is to try and understand what the director is trying to accomplish through the use of music in his film. The music is usually one of the very last elements that is added, so by the time the composer comes in, the film is pretty much what it is. It is not usually going to be changed to be entirely different. So the message of the film is there and the rhythm of the film is there.

There are always going to be inherent strong points and weak points that maybe the director will point out, or maybe someone else will point them out. For instance, maybe there is a scene that needs to be "warmer," or there is a scene that is really too slow and maybe faster music will help propel it further forward. The music is supposed to be relatively utilitarian, yet at the same time, for the composer it has a need to be artistic. So right away you get into a complicated issue as to what is your role: Are you a composer, or are you a facilitator of something that is happening on the screen?

When I first started, it was not really a collaborative venture as much of it is now. It was more of, here is a director who has a vision, and you need to get inside of his head to see what it is that he is trying to say. In the case of Bill Lustig, he and I spent countless hours at his apartment listening to Ennio Morricone scores from old Italian movies so that he could explain what he felt the purpose of the music was and how Morricone established his ideas. Which I thought were brilliant, because he could establish his creativity and yet be completely utilitarian when it needed to be.

The function of the composer is that of a team player. You are not just, like, "I'm just going to write this music and hopefully it will fit." You are writing music to achieve something. To maybe add emotion to a scene that wasn't delivering enough emotion without any musical help. If it is suspenseful, maybe it is not as suspenseful as it should be, and the music can propel that or add to the suspense.

If you want to get into "genre," the most fun, of course, is to do a horror film. Then the music, in at least the ones I've worked on, seems to be able to have its own unique personality. Whereas in some of the space dramas that I've worked on, the music is much more of a utilitarian background thing.

With horror you really have control; the composer can manipulate as much as he or she wants to. If you want to scare somebody or have a red herring moment, where you are scaring somebody when they shouldn't be scared, it is pretty simple to do with music, and it is a lot of fun to do that. It is also fun to add emotion to a horror movie that might not have had emotional intent.

In other words, if you want to talk about *Maniac*, for example, there's a guy that was an abused child, but they don't show any of that child abuse through flashback or anything. There are a few references to it by somebody mentioning that he was locked in a closet and the cigarette burns on his arm, etc. But the way it was accomplished in that film was by, instead of having slasher-type thematic music for his character, the trick was adding more of an emotional childlike quality to the theme. Which was this little flute or recorder melody, but it has a real bent harmonic structure around it, which sort of says, "Gee, I feel sorry for this guy, but he is still pretty warped." That's the joy of writing music for those types of films.

When you were working on *Maniac*, was that flute melody something you and Bill Lustig discussed and came up with together, or was that sweet and melodic aspect of the score something that you saw in the film and brought to it?

Actually, the beauty of working with Bill was that he was very trusting. He felt like he did his duty by educating me, then he just sent me off and said, "Okay, go write what you want to write."

There are scenes in that film like the opening, and then there's a scene where he's walking down the street and looking at mannequins—I think we called that piece "Window Shopping." It was almost designed for it. If Bill had the music in advance, he probably would've shot it exactly the same way. But he didn't have the music, there were no demos involved. It was, like, "Here's the film and here's the music. Let's hope it all fits." And it did.

That was done in the days when the movie was shot on film and the music was recorded and mixed on mag stock [magnetic recording tape with film-sprocket holes along its edges so that it can be synched up, frame by frame, with film stock during the editing process]. There wasn't much manipulating of the music, there wasn't much change going on. It was, like, "Here's the music. Let's just put it with the film and see what happens." And somehow it really worked! I think it worked mostly because of the emotional quality. The scary parts were pretty unique in that we did some very strange techniques.

I would love to get into the nuts and bolts of the score. Horror film scores at that time were unique, because of their blending of classical instruments and things like synthesizers. With *Maniac* you seem to really highlight the flute and a few other instruments, like the fretless electric bass. I'd love it if you could talk a bit about your decision-making processes back then, if you can remember. (I know it has been a long time.)

It has been a while, but it is really still fresh! The budgetary requirements were such that we didn't have a full orchestra. We had myself and one other person on keyboards, a percussionist, a bass player, and a woodwind player. The whole idea of the acoustic parts, with the exception of the flute and the recorder, were to make it sort of twisted and bent.

In those days, the best solution to that was to play on an acoustic instrument and then change the speed of the tape machine while it was being recorded. We had a twenty-four-track machine and it had a variable speed on it. So, if you play a piano chord and turn down the speed of the machine, the end result sounds like what they have now on keyboards and synthesizers: It is called a glissando pedal, or on a Kurzweil they have a little ribbon that you can pitch-bend.

They didn't have that back then. We used a real acoustic piano and changed the tape recorder speed. And we did the same thing with percussion. We would hit the cymbal or do a cymbal roll and change the speed of the tape or record it at half speed. These were things that were being done in serious electronic music, and we were trying to apply those textures to generate cool film music.

Also, the synthesizers then were not polyphonic [able to produce more than one pitch/sound simultaneously]. The most polyphony I think we could get was a little Prophet 5 [synthesizer]. We used a Minimoog, a Prophet 5, and to do the big string orchestra stuff we had a Mellotron [a keyboard instrument that played back prerecorded sounds], which came from more of a pop feel. It was an archaic instrument where you play a key and there is a little ribbon [a piece of prerecorded magnetic tape] that goes across a playback head. That actually had a recording of string instruments, or it had a choir or whatever bank of sounds that you bought for the instrument, and they were pretty decent-sounding. Of course, it really isn't archaic anymore, because I think they've come back into fashion [*laughs*].

How long did it take from the moment you came aboard the project to the moment you completed the last track?

I think it took about three or four weeks. I would write the music in sketch form first. I actually think we recorded the whole score in one week, in a little country studio in Weston, Connecticut. The guy's name was Don Elliott, who was a big advertising guy in New York; he had a nice little studio. The keyboard player who did most of the work was an excellent blues Hammond B3 organist. Pete Levin is his name; he was very influential with coming up with cool sounds and stuff. We had a percussionist who brought all this crazy percussion. He sort of lived inside of this shell of percussion instruments.

It was all multitrack. So no one was really playing together *per se*. We'd record one track, then add another and then add the percussion, and then the flute player came in at the very end and did his thing. Then we mixed it and added some very strange effects. It was also one of the first films to be mixed in Dolby Stereo, so we did some fancy stuff with that. I remember it like it was yesterday . . . well, plus thirty-some years [*laughs*].

Could you talk a bit more about how you scored to your notes, as opposed to scoring directly to picture? In essence you were scoring to a stopwatch.

Right! Exactly. We didn't have the facility to do so [score to picture]. The picture I had just done in London with Gato was a big studio picture, so that was scored to picture. For that film, the picture was projected while we were rehearsing and recording the music, so you could make adjustments. But with *Maniac* . . . there was just no way to synchronize a Moviola with live musicians. It just wasn't practical to do that.

So the process was that everything was written in timings. There were click tracks [prerecorded clicks, like from a metronome, that the musicians sync their playing to when recording] involved . . . and I had this huge book (now it is all done in the computer) that would covert timings into clicks, and we had a digital metronome. That was about as fancy we could get.

UREI made a very accurate metronome that we could play to. For instance, if you had 120 beats per minute, then 120 clicks on that metronome would be one minute. You could go through these complicated tables [in the book]: What if it was only 57.5 seconds? Then there would be a click equivalent that you could use. You would set the metronome to that and it was dead-on accurate. It was really amazing.

Almost all of the cues had to have a click to them, a metronome track. Then, once we recorded the metronome track, we would check it with a stopwatch to make sure it was right for the picture. And we'd check the internal hits [exactly synchronized points where certain notes or chords need to be within the overall span of the cue]. For instance, if someone was getting stabbed, you have to make sure that is in sync [the music corresponds to the onscreen action] or else it would look pretty strange.

It is a little technical, but one of the things that I learned is, in most cases, music in a film builds up to something. It may foreshadow it, but if there is a scare moment, a real "spill the popcorn"–type moment, it has to precede the action—it can't come after the action and be reactive to it. They are called *stingers*. If you're going to have a knife appear and stab somebody, you want the music to happen just a little bit before that. It kind of gets everybody's attention and then they'll watch the gore. . . .

All that timing was very critical, and we had no means other than a click track and a stopwatch to really check it out. That's why we were all amazed when we actually took it into the mixing studio and watched it for the first time with the picture and saw that it worked.

I think Bill came to one of the sessions where we were mixing, and that was about it. With all of his films, he was never hands-on with the music. He would just trust me to do what I do. It is so refreshing. Nowadays it is very different. It was really a good relationship.

Other than the Morricone stuff that Lustig played for you, were there any other direct influences on that score?

I think there were some things that John Carpenter had done around that time that Bill liked, but mostly he was a complete and dedicated Morricone fan. And some of Morricone's earliest scores were very minimalistic. They were done with weird effects on electric guitar, for example, like electric guitar and harmonica and not much more. They weren't the Morricone that we know of now, with the big, lush orchestral scores. But the early works of his were phenomenally successful with a minimal amount of instruments.

That was, I think, the purpose of the education: You don't need to have a sixty-piece orchestra to do this. And Bill was right! I think if we had sixty pieces or more, it wouldn't have been as effective for that film—that was a breakthrough film both from the way he shot it and musically. It was pretty adventurous in ways that I have not been so adventurous since.

It seems that horror film scores, especially in that era, have two things in common: There are budgetary restrictions, and the genre

seems to lend itself to experimentation. Can you talk a little more about how restrictions can fuel creativity?

If we had no budgetary restrictions, the chances of going more cliched probably would've surfaced. Everybody wants that big cinematic moment where you can have a huge brass section or screechy strings or whatever, but there is only so much space for music in the audio spectrum. You can fill it up in a myriad of different ways. The more experimental ways might be like using very bizarre percussion to make rhythmic hits, as opposed to having a full, pounding brass section do the same thing. It does fill up the same space, and you can get the same bang for the buck—you just have to be creative about how you achieve that.

One example in that score: There was a sting that was used that was very complicated in its construction. So we reused it many times, and it sounded as though it was a knife coming through you. In reality, it was a combination of synthesis, scraping piano strings while we changed the speed of the tape, and various amounts of metallic percussion that was recorded with a varied speed.

When you put all that together, it is something that a symphonic orchestra couldn't really perform; it was unique to its own genre. That's an instance where I think the score worked better than if I would've had a huge orchestra to perform it.

You often hear popular songwriters talk about how they always have music playing in their heads, and many of the composers I've spoken to describe a similar occurrence. Is that something that you experience as well? Does the music just play in your mind like a radio, and it is just a matter of tapping into it and jotting it down, or is your process more "conventional" and labor intensive?

I think I have that gift. It is pretty unique in that I hear it. When I watch a film or another type of project that I am going to score, I envision . . . or I guess it would be "en-aural" [*laughs*], the entire score in my head. I don't know how that happens, it is just there. The problem is writing it down or getting it communicated fast enough, because when I start plunking away I can forget what I had thought when I initially heard it in my head. I have no idea how that works. It is one of those mystical things. Or maybe it is always there and we are just people who are translators or transmitters and receivers. I don't know, I'm not that cosmic about it. For me, it is there, I hear it. I visualize the music all at once. It's pretty scary.

Let's use the flute melody in *Maniac* as an example. Is that exactly what you heard when you watched the footage? Or did you get a feeling that that was the *kind* of thing that you wanted, and then you sat down and worked it out and that is what it became?

No, I heard the whole melody. What I had to work out was the dissonant harmonies around it to make it still be . . . I guess you would call it almost "bitonal" [utilizing two different keys or tonalities simultaneously], in that the melody itself is very melodic and diatonic [in a standard major or minor key or common mode], but if you analyzed theoretically what the harmonic structures were on the piano, they're pretty out there. So I did have to plunk around on that to make that sort of dissonance work. For me, it is harder to write dissonance than it is consonance; I am sort of a consonant guy, and it is a fascinating concept.

This is a little off the track, but it may be helpful just to mention this. I was Artist-in-Residence at Berklee College of Music in Boston, and I had a group of master class students and they all wanted to learn to write scary music. . . . I had one young man who just did not have it in his makeup to write anything dissonant. He was from Atlanta, Georgia. He was a choir guy and everything was triads for him. So I said, "Okay, try this. Take what you're playing on the keyboard with your left hand, and either move it up a half-step or down a half-step. So now you've got triads on your right hand, but your bass line is out by a half-step."

And suddenly he discovered dissonance. It was amazing. His light bulb went off—"How did you do that?" So it is weird. Some people just don't have the dissonant concept.

When you're working on a film, do you like to score from the beginning of the film to the end of the film, or do you like to find specific moments throughout the film and use them as tent poles to then score around?

What I do, if I have the whole film, is I pick and choose areas where I am going to use thematic material. I am a thematic composer. In *Maniac* it was evident that there were three or four places that the theme could be used, so I would score those scenes first. Then, if there were an action sequence that was maybe derivative of another action sequence, I would go and do those in sequence. I don't ever start at the beginning of the film. I don't know if anyone does that.

Usually, nowadays, films aren't finished in chronological order. You have to score what you get, and so you get timings for one reel and then maybe two scenes in the next reel. It is very confusing, but at least now you sort of get a rough cut of the entire film, even though it is not completely tweaked and finished. I don't think they are ever finished now, until after they're on the screen.

I guess you could call it "tent poling," but I call it more like "selectively choosing" sections that I know are going to be relevant. Because then I will have the palette in my head, where I know, "This is what I'm using, and this is the harmonic and the orchestral palette for this, etc." So my head isn't completely twisted, like, "This is a lush orchestral section, yet this next section is a contemporary rhythmic thing." I try to prioritize pieces or cues by their tempo and their type.

Could we talk a bit about *Silver Bullet* [1985], which is both a film and a score that I have a great fondness for?

Oh really? Okay.

The Stephen King–based films of the 1980s were family melodramas in many respects, with an element of horror added. With *Silver Bullet*, I love the way that dramatic duality is represented in the music. Could you talk a bit about how you approached scoring those two aspects of that film?

It was, in a way, similar to the concept in *Maniac*. Here's this kid who is handicapped and has a belief that something is going on in this little town, and nobody really believes him. So he's very vulnerable. The scene in that movie that did it for me was when he's in his wheelchair and he's sitting and watching the other boys playing baseball, wishing he could play too. Well, I'm *guessing* that is what he is wishing for. They don't tell you that, it is not in the script, it is not in the notes from the director— but the *music* tells you that.

So that's where that theme came from, and, if you notice, that's *also* a recorder, a wooden flute, playing the melody [*laughs*]. It seems like a wooden flute is a motif of mine, my saying, "Oh this poor kid, he doesn't have everything he should have." I never really thought about that, though, until you asked me that question. . . . But that is the scene that triggered, "Yes, it is a werewolf movie. Yes, it is supposed to be really scary. But it really was about this little kid and his love for his uncle and his family."

The version of the movie that you've seen was not the original intended film. The movie was intended to be a PG-13 movie when it was finished. Paramount, in its infinite wisdom, had just come off of *Friday the 13th* [1980], which was a complete slasher film (which another one of my friends directed, so I am not criticizing it). And they saw the finished cut of *Silver Bullet* in its PG-13 stage and said, "Oh, no, it's not violent enough." So they went back in and filmed a bunch of inserts with more graphic werewolf attacks, etc. and tried to make it something that it really wasn't intended to be.

So I had to go back in and rescore all those sections to make it more "graphic"—for the lack of a better word—because they wanted an R film. I guess they saw that the *Friday the 13th* movies generated a lot more income. But the vision of Dan Attias, who was *Silver Bullet*'s director, and Martha Schumacher [the producer] was that it was a family movie about a kid that believed there was a werewolf, and there was one—but it wasn't going to be violent. When I first saw the movie, that "duality" is what came to my mind too. It's brilliant that you picked up on that; it seems that not too many people have. They said, "Well, the music is a little tame for this movie [*laughs*]."

That was an interesting film. . . . It was about werewolves, and . . . digital sampling had just, sort of, come into its own. I got a guy with a Synclavier system, and we went to a wolf farm and we recorded wolves howling. [*Laughs*] It wasn't, like, "Okay, now you, number three wolf, I'd like you to howl now," but we recorded ambience of wolves howling.

Then we took these back into the digital domain and analyzed them and, lo and behold, the melody of *Silver Bullet* came from a slowed-down version of a wolf howl. [*Laughs*] That's something that never made it onto the liner notes (although it has been rereleased on a CD and I never read the liner notes, so maybe they did talk about that).

So then we used those wolves in conjunction with the wooden flute in a few cues, and they kind of worked out together. It's almost like the wolves sort of became a member of the orchestra—[*laughs*] "Okay, cue the wolves now! Okay, here they come." And it's kind of cool because they can just play a chord on the keyboard and then you have a wolf choir or a wolf solo or a wolf ensemble.

And this film had a much bigger budget, as you can probably tell from listening. We had about a seventy-piece orchestra along with a bunch of synthetic instruments on this one.

Danial Attias had worked as an assistant director, but this was his first time helming a feature. Can you talk a bit about working with him?

I actually got involved with that film through the editor. Dan Loewenthal was the film editor on that project, and he and I had done maybe five or six features together. And when it came to discuss music, he suggested to Dan Attias that he should listen to some of my music. I lived in Connecticut at the time, and both of the Dans and their families, I believe, came to my house.

I had a little studio there. . . . I had read the script. (I also should mention that I was an avid Stephen King fan. Not that that had anything to do with me getting the job, but I had read just about everything he had done and also saw all the movies that were made from his books.) So when Dan and Dan came to my place, I just started playing a little of the theme that I had written from the script. I hadn't seen any of the footage yet, but I told them, "This is how I hear the music." He [Attias] was, like, "Oh, you did this without seeing the film?" I said, "Yeah, I just read the script, and I can envision what it might look like." He liked that.

The next thing I knew, he went back to North Carolina, and we stayed friends on the phone, talking about music, etc. I knew they were still discussing who would do it, and I was sort of hoping that I would get it because I liked the people a lot and I liked the script.

The next thing I knew, I got a call. They wanted me to come down to North Carolina and meet the producers. So they flew me to North Carolina and I met Martha [Schumacher], who was a young producer working for Dino De Laurentiis. She apologized for not having enough money to adequately do the score [*laughs*]. I asked, "What is not adequate?" and it was, like, ten times what I had seen for doing *Maniac*. I replied, "Oh, yeah, that is pretty tough, but I think I can make it work [*laughs*]."

So it was great, and we had a good relationship. I really had a good time doing the score. Again, it was not hands-on: They were all in North Carolina and I was in New York. I don't think there was a video copy to work to; it was just getting notes, and we had a rough-cut print, but we couldn't project it in the studio where we were working. Nowadays there must be studios in New York City where you can run projection, but in those days there weren't. . . .

We recorded some of it in Connecticut and some in New York, and put it all together and mixed in New York City at Sound One. We had great mixers. I went to the dub and the mix, and Martha and Dan were there. Everybody liked the music. Also, I got to meet Stephen King too—that was kind of cool.

Can you talk a bit about that? You were a fan and he is a very musical person. That had to be interesting.

I know! All he wanted to talk about was playing the guitar [*laughs*]. I wanted to know more about his writing, because I just think he's great. Are you a Stephen King fan?

Yes, of course.

Did you ever read his book called *On Writing*?

No, I haven't read that one yet.

It's a nonfiction book that he wrote about how he writes. It is fascinating. His take on the creative process is absolutely fascinating. That's what I wanted to know about. Like the same stuff you're asking me, that's the same kind of stuff I was asking him. But he'd be, like, "When you're playing the blues, how is it that you get these sounds on the guitar?" [*Laughs*] It was great. He's so prolific that I just wanted to know how he does it, and he'd say, "Well I have to write. It's not like I do it for the money. I get up in the morning and I just have to write, that's my thing."

And I envy that. I don't feel like I have to write music every day—it's not going to be a big bad day if I don't create something. But for him, at least back then, that was the way his work ethic was. He would have to write something every day, and that's pretty admirable. We didn't become, like, friends, but we hung out and he wanted to know about music and I wanted to know about writing. It's kind of like going to a foreign country: I'm trying to speak Spanish and he's trying to speak English [*laughs*]. But it was quite interesting.

As a side story about the film, I had these bell sounds that I used throughout the score. . . . So we go to a screening of the film. I had never met Dino De Laurentiis before, and he was the head guy [at the De Laurentis studios in Wilmington, NC]. He wasn't hands-on with this film, but he got it started—and at the same time they did the film *Cat's Eye* [1985], that Alan Silvestri scored. Both of the films were based on short stories written by Stephen King. (There never was a book called *Silver Bullet*—*Cycle of the Werewolf* was the name of the short story.)

So Dino sits next to me. . . . It was pretty scary, and we play the whole movie with the score, and everybody really likes the movie. Dino says [*imitating an Italian accent*], "Jay, the bells . . . bells are for weddings. You get rid of all the bells, I don't like bells [*laughs*]." So I had to go back into the score and take out every bell that was a thematic element of the score.

But it worked out, because we had to rescore a lot of the stuff anyway because they recut the film at this point—they decided it wasn't graphic enough. We went back in, they paid for all the changes, and it was very economically feasible and it worked out. It was a great experience.

I haven't worked with Dan [Attias] since. He and I both went into the television world not long after that. I went into space [with *Star Trek*], and he went on to doing other stuff. I think we met a few times in LA but didn't really hang out. It's a different world out there. The film world in Los Angeles is different than what it was in New York. In New York you'd see people that you worked with; in LA you have to get into a car and drive two hours to hang out. It was not as much a social scene as it was in New York.

Can you talk a bit about your working relationship with Larry Cohen?

Larry Cohen, as you know, was the writer of *Maniac Cop* [1988] and *Maniac Cop 2* [1990]. Larry is a brilliant writer, a very funny and a very cynical guy. He's kind of old-fashioned in that a lot of the stuff he wrote was based on experiences he had. For example, he had an incident that put him in the hospital emergency room and, as a result of that, he came up with a film called *The Ambulance* [1990]. He did a lot of really cool movies. I don't know how this one [*The Ambulance*] holds up, though. I know it did very well in France, for some reason. I'm not sure why. The concept was about a guy that gets picked up on the street in New York by this ancient 1950s ambulance, and they take him to a place above a discotheque. It is a place where they take people's organs out of them and they sell them [*laughs*].

It is a very bizarre film, but pretty interestingly done. It was shot in New York, but Larry is a Beverly Hills guy. (It was produced by Moctesuma Esparza, who also did *The Milagro Beanfield War* [1988].) He had some credentials in that genre, and he had some good people in it and it was a fun movie.

I think *Maniac Cop* was really brilliant with how he came up with that character. I'm not sure what his creative process is. While writing *Maniac Cop*, I think he and Bill [Lustig] would get together and just devise some of the most interesting schemes to kill people. Like they would kill musicians. I didn't quite get that one. Like this poor trombone player gets his face planting into the cement. They are almost sight gags, they're almost comical. I don't think that genre quite exists the way it did then. I did two of the *Maniac Cop* films. I guess there have been three, but I didn't do the third one.

Also, I did another project for him [Cohen] called "Pick Me Up" [2006], for *Masters of Horror* [a Showtime anthology series of hourlong episodes written and directed by horror film notables]. It was also a brilliant piece of writing, in that a serial-killer hitchhiker gets picked up by a serial-killer truck driver, and they kind of coexist in strange places for a while.

Larry's vision [for music] is that everything should sound like Bernard Herrmann, but with a budget of, like, $5,000. It doesn't really work to try and be experimental in Larry's world, unless it is so unique. That's, like, why the whistler thing in *Maniac Cop* was very compelling, because you didn't need a huge orchestra. Although we had some semblance of an orchestra in that film, so you could sort of fake a Bernard Herrmann sound if you wanted to, the thing that carried it was not the big orchestra stuff. It was the more intimate whistling and electronic parts of the score.

Maniac Cop has an interesting cue that gets used a few times throughout the film. It almost sounds like a music box. Can you tell me a little bit about how that cue came about?

That music box idea came from something I had heard in an early Morricone score. It is sort of a timekeeping thing. . . . The way it worked is pretty slick, in that it established time as being very regular—but also very tonal. And then, against that very tonal time-clicking clock thing, I was able to overlay these really dissonant chordal things, which pointed out the horrific thing that was about to happen or did happen on the screen.

So it achieved two things at the same time. It had the elementary-sounding tonal music that kept time, and then it also allowed me to put just about anything over it that I could imagine that could cause it to be very atonal. The end result was, like, "What's that? I hear this music box, but then there are these cluster chords—what's that about?"

The music made for horror films seems to have a particularly passionate fan base. Do you have any thoughts as to why that might be? Do you think there is a difference in the relationship between music and horror, compared to other kinds of films?

I do. I think that horror music has many more individual identifying factors than, say, action genre music does. . . . People go see a horror movie and they are generally moved by the movie—and they are moved by the music because usually you [as a composer] are asked to make the audience move. You're not asked to be neutral. "We want the audience to jump out of their seats at this moment"—and it is up to you to help this happen.

So I think the audience remembers that. They remember the emotional effect that the music generated for them. I think, if they saw, let's say, another big action superhero film—and I don't mean this as a put-down—they may not remember such a unique experience, because a lot of those scores are such hybrid scores now.

Usually a horror score is truly unique. Unless it is a sequel—which is not supposed to be completely unique—it is going to be really special and really unique, because the film is generally pretty unique in its concept. With a big-budget summer movie, is there anything truly unique in that music that is going to make you remember it? Are you going to whistle it or hum it? You might remember the special effects and who the bad guy is, but is the music so identifiable? I don't think it is, and probably for a good reason.

I am sure that some of the other composers that you have spoken to have already vented to you about filmmakers temp-tracking their movies. . . . I think the reason that my earlier movies were relatively individual is because there weren't any temp tracks. Nobody said, "Okay, make it sound like this guy. Here's what I want here."

Sometimes the editor is responsible for placing music in the temp, and many of them have large libraries of stock film music. So they place that in a film, and pretty soon the director starts to fall in love with it. Then they hire a composer and they say, "Here, make it sound like this." And the temp track that they put in might be an amalgam of a bunch of different composers. So, what happens is you have a sort of generic-sounding temp score, which is then replicated by someone that is asked to reproduce it—without getting sued. Now you have a generic [temp] score that's been replicated to be even more generic.

Nowadays you can have an action score or a scary score or an emotional score, but are they unique to this film? No, they're not. Elmer Bernstein would not do a score that was temped. He would temp it with his own music, but he wouldn't even listen to one that was temped. He'd say, "That's insulting to me." It's like you doing your book and your editor saying, "Well make it read like this guy's book [*laughs*]." It's not going to work out for you artistically.

Are you surprised that the *Maniac* score keeps on being reissued? It has found its way onto several CDs and special edition vinyl LPs. I think one of the CDs is even shaped like the movie's star and screenwriter Joe Spinell's head. It's like the score that won't die.

Yeah, I am kind of surprised. I don't know why. I have, like, eighteen years of *Star Trek* music behind me, but I meet new people and they'll go online to check me out and they'll go, "Oh! You did the music to *Maniac*!" Yes, I did that, but I've also received Emmys and stuff for other things.

But apparently it has longevity. I'm astounded that there's been, like, nine reissues of it, and probably more to come. It's the same with *Maniac Cop*—now everybody wants to jump on that one. There's another film that Bill Lustig did, which I thought was one of my best scores, and it has never been released as a soundtrack. It is called *Relentless* [1989], starring Judd Nelson. It's a very contemporary, original score and, I don't know, I guess the film didn't do as well as some of the other ones. *Maniac* and *Maniac Cop 2* are still shown in theaters—they have these screenings! It's almost like *The Rocky Horror Picture Show*, or something.

Have you seen the 2012 remake of *Maniac*?

No, I haven't seen it. Is it good?

I think it is really interesting. I went into it as a skeptic, because I love the original so much, but it is sort of an entity unto itself. Which was a smart idea on the filmmakers' parts. But there are a lot of nods to the original. I really like its score a lot—that is why I asked you about it. It's a very different kind of score than yours. It is very synth-based, which is very much a throwback to the 1980s, but it has a totally different vibe than your score.

It was hard for me to imagine it without Joe Spinell. He was a great guy and great actor, and just a cool guy to hang out with. He was always there: He was at the film mix. We took the film to the Cannes Film Festival, and he showed up there for Directors' Fortnight. I went, and it was really neat to have a film there, which actually did quite well there and got quite a bit of critical acclaim. It was truly groundbreaking, and I am proud to be a part of it.

A lot of people want to hide some of their earlier works, but this one just won't die [*laughs*]! It's right out there, and it got me started in terms of something that I did on my own. That's what got me going.

Also, that's what I loved about the New York film scene: You meet a director or editor on one film and they move on, hopefully a little bit upward, and then they remember working with people. So maybe they'll hire you as a composer, or at least introduce you to somebody. So you keep working your way up the ladder and hopefully find someone that keeps making good-quality product. That's how it worked. You just sort of schmoozed your way up the ladder and met talented people who appreciated your work.

And in those days, it was everyone—from people that were working on Jacques Cousteau specials and *National Geographic* specials to horror films and action films. I guess they all ultimately migrated out west. I did too, but I resisted heavily. I kind of wish I had done it a little earlier, but my family really wanted to stay on the East Coast. They thought California was going to slide into the ocean from the next earthquake, which it almost did once when I was there. But I loved being out there and working. . . .

I moved there. I bought a house there, but I didn't have a job. It was really the biggest motivator ever. I was, like, "Okay, now I have to go out and get a job to pay for this house." So I did! I kept hustling and did more and more stuff, and it worked out for me. So there is some career guidance: Go buy something you can't afford, and then try and find a job to pay for it [*laughs*].

You also did quite a bit of work with Joseph Zito. You may have only scored action films for him, but he is certainly known for his work in the horror genre. What was his process like?

Did you interview Harry Manfredini?

Yes, I have spoken with Harry.

Well, it was interesting, because we shared the same music editor. His name was Jack Tiller, and he worked with Harry on *Friday the 13th: The Final Chapter* [1984], and he was a character that was in his own world . . . completely! Jack would describe how he would help Joe [Zito] select music. They were working on *Friday the 13th: The Final Chapter*, and Harry had scored it and they had all the music transferred to mag [stock]. Have you ever worked with mag?

Yes I have. It's basically magnetic tape/film that is the same size as the film stock.

Yes, exactly. So Joe says to the editor, "Well which one of these cues should we put here?" And Jack replies, "Well, you see, if this is a really long scene you take one of these big, fat reels and you put it there." [*Laughs*] "If it is a really short scene, you take one of these little, smaller reels and you put that against it and it probably should work." [*Laughs*] That was their ridiculous philosophy about how the mechanics of it worked.

But for me, working with Joe, he was completely hands-off until the end. I think on some of those films, I was able to see a rough cut—I actually got a video. At that point we were moving toward the twenty-first century, so we had videos happening, with timecode and everything.

We'd spot the film with Joe, and he would wax very poetically about what he felt his failings were in a scene. Like, "I didn't get this out of this actor. So can you help me here?" Generally, he worked, I think, maybe purposely, with actors that don't ever talk in their movies. We did three or four Chuck Norris movies and a Dolph Lundgren movie together and some other stuff. And these people don't talk. So there'd be a five-second shot of Chuck Norris thinking about something, and Joe said, "Well, you know what he's thinking about, don't you?" And I said, "I have no idea." And Joe would be like, "I don't either, but you should put some music in there, so that the audience knows he's thinking about something."

That was what was going on. Joe wanted people to see the film and listen to the music without hearing any dialogue and understand what the film was about. In other words, the music should tell the story. So it was very storytelling scoring. He loved that, because he was self-depre-cating, and he'd admit, "I failed in telling this part of the story. So you have to do it with music."

From a technical point of view, I found that one of the most fascinat-ing things I ever scored was the first *Missing in Action* film [1984], in that it wasn't the first *Missing in Action* really. It was actually meant to be the second one. They didn't like the first one as much, so they called the one I did *Missing in Action* and the other one became *2*, even though that one was supposed to be the first one. It made no sense at all.

With that film, I was still working in New York and he was in LA or the Philippines or someplace, shooting this film, and he didn't get the first and last reels finished in time for us to score the film. He told me that it was going to be twenty minutes of nonstop music. I asked what kind of music we should have in there, and he said, "Well, it is an action film, and there's going to be guys fighting, and there are going to be good guys and bad guys and it is going to be twenty minutes. So take your theme and work it around, and give me something that we can cut together at the last minute."

So I go out to LA ,and I have this music with me. I show up to the editing room, and there is crazy Jack Tiller again and he's got all the music transferred to mag [stock].

I conceived a rhythmic bed of the music, which was very arrhythmic: It wasn't in 4/4, it was in, like, 7/8, some odd meter that made it easy to trick your mind into not being regimented into one-two-three-four, etc. Then I recorded all these different overlays separately. This was done orchestrally. The strings were doing the rhythm with synthesizer under it. And then all the overlays were recorded, like the brass, percussion, and stuff like that. Just these big chords—some "good," some "bad," some "indifferent," etc.

Then we'd look at the film with that rhythmic thing running throughout it, and when there was a bad moment, we'd pick out one of the "bad" overlays and just stick it on there, completely irrelevant to the tonality to what was going on. Then, if a heroic thing occurred . . . we'd stick in one of the "good" overlays.

But we couldn't hear it, because we didn't have enough playback heads on the flatbed [editing machine]. So we just stuck this stuff in and they took it up to the dub room, where they had, like, twenty dubbers [mag playback machines] running, and sat there and listened to this twenty minutes of music that we blindly created from a bunch of little pieces. And it actually sounded amazing!

I could never have written that, like that. It was just that the film was rhythmic the way it was, and these stings worked. Joe just couldn't believe it. It *was* unbelievable, which was good in one sense, but then from then on he never really finished a film. That became his technique, he wanted to do them all like that. He would do his part—and get as much of it done to a point—then he wanted flexibility in terms of where to put stuff. It was always, like, you think you're finished, but then you have, like, ten more days of aggravation in the editing room, trying to figure out how to make this film work with the music.

But it was sort of fun. It was almost like a jigsaw puzzle approach. I used the same editor all the time, and he was brilliant about how he did it. We laughed a lot and had a lot of fun. And the films were okay, some of them did okay. The *Missing in Action* one was a big success. Anyway, that is how Joe works.

Do you ever go see the finished film with an audience?

Sometimes yes and sometimes no. I always go to a theater where I think it is going to play well. But what I have always been disappointed in is the quality of the sound that comes out in the theater. You're used to hearing it in a dubbing room [final mix room], where everything is perfect, and now you've got people with popcorn and mumbling. And the music is never loud enough for me [*laughs*].

One time I went to see a film, and I went to the projection room and said, "I don't think you're playing all the music here." But that was just how the print was struck—it was a mono print being played in stereo, or something like that. It's always been kind of frustrating. I sort of hate going. . . . It is a little demoralizing to not hear it the way you had intended. . . . No fault of the director or the mixes—sometimes it is just the process, or sometimes the sound effects just eat it up so much. And the ambience of the theater can be a big factor as well.

I hate reading the reviews, too. . . . If I hear one bad one I think I failed or something. I like to write and remember it as being successful and then move on.

Are there any bits of advice that you can give to anyone who is aspiring to go into film and television scoring?

There are a few events that happen every year that, if somebody is at least interested in exploring it, they should check out. In LA there is something called the ASCAP Music Expo every April. It is a three-day seminar on every conceivable type of music, but with a special segment on film music. If you were an aspiring film composer, you could go to this and actually meet people in the industry, you can have them critique your music. It is a whole industrywide meeting ground. It's absolutely amazing, and it is not all that expensive.

I don't mean to sound like an advertisement for ASCAP [*laughs*], but they've been very important to my career. They also offer two music-scoring workshops, I believe one through NYU in New York and one in Los Angeles. I believe you have to apply for those, but if you get accepted you get to work for six weeks, studying with major working composers. You get to record one of your own cues to an existing piece of film—have it recorded by a substantial orchestra and mixed—and it is something you can put on your demo reel. Those are two things that did not exist when I was trying to figure it all out. They are absolutely phenomenal events that somebody should check out.

Fabio Frizzi

"We could say that the composer acts as a musician who writes music, and the music that is inserted into the film becomes one of the protagonists of the film itself."

The phrase "Fulci Lives!" is a mantra for horror fans around the world. Italian gore-maestro Lucio Fulci (1927–1996) does live within all of his many films. He also lives in the hearts and souls of everyone who ever wanted to see a zombie wrestle a shark. And he lives in the music that composer Fabio Frizzi created for Fulci's cinematic masterpieces.

In my interview with Claudio Simonetti, he described Frizzi's music as "a bit of a mix of Morricone and Goblin," and I can't think of a more perfect description. Throughout his forty-five-plus-year cinema career, Fabio Frizzi has injected his unique hybrid of classical-synth-rock into the works of some of his generation's finest Italian horror-genre filmmakers, including Umberto Lenzi, Luigi Cozzi, Sergio Martino, and

Lamberto Bava. But he will forever be best known and most appreciated for the sonic textures he provided for Fulci—music that Frizzi embraces today with a touring live concert program he calls "Frizzi 2 Fulci."

A longtime fan of his work, I knew when I embarked on this literary journey that I wanted Frizzi to be a part of it; so little was known in the United States about his career and artistic process. There was so much I wanted to know, and I had no doubt that the rest of his English-speaking fans would want to know it too. I was determined to be the one who would spread the gospel of Frizzi to his non-Italian disciples. What I failed to realize was that the very reason a definitive English-language interview with the Maestro did not exist was also the reason I could not do one—the language barrier.

During the period when I interviewed composers for this book, Frizzi was in the midst of fulfilling live concert commitments as well as composing and recording new material—he was for all intents and purposes a very busy man. But in a great act of generosity, he offered to participate in my project anyway. We decided to perform the interview via email. I submitted a manageable number of questions, and in return he sent his answers to me in the form of an audio recording, in Italian. I then had his recording translated into English, which is what is presented here—a short but informative look into the work and process of one of Italy's most beloved horror film music composers.

(On a side note, Frizzi congratulated me for asking some questions that he has never been asked before, which is a compliment I accept proudly and with great honor.)

SELECTED FILMOGRAPHY

1975   *Four of the Apocalypse* (aka *I quattro dell'Apocalisse*; with
              Franco Bixio and Vince Tempera)

1977   *Godzilla* (Luigi Cozzi's Italian-dubbed, colorized,
              expanded-with-additional-footage version of the
              1956 film *Godzilla, King of the Monsters!*; with Franco
              Bixio and Vince Tempera as Magnetic System)

              The Psychic (aka *Sette note in nero*)

1979   *Zombie* (aka *Zombi 2,* aka *Zombie Flesh Eaters*)

1980   *Contraband* (aka *Luca il contrabbandiere*)

              City of the Living Dead (aka *The Gates of Hell*, aka *Paura
              nella città dei morti viventi*)

1981   *The Beyond* (aka *Seven Doors of Death*, aka . . . *E tu vivrai
              nel terrore! L'aldilà*)

1982   *Manhattan Baby*

              The Scorpion with Two Tails (aka *Assassinio al
              cimitero etrusco*)

1984   *Blastfighter* (aka *Blastfighter: The Executioner*; credited as
              "Andrew Barrymore")

              Devil Fish (aka *Shark: Rosso nell'oceano*, aka
              Monster Shark)

1990   *A Cat in the Brain* (aka *Un gatto nel cervello*)

2013   *House of Forbidden Secrets*

What were some of your early musical influences, and how did you become interested in creating music for films?

I come from a family of filmmakers. My father was a fairly important man in the film world in Italy—a distributor and producer. So clearly the passion for movies and for film scores was already in my DNA. Also, everyone in my family had a deep passion for music. My first influences were "traditional" ones, folk songs and things of the sort. As I grew up, I began to acquire more influences, such as Bach and the Beatles. Eventually I moved toward musical scores.

In your opinion, what is the job of the film music composer, and what is the job of the music within the film?

The role of the film score composer and the role of his or her music within the film are two very interconnected elements. The composer is first a musician, with all of his experience and sensibilities, but when he comes in contact with a soundtrack, with a film that needs music, his sensibility must be put to use for the final product. Therefore, when he begins to create the music, he also begins creating something that will later belong to the life of the film itself. We could say that the composer *acts* as a musician who writes music, and the music that is inserted into the film becomes one of the protagonists of the film itself.

How did you first meet Fulci, and what was it like working with him for the first time on *Four of the Apocalypse* [1975]?

The first time I met with Lucio Fulci was so that we could talk about the soundtrack of *Four of the Apocalypse*. At that time I was part of a group, Bixio-Frizzi-Tempera, and we had this meeting during a spotting session. We understood his personality right away: He was a very determined man, a man who knew what he wanted, with an absolute perfect knowledge of every aspect of the filmmaking process. *Four of the Apocalypse* gave me the chance to not only write film instrumental themes but also many songs [with lyrics]. The producers and Fulci himself asked us to write folk songs for the film in order to make it more appealing to international markets. I loved that kind of music, so I really enjoyed doing it.

You have said elsewhere that Fulci "was not an easy man to work with." Can you explain what you mean by this?

Yes, as a matter of fact, I have often said that Lucio Fulci was not an easy man to work with. But this statement didn't have and has never had a negative meaning. Essentially, I was highlighting—and continue to do so today—how the expertise of a person such as Fulci sets a certain standard for the entire crew. He was passionate about his work and was hands-on. If he was not happy with something or felt that something was missing, he would let you know.

Can you talk about how your collaborative relationship with him worked?

The way we worked was very traditional, but that was the way things were done in the Seventies, Eighties, and Nineties. Basically, I would read the script, discuss with him the musical themes and the characters. Then, in the editing room, we drew a sketch of the timings and I took notes that were later examined and refined, along with the durations of the individual compositions. Finally, of course, came the musical planning phase, which had to pass a few tests—simple ones, really—as at that time we didn't have the resources and electronic technology we have today.

Then came the draft approval, and we would often find ourselves together in the recording studio. Fulci's distinctive trait was that he had this instinctive perception about everything his movie needed, not only in regard to music, but also the sound design, like the voice-over work and the sound effects. So, in that sense, he was a great coordinator and a truly great director.

Can you talk in some detail about your actual creative process of composing, especially back when you were working on films like *Zombie* [1979], *City of the Living Dead* [1980], and *The Beyond* [1981]?

The process of creating music for Fulci's films was, more or less, always the same. In particular, for *Zombie*, I came on at the end of filming—so the discussion actually began during postproduction. That happened for *City of the Living Dead* as well. For *The Beyond*, I was actually on set during the filming quite a bit. So, for that film, I was in contact with the actors, with the people on the crew, the director of photography, Sergio Salvati (a dear friend of mine), etc.

Usually I would read the script before watching a cut of the film, but actually seeing the shot film, the footage, even if it is very rough, is always very different from reading the screenplay. The script is written one way and the film will always have its own flavor. Also, there's usually a bit of time between the reading of the script and the watching of footage, so feelings about the film and story can change.

Then, after I watch a rough cut of the movie, the first thing I would do is look for the inspiration. I would talk to Fulci about the story. My main instrument is the classical acoustic guitar, but like all composers, I play a little bit of everything. When I am writing a film score, I mainly use the piano. My idea has always been to jot down the instinctive ideas that arise from a character, a situation, or a specific scene and then go back to the studio and work those original ideas out, into more defined pieces of music.

These films were not big-budget pictures. Can you talk a little bit about working on a limited budget?

In Italy at that point, the time spent on a soundtrack was much shorter than for the bigger American films. For example, let's say the average amount of time, from the beginning of the job—from when you first started watching footage—to when the score was completely finished was really only a couple of months, sometimes a bit longer. Sometimes it was even shorter. With regard to budgets, the soundtracks of that era were absolutely smaller, much smaller than the big international productions. During that period we had small producers who loved cinema and great films were made, but the budgets were absolutely laughable. And at that time I didn't even have an agent managing contracts for me. So costs of actually recording and producing the score affected me financially and were distressing for me, which in turn affected the creative process.

Where did you find your inspiration for these horror scores?

The inspiration to write the music for these films could have come from a number of places. But above all else, the creations started within me. Maybe that is why these soundtracks are so loved, because they were personal, instinctual. A musician who definitely inspired me to find my path in that period was the English composer Mike Oldfield, and his album *Tubular Bells* [1973]. However, my musical culture had a strong classical foundation, and I had a lot of passion for the great pop artists of the Sixties and Seventies. Everybody knows that I'm a big Beatles fan, but they certainly weren't able to inspire the work I did in horror or fantasy.

Was Fulci a director who could easily communicate his musical ideas?

Lucio was someone who knew music. He used to play, mostly jazz, and had a lot of connections in the Italian pop music industry of the time. He had even shot musical films, fun ones, [a subgenre] that in slang we call *musicarelli*. But even with those, he had a very clear idea about what he wanted, in the sense that he knew how to give directions from a specific point of view. So he was certainly the kind of person with whom artistic interaction made sense. There are many people who don't know music that try to talk to you about their musical passions. Lucio was someone who knew a bit more, and so he was an excellent person to collaborate with.

How do you think that the Italian and American ways of scoring differed during the 1970s and 1980s?

The fundamental difference between Italian soundtracks and American soundtracks in the postwar years all the way up to when I started working was, in my opinion, that of a more directional thematic musical journey. Meaning that in the US there are extraordinary composers, many of whom are a great inspiration for us here in Italy, but the American musical element is more focused on a general accompaniment to the story—from the first frame to the last. During those years in Italy, however, there was a theme dedicated to the character, to plot twists, or to a subplot within the story. So the themes were more melodic and drew some inspiration from our musical history. The composers aimed to leave the viewer with a memory, even after they left the theater. For example, Nino Rota's pieces were extremely beautiful, but also extremely popular; the works of Ennio Morricone were as well.

How did the musicians you used in the studio affect the overall sound of the end product?

Musicians have always been important in my career as a composer. I've often said that a good composer is nothing without good musicians. Over the years, my composing style has obviously changed quite a bit. During Fulci's collaborations, I would go into the recording studio alone for the first couple of days, to create the blueprint for the job, beginning with the rhythmic parts, I focused on the first stage of creation of the musical base, and then I would later add the orchestras and soloists.

A few of the important musicians that I have collaborated with include [members of the band Goblin] Maurizio Guarini, Fabio Pignatelli, and Agostino Marangolo, who is a very good drummer . . . but over the years I've had so many great talents playing next to me.

In recent years I've decided to write much more, meaning that I go into the studio with scores that are practically complete—kind of how it's always been done in the US. I do this mostly because, doing it this way, production times are decreased. You don't have the same kind of group creativity that we had back in the old days, but when everything is pre-planned, already decided upon, you can go straight to the recording stage and start recording.

I've heard that you collaborated with the members of Goblin on a film called *Perché si uccidono* [1976, aka *Percy Is Killed*]. Is that true?

Actually, Fabio Pignatelli, Claudio Simonetti, and I wrote a soundtrack a few months—maybe even a few weeks—before Dario Argento asked their group [Goblin] to write the score for *Profondo rosso* [1975, aka *Deep Red*]. Our producer, Carlo Bixio, asked us to work together as an experiment, and we were thrilled to do it. The film title was *Giro girotondo . . . con il sesso è bello il mondo* [1975]. Our work for it was actually released on the record for the soundtrack for a film called *Perché si uccidono*, which was an entirely different film. So that is where the misunderstanding came from.

Did you like writing with them? Do you think that you have similar styles?

I enjoyed working with them, and I was with them when Goblin began writing the music for *Profondo rosso*. Because I have worked with some of the band's members for a very long time, there definitely is some similarity in our creative styles.

In recent years, music made for horror films has attracted a large and loyal fan base. The success of your live "Frizzi 2 Fulci" shows and the fact that so many of your scores have been recently rereleased on special edition vinyl is fantastic proof of this.

Yes, actually, during recent years there has been a great resurgence and a great opportunity to tell this story, to talk about my experiences working with Lucio Fulci. The idea for the "Frizzi 2 Fulci" show came about many years ago, because even before the Internet there was great evidence of affection and appreciation from fans all over the world. But the Internet really expanded the opportunity to launch this project, because the amount of supporters pushed me to bring the idea to fruition and finally bring it to the stage.

Is it particularly gratifying to see how beloved your music has become after all these years?

All of this is very gratifying. For every musician, recognition from the audience—their enjoyment and appreciation, a following, and the fact that they love the music—is one of the most important things.

Why do you think there is such a huge fan base for horror film music?

Maybe because among younger generations—not just young people and teenagers, but rather the people who are passionate about film—there's a large group that loves this genre and who want to recognize certain Italian directors for their excellence who weren't, perhaps, so appreciated at home. This is all so beautiful. Wherever I go in the world, I find people who come to me with great admiration and deep friendship, which is why in the upcoming seasons "Frizzi 2 Fulci"—which is only one of the shows I'm working on—will continue to be the center of my endeavors.

I also have many records and other projects in the works. The band and I have been working a lot. A double album has just come out from the Union Chapel's [London] concert in 2013, but we are working on other unreleased material as well, from both the past and today.

JEFF GRACE

"At the end of the day, the composer's job is to give the filmmakers
what they want. Even if they asked for a 'blue fence' and then
they decide that what they really need is a 'red fence'. . . . But,
to be effective, you still have to balance that with being passionate
about what you do and passionate about their projects."

A S A FREQUENT COLLABORATOR WITH the New York–based Glass Eye
Pix production company and such filmmakers as Larry Fessenden,
Jim Mickle, and Ti West, composer Jeff Grace provides a strong musical
voice to a new generation of independent horror.

He began his film music career as an assistant to the great film composer Howard Shore, aiding him on films directed by David Fincher,
Martin Scorsese, Peter Jackson, and David Cronenberg. As a composer
in his own right, Grace has scored some of the most well-regarded
horror films released in recent years and continuously broadens his
musical palette.

With experience as an orchestrator, music producer, music coordinator, and music editor on massive Hollywood productions, and as a
composer on modestly budgeted horror films and dramas, Grace has

had an intimate professional glimpse at both ends of the film-scoring spectrum. His eclectic résumé gives him a well-informed perspective on what it is like to navigate through the creative and collaborative aspects of today's film music industry. As an interviewee, I found him to be honest and open—willing to pass along what he's learned, through advice and anecdotes that may be particularly helpful for those considering film scoring as a career.

SELECTED FILMOGRAPHY

2005	*The Roost*
2006	*Joshua*
	The Last Winter
2007	*Trigger Man*
2008	*I Can See You*
	"Skin and Bones" (*Fear Itself* TV series)
	I Sell the Dead
2009	*The House of the Devil*
2010	*Bitter Feast*
	Meek's Cutoff
	Stake Land
2011	*The Innkeepers*
2012	*Hellbenders*
2013	*We Are What We Are*
	Cold Comes the Night
2014	*Cold in July*
2016	*In a Valley of Violence*

Tell me a bit about some of your early influences, passions, and memories regarding music?

I grew up playing all different kinds of music. I actually played a lot of jazz as a kid, and I studied classically and then I also played in bands. Then I went to college, and where I went to school there was a lot of interdisciplinary art stuff going on: We worked with dancers or theater people or whatever, doing music.

I like a lot of different types of music, and then I do this thing of creating music for other mediums. That's one of the things I love about film: Oftentimes you get asked to do different things. When I was a kid, it didn't even occur to me that it was some guy's job to go and write music for movies. I mean, I knew about John Williams, of course—I think everybody I grew up with had the *Star Wars* [1977] soundtrack [*laughs*]. But it just didn't occur to me. And then I studied composition and performance, and when I was graduating from college I had a friend who had a family friend that owned a music house [a music production company]. So I started working there. At that point, I was obviously aware that there are composers that write music for films and stuff [*laughs*]. It seemed like, "Oh, that's a possible job!"

I think, for me, one of the things about memorable music is the mood that it creates. I remember seeing *The Shining* [1980] and being really freaked about how powerful the film and the music were. When I saw *Psycho* [1960], I remember thinking, "It is just an old black-and-white movie—how scary could this possibly be?" Then I remember being really freaked out by it. I saw it during the day, and someone came up behind and went "Blahhh!" as a joke, and it scared the crap out of me. Those are some early memories about movies and music, but as a kid I liked *playing* music. It was like getting on a bike: Once the thing is up in the air and going, almost on its own, it is a pretty amazing thing.

Do you think your early love for jazz has influenced your film composing?

I don't think in any way that is identifiable as that. These days I am a terrible jazz musician [*laughs*]. It is one of those things where you have to keep up with it. But I think it has influenced me in a lot of ways. First of all, I think you really have to depend on your ears a lot in jazz, and you need an ability to generate material and come up with ideas very quickly. I think those things are also very important for a composer.

Also, I think, rhythmically, in terms of tonality and harmony, and things like that, it just provides me with more things to draw on to come up with variety or to come up with different ideas. When you start to take one element from one area and you transplant it into something else, just by the nature of doing that, it becomes something else. I think that applies to art in general. So it is a good way to come up with different ideas or try different sounds and things like that. It's a type of cross-pollination. It's taking an idea from "here" and doing it with other things.

I think all of those things have had a really big influence on how I approach things. But I also think it is that thing of when you are told there are rules, you're like, "Oh, okay. What are the rules? What is the edge of the rules? How can I break those rules and still have things work? Why is that a rule? Is there a benefit of having that as a rule?"

For music, there are a lot of benefits of having that kind of stuff. But when you start to look a little deeper, you try to understand, "Why is that the rule? Oh! It's the rule because if you do *this* it sounds bad, because it does *this*." Then maybe you can figure out that there are ways around the rules that come up with different sounds. And for jazz musicians, that is something that you're constantly pushing against. It is like bringing things outside of tonality or rhythmically pushing against where you are "supposed to be". . . . That is very important for creating tension in music, just as a general concept. So, again, jazz is just more ammunition to help me try and come up with ways of doing things creatively.

How did you come to work for Howard Shore, and what was your role?

It was just through a friend of a friend. They were looking for people, and a guy that was working for him [Shore] at the time just happened to come over to my house. He was a former classmate of my roommate. I was working on something in Pro Tools [a digital music recording, editing, and processing program] or in Finale [music notation software] or something like that, and he just happened to pop his head in. We talked for a while and he said, "I work for Howard Shore and we're actually looking for people. Maybe you'd like to come up and meet him." So eventually that turned into my working for Howard. The first thing I did was the copywork on a film called *The Score* [2001], and then I came on full-time for *Lord of the Rings* [*The Fellowship of the Ring*, 2001].

Then it was just like how working in music for film is, in general, nowadays. You wear a lot of different hats. Our job was really to do *whatever*, so that Howard could focus on writing and orchestrating. I find that the technology that my generation grew up with often doesn't come as easily to the people of his generation, simply because they didn't grow up with it. So I got a lot of jobs just by virtue of having some sort of technical knowledge and then also having a musical background.

A lot of it was music-editor kind of stuff: "Okay, here's the spotting session. Take the notes for the composer." But a lot of technology was shifting then. Audio was going from analog to digital, faster Internet was starting to become available. I tried to streamline things for him and handle things like picture change and all the notes from the director as well as programming, copywork, and any kind of technical thing that needed handling: "How can we utilize the current technology?" I also worked on a lot of the songs for *Lord of the Rings*, putting demos together, recording, editing, whatever.

How long did you work for him?

Three and a half years.

After that is when your film-scoring career started?

Yeah. In New York they have the Independent Feature Project, and I used to go to try and meet people all the time. They used to have these monthly things. I don't know if they have them anymore, but they used to have these monthly things that they called "Buzz Cuts," where they would show works in progress by young filmmakers, or maybe a short—things like that. They'd present a whole bunch of stuff on one night. I used to just go to those things and meet people, give them some of my music, etc. So I met a whole lot of people there, and one of the people that I met there was Peter Phok. Now he works with Larry Fessenden's company, Glass Eye Pix, but Peter went to school with Ti West. So he introduced me to Ti, and then Ti introduced me to Larry. And now, here it is ten years later and I'm working on my fifth or sixth film with those guys. After we did Ti's first film, *The Roost* [2005], they just kept calling me to do stuff.

It [Glass Eye Pix] was a really interesting group of people, because they're all very talented and they have a wide range of skill sets. So somebody might be a director on one film and then on the next film they're the sound designer. They are all really good at all those things. . . . You have these filmmakers who are really super-well-informed about the filmmaking process.

It was just a really interesting bunch of people and interesting projects, and I think that Larry, as a sort of figurehead for all that, is great. In a creative way, he is very supportive, and he's kind of hands-off in a lot of ways, which is great creatively. He will definitely let you know how he feels about something [*laughs*], but at the end of the day he's also a director—and a very good director. So he appreciates not having people monkey with your vision and things like that. He has mentored and helped to shape a lot of people there, and not just in horror.

A lot of people in New York know him and respect him and ask his opinion on things. He's very well respected by the people that know him—and he knows everybody too, which is great in terms of meeting people and getting projects off the ground and stuff like that. With Ti, Larry did *The Roost* and *Trigger Man* [2007]. Then he got *House of the Devil* [2009] going, as well as *The Innkeepers* [2011]. So there's a lot of stuff—and that's just one person!

Then there is Jim Mickle, with *Stake Land* [2010]. Jim has his own producing team. He already had a producing team, but if he hadn't had that, I am sure he would've just kept right on going with Larry. Those guys get along great. Larry is also a good friend of J.T. Petty [*The Burrowers* (2008) and *Hellbenders* (2009)], who is another great filmmaker. And Glenn McQuaid, who did *I Sell the Dead* [2008] . . .

Before we get into specific films and projects, let's talk a bit about your process. I'm sure it differs from film to film, but at what point during the making of a film do you typically come aboard?

Oh, yeah, that can range unbelievably. [*Laughs*] I actually started before a script was even finished once, and then there have been instances where I had five weeks to do a score and I didn't really know much about the project beforehand.

With independent film, what usually happens is, there is a finite amount of money and they kind of know their schedule, because they're usually heading for a festival or something like that. If you work backwards from there, you can figure out how to do things—and *then* they just can't keep editing and keep editing and keep editing. It's more difficult for them, but the flip side of that is, those films have fewer cooks in the kitchen, so you get more of a singular vision, which is easier to deal with.

Locking picture actually exists in the independent film world. A lot of times, in my experience, people will want me on for locked picture. If it is somebody I have worked with before—and I do work with the same directors a lot—I will oftentimes get a script, and then they might even need music on set for something, or they might just say, "Hey, maybe you can start working on some themes." For the film I am doing now, I actually wrote a huge amount of music before they finished shooting, because the director didn't want to cut temp with existing stuff. That's great, because now he is fairly far along with his edit, but all the themes are done and I am already scoring scenes. With a lot of the scenes, the music dropped in just fine. So we are very far along in the process already.

Who is the director?

That's for Ti [West], but again this is somebody that I have worked very closely with for years. That's much easier. If it is somebody that I haven't worked with before, that is much more difficult. I have tried it, but unless they are really good communicators and unless you know their process, trying to figure out what they're talking about can be just like two ships passing in the night. Or with less-experienced filmmakers, they've got enough on their plate during production and early editing that the music becomes too much to deal with if it is started too early.

With Mickle, the last two films that we did were *We Are What We Are* [2013] and *Cold in July* [2014]. With *We Are What We Are* he needed music on set. So he had three or four themes from me when he shot the movie, and then they all ended up in the movie.

Do you know what he used them for on set?

There was supposed to be this song that the mother sang to the kids, and then the son wants the sisters to sing it to him after the mother passes away. It is in the movie very, very briefly now, but it was a bigger deal in the initial script. There was a piece of music for that. . . . There was going to be this whole thing built around that. It was going to be this recurring thing, but like so many things in filmmaking, it didn't end up that way. It is in there in a very small way, but that kind of influenced another theme that I wrote, which ended up being in the movie a lot. So it ended up getting all rearranged, but it is that thing of getting the ball rolling.

Cold in July is not a horror film, but his [Mickle's] background in horror seriously influences his filmmaking in whatever he does, and certainly that is the case with *Cold in July*. He initially talked about having more of a Dustbowl vibe for the score, and we talked about having a piano theme. So I wrote some stuff along those lines. And then he started thinking, "Well, maybe it would be cool to do some synth stuff," because it is set in the Eighties, and then *that* conversation started.

So I took the piano theme and I put in a synth [*laughs*], and then it just went in that direction. In the movie he uses both. Then I ended up putting a pulsating synth underneath some of the other stuff that was more guitar-based.

It is funny, because people just instantly think of John Carpenter for that score, but actually those themes were done before we added the synth stuff. But it is kind of hard not to think of Carpenter, especially when there are certain things that are going on in the filmmaking that also bring him to mind.

Some of the composers I have been talking to seem to actively try to avoid reading the script. Do you like to read the script first, or see a cut of the film first?

It depends on when I am going to get involved. If some sort of cut already exists, even if it is a little rough, then reading the script is kind of useless. That just shows you intent, but what they actually got [when shooting the film] might be something quite different.

So I will read it if nothing else exists. But, like I said, if there is a cut, I don't need to . . . unless there is some reason to. They might have a cut, but in their mind it might clearly not be there yet and it needs to be a lot tighter to have the right mood. Then you read the script and you're, like, "Oh, yeah. Okay. I've seen this guy's other movies, and in the script it is like this, so it will probably be like that in the movie." That can be helpful. But if they already have a cut of the film and it is in decent shape, I think the script is a distraction.

When you are ready to sit down and begin working on the music, can you walk me through the process? For instance, do you typically write at any specific instruments? Do you record what you're doing, or do you notate it?

I think it really depends on what the score is and what the sound palette is. If it is more of an orchestral score, I will try and figure out specifically what kind of instrumentation I will want or want to highlight. I will just try and keep in the back of my mind, "Oh, maybe I will want to use this kind of sound for this." Then I will try and sketch things.

I do end up just staring at the screen [*laughs*] and watching the movie over and over and over again. And a lot of times, even though I am working on one particular scene, I may watch five or six different scenes, because the music needs to be connected between those or there is some element of the story that is connected.

I think that one of the really big things that a good score can do is unify a film. In order to do that, you have to be aware of what is going on in other scenes, etc. Of course [*laughs*], you can't do that if those things don't exist yet. But, if they do, I tend to bounce around a bit, even though I know that, "Okay, I am supposed to be working on this right now, that's really the focus. But maybe I will get some ideas from this too." So I will watch the scene, but the more that I do this, I really try to just hear something. The first thing and the easiest thing to do is figure out some kind of tempo and go about it that way, and then try and hear some kind of melodic line and find a way in that way.

In terms of what instrument I use, I try to mix things up, because if I just do one approach, it is easy to get stuck in things. My first instrument is piano, so I will definitely spend some time with a piano. But if it is a guitar thing, if you want to do something idiomatically for an instrument, it is good to not be saddled by just the piano. Or if you're writing something orchestral on just a piano or a guitar, you are limiting yourself. So I try to get away from that as well.

When I am sketching things and I am getting the basic musical ideas, I find that writing on paper is way, way faster. For me, I can work things out much quicker if I do that. And then you need to see how it is going to hit picture pretty quickly too. So once I have got an idea taking shape, I will then hop in front of the film and hit RECORD and just play through it up against picture and see what happens.

Then, from there I see what ideas come for fine-tuning it. It is a back-and-forth process of trying stream-of-consciousness to get to some idea and then work it out a little bit, and then step back and look at it and see what my intuitive reaction to that is, and then say, "What needs to happen next? What is working? What is not working?" There is the process of coming up with the germinal material, and then sort of a different process of scoring that material to a scene.

I met Johan Söderqvist [composer of the music for *Let the Right One In* (2008) and many other scores] at a film festival in Switzerland, and [*laughs*] I think he said this [when] somebody asked him what his job was: "My passion, which I do at night, is writing music for films, but my day job is just dragging notes around in music software." Which is so bang-on! You spend two hours writing this music and then spend eight hours [*laughs*] trying to program it!

So I try to get it as clear as I can. It is like orchestrating: Compositionally, you want to know what you're doing first and get that in good shape, and then you go and start to orchestrate it. If you go and try to reverse-engineer that, it is just, like, a quagmire. The technology is great; it can be fantastic for a lot of things, but it can really hamper you if you let it. If you're not careful, it can quickly turn into quicksand.

I have been finding it very interesting just how differently each composer's mind works. Synth guys like John Carpenter and Claudio Simonetti explain that their process is very rooted in improvisation, while guys that have more experience working with orchestras, like Charles Bernstein, Harry Manfredini, and Jay Chattaway, describe that it is more like they can hear the music while they watch the cut and then it is just a matter of getting it down on paper or "tape."

I think it depends. . . . One of the interesting things about working with film is you're asked to do so many things. But if you're asked to do an ambient score, in a lot of ways the parameters are defined by the technology.

For instance, I can't get to a "sound" in ambient stuff with just hearing it in my head and then just get to it the way that I can if I hear a note or a line. If I am writing a theme, I sit there and I just try to hear things or try to let them come, and eventually something takes shape. Then I go to the piano and work stuff out. I think that with any trained musician, that is part of the training. But that process, whether you're hunting and pecking it at the piano or whether you're doing it in your head, I think that is just a matter of experience—the more you do it, the better you get at it.

[John] Corigliano [composer of the music for *Altered States* (1980)] has a great quote in some interview that he did. He was sitting with a composer friend of his, and they were geeking out and looking at each other's scores and saying things like, "Oh, I was wondering why you did this here." And his friend was, like, "How did you come up with that, it is just so John Corigliano?" And his response was, "What do you mean 'Corigliano'? There's no John Corigliano. I am a chameleon! That's my problem—I have no musical personality."

And his friend said, "What? No, that is completely wrong." And he pointed to five or so things in a minute—decisions that only Corigliano would make. The conversation then became about how style is the choices that you make, and I've never heard it put better. I think that most people's experience with that is that those choices that you make come from whatever your musical experience is and essentially how much you've worked at something and how much music you've taken in, and also your likes and dislikes.

I always try to learn more. Hopefully, most musicians will try to keep learning more and more and more about music. And even as I do that, there are still things, from since I was young, that I just consider a certain way. Not that it makes me blind to certain things, but there are just things that intuitively you just head towards. I think that those are things that influence those decisions that Corigliano and his friend were talking about. Then there are also things that are very conscious. And the interesting thing is the combination of those two.

I won't say it is harder, but I will say that the ambient stuff that is less note-dependent is more time-consuming and less predictable if you want to do something interesting. You have to monkey around and sort of get under the hood with synth things and whatever technology you are using to come up with a sound.

If you're doing an ambient score or an orchestral score—on the face of it, they could be, like, miles apart—there are things that are common to make an effective score. You don't need the "Indiana Jones Theme" to have an effective score, but you do need to have recurrent material that an audience can latch on to. It can be a great theme or it could be like that [György] Ligeti piece [*Musica ricercata II: Mesto, rigido e cerimoniale*] in *Eyes Wide Shut* [1999]. It's only, like, two notes, but it is the way that it is used that makes it very, very effective.

In that piece, you have the use of space and the way that it is recorded. All of those things become part of that. In the same way, if you're writing an orchestra piece, it can be very tonal. It can have a theme, like the "Indiana Jones Theme," or it can be like Ligeti or [Krzysztof] Penderecki or something that is a lot less immediately identifiable. But when you start associating that with images and parts of a narrative, then it functions pretty much the same way.

Getting back to the electronic and the ambient thing, unless you have an ability to go and just know how to mess around with the technology, it can be tough. Some guys are just good with synth programming. I'm not afraid to get under the hood and do that stuff, but I am not as fast with that as I am with just writing a theme. So it can take some time. But, to me, getting a sound palette is a big part of the equation. When I start working on a project, it is just wrong until it is right. You just start chipping away at it and throwing things against the wall until something works.

With some projects, it is just very, very clear what it needs to be and you're off and running. With other projects you're just banging your head against the wall for two weeks, and then all of a sudden you write a cue and the cue doesn't work, but thirty seconds of it works [*laughs*]. Or you write a cue and the director says, "It totally doesn't work there, but it works great over here." And you weren't even thinking about that, but he's right. When things like that happen, it is great, because then you can understand where the director is coming from in a different way.

Let's talk about directors. When you meet with a director to get started on a film, do you have a checklist of certain recurring questions or specific things you'd like to discuss before you go off on your own?

It falls into two camps for me; it is like "check the box." Is it a director I have worked with before? Yes. Okay, go over here. Is it a director I have worked with before? No. Okay [*laughs*], then here is a list of questions.

Okay. So let's say it is someone you haven't worked with before.

If it is someone I haven't worked with before, I am listening to what the person is saying with a different type of attention. Some people know exactly what they want and they know how to communicate that very well. Maybe not necessarily in musical terms, but in clear terms. That's what is important. I don't care that people talk to me about things in very specific music terms, unless it has a very specific point. For instance, if a director actually knows about music and he says, "Yeah, the harmony right there, that chord. That doesn't work."

But what is most important is being able to talk about it in terms of the narrative and the characters, both dramatically and emotionally. I just keep in mind, "How does this affect this particular scene?" and, "How does it fall into the overall story in terms of both the film itself and the score?" You can score a scene and it will work fine in isolation, but when you put it into a larger context it doesn't work—it creates other problems.

Working with a new director falls into two camps as well. How experienced is this director? Is it a first-time director, or is it a director that has made a bunch of films before and worked with a composer before and knows a process? So I look at, "What is the person actually saying about their film?" and, "What are their musical ideas?" And then I am also thinking about, "How does this person communicate?"

That is one thing that I learned when I worked for Howard [Shore]. You watch the way Peter Jackson and Fran Walsh communicate and then watch the way that David Fincher communicates, and you watch the way that David Cronenberg communicates and then Martin Scorsese. They are all different, and their approach to film is different and their approach to music is different. Some directors may know an amazing amount, basically every part of the filmmaking process, but when it comes to music they are a total fish out of water and they don't like it.

So you have to be careful about that, because some people really don't like giving up control, but with the music they're faced with a task that they can't do themselves. So clearly they have to rely on someone else. The best people are people who hired you because they want you there and [*laughs*] not because they couldn't get the person they really wanted. Hopefully, you're there because they liked some other thing you did or maybe you've worked with them before, etc.

I find that with the best people it is like you throw something to them, and instead of just stopping it and throwing it back in your face, they just kind of guide it. Jim Mickle is amazingly fast with this. He will just say the smallest thing, but it is so insightful and it gets to the heart of what the scene needs, what he needs, and what is working and what is not working for a piece of music that I wrote for him. It is just, like, *bang!* Very rarely do we have a situation where I write something and it gets completely scrapped; off the top of my head, I can't even think of one. He is just really good at it. First of all, he brings people to the table that he wants there, and he just has this insightful way of very quickly communicating that stuff.

With Ti [West]: Whenever we do a film, he is always pushing for the next film to be different than the last one, and the music has to be different too. Everything has to be different. We're trying to do something different and find a different approach all the time. So, in the beginning we end up with stuff that doesn't work, or, like I said earlier, "It doesn't work in that scene, but it works great in this other scene, though [*laughs*]!" I have found that we do much better with each film we do together. We have a bit of history, and it is, like, "Remember when we did that thing in this scene in this movie? Maybe do that with this instrument or do that with this kind of thing."

When you worked with Ti West for the first time, on *The Roost*, which was also his first feature film and your first feature-length score, what was that discussion like? Did he play you music that he likes? Did he use a temp score to illustrate his ideas?

I am not a huge fan of temp music, but I see its point and I always like to have it, but generally only start with it. I will watch a screening of the movie, and then after that I will shut the temp track off. If I need it, like somebody makes a reference to it, I might listen to something, but I try to get away from it as quickly as possible.

I am a fan of generally talking about music, especially if it is somebody that is not a musician, because it is just a way to get the conversation going. "This piece is cool," or, "This ten seconds of this piece is cool." "I like the instrumentation of this." "The feel or the mood of this is great." Just those kinds of things are helpful.

So I encourage directors, if they have any thoughts on music, to talk about things and maybe we can listen to some stuff, in the beginning. I do like to move past that, but I think that is a better place to start than showing me this other score from some other movie playing under a scene from their movie and then they say, "Make it sound like that." I don't think that is fun in anyone's book.

One of the great advantages of having your own score is that it is catered to your film. You can do amazing things. Look at John Williams, the way he hits picture. It is crazy, it's insane, it is amazing—it is so well sculpted to the picture. Music also brings unity to the movie. Obviously, the easiest example is a montage. [*Laughs*] A montage without the music is just a bunch of random shots, but when you put music to it, it can be this amazing piece of cinema. So, to a certain extent, I definitely don't shy away from listening to music, because it can get a dialogue started.

Do you remember what those discussions were like for *The Roost*, and how you arrived at the idea of using a string quartet?

Yes. That was very simple. They said that they had a tiny, tiny budget and that they could give me X amount of money [*laughs*], which was a very small amount of money. So I was thinking to myself that maybe that was enough money to hire a string quartet [*laughs*] for, like, a day and half. Ti did say that there should be some synth-electronic kind of stuff, à la *The Evil Dead* [1981], for just mood and the sinister nature of this thing. But he also said he would need something to deal with the more action-oriented stuff, where the characters are running around and everything is frenetic.

So I looked at the budget and I thought about what he said, and I was, like, "The synth stuff, no problem; I have synths." For the action stuff, I said, "Bang for the buck, the best we're going to do—and I think it could be really interesting—is a string quartet. But it is not going to be a Beethoven string quartet."

Then I played him some modern classical music, some concert music. I played him some Ligeti, some Penderecki, and stuff like that, and he said, "Yeah, that's great!" The stuff I couldn't really explain to him so well was what I wanted to do for the more action-oriented stuff. I was thinking to myself, "It's a string quartet. That is not a very big sound. So I need to get as much sound out of the quartet as possible." Then I just started thinking about ways to do that.

I used a lot of tremolo, a lot of multi-stops. I was really, like, "What can I do to get as much sound out of these instruments as possible?" That became the jumping-off point: "What can I reach on this instrument [*laughs*]?" And it's, like, "Okay, yeah, I can do this kind of harmony, and that will work." There's this scene at the end where the brother grabs the sister, and he's running and he takes her into the car, and it is all multi-stops and rhythmic. That whole thing came out of, "Okay, I need to keep building and I need to get more sound out of the quartet! How do I do that?"

So I just wracked my brain to figure out a way to do that. Getting back to talking about the way that jazz has influenced things for me, rhythmically there in that scene, what is going on—the way the beat kind of flips around with some of those hemiolas [a musical term that denotes any of a number of ways to alternate and/or superimpose three pulses with two pulses, such as when six eighth notes alternate between being heard as three groups of two (implying 3/4 meter) and two groups of three (implying 6/8 meter)] and stuff—I'm sure that completely comes from having a background in jazz, but it doesn't sound like jazz. That was the process there, and in independent film that is very often the process.

Let's talk about Ti West's _The House of the Devil_. It is an interesting film in terms of rhythm and pacing, with its slow and steady buildup to its crazy third act. When it comes to scoring, especially a film like this one, there can be a very fine line between having the music support the film and having it get in the way, and I think your score is very successful with staying on the correct side of that line.

Well, thank you. Yeah, it's funny, Ti and Graham Reznick grew up together, and Graham is actually a great filmmaker in his own right, but he is one of those Glass Eye guys that I talked about earlier: One day he's wearing one hat and the next day he's wearing another hat. But he's a great sound designer, an awesome, awesome sound designer, and he's also a really trusted confidant of Ti's.

He's also a totally competent composer and musician. With his movie _I Can See You_ [2008], he did half the score and I did half the score. He writes great synth music, fantastic. So he has a certain understanding of music. But they're both so tuned in to what is going on in terms of sound and music in a film that when they watch films, it is a really big thing for them. And in making a film it is a huge thing for them. Ti always says, even when we did _The Roost_, "I'm really hesitant to show this movie to you, because there's no sound, and to me sound and music is, like, ninety percent of a movie. But you can't do your job without seeing the movie, so . . . [*laughs*]"

The House of the Devil was our third movie together. He does not usually temp his films, but on that one I think we had to submit it for something, so there was a cut that had some temp music. And then maybe, like, two of those pieces of music were eventually played for me at some point and then quickly turned off.

So he doesn't really temp, but we did talk about the 1980s thing, and said, "In concept, it is this and I am going to try and get these songs, etc. The film is about a girl babysitting at a strange house by herself. And the film is called *The House of the Devil*, so we know something is going to happen. It is just that we're completely messing with the audience about *when* it is going to happen."

We were working on *The Roost*, and he commented, "Oh, you're exposing that too early in the music—hold off on that." And I said, "Oh, you mean I am tipping the hand." And he said, "Yeah, yeah, *tipping the hand*." So from then on [*laughs*] that always became the joke: At what point are you *tipping your hand* too soon? So with that, we just wanted to go right on the line with *The House of the Devil*.

On *The Roost* we did synths and the crazy, over-the-top string quartet with some percussion. Then, on *Trigger Man*, it was all this cello stuff run through a delay. Most of the cello stuff was strummed or plucked. So that's what we did on other scores, and he said, "Let's try some piano stuff."

I know he loves that movie *The Changeling* [1980], and so he mentioned something about that. And then he said, "We need to figure out a way to hold these really pregnant pauses." So I thought, because he never wants to do what we did before, it would be really cool to do something with prepared piano [a piano that has objects, i.e., preparations, placed on and/or between its strings to alter its sound]. As I started to work with that, I doubled the prepared piano with a regular piano, and it made this weird sound. Also, I think I had written another theme that wasn't quite right. It was just a little too down-the-pike, and in his response to that I went back and started rethinking stuff.

I remember that with the prepared piano, certain notes would get different harmonics. So certain harmonies would work in certain keys and not in others. I started noodling around with that, and there was something about the arpeggios in that that made me think, "Well, that note really shouldn't go there, but what if I go there [*laughs*]?" I just kept doing that, and I did the left-hand thing, and then I wrote the melody on top of that. So I came up with the harmonies and then I came up with the melodies, and that was a reaction to how the overtones played off the prepared piano. He heard that and loved it.

That became one whole thing for the isolation that her character was experiencing. Then there was the string stuff that is much better at sustaining; you can hold one note as long as you want. Also, with a larger ensemble you can get a larger variety of sounds. And we had more of a budget—it wasn't a huge budget, but there was some budget. Then it became only strings and piano until she gets down in the basement. Then you get more stuff. Then it was just, like, "Go crazy!"

But it was constantly that discussion of staying one step ahead of the audience. Ti is very cognizant of how knowledgeable audiences are about film and how much they expect and want to be ahead of the film. So his thing was, "I am not going to let them be ahead of the film [*laughs*]—I am going to make them wait." It was about drawing out things. How can we mislead them? But it definitely took a few weeks of trying things out to get there.

The Innkeepers has a much different tone. Even though it is a Ti West horror film, it starts out much more lighthearted and almost comical, compared to the other films you did with West. Did you find that to be a challenge, or was that change of pace refreshing?

That was definitely a challenge. Usually when you have a horror/comedy film, you play up the horror to make it funny. But in this case, the film is something that starts out kind of comedic and then heads south—which is different. In the beginning it was that question of, "How comedic do we make it?" [*Laughs*] I remember Ti was just, like, "Nope, you can go more, you can make it goofier. She's pretty goofy."

I remember I played him, like, the third version of something and he was, like, "Oof. Wow—that's pretty bold." And then we watched it, and he said, "But it works. That's what it needs to be." At that point it was our fourth movie together, so I trusted him completely. But, yeah [*laughs*], that was definitely a topic of discussion.

The beginning has the opening titles, which is not comical, but then we have all the stuff where we're meeting the Claire character, when she goes next door and sees Lena Dunham's character and all that stuff. And there's the exposition of her and Luke, just getting their characters across and stuff. Yeah, we had to right-turn it [*laughs*]. In a way, it reminded me of [Glenn McQuaid's] *I Sell the Dead*. I don't mean that literally, in terms of the film, but in a problem-solving way. *I Sell the Dead* has these little episodes. They each tell a story, and then there's a narrative that goes over all of that.

It is really hard to revisit material when it is all changing, so I always look for ways that I can plant seeds and have things organically come out of something else or relate to something else. At times you're asked to go and remind the audience of something that happened earlier in the film. Maybe you're making a reference to something that will happen later in the film, and you need to do it in just a couple of seconds. So you need these little nuggets that you can do that with. Through the music you can transplant the audience very quickly, without taking them out of where they actually are in the film.

Fortunately, with *The Innkeepers* the scenes themselves planted enough of those seeds that, to me, it didn't feel too broken apart. In the opening titles there's a more ambient part that goes into the thundering version of the theme. That material that plays at the beginning comes back when she's at the desk, and then it has this little piano motif that comes back later. Just those little things, to me, go a long ways with pulling things together. But it was a challenge—it certainly was a challenge.

Your work has not been exclusively in the horror genre, but it is what you're best known for. Do you like working in the genre? It seems like a place where you might have more freedom to experiment.

Yes, but I can see instances where that is totally not the case these days.

I think, ultimately, for me, it is all about the filmmaker and the material. I think that I have been really fortunate in that I've worked on a lot of interesting projects. They are interesting to me, like the stuff that I have done for Larry Fessenden's company, for example. I think he likes films where you're invested in the character. If you make a horror film about somebody that you don't care about, when bad stuff starts to happen, at least for me, I am not as invested.

There's a segment of the moviegoing public for whom that is entertaining, and that's fine, but I think he and the guys that he supports look at things like they're filmmakers and they just happen to frequently work in horror. Things are much more horrific if you're actually invested in the characters, and one of the ways to do that is to take a more or less normal situation and then introduce one element of the supernatural or the horrific into that situation. In *The Last Winter* [2006] it is these people that are drilling for oil and then they start to see something. That's another thing that Larry likes a lot—the whole reliable/unreliable-narrator thing. Are they actually seeing what it is that they are seeing?

In terms of being creative musically, that film is a perfect example, because you use instruments in a way that is perhaps unconventional, and that is something that you probably wouldn't be able to do in another type of film.

Oh yeah, absolutely. Like in *The Roost*, who else would have a crazy, strident string quartet with that kind of tonal language [*laughs*]? And that was my first feature film. *The Last Winter* was the third movie I did, and, again, its musical language is kind of demanding of the audience. But I think that is what the film required. But it is great!

Like I said, I like working in film because you get to do all of these different kinds of things, and I like a lot of different kinds of music. There's a lot of modern concert music that I really, really love, and it is great to be able to match some of those sounds with imagery.

Have you experienced some of these films with an audience and seen their reactions?

I go to see most of the films. It is always interesting to hear the mix. It is like when somebody has a script: They say you write your film, you shoot your film, and then you edit your film. With scores, I think it is the same kind of thing: You have a conception of your score, you go and make that score and you record it and then go to the dub with it, and they mix it into the movie, and then it's not quite as prominent as you might've hoped [*laughs*], and then you go and see it in a theater.

Some theaters sound great and some theaters sound terrible. Some mixes translate well, some don't. And at the end of that, you see the reaction of the audience. Sometimes you realize, "Oh, you know what, we didn't leave enough space there for that line to register with the audience." Or, "That 'thing' is cutting it a little too close—it gives away what is going to happen. We started the music a little too soon there." You know, all those kinds of things. It is a good opportunity to gauge that stuff.

And when seeing things projected, you sometimes see things that you don't when you're watching it on a smaller screen. Now having a bigger screen [to view the picture while working on it] is easier than, say, five or ten years ago, but it is still not the same. I do really enjoy just sitting back and watching the movie that [*laughs*] I spent a lot of really long days working on.

When I was in film school, we were still working on actual film. So you'd shoot and then you had to get the film processed and then you had to edit it, etc. It was a very long process. Most of my friends were in the music department, and I used to tell them how jealous I was of them because they could play live and get instant feedback, instant gratification from an audience. But as a film music composer, you're saddled with the same hindrance as the director: You may have the filmmaker's feedback throughout the process, but you still have to wait, sometimes several months, to get the audience's response.

Oh yeah, and you don't always remember every single thing—and then there are some things, you wish you could forget [*laughs*]. Sometimes it is, like, "Oh, I wish I could go back and change that." Fortunately, that doesn't happen too often. We try to put a lot of effort into stuff. And the vast majority of the filmmakers I have worked with have been great. We tend to see eye to eye.

At the end of the day, the composer's job is to give the filmmakers what they want. Even if they asked for a "blue fence" and then they decide that what they really need is a "red fence," it is your job to give them a red fence. But, to be effective, you still have to balance that with being passionate about what you do and passionate about their projects. So, yeah, it is kind of a funny balancing act...

I am probably doing my twentieth or so film right now. Definitely, the more you do that process, there are things that you can see. And having worked for Howard [Shore] . . . (I also worked for Angelo Badalamenti, and there are other composers I have worked with as well), you see how differently people do things. Different people work different ways, and you can say, "Oh, *that* thing works well for me, but *that* thing doesn't. I can't work that way." Then, as you do more films, you might also see an issue arise that you never really thought about before . . . and, like you said, sometimes, especially with bigger pictures, you're not seeing that thing until six months or a year later. With smaller films, though, like for film festivals, it tends to only be a few months. At Sundance [Film Festival] sometimes you finish the mix, like [*laughs*], a week before the movie premieres.

You've been doing this for ten years. Are there things that you do that you now recognize are influenced by the other composers you've worked for? For instance, are there any specific things that you do that you can tell were influenced by Howard Shore?

I think he and I are actually pretty different in the way that we approach things. I think every person has to find his or her own way. But what was really helpful [for me when working for Shore] was just seeing how somebody gets a large amount of stuff done, especially *The Lord of the Rings* stuff. That's a lot of music. It is a big job, and to have a sustained effort for a really long period of time and then to see how that gets broken down on a monthly, weekly, daily basis, that was really helpful.

Again, creative people work different ways. I love Stephen King's book *Stephen King on Writing*. Half the book is just him talking about his daily process. It's great. And a lot of it translates to any kind of linear art form. In there, he talks about being what I think he calls a "basement person," where he pulls the blinds and he blocks out the world and he just gets in his zone that way. Now, Howard is more the opposite: His house is in the woods, and he likes to look out the window and that kind of stuff.

Which is also a type of isolation.

Right. But if we both want to go to London, well, you can go east or you can go west. Eventually you're going to get there [*laughs*]. One way might be preferable to one person or, depending on where you're coming from, it might be better to go the other way. . . . I find, for myself, sometimes I am more of a basement person, and sometimes I am more of an expansive person. What is difficult about working in film is, you don't really have the luxury of getting stuck. So you have to figure out ways to get around being stuck.

Getting back to what you were saying about process, I'm saying sometimes I'm sitting at the piano. Sometimes I go for a walk or a run. I find that sometimes physical movement is good, but sometimes it's helpful to just sit somewhere and let myself more or less space out and see what comes to me. It's giving yourself the space to allow something to take shape. I find, for me, it is good to be able to switch it up, because if I am trying to get stuff in one way and I'm not really getting anywhere, then I can change it.

Did you grow up being into horror films, or is it just something you fell into?

I got into the horror thing, essentially, by being asked to do it. I met Ti [West] and then I met Larry [Fessenden], and then Larry started his banner called Scareflix at Glass Eye Pix. He started finding younger filmmakers and helping them get their movies made. They were all interesting projects to me. And all those guys have a lot of respect for music, they like music. To them it can play a really big role in a movie, and they are all kind of adventurous. So it just had a lot to offer.

As a kid, I grew up outside of Boston. And a friend of mine who lived down the street, his dad, as a side business, had one of those video vending machine companies. They used to have every B-movie you could think of just sitting there in their basement. [*Laughs*] And even though my friend's family was pretty well off, he was just too cheap to go to the movies. He'd go, "We have all these movies down in my basement." So I watched every single one of those. I've seen so many B-movies [*laughs*]; some of them were just awesome and some of them were just terrible, and there is a certain appreciation I have for that.

You experienced every true horror geek's dream, in that you got be a fly on the wall while David Cronenberg and Howard Shore were working together.

Yeah, that was on *Spider* [2002]. Actually, what was interesting on that one was that those guys have worked together so much that I don't think they even spotted *Spider*. They just talked it out on the phone, and then Cronenberg came to the recording sessions. That's the rapport that they've developed. I think the only Cronenberg film Howard didn't do was *The Dead Zone* [1983], which Michael Kamen did. It is not like they didn't communicate—it is not like Elmer Bernstein and Martin Scorsese [*laughs*] on *Gangs of New York* [2002]. They [Cronenberg and Shore] communicated, but they have a serious shorthand because they've worked together so much. I think *Spider* is a great movie, but it is its own movie, it's a very different thing. (I wasn't there for *A History of Violence* [2005], which would've been great.)

It is interesting to see people that have worked together for a long time—and those guys have known each other since they were teenagers. So that is different than when he [Shore] is working with Peter [Jackson] and Fran [Walsh], because *Fellowship* [*of the Ring*] was the first movie they did together. With *Gangs of New York*, Howard had worked with Scorsese once before—in the Eighties they did *After Hours* [1985]—but that was it. So it was a different thing.

With *Panic Room* [2002], he [Shore] had worked with [David] Fincher a bunch [on *Seven* (1985) and *The Game* (1997)]. That was probably, in a lot of ways [*laughs*] the most normal project. "Okay, we're scoring in LA; we will just show up to Sony and record at Sony for a week"—it was that kind of thing. Fincher was there, and he would have his comments: "I don't like that theme in the horn," or whatever. And Howard would make some adjustments. Out of all the films I did with Howard, I would say that one was probably the most normal. Lots of good projects, though.

In recent years horror film music has acquired a large and loyal fan base, maybe larger than for any other genre of film. Many composers of classic horror scores, some of which I've interviewed for this book, are even hitting the road and playing their music live for sold-out audiences. You're still comparatively early in your career, but do you have any opinions as to why horror film music attracts fans?

Umm . . . well, first, I think it's awesome [*laughs*]. In case it wasn't clear, I should preface it with, I definitely enjoy doing horror films. It is not the only thing I enjoy doing, but it has been great. Like I said, I think a lot of that has to do with the particular collaborators and the particular projects I've had. But, I think, just historically, horror and sci-fi have just been the best social commentary. It is such clever, clever filmmaking, and it is done on so many levels and in such a wide variety too. From the look of it, it seems like, "Oh it's *this*," but it is not.

There are so many different voices and there are so many different things and eras. Look at what is going on with horror today versus even five years ago or ten years ago and then thirty years ago. It is a really interesting animal, and I think that there has always been a bit of that "misfit" aspect to it too. Of course, now you have the studios trying to do their thing with it and make all the money, blahblahblah. . . . Maybe this is just my impression, but it seems like that kind of approach is least successful with what you're talking about.

Vinyl records are making a big comeback, and one of the trends with it is pricey reissues of film scores. Even though non-horror scores are also getting rereleased, horror definitely does seem to be the primary focus of this trend. So, clearly, there is a market for it; people are buying them.

Well, at the end of September [2014], actually Death Waltz, Spence Hickman's company, had us come out for a double bill: *The Texas Chainsaw Massacre* [1974] with a live rescore, then they screened *The House of the Devil*. They had a vinyl release for *The House of the Devil*, and they did an amazing job with the vinyl—it's really, really cool. I don't know if you've seen it [*laughs*], but it is totally insane!

All of their stuff is really great.

The audience seemed really into it. It was well attended, and I thought it was a really cool event. I think it is great. I think there is a real sense of community that doesn't exist other places. You have your Trekkies and you have the *Star Wars* fan base, but those are very particular . . . I don't want to say *franchises*, because it cheapens the way people think about them, but they have a particular identity. Whereas, I think, with horror there is a culture to it, and I think it connects with people. It is a bit broader, and there are also so many just wildly different things—both in filmmaking and in music—that have gone on in horror. Also, people have tried to trivialize it so much. But in terms of cult status, there are so many more horror films [*laughs*] than there are anything else. There are things about the films that connect with people.

So the music is just an extension of that?

Sure, but I think a lot of the scores have a lot of personality, because the films have a lot of personality. Look at *Suspiria* [1977]—that is a crazy movie, and the music is totally nuts! But it is awesome, it is great. It is so over-the-top, but that's the whole point. That is a beloved movie and a beloved score, and there are plenty of things that you could cite like that.

So I think it is great, but I also think it is just sort of where things are with the music industry. Because they can do special-edition reissues and things like that, it actually makes some sense to do a vinyl release or do a rerelease, whereas these days CDs are actually really hard to put out. First of all, people aren't buying them as much. . . .

I think about when I used to open vinyl as a kid, it was an experience. You cut open the cellophane and you check out the artwork, and you read all the stuff and you hold the record in your hand. You want to be very careful with it; you put it on the player, and you're very careful with putting the arm down. It was an experience, and it also has its own sound and all that stuff. There is a lot of intent that goes behind all of that. I think that people appreciate that, and it resonates with people. . . .

Again, with horror I think there is some sense of community with it, and there's a bit of the outcast thing as well. Some people don't think of it as real filmmaking, or whatever. And I think there are plenty of people that can make a good argument against that [*laughs*] nowadays. I think it offers up more personality, in an era when there are a lot of things that really don't have a lot of personality.

Since you've worked with so many great people, including other great composers, are there any bits of advice that you have cherished that you'd be willing to share with somebody who is just starting out and looking to score films?

Certainly one of the best pieces of advice that I got was when I was leaving Howard [Shore]. I asked Paul Broucek, who was the head of music at New Line at the time (but he is now the head of music at Warner Bros.) what advice he had for someone like me, and he said, "My advice is to not try and be like Howard Shore or John Williams. They are great composers, but the reality is, in your lifetime, if you ever get to the kinds of budgets that they get, it will be a long time from now. And what is going to be most helpful is learning to work creatively within a budget that you realistically will have to work with. If you can go and do that, people will respond to that."

That's been easily one of the best pieces of advice that I've received. And I will just say that it is a ton of work, so [*laughs*] you've got to like it.

Maurizio Guarini

*"We were in our twenties and the world was simpler and
everything was quicker. We didn't have much time to think about
what kind of sound we wanted or what sampler or what technology
to use. We only had a few instruments. So we didn't have to spend
much time choosing. We just started playing and making music."*

I N 2013, I HAD THE PRIVILEGE of seeing the great Italian progressive
rock band Goblin in concert twice. The second show took place on
a cold December evening, in an early-nineteenth-century church near
Yale University. The band rocked their way through all of their most
beloved Dario Argento movie themes, while the "Italian Hitchcock's"
most stylized moments of blood-soaked carnage were projected onto a
stained-glass portrait of Jesus behind them. To say that the experience
was surreal would be a gross understatement.

At this show, I sat in an old wooden church pew, directly in front of
keyboardist Maurizio Guarini. I once heard somebody describe him
as a "mad scientist," and as I watched him attack layers of electronic

keyboards—turning knobs, punching buttons, and pounding keys—with artistic intensity, I could see why.

As a member of Goblin, his most significant film scoring contributions were made during the band's lesser-known (and underrated) post–*Dawn of the Dead* (1978) period. As one of Italy's leading session musicians, he has worked with such esteemed composers as Pino Donaggio and Fabio Frizzi and has contributed music to films by directors Mario Bava, Lucio Fulci, Luigi Cozzi, Ruggero Deodato, David Schmoeller, and Dario Argento.

Maurizio Guarini may not be as recognizable a name as some of the other contributors in this book, or as accomplished a film composer in the most traditional sense, but as an esteemed member of (arguably) horror's greatest band and as a highly in-demand professional studio musician, he offers a unique perspective on the heyday of Italian horror cinema, as well as insights into Goblin's lesser-known works and the process of creating film music as a member of a band, among other things.

Selected Filmography

1977   *Suspiria* (as a member of Goblin)

              Shock (aka *Schock*, aka *Beyond the Door II*; keyboards, uncredited)

              Martin (Italian version; as a member of Goblin)

1978   *Patrick* (Italian version; as a member of Goblin)

1979   *Buio Omega* (aka *Beyond the Darkness*; as a member of Goblin)

              Zombie (aka *Zombi 2,* aka *Zombie Flesh Eaters*; keyboards)

1980   *Contamination* (as a member of Goblin)

              Contraband (aka *Luca il contrabbandiere*; keyboards)

              City of the Living Dead (aka *Paura nella città dei morti viventi*, aka *The Gates of Hell*; keyboards)

1981   *The Beyond* (aka *Seven Doors of Death*, aka . . . *E tu vivrai nel terrore! L'aldilà*)

              St. Helens (as a member of Goblin)

1983   *Spy Connection* (aka *Notturno*; as a member of Goblin)

1984   *Murder-Rock: Dancing Death* (aka *Uccide a passo di danza*; additional keyboards)

1986   *Crawlspace* (keyboards, uncredited)

1987   *The Barbarians* (keyboards)

1988   *Phantom of Death* (aka *Un delitto poco comune*) (keyboards)

              Catacombs (keyboards)

1998   *The Phantom of the Opera* (additional music)

2010   *The Solitude of Prime Numbers* (opening titles; as a member of Goblin)

Tell me about your early musical influences.

When I was around fifteen I mostly listened to rock bands like Deep Purple. Then I started to a get a little bit more into English jazz-rock and what is now called progressive rock . . . but at the time it didn't have a name, it was just a different kind of rock. I was playing keyboards, so I was following bands like Emerson, Lake & Palmer. I also liked Genesis, Gentle Giant, and other bands playing that kind of music. Then, maybe in the late 1970s or maybe 1980, I started listening to more jazz and fusion, like the band Weather Report—that is one of my all-time favorite bands.

How did you meet the guys from Goblin and end up joining that band?

I met them through common friends. At that time, in the spring of 1975, I was playing in Rome a lot, and they were at the end of recording the music for *Profondo rosso* [*Deep Red* (1975)] and they needed to set up a band. They didn't actually have a band to play live, they had just done things in the studio. Through common friends I met Massimo [Morante, one of Goblin's founding members]. We talked and played together. We got to know each other musically, and then they asked me to join the band. That was the start of everything. We started playing live together late in the summer of 1975.

Were you familiar with Dario Argento's work when you joined?

Yes, I saw the two or three previous films by Dario Argento. I was a bit less familiar with horror; I was more into science fiction. There is often some horror in science fiction, but not always. I was not really a horror fan. I did like thrillers, though, and science fiction.

Do you have any favorite science fiction films?

Yeah, of course. *2001: A Space Odyssey* [1968] is one of my favorite movies ever. I like that movie in particular because the author, Arthur C. Clarke, participated with the movie. So there are no scientific errors. I always thought that film was amazing in general. Also, *Blade Runner* [1982] is another one of my favorite movies.

So you joined Goblin to basically play with them live, but later the band began work on *Suspiria* [1977].

Yes, exactly. The first need was to set up a live band, and we started touring in 1975. In the meantime we started composing an album called *Roller*. That was released at the beginning of 1976. And it was also in 1976 that we started working on *Suspiria*. I believe Dario Argento contacted us in the summer of 1976.

What was the band's process for composing the music for *Suspiria*? Was there someone who took the lead, or was it completely collaborative?

In general, Goblin has always been collaborative in the studio, but it depended on the work and how the work started. In that particular case, I was only involved in the first part and not in the second. We were required to write the main theme before seeing the movie. So, in that case, I remember being in the studio and working on this sort of lullaby with the celesta [an acoustic keyboard instrument that produces delicate bell-like tones]. That was a more collaborative theme. No one brought that specific theme into the studio. We built that together, of course following the suggestions of Dario, because we hadn't seen the movie yet.

What normally happens in the studio is, the initial idea does have to come from one mind. Let's say the melody, for example. The melody is the root for the music, but the real music, the actual piece, is an overall work by the band. So you can have all the arrangement, the instruments, the choice of phrases, whatever, but we always built it together as a band. It is not like an arranger that gives all the parts written out to all the studio musicians. So no matter who is the real composer of the melody, it is always a process of collaboration between the members of the band, of course.

There's a rumor that you guys composed and recorded music before Argento even started shooting *Suspiria*, and that he played that music on set while he was filming. Is that true?

I remember having been in the studio while Dario was filming. I remember that he was listening to the music, and I think that he did use some of the music while shooting. I believe that is true. Unfortunately, that was forty years ago, so even though my memory is pretty good,

I can't remember all the details. It may be a famous movie now and some people may say, "How can you not remember this?," but keep in mind that at that time, we didn't know that *Suspiria* was going to be the sort of movie that would last forty years. We were working a lot, on different productions, maybe one day on one and then one day on another. We didn't think that it would be something that in 2014 people would still be talking about. So, of course, there are things that I can't remember.

A few moments ago you mentioned that *Suspiria*'s main theme was written before the band saw the film. Was that the case with other parts of the score as well?

No, just the main theme. And actually, in my case, we had an argument and I left the band after only a few days in the studio—that was November 1976. I still have the day-by-day agenda with all the studio times listed, so I can tell you the dates. After that I left, and they kept working on that into 1977. In that case, I have to say that there are no real other themes. *Suspiria* is one of a kind; it is atmosphere, and the music perfectly matches the imagery.

There are some unique instruments used in that score. Do you remember what inspired their use?

Yes, because the witch in the film is Greek, we decided to use Greek instruments. Instead of the guitar, Massimo used the bouzouki. It is like a guitar, similar to a mandolin; it is Greek. We used some ethnic sounds, like a *toubeleki* together with a synthesizer, to create some unique sounds. So it was inspired by the fact that the witch in the film was Greek.

Do you have any recollections regarding Argento's style of working with and communicating his needs to the band?

Dario is normally really communicative. He can explain exactly what he wants in terms of music. Maybe not speaking specifically in musical terms, because he is not a musician, but while talking he can explain exactly what he needs. In that case we went to visit him at his home, and he explained the story of the movie. He's always very enthusiastic. He can really transmit his needs to us. I have to tell you that, in general, when we are called to work on a film, we are left free enough to do what we want; of course, that is after following the initial oral guidelines from the director. If they call us for the "Goblin sound," they have to give us a certain level of freedom. They can't be too specific.

For you, personally, had you considered scoring films before you joined Goblin?

Yes, I think I had thought about it, but it was not really a plan. When I was a teenager, thirteen or fourteen, when I watched movies I was already listening to the soundtracks. Sometimes people watch a movie and don't pay attention to the music, especially at that age. Sometimes I was just focusing on the music, and I did think to myself, Yeah, maybe one day I might write a soundtrack, or maybe even just something that is not "easy" music that you can listen to on the radio. Because the music in movies is always more articulate, more complicated. It's more interesting in some ways, like classical music. Yes, I was interested, but not professionally until I joined Goblin.

After *Suspiria*, you worked on Mario Bava's last film, *Shock* (1977).

Yes, but I was not part of Libra. (Libra was the band that did the soundtrack.) But for some reason I was called into the studio—because maybe Sandro Centofanti, the band's lead keyboard player, had to do something else? So I ended up playing keyboards on that album, but I was not involved directly with the composition or anything with Bava on that. I was just sitting in on keyboards for the guys in Libra, who I knew and was friends with. It was sort of a random thing that I participated on *Shock*.

Later you rejoined Goblin, but the band's lineup was different. Did it feel like Goblin, or did it feel like a whole new band?

In our case, and I bet in most cases with bands, the overall sound of the band . . . comes from the single elements of the band working together. So, whoever brings his soul to the overall sound, at the end of the day, contributes to the sound of the band. Without having Claudio Simonetti and Massimo Morante in that particular lineup, their elements were missing, so it felt like it had a little bit of a different sound. But the approach was the same and, of course, the rhythm section was the same.

But you can instantly recognize the work that was done with that lineup of the band versus the other lineup. So, to answer your question, I would say yes and no at the same time: Yes, because we changed the elements and the sound changed; no, because it was still Goblin. We had the same approach, we still had the same rhythm section. Fabio Pignatelli and Agostino Marangolo and I were there. With that lineup, I think we moved a little bit more toward the fusion side, instead of rock.

When you rejoined the band, Claudio Simonetti had left and you were the only keyboard player. Did that result in your taking on an even bigger role in the composing of the music?

Well, it depends on which movies we are talking about. In some movies I was just in the studio. Of course, I was contributing in terms of playing and arranging the keyboards, but Fabio may have been the one creating the main melodies. During that period, I didn't want to be a literal member of the band and sign with their record label—to tell you the truth, I had a problem with their record label. So I always participated as a contracted musician, like an external studio musician.

Artistically, though, there's a slight, tiny difference between being the composer and being part of the composition. If somebody writes four lines of melody, he is the composer, but if you're in the studio working on a song, the "sound" is made by who is playing that, because there is no arranger.

So, if you're asking if I was the composer—as in writing the melody—I was not the composer on some of those albums. If by composing you mean collaborating and contributing to the overall sound, then, yes, I helped compose, because we all did. This was for *Patrick* [1978], *Buio Omega* [1979], and *Contamination* [1980]. There are other movies also.

***Patrick* was a film that was made in Australia with a Brian May score. Then Goblin did a new score for it for its Italian release. Had you guys seen the movie? Did you hear the other score, or even know there was another score?**

I don't actually remember. *Patrick*, for me, was a very short collaboration . . . as were the other films as well. For some reason we were quicker in those days. It would sometimes take us a week to do everything—composing, going into the studio, recording, mixing, etc. And we did tons and tons of studio work every year. I cannot remember how the *Patrick* soundtrack came about, but I do remember being in the studio working on it. I think we did know that there was another soundtrack, but I am not sure.

The score for *Buio Omega* is likely the most famous score by that particular Goblin lineup. Do you have any recollections of recording that music?

We were probably in the studio for only a week total, including composing, recording, and maybe mixing. As I said, we were quick back then. Today the technology allows you to do infinite things, so actually the result is a slowdown in the process of composing—not just for movies but for albums too. It can take months and maybe a year now to make an album.

In the old days, maybe it was because we were younger and quicker, but we were producing a lot of things every month. We were in our twenties and the world was simpler and everything was quicker. We didn't have much time to think about what kind of sound we wanted or what sampler or what technology to use. We only had a few instruments. So we didn't have to spend much time choosing. We just started playing and making music. In that way, it was a more productive period. I think that is why we were quicker.

Do you remember the actual creation of the *Buio Omega* theme—who came up with the melody and what was your contribution?

I remember composing parts of some of the melodies. Some themes don't really have a "melody"; they're just something that we built in the studio. I remember playing one song called "Quiet Drops." It is very slow, with very interesting and intriguing chords. I can even remember playing the chord progression of the main theme, but I can't remember who actually composed that theme. If you think about it, the main theme of *Buio Omega* is just a few notes, with a progression of chords played under them.

Can you talk a bit about working with directors and the actual scoring process?

The overall process starts with talking to the director, and you see a cut of the movie. Sometimes it is not the final cut and sometimes it may be. Sometimes when it is a rough cut, that is when you have the most intense collaboration with the director, when you have to identify where to put the music and what kind of music you will need to compose or write. Then, during the process of composing the music, the director is not normally involved. Now, today, the process may be a bit different, because there is more communication. But in the late Seventies somebody might've lived in another city, etc. There was no Skype, no email, or anything like that, so communication was lacking in some ways. There was less director involvement, especially in the studio.

You played as a session musician on the scores for some of Lucio Fulci's most beloved horror films. How did your working with Fabio Frizzi, who composed those scores, come about?

We were friends, because we worked together on other films that were not related to horror and we played together often. More than just a being a player, I would collaborate with him . . . again, from the aspect of the "sound." Fabio didn't give me or the other musicians written charts or tell us what to play. It was similar to the Goblin process of composing. Fabio would have an idea, some chords; he would have a melody. We would meet in the studio at 9 A.M. and we would sometimes play for a while, just to see what would come out.

It was more a process of creation in the moment. Everybody's creativity was left free to explode in some way—that's why there are some ideas on those movies that cannot come from just one single brain. That is, of course, excluding the fact that Fabio was the one meeting with Fulci beforehand and talking about the themes and having the melodies written and a lot of the work pre-done.

But working with Fabio was a very creative collaboration. Fabio and I were friends, so there was no problem at all with communication. We did a lot of work together, including Fulci's most famous movies. I think I worked on three or four of them, but not only me, also [Goblin bassist] Fabio Pignatelli.

So, Frizzi would come in with some ideas and melodies, but then, when you and the other musicians would play, the music would take on a life of its own?

Yes, I'm not saying that Fabio didn't compose the music. Of course he did compose the music, but I'm saying that the overall sound was our sound, not necessarily Fabio's sound. We were collaborating with him to create the sound. I don't want to diminish the value of the composer, but I am just saying that musicians are, in this case, important to how the overall soundtrack sounds.

You are a musician, right?

Yes, I am.

So you can understand how a different arrangement and who you are playing with can totally change the same song. That is what I am talking about here.

I find this interesting, because people traditionally think of film music as being orchestral, and in those cases you are dealing with a composer and an arranger and an orchestrator and sheet music and a group of classically trained musicians who are playing exactly what is on the page. However, getting into the 1970s and 1980s—not just in Italy, but everywhere—many scores where done by bands. You point out that there are certain characteristics with a band and the dynamics and chemistry between its players that can help shape a piece of music.

Of course! It is different. One time we [Goblin] did a score with a symphonic orchestra, in 1980 or 1981. It was for a film called *St. Helens*, about Mount St. Helens, the killer volcano. I don't think it was released in theaters, but we composed the themes. That was written music, note by note, for the orchestra. So we have worked with an orchestra before, but in most cases, as a band, we were creating on the fly.

Were the Fulci scores done very quickly, like the Goblin projects were, or did they take more time?

It was always quick. During that period it was always a very short time. I remember that Fulci was often in the studio during the first two or three days, when you just set up and play the main instruments, like drums or bass, keyboards, etc. Then there are a few additional days when you just work with keyboards, adding sounds, atmosphere, and effects to what was recorded on the previous days. On those days you're not just working on the side of the studio where there are instruments, but you are also working in the mixing area. And I remember that Fulci was often there during the final retouching before the mix.

You've also worked quite a bit with composer Pino Donaggio. Was that a similar process, or was your dynamic with him different?

With Pino it always involved an orchestra, so the process was a bit different. We were meeting Pino . . . (I say "we" because at that time I was sometimes working with my wife, who would help me with things on the computer). Anyway, Pino would come two or three days in advance. Since the soundtrack was going to be played by a big orchestra, we had to prepare all the scenes on synthesizers and piano and even prepare the click track for the orchestra. It was the beginning of when a computer was being used to synchronize movies with music. Before that we were just going with a timer. (In the early Eighties we started working with computers.)

Pino would come to my place. We would prepare the cues for the orchestra, plus we would find samples and sounds with the synthesizers. This was a way to make the process much, much quicker and less expensive. The session recording with an orchestra is, of course, very expensive, because we are sometimes talking about forty or fifty musicians. So the shorter the time, the happier the production is, because you are saving money. We did this kind of thing many times with Pino Donaggio on his scores.

When you're working with various composers, like Frizzi and Donaggio, who are now beloved for the work they've done, do you learn from them and do you start to look at your own composing in a different way?

Not specifically. But it is true in general. I think all musicians "steal" from everybody we listen to. So I can even steal from somebody I hear on the subway, or whoever. We are a sort of input for information and technique and ideas—and we take from everybody. So of course I get some things from them, but nothing specific. If I go to a concert and see a piano player, I may take a note of something he did and maybe adapt it for myself. It is a general process that I use, and I think everybody does . . . more or less.

Of course, Fabio and Pino use totally different techniques. Donaggio was very accurate and knew exactly what he needed to do in terms of the orchestra. He also had orchestrators who would write out the stuff for him. Frizzi had more freedom, because there were more synthesizers and keyboards involved.

The score for Fulci's *Murder Rock* [1984] was by keyboardist Keith Emerson, and you added additional keyboards. Did you work directly with Emerson, or did you record your parts after the fact?

We were working in the same studio on two different projects. I can't remember which project I was working on. It was Trafalgar Recording Studios in Rome. . . .

I met Keith before, because we would run into each other every day while we were working in the studio. I did additional keyboards just because I was there. The sound engineer may have told me that Fulci needed some additional keyboards and effects, but Keith was not there for that, otherwise he would've done it himself. I did it because he already left. Actually, Fulci even asked my wife to do some screams for the sound effects.

You are also credited with doing "additional music" for Dario Argento's *Phantom of the Opera* [1998]. Was that a similar situation?

My wife, Cinzia Cavalieri, was working as a music editor with Dario, and during the composition there were a couple of scenes where they needed ambient music. It was not part of the original music composition, but more like background music, and I was asked by the production to compose it. Dario listened to the songs, he liked them, and he put them in the movie. It was additional music, it was not overlaying keyboards on existing music. They were separate songs.

Do you have a favorite recording session? It doesn't have to be your favorite score, just a favorite recording experience.

There are several things that I remember. First is the soundtrack I was talking about earlier for the film *St. Helens*—the one that was played by an orchestra. It was an American production, and the experience of hearing my music played live in the studio by a forty-eight-piece orchestra was something I really enjoyed. It really touched me. We were relatively young, and when you hear your music played by that many people in an orchestra, it is very touching.

Many of my other good memories are from playing live. Playing live music is always something that enriches you. You get a chance to create good memories and energy every night. For example, in 2011 we [New Goblin] had the chance to play with Steve Hackett [lead guitarist from the band Genesis]. He played "Profondo rosso" with us and we also played "Watcher of the Skies." That was a sensation—I was playing with someone I admired very much.

There are many special moments when you are a musician, because music is always emotional. It has to be emotional, otherwise it is useless. Every moment is good. There are not many specific moments that I remember. I have spent most of my life sitting behind a piano or a keyboard in a studio, so there are too many to say.

Do you remember when you started to realize that there was a passionate audience for all this soundtrack music that you recorded decades ago?

Yes. I don't remember the exact moment, but I remember the process. I started realizing it when the social networks were beginning to become popular and the Internet was expanding. I would say it was maybe ten years ago or even a little more.

I started realizing it when I was meeting people here in Toronto and they would ask, "Are you really part of Goblin?" They would praise the band and express disbelief that I was part of it. I noticed that the diffusion of the information through the Internet was the start for a new era. Things that were totally dormant and forgotten were about to be rediscovered by younger generations and reborn.

Now we are talking about all these movies, but if you were to ask me about this fifteen years ago, I would've been surprised—and not just me, also the other members of Goblin, because we had been forgotten. Now there is a sort of scanning of what happened in the 1960s, '70s, '80s on the Internet. There are armies of people that want to know more and more and more, because, I have to admit, those years were very creative.

So I started to realize this was happening around ten years ago, when I actually was asked to put together a band here in Toronto and play the most important Goblin themes. I put together a trio here and we played live Goblin scores, a bit rearranged, a little more experimental. I was asked to do it, and at the time I thought, "Who is going to listen to these songs? Nobody, because they are weird. They are not easy songs."

But actually, I discovered that there was a huge amount of people that loved them. That was 2003 or 2004, and that was also when Massimo Morante and Fabio Pignatelli decided to re-create the band . . . after so many years of doing nothing. That is when we re-created a new version of the band called Back to the Goblin.

More recently you've toured other countries—the USA, Japan, Australia, and England—with different lineups of the band. Even though you were already aware that there was a fan base for the music, were you surprised to see just how far the band's popularity has spread?

Yes. But now we are getting used to that, because we've been touring now for five years. But at the beginning, as I said, we were very surprised at our success everywhere. We started in Europe and we were so surprised. I kind of knew, but I tried to force the others to do this kind of thing, and at the beginning they would say, "Nobody is going to listen; the place will be empty if we try and play. Who is going to be interested in our weird themes with odd time signatures?"

And it's not true! Everybody is crazy—and they like it everywhere—and we were surprised. We were surprised last year by the audiences in the US. Concerts sold out in hours in New York and Los Angeles. Of course, after such a long time, what can you be if not surprised?

Horror film music seems to attract a large and passionate fan base, and the fact that Goblin can sell out shows all over the world is proof of that. What is it about this kind of music that attracts such loyal fans?

I've asked myself this very question, but I actually don't have an answer. Maybe it is because, particularly with our music, there were heavy metal bands and hard rock bands that we've influenced, and they helped make the sound popular. So maybe there are younger generations that are discovering our music through these other bands. We are also sort of considered a milestone, or the ones that created the "sounds for horror." Maybe that is true or maybe it is not. I don't know. But I agree with you that only horror film music seems to have such a huge following—not only Goblin's music.

Maybe it is because the "Goblin sound" was one of a kind and has become a sort of signal to detect that "this is the real horror of the 1970s." If that is the case, we would be happy to have that label.

Tom Hajdu

"We've always had that connection to the edges of culture, rather than what's happening 'today,' if you will. We've always been more interested in what's burbling up from under the surface."

As one half of the groundbreaking multimedia scoring team tomandandy, Tom Hajdu has contributed to projects ranging from TV commercials and the original MTV Video Music Awards to big-budget Hollywood action spectacles, iconic indie film favorites, and modern horror masterpieces. He and his creative/business partner, Andy Milburn, have collaborated with such notable filmmakers as Oliver Stone, Renny Harlin, Roger Avary, Paul W. S. Anderson, Mark Pellington, and Alexandre Aja.

Hajdu's musical history, combining computer-based and academic music with the sounds of underground club scenes, is fascinating. His perspective on music and the art of film scoring is unlike that of anyone else I have spoken to. As an interviewee, he was open, candid, informative, and exceptionally generous. He showed a great amount of enthusiasm for the project, and he even offered to put me in contact with other composers. I did not end up needing his help in that capacity, but his offer was genuine and I am very thankful for his generosity and participation.

SELECTED FILMOGRAPHY
as tomandandy, with Andy Milburn

1991	*JFK* (additional music)
1993	*Killing Zoe*
1994	*Natural Born Killers* (additional music)
1995	*Mr. Stitch* (TV movie)
1999	*Arlington Road* (additional music)
2002	*The Mothman Prophecies*
	The Rules of Attraction
2006	*Right at Your Door*
	The Hills Have Eyes
	The Covenant
2007	*P2*
2008	*The Strangers*
	The Echo
2010	*Resident Evil: Afterlife*
	And Soon the Darkness
2011	*I Melt with You*
2012	*Resident Evil: Retribution*
	Citadel
	The Apparition
2014	*Animal*
	Girl House
2015	*Sinister 2*

What were your chief musical influences while you were growing up?

Growing up, my parents listened to Muzak, which made me feel physically ill most of the time. I remember that, as a young child, I just couldn't believe that they were listening to this stuff. It was one of the many reasons that I felt like I was alien in that family somehow.

What happened was, when I was a young teenager, the punk scene in Vancouver started to take off, which I immediately glommed on to. The punk scene was really emerging in Vancouver, also across the world, but there was a hotbed of punk in Vancouver at the time—everyone from D.O.A. on one end of the spectrum to Skinny Puppy on the other end of the spectrum—that really wasn't punk, but it was more industrial. There were just a ton of bands, and so I started playing in bands.

I played in a number of them that were kind of interesting. The most interesting was called *e*, just the small-case E, like the math symbol, which consisted of a number of punk veterans—but we all played synthesizers. So it was kind of like Throbbing Gristle without a rhythm machine, which was kind of fun.

Then I took this hard right turn into academic music, and I went to the University of British Columbia and got a degree in music composition. At the same time, I went to Simon Fraser University and got a degree in computer music—it was a joint kind of thing. At Simon Fraser University there was a computer music program led by a guy named Barry Truax, who was one of the pioneers in computer music at that time. From there I went to Princeton University and started working on a PhD in that. So it was a very strange combination of rebellious, noise-based music and academic music, which in the past has been considered primarily pitch-oriented.

Andy's [Milburn] background is very similar, except that his parents were academics and very open. As a result of that, he found the whole punk scene very naturally, as opposed to in a contrarian fashion. He ended up at Princeton doing his undergraduate degree, studying computer music. Then we met at the graduate school, doing basically the same thing and coming from the same background. We had a couple of professors who were quite influential in the academic world and in the computer music world who embraced these types of contrarian positions.

So it was just luck, because what's the probability of going to one of the best university institutions in the world, with one of the strongest computer music programs in the world, and then being allowed to experiment in a way that was fairly contrarian?

That was really fortunate, and the two professors were J. K. Randall and Paul Lansky. J. K. Randall was one of the strongest minds in academic music but was really rebellious. In his day, he kind of rejected traditional academic music and started working with people like the Grateful Dead. And Paul Lansky was one of the pioneers of computer music, who just recently retired. (Radiohead sampled Paul Lansky's work and gives him credit.) We were just really lucky to have been in that environment, because we were able to work very, very hard and grow a lot.

And around what years was that?

That was 1985 to 1989. We were heading toward these professorial positions, which we didn't realize at the time, but we kind of figured it out during our last year at Princeton. So we decided to make our lives as uncomfortable as we could, and we both moved, together, into what was basically a garage. It had no heat, no bathroom, nothing . . . and this is in Princeton, New Jersey, where it gets pretty icy cold in the winter and pretty hot in the summer. We lived above this two-car garage, in this tiny attic area.

So it was like Fonzie's apartment in *Happy Days*.

Well, it was a lot less gorgeous than that. It was just basically wood planks and that was it. It was very uncomfortable, so we started going to New York. Well, actually, I guess the last straw, the real indication that we were on the wrong path, was, I was in theory class with a very well-known American theorist who was at Princeton named Peter Westergaard, and the first thing he said at the very first class was, "All music has a beginning, middle, and an end." And as soon as he said that, it just seemed like a ridiculous statement to make.

So Andy and I started making music together that was fifteen seconds long that was just, like, a wall of noise. It just was nothing; it was like [*makes a loud static noise with his mouth*] and that was it.

There was a concert at Princeton with this well-known academic composer named Barry Vercoe. He had this thirty-minute piece for violin and tape. It was just this ridiculously long and hard-to-listen-to, complicated piece that this violinist was struggling through with this computer-music tape. And then, after this thirty-minute piece, we put on one of these fifteen-second blasts. That was the whole piece: It was this fifteen-second wall of noise, and in the concert hall obviously it was completely ridiculous to do. But it made it really obvious to me that this was the wrong context to be in.

And it was based on *that* that we went to New York and to MTV and said, "Look, you guys, what you're doing is really cool, but your music just sucks." And they said, "Oh, well, if you think you can do better, let us know." And they hooked us up with an assistant producer, basically an intern, named Mark Pellington, who then went on to be the director of *The Mothman Prophecies* [2002], *Arlington Road* [1999], etc., but at the time he was just a PA [production assistant]. And between Mark Pellington and tomandandy we created the interstitial moments during the Music Video Awards, which was the first time at MTV that it was kind of nonlinear and cut-up and swishy and zippy.

And we realized we were onto something. Shortly thereafter, we did the music for an international TV show with Mark called *Buzz* [1990]. As of a result of that, we ended up working with a lot of people—really well-known artists like Jenny Holzer—and we expanded from there.

I'm sure there is a little bit of luck involved in everyone's career, but it seems exceptionally fortuitous that you would meet somebody who was such a kindred spirit creatively.

Yes, I would say that too. And then we were just in the right place at the right time, which happened to be in New York, where they happened to be doing MTV, where they happened to be just in the cultural shift. So, from an intellectual perspective, what we did was actually quite intentional, because we appropriated the aesthetics of the avant-garde—the Dadaists and the Futurists of the early twentieth century—and brought them into pop culture very consciously. . . .

We ended up meeting a lot of the artists in New York—like Lou Reed, Laurie Anderson, David Byrne—who also had in some ways bridged the gap between art and pop culture. And that was our thruway into what we're doing. It's kind of an unusual pathway.

How does the creative collaboration work for you two? Has it evolved over years, or does it differ per project?

Well, you have to understand that tomandandy became essentially a brand in New York and LA. It became one of the largest production companies in the world, with almost 100 people working . . . on various kinds of projects—primarily TV commercials in the Nineties, actually. Then it was a few years into the Nineties that we started to work on films. The first movie that we worked on was *Killing Zoe* [1993], with [writer-director] Roger Avary, which wasn't a horror movie, but it is a well-regarded cult movie.

That independent film movement of the early to mid-1990s was a very interesting time for American cinema.

Yes, I totally agree.

And Roger Avary was fixture of that period.

Yes.

How did you meet him and come to work on that film?

I don't remember [*laughs*], I just don't know how that happened. Somehow we got hooked up with them on this project, and we've been working with Roger ever since—just like we've been working with [Mark] Pellington ever since . . .

Killing Zoe was the first time you guys were the "composers" on a feature-length film?

Yes, and we didn't have a clue what we were doing.

Then how did you do it?

I think we just basically kind of did what we wanted and it all just ended up in the movie. The thing that's strange about it is that to this day there are people who think of that music as being very contemporary, like it was written today. It's very weird, and people sample it and remix it somewhat regularly. I think, like a lot of good things, it was just the strength of being very naive.

It is interesting you say that, because it is a "sound" that became very popular for films like *The Matrix* [1999] a few years after you did it.

Right.

Was that type of music something you guys were hearing else-where and were just into?

Yeah, I think it was just what we happened to be into at that time, because we were in New York and always feeding from what was going on in underground culture. We've always had that connection to the edges of culture, rather than what's happening "today," if you will. We've always been more interested in what's burbling up from under the surface. That's number one. Number two—and this is kind of similar to Brian Eno's position and very different than most composers that I know of—we're very much not into authorship.

For instance, if you listen to a Danny Elfman score, you know exactly who that is, or Hans Zimmer, for example. We're not like that; our orientation is the opposite of that. In that regard, it's similar also to [Marcel] Duchamp's position, which is that if we've already done something, we don't want to do that again. We'd rather do something that we don't know how to do or we haven't done before in some way. So in that regard it's like Duchamp.

Our own position is that we really try to look at a project from a strategic perspective, which is, How can our participation make this project better than it would be *without* our participation? It's not about putting our fingerprint on it, but rather creating a bigger opportunity for the project as a whole.

But don't you think that composers just happen to have distinctive styles? Since you brought up Danny Elfman, for example, don't you think it's possible that he approaches a project with similar goals—he just also has a distinctive style? I haven't spoken to him, but I don't think he goes into a project thinking, "I'm going to Danny Elfman the crap out of this baby."

Oh no, of course not, I don't think so. But I guess my point is that I'm not even sure it's ever even brought up. I guess what I'm trying to say is that if you follow the trajectory of academic music thinking, it kind of splits in and around the early 1900s, when modernism comes in and you have this sort of sense of continuity. Well, there's a lot of issues at that split, and I don't want to go into a lot of them, but the one I'm speaking to specifically breaks at [John] Cage, right where Cage basically says, "Everything is music." The implication there is that if everything is music and nothing is music, you don't own anything. You are just partici-pating in the "everything" that is around us. So the idea of authorship is presumptuous and just false.

Now, on the other side of the argument is, "Well, no, as an artist I'm connected to God, and he is writing through me and this is his voice, so I'm his tool and I know better than you do, and that's why you're the audience and I'm not in the audience." And that's the sense of authorship.

And these are implied or known consciously, but these are among many types of diverging thoughts that occurred in the early twenti-eth century. Those are two of them, and we have kind of fallen to the Cage side.

In the 1990s, tomandandy did some work for Oliver Stone.

Yes [*laughs*], and that was very different than working with Roger. There's a third person that needs mentioning that was involved in the way in which media started to change with sound—with cut-up sound and cut-up music and cut-up visual images—and that's a film editor called Hank Corwin. (He owned a company called Lost Planet.)

What happened was that Mark Pellington, Hank Corwin, and toman-dandy were all working on commercials. We kind of had one foot in commercials and one foot in movies at that time. And Hank was hired to work on *JFK* [1991], as one of the junior editors. But what happened was, he is so nonlinear and so interesting in the way that he works that he really seriously influenced *JFK*. We ended up working on the assassi-nation scene of *JFK*, because of Hank. But then after that, Hank became the main editor of *Natural Born Killers* [1994], and so we ended up going in and doing some work on that as well. That's how we met Oliver Stone. It was because of Hank Corwin.

Were you working under the direction of Corwin?

No, it was really both, but we were brought in because of Hank. Hank had worked with us on so many other projects, so he knew that some-thing interesting would happen.

How would Oliver Stone communicate to you what he wanted?

We would just go in and play him some stuff, and he would say if he liked it or didn't.

When did you guys start working with orchestras for film scores?

I guess *The Mothman Prophecies* [2002] was the first one that was a big orchestra. And that was an interesting collaboration too. That was a combination of orchestra and Glenn Branca, who at the time was writing these symphonies for electric guitars. That was another example of reaching into the underbelly of the New York art scene and pulling Glenn Branca into that process.

What led to the decision of using an orchestra for the score?

I think it was a conversation that we had with Mark Pellington [the director], and we were fine with it, of course. But we wanted to do something that was slightly less traditional than what people were doing with an orchestra in scoring.

Was it intimidating at all?

No, no, because we'd been doing stuff like this in graduate school and undergraduate school for many years, and also in commercials. That's the other thing: I think part of this idea of questioning authorship and questioning context came from doing these commercials and the interstitial stuff on MTV, because these commercials or weird cartoons or whatever would just sort of randomly show up inside your house. You didn't go to a concert or to a movie and pay your ticket and sit there and wait for all the lights to go down and then the show starts. These are things that go into your house anonymously, unannounced. They randomly show up and leave, and you don't know what they were or who did them or how long they were going to be there.

I mean, it was a completely different approach, and during that process we were able to do everything from big orchestral scores to crazy little noise things. It was, for us, a tool set that we brought to the film-scoring world, which is a little bit unusual. Now I think it's not so unusual for film directors to go from primarily doing ads and music videos to features. But in our case, I think at that time anyway, it was a little bit unusual.

At that time, if you were a recording artist you made records, if you were a film music composer you made film music, if you were a TV music composer you made music for TV shows. If you were doing commercial music, you were doing that. If you were doing underground club music, you were doing that. We were kind of doing a little bit of everything, and that's what made the brand so successful. Today it is not that unusual, but in those days it was extremely unusual.

As you now work more and more in film, you're creating music for projects that focus on narrative storytelling. You've mentioned that on each project you try to do something different and that you look for ways that tomandandy can make a project better. Does working with a long-form narrative structure affect your process?

Well, what we are not necessarily doing is looking at what's the most obvious way that other people are doing that [*laughs*]. That would not be the first choice. And if anybody has any other suggestions, great, let's try that [*laughs*]. The tried and true? It's fine, but is there something else that we can do?

Part of the irony is that a handful of reviews—I think for *Arlington Road* [1999], and there have been a few other examples—actually referred to our work as being similar to Bernard Herrmann's work. Which I find super-ironic, because that's about as narrative as you can get. I mean, I think they're referring to some bombastic stuff, which is fine. It's fine. It's a great comparison, but narrative-wise? No, I wouldn't say there's a similarity. So, yes, we can do that and we have done that and we have no problem doing that. But if somebody has a different idea that nobody has ever done before? Yeah, we'd love to try that too. And see which one works better.

Let's talk about your process. How early or late are tomandandy typically brought onto a film?

You know, it really does differ. On some projects we get brought in before the film is shot. When I say before the film is shot, I mean we've been on projects where they're playing our music on the set while they're shooting. On other projects it's been in the eleventh hour, where things are kind of crazy or even where things are being all thrown together at the same time, where nothing is actually completed, everything is just sitting on the—you know, not on the cutting room floor, that doesn't exist anymore, but on computers.

So it really depends, and I think each project has its own life, they have their own beginning, middle, and end. They're all kind of unique in that way, and that's interesting. So we try to be sensitive to that and figure out, "How can we make all this work in an interesting way?"

Do you guys find the script to be a useful tool? I've found that some composers don't even want to read it, while others find it to be very helpful.

I think it can be useful, but things don't always end up the way you think that they're going to end up. So I think it's a valuable beginning, but it doesn't necessarily mean that it's an indication of how things will end up.

I think what makes us a little bit unusual . . . I think your focus is mainly horror scores, is that right?

Yes.

I don't know how many composers who do horror scores do comedies regularly and have commercials and have worked with artists and etc., etc.—*and* come from this type of an unusual background. By the way, that's not a negative or a positive. You don't lose anything, right? You bring everything with you. So we embrace all of that in coming into a horror project, for example.

So, if you look at two horror scores that we've done, let's say *The Hills Have Eyes* [2006] and *The Strangers* [2008], they don't sound anything like each other at all. And also *The Mothman Prophecies*. If you use those three films, I would say they have nothing in common aesthetically. They don't sound the same, they don't look the same. Music doesn't function in the same way. I mean, they're just different sounds, they sound completely different. And that's because of that background that we bring to the project.

I'd like to talk about your writing process. You've said that you are actively trying to avoid what may be considered typical. So where do you start?

It's not thought-through in the sense of . . . you know, some composers, as I understand it, create, like, a tempo map and try to figure out where these things happen, etc., etc. We don't really do that. It's pretty "Cagey" [referring to John Cage] in that way. It's like throwing stuff up against the wall and seeing what happens. So, it's ironic because, of course, given our strange background, you would think that we would be much more structured and organized, and we're not, necessarily. I mean, we can be, but not necessarily.

Besides the guys from Goblin, who work in a band dynamic, you're the only composer I'm interviewing who has a creative partner. How does that work?

It just really depends on the project. In some cases Andy will do something on his own or I will do something on my own, or he might help out or I may help out or we might work on it together. It really depends on what's appropriate and what makes the most sense in terms of the direction of the project. So it's very contingent on a project-per-project basis.

Do you write to the film, or do you write cues and then alter them to fit?

It depends. Obviously, if a cut of the film exists, that's very, very helpful, and we would probably write to the film—we *have* to write to the film. It's important to do that, but we might also make some music and then try and make it fit into the film, as opposed to just following it religiously. Sometimes we get happy accidents that you never would've imagined. But at the end of the day, of course, we want to honor the film itself.

For you (recognizing that you may not be able to talk for Andy here), where does the music, its inspiration, come from? Some of the composers I've spoken to describe that they just hear music all the time, or when they watch footage, they hear music and then they just need to write it down or record it. How does it work for you?

I think, for me, it's probably the fact that I rebelled against listening to Muzak as a child. . . . It's this existential dread or something from which this music emerges. It's sort of a dissonant clash between light and dark or something, the world not being as consonant as we would all like it to be.

But I don't hear melodies or anything, and I'm sure Andy doesn't either. We don't walk around singing tunes or anything like that. It's more of a philosophical position, I think, than a craft or a trade.

When you start working out specific pieces of music, do you use a keyboard?

Yes. We do everything.

Because of our background in computer music, we have always tried to push the edges of technology whenever we are working. I don't know if you remember this, it might be before your time, but there was a time when Steve Jobs left Apple and he created a computer company and a computer called the NeXT machine. Andy actually spent some time with Steve Jobs, and we became the first private owners of the NeXT machine; we actually helped to create the music engine for that computer platform. We've always tried to be as out-front as we could be in the technology that we use.

So, as a result of that, for several years now, we've worked just on computers and used just a tiny little keyboard as a triggering device. We've been doing that for many years, but at the time when we transitioned to that, most people were using a tremendous amount of outboard gear and had huge rooms filled with lots and lots and lots of different kinds of gadgets and speakers and padding and all that stuff. We haven't done that for years.

You said "outboard" gear?

Yes. That's the stuff like the reverb units and the compressors, etc. There are still some musicians that swear by that stuff, but we left that world a long time ago—we were in the digital world.

We were just at Ted Cohen's house yesterday. He used to be senior executive VP at EMI. He is a senior strategy expert in digital entertainment. . . . That's the only other person we've ever known who ever owned a NeXT machine. You really have to be into gear, like on the edge of digital gear, to know and certainly to own something like that. So we're kind of outliers in that regard, I think.

When you're sitting at the keyboard and your computer and you're composing, how do the tone and the sounds you're using affect your writing?

I can't speak for Andy on this, but that process for me is very timbre-related. (I'm sure that's true for Andy too.) For me it's kind of like I'm pulling on a thread or I'm following a thread. So, in other words, I feel like I'm doing a lot of listening in a way, kind of trying to listen my way through what's happening.

The irony of that, of course, is, it completely goes against my prior statement about musical aesthetics and where this stuff comes from philosophically. Because there I really am trying to listen; I'm not really trying to lead. And that is kind of more like the very traditional philosophical perspective of how art is made. . . . So, I just feel like we're sort of a series of contradictions.

One of the things that my teacher at Princeton, Jim Randall, told me a long time ago . . . and this is actually literally his quote, "You're not going to go up to the Butthole Surfers and say, 'Hey, man that's a really good F chord you are playing.'" That guy doesn't necessarily hear it as an F chord; he hears it as a thing, but that thing sounds like that. So we occupy this weird space where we're straddling both the academic side as well as the underground side of culture. We don't really fit in either or fit in both irregularly . . . or something. It's a very interesting space to occupy. It's like having multiple passports or something.

Let's talk about the 2006 remake of *The Hills Have Eyes* and its director, Alexandre Aja. How did tomandandy come to work on that film?

He approached us. He moved to LA from France, so we rented a house near where they were editing and we actually set up a studio with a couple of workstations. Andy was working in one room, I was working in another room, and we started making music. The approach that we came to—and I was very surprised that the press picked up on this and commented on it—was that we were trying to do sort of a postmodern Morricone score . . . in a postmodern Sergio Leone movie. That's really what we tried to do, and we told him [Aja] that we wanted to do that. I think it turned out well.

What made you guys go in that direction? Was it as simple as that you're watching the footage and you see a lot of dust and desert?

[*Laughs*] No, I don't think that we're just as simple as that. But I do think that it emerged over watching the picture and getting a sense of where we were in our culture. You know, what does that film mean in our culture? To do a remake of *The Hills Have Eyes* and the way in which it was done . . . I mean, you have a guy who is from France who I don't think was alive when [the original] *The Hills Have Eyes* was made, redoing that film in the desert of America—it's already postmodern by definition. And it's very dark. I don't think that we consciously analyzed it that way, but it just ended up having a "sound." And that was that. I think the sound of it is probably more of a postmodern Morricone score than the look of the picture is—you know what I mean?

Can you talk a little bit about what you mean by "postmodern"?

Well, I think it's "after modern" [*laughs*] in the sense that it's making reference to or it can be making reference to something that exists before it and is taking that thing that exists before it and making it into something new by its reference . . . like a Campbell's Soup can or something.

How far along was that film when you guys joined the crew?

They had just finished shooting and were putting together a rough cut. And we just started to try different kinds of things. We tend to work from left to right in a project or, in other words, from the beginning to the end, because we're trying to find the voice of the film, and by the time we get to the end the voice is very clear. Then you can go back and make adjustments if you need to. That film has this big Morricone twangy guitar purposely; we brought in a guitarist named Jeremy Drake for that.

We knew what we had by the time we got to the end, and then we could go back and make adjustments. But we didn't know that when we started.

So it's a process of laying it down, and when you get to the end you see where it ended up, and then you go back and fine-tune what you've already done?

Exactly, or maybe try to be more clever, like, "Wait, this is giving something away. Let's just change that. Let's make that a little darker here or not as revealing."

On the other hand, in the case of *The Strangers*, that film we did from left to right, and that film actually has a very unique sound in that, right from the onset, the idea was to make all the instruments that would normally be played softly, loud, and all of the instruments that would normally be played really loudly, soft. So, there's really distorted electric guitar, but it's extremely quiet. And there are very soft cello harmonics that are very loud, for example.

So, the perspective is completely out, and the orchestration or the instrumentation is quite fractal as a result. There are only a few instruments, and their perspectives are all skewed. But by the end of the movie, it's a massive live orchestra score, so it kind of emerges at the end.

It builds . . .

It builds, yeah. I don't think people remember the tone of it as being that building part; they remember the way those instruments worked together in an unusual way.

What was it like working with Bryan Bertino [director of *The Strangers*]?

Great. I think Bryan is one of the most unrecognized talented directors and writers in Hollywood. We've been lucky to work with a lot of really talented writer-directors. Roger Avary is another one.

From what you've said so far, it seems like you and Andy tend to drive the style of the score's sound, as opposed to the directors telling you what they want. Is that true with most of the projects you work on?

No, it depends. Sometimes people know exactly what they want, and sometimes we do exactly what they want and then sometimes the studio will change it. So it very much depends. It's just not as cut-and-dry as it might sound. We're very open to whatever the process is—that's kind of built into where we're coming from.

How did it work on *The Strangers*?

Well, see, that's an example where we had this idea that turned out to work. But an example of the other way around would be this series of motorcycle films we worked on by a director named Mark Neale, who is originally a music video director [*Faster* (2003); *The Doctor, the Tornado, and the Kentucky Kid* (2006); *Fastest* (2011); *Charge* (2011); *Hitting the Apex* (2015)].

A number of years ago he wrote the first motorcycle documentary on high-performance motorcycle racing. It was called *Faster*. It was essentially for motorcycle racing what *The Endless Summer* [1966] was for surfing. It [and Neale's subsequent motorcycle racing films are] the definitive series . . . and we've done every one of those documentaries, and that has become like a cult thing, which among the motorcycle world is very well known. There are millions and millions and millions of motorcycle enthusiasts around the world, not so many in the States actually, but many in Europe and Asia, etc. In that case it's ironic, because we've done all the music. People have licensed that music for different things.

The director oftentimes presents directions that are not typical of us, and that's fine. That's an example of having already created a tried-and-true brand, where the director is making suggestions that we never would've thought of. And we have no problem with that. We think that's great.

With *The Strangers*, at some point the decision had to be made to use an orchestra . . .

That wasn't our decision, that was the decision of the producers and the director, to make this a very big, over-the-top, large orchestra ending. So that is another example of a collaborative effort when we started in one direction but we ended up somewhere else.

I feel that *The Strangers* is a perfect example of how silence is just as important as sound.

Yes, that's true. [John] Cage makes that comment that essentially the music is the silent part—and the sound is what is punctuating the silence, which is actually not the music at all. *The Strangers* kind of speaks to that a little bit. We're big fans of silence, which is ironic since we've worked so much with noise. I think silence can be very valuable, and I think *The Strangers* is an example of that.

Another example of that is a Mark Pellington film that we did called *I Melt with You* [2011]. It's a really interesting movie with a lot of great actors in it. Rob Lowe is in it, so are Thomas Jane, Jeremy Piven, and Sasha Grey. It was a really interesting group of people, and it was all shot on the [Canon EOS] 5D Mark III. Everybody had these small cameras all around them. It was shot in Big Sur. People either violently love it or hate it. I thought it was great, personally.

On the surface, your job is to add sound to the film, so how do you decide where you're *not* going to add music—where you're going to let the silence dominate the soundtrack? Is it by feel?

Well, I think it depends on the project. In *The Strangers* that was something that was discussed right up front. Like, "It would be really cool if there were not a lot of music", "What if it was, like, really brittle?"; "Maybe there will be an old radio playing or something." We actually had a similar approach to scoring in a movie called *Right at Your Door* [2006]. That was a movie where we had decided very early on that the music and the audio would be essentially a character in the story—where you're getting some information and you are not getting some information. It's always kind of there, but it's not really functioning in a normal way. Then it just stops, and nothing happens for a while. I think it's great when we incorporate silence in a score. It's very powerful.

Can you talk about your collaboration with Paul W. S. Anderson on the *Resident Evil* films, both *Afterlife* and *Retribution*?

We went in there and just started making music. Obviously, that franchise has a long history and a very successful history with very successful scores made by very talented composers, so our goal there was to just create some sort of a continuity—respecting what they've done and hopefully making it more contemporary. If you listen to the various scores for those films, they're all really good. Our hope was to make something that was as good as the scores that we were following, but also unique.

And I think what's really interesting is that the fans really responded positively to that, to those scores. Those movies are geared toward a younger audience, and if you go on Twitter and type in "tomandandy," just about every day kids are tweeting about us. Oftentimes it's about the *Resident Evil* films, but not always. Some kids are saying that their favorite composers are Hans Zimmer, tomandandy, and whoever, while others are saying their favorite groups are Daft Punk, Nine Inch Nails, and tomandandy, etc.

Why is this happening? I mean, we're not young guys anymore, we're not twenty-six-year-old guys. I think it goes back to what we were discussing earlier: I think it's happening because of that bizarre background that Andy and I have had, and I take that as a really good sign that the background that we are coming from and the approach that we are taking is effective.

With *The Strangers* you guys took an orchestral approach, but with the *Resident Evil* films you went in almost the completely opposite direction.

Yes, with the first one, that we did. *Resident Evil: Afterlife* [2010], it was obviously kind of a post-apocalyptic, industrial approach, which worked for that one. Then for the second one [*Resident Evil: Retribution* (2012)],

Paul actually didn't want to take an orchestral approach. But if you listen to the opening of the second one, it's actually quite orchestral. It's actually a hybrid, but it's almost like a James Bond track or something, a big orchestral score, and then we pulled it back. We were asked to pull it back somewhat, to be more like what we had been doing.

But, yeah, that was just a process of trial and error. You know, we would bring in stuff and play it for Paul. The great thing about working on the *Resident Evil* series is that you have a lot more time. The music portion of those projects can last six months, so you have the opportunity to explore a lot of different directions, which you might not have on a score with a more limited timeframe.

Do you find that larger budgets help spark more creativity?

I don't know if it necessarily matters, because look at *Killing Zoe*—you know, it has had longevity. I think it really depends. It's a kind of a magic that comes back to, "What is the life of this project, and how can we participate? How can we help it?"

Would you say that less resources fuel creativity in a different way?

Yes, sometimes it does, sometimes you can come up with some good solutions. On the other hand, sometimes it can be debilitating. For example, let's say you have a small-budget film that requires a Bernard Herrmann–type orchestral score—that has happened to us before. So now we have to create this very large sound, which is quite elaborate, but we don't have an orchestra. Even with an orchestra, you would need time as well as money, because you have to orchestrate it and record it and etc., etc. But if you don't have the time or the money, now we have to approximate that with digital instruments. And sometimes it's successful and sometimes it's not as successful.

Approximate in what way? Are you talking about using orchestral pads and samples, or are you talking about just trying to get that orchestral feeling with totally different sounds?

No, just getting that feeling with those sounds. There's an art to just that. I mean, just getting digital instruments to sound like organic instruments takes time and is an art unto itself, apart from what the score is doing. It can be done and it can be good, but it's never going to be as good as an orchestra. Well, I shouldn't say *never*—it currently is not possible, but it may be someday. So it's almost like you're fighting with two hands tied behind your back. Everybody knows what they're trying to achieve, and it can be difficult to achieve that.

Given your background, I am sure there are also times when you are attempting to take organic instrument sounds and make them seem inorganic.

True. Well, that's a lot easier [*laughs*]. That's a lot easier to kind of mix them, blend them, and do stuff like that. That's what becomes a lot more fruitful. But it's understandable that if the vision of the project is to have a large orchestral score, of course we will do that and we can make it the best it can be. And sometimes it's extremely successful. At that point, it really depends on the mix and how much it's in the open, etc. There are lots and lots of factors: how the sound design is interacting with it, what are the frequencies of the sound design, etc., etc. But I am very sympathetic to the budget constraints that can happen and want to provide the best solution possible.

Now that you've been doing this for over twenty years, are you finding that it is getting more difficult to find new and different ways to score films and other visual mediums because you've already explored so many avenues?

No, I don't think it is necessarily getting more difficult. It's just, what are the expectations for the project? In other words, what are the criteria for the project and what can we bring to it?

And not all projects require doing something completely insane, like only using an eight-bit synthesizer or something like that [*laughs*]—which, by the way, nobody has ever done! (That'd be an interesting project right there.) But, for example, *Birdman* [2014] was just one shot and a drum set. That was really cool, but something like that doesn't necessarily happen frequently.

I think that the music that you and Andy make—specifically the electronic stuff—is akin to what people like John Carpenter and Tangerine Dream were doing in the 1970s and 1980s, but a more contemporary version of it.

Yeah, I guess that could be true. And, you know, the funny thing about it is that also you've got a lot of these crossover artists like Lisa Gerrard [*Gladiator* (2000), *Layer Cake* (2004)], for example, or Clint Mansell [*Pi*

(1998), *Doom* (2005), *Moon* (2009), *Black Swan* (2010)]—people that come from a rock background that are doing really interesting stuff in film. Lisa Gerrard was in a band called Dead Can Dance, and Clint Mansell was in Pop Will Eat Itself. In a way you could argue that Andy and I are really closely aligned with where they are coming from. Now they are actually doing concerts where they are playing some of their film music live, but we're not going to do that.

We don't really fit into any one thing; we fit a little bit into a few things. It's a little bit like the Groucho Marx thing: "I wouldn't ever want to join a club that would have me as a member." That contrarian position is, kind of like, Buddhist or something [*laughs*]. You embrace everything and nothing.

Do you think that music plays a different role in horror films than in other genres of film?

I think that there is a perception that it does or it should. But I think what's going on is just, like, these different industries of music that have collided, like pop music and film music and scoring and live performance and commercial, etc. I think the same is true with the expectations with the way in which music functions in the different genres of scoring.

So, for example, you can have a source cue that's just playing in the background, and then there can be a horror scene or a slasher event and that song just gets turned up, and it can be really effective. I think the traditional expectation is that music in horror movies is this external narration, and one of the things we've tried to bring to the horror movies we've worked on—and I'm sure other people have done it too—is that it actually can be interior as well.

But my point is that the expectation, whether it's interior or exterior, is sort of fracturing in all these different other ways too. Like in the example that I just used—source versus score or score being played as source! And we are all for that, that's kind of our position. We're much better at breaking things than we are at building things. There are people who are really good at those specific things. We are kind of trying to look at where those expectations can be not fulfilled [*laughs*] and made into something new.

Can you explain what you mean by exterior and interior?

Let's say, for example, you have a chase scene. Somebody is being chased in a movie and the music is moving very quickly and very aggressively, scoring the pace of this chase scene. We're watching the scene, and we can identify with the fact that this person is running and is being chased, and so this music is functioning to accompany the scene as we see it, from the world outside, watching. I think that is probably the most common expectation of how a horror score works.

An interior version would be, something's happening in a scene and I'm really scared, but rather than scoring the excitement or the fear, you could be doing something that is soft, being played softly. And what we're doing is, we're getting inside the head of the protagonist, who is feeling that or going through that experience. That's typically less common in horror movies, and we're all for that.

Now, there's also the example I gave you where you have something that's just being played as a piece of music that is a part of the scene, like a song, or it could be a piece of score that's just kind of playing and accompanying. You're not sure what that is. And it can start to change its position, and you could also do the same with going from an interior score to an exterior, which is kind of interesting. So, just playing with all those boundaries is, I think, more common now than it has been in the past. What do you think?

I think you're right. In hindsight, the music that is more overt and "exterior" is more memorable, but I also think that the "interior" music, as you put it, has been a fixture of horror movies forever. It is just that it is not as recognizable and as iconic because it is not as much in the forefront. I would say that with John Carpenter, for example, a lot of his music is very minimalistic.

Right, that's true.

And I think we remember the more overt music and the music that is easier to link to a specific scene that we can remember from the movie, like a woman being chased or even the opening titles.

Yes, I think you're right. I think your answer is better than mine [*laughs*]. On the other hand, I guess, I would just say *The Strangers'* score is known for its sparseness—and that's all interior stuff—but that might be an outlier or might be just a sign of the times. Maybe that project just worked better that way, so that's what we remember. Which is ironic, because the whole second half of the film, or certainly the last third, is completely exterior.

That film has such a slow build, and what we remember about it are the scenes like the one where the guy in the mask is standing in the background while Liv Tyler is in the kitchen. That film is an interesting example, because so much of what we as the audience remember about it is much less action-driven than what we remember from many other films.

That's true, and it is built into the film. But when you see the guy in the mask you don't hear us *bum-bum-BUM!* [*mimicking an over-the-top music cue*]—in fact, you actually don't hear anything. It really is working with the silence, or working against expectation a lot of the time, and it's really only in the last third of the film that those expectations are fulfilled. I actually think the last third is not as interesting as the first two-thirds. I think you don't remember that as much.

Have you found that horror is a place where you can be a little more experimental?

I think, for us, how experimental we can be really just comes down to the project and the people that we're working with. Certainly it's an active space, so there are going to be people in there, like Bryan Bertino, where you can be experimental. And, of course, if you're working on something that is using new technology, like an Oculus Prime project, that is by definition experimental. So I think it really depends.

Since horror is not tomandandy's primary focus, you may not be aware of this, but the music created for the genre is having a bit of a renaissance. Why do you think that might be?

My feeling is that scoring, in general, is becoming more and more acknowledged as something that people really think is interesting. For some it's video game scores, for others it is documentary soundtracks. They can sometimes end up becoming really successful. It's funny, because as music sales have diminished radically over the years, music in media seems to be becoming more elevated, and I don't think it is just horror. I think that, certainly, horror is one of them, because horror is such a big market segment, but I think it's across the board. I mean, there are kids who play video game themes on a loop for, like, seventeen hours.

Horror may be part of it, but I think it is part of a larger wave. Let me give you an example: I just spoke to the CEO of the Adelaide Film Festival last week, and their theme this year [2015] is "Film and

Music." Why? [*Laughs*] That's how I know Lisa Gerrard is doing a live performance, because she is doing a live performance in Adelaide, and obviously she is not the only one. That kind of thing has been going on around LA for the last few years.

Are you guys currently working on anything horror-related that's particularly interesting?

Right now we're finishing up *Sinister 2* [2015]. Ciarán Foy is directing that second installment of *Sinister*, which I think will be pretty good. We did a film with him called *Citadel* [2012] that did very well.

Is there something different about coming into a project that is part of an existing series?

I think there is, because we want to honor what happened previously. We want to acknowledge that and honor that and only do what's best. Did you see the first *Sinister* [2012]?

Yes, and I'm actually interviewing Christopher Young, the composer for *Sinister*, for this book.

Oh, that's great. I'm a big fan of his work. We've orbited in and around a lot of Chris Young's work, where he's done one and then we've done the other or he was going to do it and decided not to and we ended up doing it. That's happened a few times.

Anyway, going back to your question. For example, in the *Sinister* movies there are those interstitial things—those little films within the film that are happening—and I would've loved to have made some interesting, stranger, weirder, unexpected music for those. But it wouldn't make sense, because that's kind of the signature of the film, and it has to be what it is. So, there's an example of how, while it would be really cool to do that, I don't think it would be the right thing to do.

So it is limiting your creativity?

I don't know if it's limiting, I just think that it comes back to that approach of looking at it strategically and what's the best thing for the project. It that case, I think it's best for the project if we don't [*laughs*].

Even though you'd want to.

Even though it will be cool, yeah. But it's not about authorship, it's not about the personal. It's about how to make this great.

When working on a sequel, is there a temptation to take what has already been done and just expand on it, or do you guys come at it with a totally different approach and just try to match the earlier tone in your own way with all-new music?

In the case of *Sinister 2*, Andy is working with Ciarán, and they've worked together before. So they're finding the voice of the film together, because they have a relationship that started previous to this project. But those sequences I was talking about earlier, those films within the film, are not part of that existing relationship. Those are kind of found elements, and you have to be true to what came before.

Do you have a particular session or working experience that is your favorite?

There was a session in *The Mothman Prophecies* where I was up in Seattle recording with the Seattle Symphony. There was a bunch of music that was written and they played it all, etc., etc. And *then* I gave them some sheet music that had basically a bunch of scribbles—you know, literally scribbles—on the page. Not any notes, just literally scribbling, drawing, and then, like, black blocks and then blank spaces. And I got them to do this sort of avant-garde score.

I wanted to include some of that type of material. If you would write out something that was as chaotic as that, you would never get them to be able to play it as energetically. It's very complicated to actually do that. It sounds like, "Oh, it just might be random." No—because you can have some fixed things where all of a sudden they hit octaves at a certain point. You can give them hand signals to do that, and I've done that a couple of times.

It's really great to do with a really talented orchestra, because they don't know what the hell is going on. They're not used to doing that. They want to be told what to do, and all of a sudden now they don't know what they're supposed to do. So that's been quite fun [*laughs*].

What might people find unique about your process?

I think our process is just unique in that we are kind of all over the place, and that we really push the edges of underground pop culture to academic culture, and those two paths don't normally cross.

ALAN HOWARTH

*"Sound effects are still music to me. One of the great definitions
of music, in the broadest terms, is that it is the alternation
of sound and silence. With that broad heading—working
with sound, whether it's music or sound effects—it's the same
equipment, it's the same studio. It's just applying it differently."*

M Y FRIEND DAVE ONCE TOLD ME that when he was younger he
used to "dream about moving to Glendale, California, and hanging out in Alan Howarth's studio, sleeping on a cot—just being there
with him and John Carpenter."

For some fans, Alan Howarth is just a name billed under John
Carpenter's on an LP cover. But those of us who are real Carpenterphiles
know that he is the technological genius who helped make the bulk of
Carpenter's 1980s musical catalog possible. His passion and aptitude
for synthesizers, sequencers, and tone made him the perfect yang to
Carpenter's creatively oriented yin—and also helped establish Howarth
as one of Hollywood's go-to guys for "special sound effects."

Going into this interview with Alan Howarth, I wasn't sure what to expect. He has worked with everyone from John Carpenter and Sam Raimi to Steven Spielberg to Robert Wise, and he single-handedly built the studio that not only birthed some of the greatest horror and sci-fi film scores of all time, but also created the sounds of the *Enterprise* for the original *Star Trek* films.

What I found was an ex-rocker with a fascinating professional past who was refreshingly open and full of knowledge, stories, and modesty. As someone with working experience in almost all aspects of post-production sound, Howarth has a broad and interesting perspective on the role of music and sound in film. And with such an accomplished résumé, he was also able to offer insights into the making of some of the most beloved films of the last thirty-five years.

SELECTED FILMOGRAPHY
Music

1980	*The Final Countdown* (additional music, uncredited)
	Battle Beyond the Stars (additional music)
1981	*Escape from New York* (with John Carpenter)
	Halloween II (with John Carpenter)
1982	*Halloween III: Season of the Witch* (with John Carpenter)
1983	*Christine* (with John Carpenter)
1986	*Big Trouble in Little China* (with John Carpenter)
1987	*Prince of Darkness* (with John Carpenter)
1988	*Halloween 4: The Return of Michael Myers*
	They Live (with John Carpenter)
1989	*Halloween 5*
1995	*Halloween: The Curse of Michael Myers*
1996	*The Dentist*
1998	*The Dentist 2*
2005	*Boo*
2007	*Planet Terror* (additional music, with John Carpenter)
2012	*Brutal*
2013	*Zombie Night* (TV movie)

Sound Department

1979	*Star Trek: The Motion Picture*
1980	*Battle Beyond the Stars*
1981	*Raiders of the Lost Ark*
1982	*Star Trek II: The Wrath of Khan*
	Poltergeist
1984	*Star Trek III: The Search for Spock*
	The Adventures of Buckaroo Banzai Across the 8th Dimension
1986	*Star Trek IV: The Voyage Home*
1987	*Running Man*
1988	*Phantasm II*
1999	*Star Trek V: The Final Frontier*
1990	*The Hunt for Red October*
	Total Recall
	RoboCop 2
1991	*Star Trek VI: The Undiscovered Country*
1992	*Army of Darkness*
	Dracula
	Fortress
1994	*Stargate*
	The Mask
1996	*The Dentist*
2008	*The Spiderwick Chronicles*

L et's start with discussing your musical education and your early days as a rock musician. I read that you opened for some pretty big acts, in the 1960s.

All this took place in northeast Ohio, in the Cleveland area. My first instrument was, at [age] five, the accordion, which came and went. Then I played alto saxophone in the high school band. I got involved with the marching band and dance band. But my original direction, personally, in terms of passion, was, I was going to be a visual artist—a painter/sculptor guy. And through the oddest of circumstances, a girl who was in my art class had a boyfriend who had a band. He invited me to go out for a sock hop and sit in, playing saxophone on dance band music—like Glenn Miller and Tommy Dorsey [sings "Boogie Woogie Bugle Boy"], you know, that kind of stuff.

But at the end of the night he handed me eighty dollars, and that was it—that was the moment of decision as to whether I was going to be in music or art. I sold out for eighty bucks, and that started me on the path to music. The guy actually turned around and had a rock band after that.

So I picked up the bass guitar, and about three bands later . . . this would be 1964–65. This was the time of the British invasion, and everyone wanted to grow their hair out longer and wanted to be like the Beatles.

The first of the big performances was when I was with a band called The Tree Stumps. We opened for Paul Revere and the Raiders at Public Hall in a Cleveland battle of the bands. In the Tree Stumps, the lead singer, a fella named Woody Leffel, and I then branched off into another band called Renaissance Faire. This was more focused on things like the Doors—more of a West Coast twist. We opened for the Cream on their *Wheels of Fire* tour at Ohio State University.

After that, the original Tree Stumps band had gone through a couple changes—changed their name to Silk and added a fella named Michael Stanley, who is now a pretty famous guy in northeast Ohio. (He is a television personality and still has his bands.) We were produced by Bill Szymczyk, who at the same time was producing the James Gang with Joe Walsh. During that phase we had a record deal with ABC Records. That was when we opened in the region for the Who when they were on the *Tommy* tour in 1971.

So, at the time I thought I was going to be a rock star. And, like the usual cycle, if your band doesn't get a big hit, then eventually the band dissipates and you go off and do other things.

Do you have any stories about opening for those bands?

We only did one show with the Cream. So that was a pretty big charge, but very compressed. With the Who, we opened for them for several shows, so there was more of a progression.

I remember the first night, it was at Ohio University and it was in the gymnasium—and it was the Who! So we set up, did our set, and we get off. And then the Who sets up . . . and it was *the Who!* Holy mackerel! You watch them do their thing and you're impressed, but you're in and you're out and then everybody packs up, and a couple of days later we wind up in Syracuse, New York, and they do it again! I remember just having the impression that, "Oh my God. This is world-class rock 'n' roll, these guys do this every night. They create this much excitement, this level of performance, and then they pack it up and they do it again."

The other thing is, as a bass player at the time, John Entwistle [the Who's bassist] was pioneering this bass guitar string called a RotoSound . . . and this was before it was available in the US. He was bringing them in from England. It was very distinctive for his sound because it had this big, bright guitar clang to it. It wasn't a [*mimics a standard bass guitar sound*] kind of bass string; it was like a big guitar string.

Because he was on tour, he had a lot of them. His road guy was changing strings, and he gave me a set of these RotoSound strings. So I was, like, the first guy around [in the US] to have these strings, and I nursed those things for, golly, maybe a year, trying to keep them alive. They were RotoSounds—I couldn't just run out and buy another pair—and also, I got them from John Entwistle. It was huge for me. It was a great time to be around those guys.

And what was the Braino?

The Braino was the first of my original bands. I went to California for a bit and played with a bunch of bands. I played with Gene Vincent, an old rock 'n' roll guy known for the song "Be-Bop-A-Lula." Then I decided to go back to Cleveland and hunker down, get a tape recorder, and start recording all my own stuff.

In the LA journey I picked up an English drummer named Tony Ashdown. So now Tony Ashdown and I are in Cleveland and we start this band called Braino, which was an original band where I played guitar and synthesizers and I sang. . . . We were writing songs and singing original music. It was in the vein of Pink Floyd; we kind of became the Pink Floyd of Cleveland at the time, and we wound up having this engagement at a place called the Smiling Dog Saloon. We were the house band every Tuesday night. We lived in a band house and we all just jammed all the time.

The interesting part of the Smiling Dog Saloon was that they would book a lot of very famous jazz acts. So the club owner was a curator who was able to pick up pretty famous acts touring from New York to Chicago, and because we just left all of our equipment set up all week for our Tuesday night gigs, Braino became kind of the house sound guys for all the other acts that came through.

At the time we were in quadraphonic. We had our own sound guy who was actually integral to our band; we thought of him as part of Braino. He wasn't just a roadie, because we were using tape playback during our shows and echo. We were doing all kinds of elaborate, experimental stuff, and in a sense he was kind of jamming with us. His name was Brian Risner.

What is quadraphonic sound?

Well, we think of it as "surround sound" today. Basically, there were PA speakers on either side of the stage, and then there were also PA speakers in the back of the room, and part of the thing was to manipulate sound to go around you and have the audience be more immersed in the music.

I heard that you still some have old Braino recordings.

Yes, that's true. There are still Braino tapes that are unreleased from all these live gigs we did that I still have to transfer. Even though my wife wants me to throw them away, I have saved them. They represent an experimental period when I got my first synthesizer and Echoplexes [an analog tape-delay machine]. And I had a Leslie [a speaker system that provides tremolo and swirl effects] on my guitar. I was actually singing and writing songs, and I kind of went out to be the front man for a while.

After the Braino you had a band called Pi Corp, but you also had a store called Pi? How are they connected? Which came first?

Pi the store came out of Pi the band. I had a music store in the Cleveland area with my partner David Yost called Pi Keyboards & Audio. At the time, we were being sort of revolutionary. We did the equivalent of what you'd see now as Pro Audio at Guitar Center. So, rather than things like violins, we would handle the tape recorders and synthesizers, mixers and sound systems, etc.

But that came out of the fact that the Braino had evolved into this other band called Pi Corp. The lineup of Braino had sort of modulated, swapping out our bass player and drummer. So, from Tony Ashdown and some other guys that played with us, we wound up with Guy Bickel (bass) and Denny Geffert (drums). We rented an office above a pawnshop in a really seedy neighborhood in Cleveland, on East 52nd Street. It was cheap, and we used to go there and jam every night and just tape-record our jams. And it was those jams that eventually modulated into the Pi Corp. We didn't play clubs anymore, we just got together and jammed all night. We were just living music.

Then we moved from the sort of jam studio we had into a warehouse on East 25th Street, across from the Agora, which was a very famous rock 'n' roll club. We set up shop there. We had a studio, then we started a synthesizer repair place. And then that became the store Pi Keyboards & Audio.

So this is where it all started for you, both as a composer and sound technician?

Yeah, it was really the start of coming into my own, from being in a cover band or playing in somebody else's band to actually writing my own music and figuring out what was going to be my music. When you hear the Pi Corp stuff, you'll hear me figuring out all the technology, all the stuff that eventually went into my film scores decades later.

And all the Pi Corp stuff came out of jam sessions?

Yes, Pi Corp was entirely spontaneous. We'd literally get together, not knowing what we were going to do, turn our tape recorder on, and just start playing. And some of those jams were amazing. There was no rehearsal or even discussion about what we're going to do. We'd just start listening to each other and going for it. . . . Guy Bickel took all those jams and edited them down; there is actually a Pi Corp website and a CD that's available.

So if we were to listen to the CD, we would be hearing inspiration happening?

Correct.

So how do you go from jamming every night and owning a music store to working on sound and music for movies in Hollywood?

Brian Risner, Braino's sound man, had gone on to work for a jazz band called Weather Report. Around 1976 he invited me to go out as a roadie-tech guy to take care of all the synthesizers for Joe Zawinul, the keyboardist. He had five or six synthesizers that had to be tuned up every day. They were studio gear, and putting them on the road required somebody that knew about maintenance, etc. So it was actually the Weather Report association that got me to Los Angeles.

Then, around 1979, the band went into a long studio phase; there wasn't a lot of roadwork. So I started to look for other stuff going on, and another Cleveland connection, a friend of mine, Pax Lemmon, who was this big burly biker character, was working at Paramount films in the transfer department, just making copies of tapes. One day when he was just doing his job, two guys that were standing behind him said, "We need someone that knows about synthesizers."

Pax turned around and said, "Oh, man, you need to talk to my buddy Alan. He works for Weather Report." And they kind of looked at him weird and said, "Is that the one at eleven o'clock or seven o'clock?" Nonetheless, he gave them my number and they called me up. I went down there and asked them what they were doing. They said, "We're doing *Star Trek: The Motion Picture* [1979], and we need someone that has the skill set to come make us space and futuristic sound effects."

The task was to make the sound of the *Enterprise* going from Warp 1 to Warp 7, as well as some other effects. I made an audition tape on my little Prophet 5 synthesizer, in my dining room, with a four-track recorder, and that tape became the sound of the *Enterprise*. So, without ever expecting to be in the movie business, that sound-effects job for *Star Trek* launched my career in film.

Well, they were very pleased with my work, and I went on to do five more *Star Trek*s. I was one of the staples in what we called the "special sound effects" area—someone that would make a library of things you couldn't record with a microphone. Today we call it "sound design." So that got me launched.

Then the picture editor of that first *Star Trek* film, a fella named Todd Ramsay, his next movie was *Escape from New York* [1982], with John Carpenter. He knew me as a sound effects guy, but I kept giving him cassettes of my music, etc., etc. It turns out that on *Escape from New York* John was looking for other collaborators, potentially for the score. So, very casually, I just invited John to come over to my little rented house in Glendale.

I had everything set up in the dining room, and John came over. We spent a few hours hanging out. I played him some sounds and some music, and as casual as that, John goes, "Yeah, let's do it." All of a sudden, I was now working with John Carpenter, on *Escape from New York*, on my first film score. So I've been very blessed on my journey.

It was a good relationship. John Carpenter had his movies and his visions, and he's John Carpenter. You can't take away from that. He's also a musician. He plays, but he didn't want to know anything about the technology. So initially I was totally responsible for the studio, the recording, all the mechanics of it as the engineer. But because I can also play, he shared with me the ability to write things and get involved. He was very supportive and he was a really good friend. So that is what got me launched in film music.

Once you moved past the position of just being the engineer and you two were actually collaborating on the music itself, how did it work? How did you write together?

It was pretty improvisational. It's John Carpenter and it is *his* movie. Pretty much, the sessions would start out with him playing first. He lived the movie and he knows what he wants, so he would do the first pass, very often.

The guy is a master at themes. (Obviously, the *Halloween* [1978] theme itself was from before I ever met him.) He really understands simplicity—maximum simplicity, I guess. He gets more out of a little bit of music than some people get out of a whole lot of music. Those themes, the *Escape from New York* theme [*sings the theme*], that's John Carpenter. I'm the orchestration [*sings a different part of the theme*]. He would come in with a sketch for a basic stab [short music cue], then I'd jump in and produce around him. I'd add more stuff to it, and that was kind of the way we worked.

On *Escape from New York* I brought in the idea of actually running a videotape of the film. Which seems like, "Well, of course you do that," but this was long before that was common. Before that, he would score literally to a stopwatch. He would need a piece of music that was two minutes long, and then you'd figure out a tempo and you'd record a piece, and later on put it up against the picture and see what happened. And now we're actually putting up the movie and watching and playing music to it.

He really enjoyed that; he referred to that as the "electronic coloring book." So now we could improvise against picture, which then was the basis of how we did it and the way many people do it today. But again, remember this is 1980—we were ahead of the curve.

To the best of your knowledge, that hadn't ever been done before?

Well, it would've been done on a scoring stage, with 35mm film, an orchestra, and a big budget. But for a couple of guys in a small home studio environment, no, that hadn't occurred yet.

Were you familiar with his work before you met him and began collaborating with him?

No, it was pretty much just guy-to-guy level, and he liked that. You know, if someone comes into the room and they're all impressed with John Carpenter, he kind of classifies them as a fan as opposed to a collaborator. So we were just two guys doing our thing.

Shortly after *Escape from New York,* you worked on *Halloween II* [1981].

We had done *Escape from New York* and he was very pleased with what we had come up with. For what it was at the time, it was groundbreaking in its own way. His next assignment was *The Thing* [1982]. I remember one of the days that we were wrapping up *Escape from New York* and he was talking about what he was going to do next. He said, "Alan, I've got this movie *The Thing* that I'm going to be doing. And at the same time they want to do the sequel to *Halloween*. So you're going to do *Halloween*—I'm too busy!" So that was it. I was assigned to be the *Halloween II* guy by John.

The process was, I had these iconic Carpenter themes from the original *Halloween*, and I used his original score as a model. Then I rebuilt against it with my own sonic textures, and a couple of times I had to write some music for places in the movie where there wasn't anything that worked from the first *Halloween*. I had to make a couple new things up, but for the most part the producers just wanted to recycle his iconic score, because this was the sequel, and in a sequel you want to duplicate as much as you can. That all transpired without him being around. I was just on my own and worked pretty much directly with [producer] Debra Hill on that, and Rick Rosenthal, the director.

It sounds like your solo process on that film wasn't all that different from when you worked directly with Carpenter and you would orchestrate around his existing themes. It seems like the biggest difference in the case of *Halloween II* was that he just wasn't in the studio with you.

Yeah, that would be accurate. As we continued on over the next five or six years he gave me more and more space to add into the scores.

Rick Rosenthal was a first-time director when he made *Halloween II*. Reportedly, there was a bit of conflict between him and Carpenter during postproduction, resulting in some recuts. What was it like working with a first-time director, and did any of that conflict affect your job?

Rick was totally open to whatever I added. Also, the *Halloween II* score was essentially the first *Halloween* score revisited, with more orchestration and new sounds synthesizerwise. There were standard cues that were going to be used again in the second movie to make it a sequel. I didn't participate too much in any sort of tension. I was a service provider; I turned in my stuff and those guys dealt with it in editing.

A score that I like a lot is *Halloween III: Season of the Witch* [1982]. I've heard that you are particularly fond of it as well.

Yes. *Halloween III* still stands out as one of those things that really hit the mark in what we will call synthesizer scoring. I remember when we started *Halloween III* . . . (you have to remember, this would be after *The Thing*) . . . John comes over and we have a little warm-up, just getting comfortable in the studio, and we play the latest Tangerine Dream LP, just to see what's the latest in electronic music. John looks at me, and he says, "Well, Alan, this is going to be pretty easy. We're just going to rip off ourselves—which means, let's just do what we did last time and do more of it."

That opening sequence with the chase was really our first thing. I dialed up the sequencing [*sings a bit of the theme*] and he really liked it, because it wasn't *Halloween* but it was *Halloween*-ish, and that was the launch point. From then on we just basically improvised against those textures to create that score. For most people, that movie was not successful, because it didn't have Michael Myers, etc., etc. Had it not been called *Halloween* and just been called *Season of the Witch*, it would've been a fine movie. So it just wound up being what it is, but the score lives long afterwards as one of the most popular scores that we did.

Carpenter produced *Halloween III* and you two collaborated on the score. How involved was director Tommy Lee Wallace in the musical process?

John had a band in college, which was Tommy Lee Wallace, John Carpenter, and Nick Castle, called the Coupe De Villes. So they were already buddies from way back in the *Dark Star* [1974] days. Tommy came by. Still, the scoring was John and I. But then we came to the Silver Shamrock commercial [an insidiously catchy TV commercial that plays in the film] . . . Tommy came over, and Tommy and I dialed that one up.

It is kind of funny, because Debra Hill said, "I don't want any copyright issues, so I want you to use the melody from 'London Bridge Is Falling Down.'" So . . . [*hums the melody*] that's the melody we used—we knew that was public domain. And then Tommy had a little piano exercise that he dialed up and played in there. The singing is actually Tommy and I, using the chipmunk technique of slowing the tape recorder down, singing it, and then speeding it back up. And the announcer was Tommy. So in the case of that particular cue, it was really Tommy Wallace and myself that created that one.

Ennio Morricone did the score for *The Thing*, but you and Carpenter also recorded some music for the film.

Yes, I was in for one afternoon session. John came over and we did about four cues, which were for when the guy burns up and some of the filler sustain-y things, which I included on the recent rerecording I did. I rerecorded all the Morricone stuff and resurrected the Carpenter cues for a CD. It is all on there.

The Morricone story is, they had him score the first version of the film with Morricone stuff. Now, obviously, John loves spaghetti Westerns, so Morricone was his hero, but there was just something that John was looking for that didn't come in that first pass. So he played Morricone our *Escape from New York* stuff and said, "Can you give me something like this?"

That prompted Morricone to go back in with another keyboardist and design up what is now the very famous "Thing Theme." That came in scoring session number two. And then John came over, and number three was a little supplemental scoring session we did at the very end.

I've always really liked the score to *Christine* [1983]. Can you talk a little bit about recording it?

The score to *Christine*, kind of, is hinted at with those few spare cues that we did for *The Thing*. Chronologically, I did *Halloween II*, John [Carpenter] went off to do *The Thing*, and after that he did *Christine*. So there was a bit of what the studio was going to sound like—the tonalities and the way things were going to work—previewed in those [*Thing*] supplemental cues.

Christine was a little different, because it had all that rock 'n' roll in it. So when the soundtrack album came out for *Christine*, the music by Carpenter and myself was only one or two cues. The rest was "Bad to the Bone" and all these rock 'n' roll things. . . . (At the time it was an LP, before CDs.)

Only later on, and just sort of as an afterthought, I had taken all our score cues and put them into an assembly. And then somebody came back a couple of years later and said, "What about all that music you guys did? We'd like to do another *Christine* album and just put that stuff on it." So that's what we have today, and I think that particular CD is still played and referred to often. Scoringwise there were a lot of things that didn't have rhythm in this case. There were a lot things that were just sustain—drones and tension—and only the *Christine* chasing stuff is where there is the sequencer action music.

People have come back to it. In fact, I think there is a *Christine* convention coming up this year in North Carolina, and they are going to have the car and some of the actors. I've been invited to come and maybe do a live performance of that score. So it lives on.

Did knowing that the film was going to be full of licensed rock music affect how you guys approached the score?

I think we approached it in the same fashion as the other scores. But because we knew that stuff was going to be there, we did a lot less. Let's say that sometimes a film has forty-five to sixty minutes' worth of score, but I think with that one it might be only about thirty to thirty-five minutes. There were a lot of temporary placeholders in place, because of the rock 'n' roll.

Were the tones of those early Carpenter scores dictated by budget, or was that exactly what you guys were striving for?

I think what we were striving for we got. We knew that there wasn't going to be an orchestra or live players. It was all going to be done with analog synthesizers and drum machines and guitars, which gave some of it a little rock flavor. So I think we achieved what we wanted. I don't think there were real budgetary constraints from that standpoint. In those days, we were just doing it, and we were happy with what was coming out.

I've heard both you and Carpenter refer to the score for _Big Trouble in Little China_ [1986] as being bigger and more ambitious than the other scores you worked on together. Can you talk a bit about that score and why it was different?

Sure. The picture drives the music, so in this case there was a lot more scope. It actually did have some humor in it as well as some scary stuff, action, and some Asian culture–influenced stuff. And at the same time there was a little bit more time to do it: Normally we had six to eight, maybe ten weeks to score something; in this case it was a little more elaborate because we had fourteen weeks. Also, we had a rock tune that we were going to do. You know the _Big Trouble in Little China_ theme song was included. That involved Nick Castle and Tommy Lee Wallace in the Coupe De Villes production. So that was kind of folded in there.

There was a nexus of technology, too, because this was the first time we had the full flotilla of analog keyboards, digital samplers, drum machines, etc. Everything in the studio was in its heyday. The only piece that was added after *Big Trouble* was the Synclavier system, which was another big digital sampler.

Also, it was the first time that we really realized the power of MIDI [Musical Instrument Digital Interface]: You could push one note on one keyboard and fire, like, nine of them [other synthesizers or samplers] at the same time. The restriction of twenty-four-track tape recording was eclipsed, because it [MIDI] was a multiplier. . . . If it had nine keyboards per pass, multiply that by twenty tracks, you've got 180 instruments. It got a lot bigger and a lot more elaborate.

Also, because we had more time, we had the luxury of finishing and then having a chance to go back to the beginning and review what we did. A lot of the times you do this stuff and then you just turn it in. In this case it actually sat; it had a chance to kind of ruminate, and we were able to take some of the things that we later came up with toward the end and then salt-and-pepper that back into the beginning to make more cohesive textures and themes happen. There was just more production.

I've heard from a few film music composers that often they remember a particular score because of a particular new piece of equipment they had at the time that they did it. With *Prince of Darkness* [1987] it seems that you and Carpenter are experimenting with a lot of choral effects and tones. Was this due to a new piece of equipment for you, or was the use of those sounds dictated by the film's content being religious in nature?

It was a combination. Every score through that decade had some new piece of equipment that gave us another texture that wasn't in the last one. And because I was really into equipment—the latest, greatest—I tried to get something new for each show. That gave us a new "something." The one that appeared in *Big Trouble in Little China* was called the Prophet VS [synthesizer], which had digital oscillators but analog processing in it. That keyboard had a couple of sounds that were actually featured in *Prince of Darkness* prominently.

As for digital samplers, we had a Kurzweil 250 and then some Emulators [E-MU Systems' digital sampling keyboards]. I think at that point I was up to the Emulator 2, and so we had choral samples, and we were able to take advantage of the choral samples in the *Prince of Darkness* score because the film had the semireligious overtones—you know, with the return of the Devil and stuff like that. So it was a combination of content and equipment.

One of the things I find interesting about John Carpenter is that in interviews, he consistently downplays the passion or artistry that he has for filmmaking and music composing. He often says things like, "It was a job, so I did it," or, "I was the fastest and the cheapest guy to do it, so I did it." Did you guys at least have some fun when you worked together?

Oh, absolutely. In fact, a couple of times he told to me that the most fun he would have when making his own movies was coming to the studio and being the composer, because for him it was like being on a vacation. The attention level and whatever it takes to write a movie, go out and shoot it, get it into editing—that attention level went way down, and he could literally turn the phone off and be just a composer for a little while and relax.

I'd say that we had a lot of fun. They were some of the greatest times in my memory: just working with him, just he and I in a room working on these various movies, doing our stuff. And I think that is reflected in what comes out on the score. It was not a job. It didn't feel like a job at all.

Is there a specific reason why your collaboration with John Carpenter ended?

I think just directional changes. John had a major personal, directorial, etc., change in about the beginning of the 1990s. And I think you see differences in his movies. So he elected to get new people. Some people were in, some people were out. He made some changes, etc., etc. So we just haven't worked together since then. Not that I wouldn't love to, but he's the director. He decides what he wants to do.

You went on to score many films on your own.

Yes.

In your opinion, what is the job of the film score composer?

Making music for a movie is musical storytelling. You could go all the way back to classical stuff like *Peter and the Wolf* [composer Sergei Prokofiev's children's tale for orchestra and narrator]. There's a theme for every character. You weave your themes based on what the character is doing in the most basic way. In fact, if you think about it, in some ways the original film music composers were the classical composers that were telling a story entirely with music, with symphonies and stuff like that. This is all translated forward to make music for images, and that's where I have strength. Having been an artist/painter-type of guy prior to getting bit by rock 'n' roll and then winding up in the film industry, when I watch images, the music that goes with those scenes just kind of flows.

Among the films you've scored, you did several of the *Halloween* sequels. When you're scoring sequels, a lot of the groundwork is already laid down for you, and in the case of the *Halloween* films you've had some pretty iconic music to work with. Does that make your job easier? Or is it a bit of a hindrance? Or both?

It is kind of a double-headed dragon, because the producers definitely want the familiar *Halloween* themes in there. The challenge is, How do I redo this theme again and make it somewhat different? (Otherwise, why record it again? Just use the old music.) Especially on *Halloween 4* [1988], because it was my first adventure to depart from what was the John Carpenter *Halloween* stuff and give my own take on it, and make it a lot more, let's say, Alan Howarth-ish.

And that comes from my influence as the rock guy—the Who, Pink Floyd, King Crimson, and the Moody Blues and stuff like that, and putting these other textures in. And also being a sound effects guy in parallel to that, doing the sound design for the *Star Trek*s and *Raiders of the Lost Ark* and going on to do some sound effects, even for the Carpenter things.

For instance, I did the spaceship in the beginning and some of the stuff for the dogs in *The Thing*, you know, just as sound effects. Sometimes I'd integrate the sound effects into the score. Because I had both skill sets, I started to combine the two things and it came out really nice. It had nice textures.

On *Halloween 5* [1989], the director [Dominique Othenin-Girard] really wanted to go "back to the beginning"; he really wanted a piano-oriented score. At that time, technologywise, I had just acquired a Synclavier system—the first of the really big digital samplers, where you could have a lot of sampled sounds. So, opposed to only the analog synthesizer stuff, we started to include high-quality samples. For the theme, I had this giant piano: I overdubbed the piano two or three times on top of itself—you would've needed sixty fingers to be able to play these parts.

Then there was *Halloween 6* [*The Curse of Mike Meyers* (1995)]. In the first version, I did my thing and I made it more rock. I started adding some drums and some electric guitars and taking it in another direction. The director and ultimately the producers and the Weinsteins at Dimension Films wanted a different ending. So there was ending number one and then there was ending number two, which I redid for the new cut. There were actually two versions of the score.

Do you think that music in horror films plays a different function than in other genres, or is it all the same?

Functionally, it is pretty much the same. Although in a horror movie we've also got a lot of scenes where there is nothing being said: It is all images, and the music is telling us to be scared or to beware that something nasty is around the corner.

I think one of the most difficult things to score is comedy, because it has been done so many different ways. What is funny and what is cliché and how you make all that stuff work is a bit of a challenge. I remember, not scoringwise, but doing sound effects for the *Airplane!* series back in the 1980s. The only way to play that stuff from a sound standpoint is to actually play it seriously. You wouldn't put in *boinks* and *dinks* like a cartoon; you play it like it is real, and let the circumstance be what you laugh at.

The content dictates. The music needs to be appropriate. Or sometimes it plays *against* what you are watching: You can have scenes where the director has decided that what you're seeing is horrible, but you want to put a classical piece underneath it to sort of play against it, in juxtaposition. It is on a case-by-case basis.

But horror, for sure, has sort of a standard way to do it, which is take everything very seriously and load tension, then really play contrast. Don't keep the music on "10" the whole way. Sneak around, be quiet. Actually let it go quiet, or have no music at all, and then when something big happens—*boom!* Something loud and scary happens.

Can you talk more specifically about the job of the sound designer?

The term "sound designer" was a title that was a little taboo at the time I started, because it implied that you would be in charge as well as be creative.

Traditionally, in a movie the soundtrack has three divisions: There's the music, clearly; there's all the dialogue, which is everything everybody says; and then there's the sound effects.

The sound effects have three subsets: First, the big sound effects—things blow up and things crash and fall down and get shot, etc. Then we have the backgrounds, which is the ambience that goes with each scene. And then there are a lot of smaller, detailed sounds that are called Foley effects, which are the subtle effects that help pump up the reality [e.g., footsteps, squeaky hinges, etc.].

When I came on board on the first *Star Trek*, my role was called "special sound effects." So, in those three categories there was still this new category of sounds that you couldn't record with a microphone, because they didn't exist; they had to be *created*. Much like Industrial Light & Magic [the famed visual effects firm founded by George Lucas] was specializing in special visual effects, I was doing special sound effects. That's where the role popped up on *Star Trek*, and I went on to do six *Star Trek*s [films].

As I mentioned before, my role was to make the sounds of the *Enterprise* and the lasers and the transporters, etc. These were all things that had to be created, and they were made with elements and layers of other sounds. So I came on as a specialist. To call yourself a "sound designer" meant that you were sort of a boss, and I was at this point a service provider.

Over the 1980s and in the '90s, I grew into being a sound designer-sound supervisor. I had a crew and was in charge of the entire movie. A good example of that was on *Army of Darkness* [1992]. That was soup-to-nuts: I worked from the beginning, I made what we call temp dubs of the movie for screening purposes, and went through the whole nine yards of dialogue, sound effects, Foley, took it all the way through the mix stage, got it all mixed, and made the final soundtrack. Joe LoDuca had done all the music, and in this case I was across the table from him, providing the sound design.

Today, *everybody* is a sound designer; it became the generic term. The term was actually coined by Walter Murch on *Apocalypse Now* [1979]. I think that was the first time that title was used. His view was that the sound designer was kind of like the production designer—the guy that got the overview of what this movie is supposed to sound like and contributed to the entirety of it, as opposed to some specialist. That is where it evolved from.

Now everyone uses the term "sound design" to mean sound effects . . . whether it is just a little bit of sound effects work or being the sound supervisor. Sometimes I use both credits, sound designer and sound supervisor, to make it clear that I ran the show as well as created the cool stuff. On a lot of movies, though, I was only a sound effects specialist (which we call "sound designer" today), where I got to do all the cool stuff—whether it is the sound of the silent drive in *The Hunt for Red October* [1990] or the weird noises from *Dracula* [1992], or the *Back to the Future Part II* [1989] hoverboards.

Directors often would gravitate to a direct dialogue with me, telling me what they wanted, and the sound supervisors, who were really the bosses, in some ways got a little concerned about that. In some ways they felt it usurped their authority. So I had to be careful in my communications with the directors when I was part of a crew. It is kind of like the captain is supposed to steer the ship, and then the owner of the ship shows up and starts talking to one of the guys down in the engine room. There were some politics to that, but in the end I'm a pretty nice guy and people seem to like me, and I never meant any harm. So I was able to manage that stuff.

Do you approach sound design in the same way that you do composing music for film?

Yes and no. Sound effects are still music to me. One of the great definitions of *music*, in the broadest terms, is that it is the alternation of sound and silence. With that broad heading—working with sound, whether it's music or sound effects—it's the same equipment, it's the same studio. It's just applying it differently.

Certainly [with] sound effects, as far as a discipline, there are a lot more layers and often I was part of a crew. It is not something you can sit in a room and do by yourself. Whereas as a composer, you could sit there by yourself or with one other person and crank out a great product. . . .

For me—remember I mentioned earlier that I was an art student—when I finally started to make music or sound for images, that's where I really found my strength. As opposed to a guy that could write a three-minute song and make it a hit in rock music, it took a little longer for me to drift around until I bumped into the idea of soundtracks. And then, all of a sudden, that's where I had special talent. That is what I knew how to do. So when I'm watching a film, what goes with it sonically just is there. It's not a head-scratcher, I just kind of know.

In your experience, do the sound designers and sound editors collaborate with the composers, or is there not much communication there?

In that very first *Star Trek* movie, when I was Mr. Sound Effects, obviously there was a very big crew, and the composer was Jerry Goldsmith. It was my first film, and I didn't really know what I was doing, I was just making stuff and turning it in. But I did go to a couple of the scoring sessions. I was very privileged to go. Bruce Botnick was the recordist and I knew Bruce, so I was allowed to see the score go down.

Jerry Goldsmith was one of the great ones. That was a big education for me . . . and it did give me a chance to see what the music was doing and then consider what opportunities there were in the music.

There was no communication between the music department and the sound effects department at that time, so basically you arrived at the mix with a lot of duplication. Big moments in the movie were covered both by sound effects and by music, and there needed to be some decision as far as who was going to prevail. When we got to *Star Trek II* [1982] it was James Horner, and I knew James from working with him on *Battle Beyond the Stars* [1980] before. I'd actually call him up and talk about, "In this part, where this is happening, what are you doing musically? This is what I've got sound effects–wise."

And I carried that through *Star Trek III* [1984]. As an example, we had planets blowing up and earthquakes and stuff like that on that film. So there was some discussion about Horner staying out of the low register because we knew the sound effects were going to occupy that register. We sort of got into frequency range deals: He would keep higher and thinner because he knew the planet was blowing up.

I did get to speak with Jerry [Goldsmith] about it also, regarding the first *Star Trek*, but it was unfortunately after the fact. During that film's climax, I'm pretty sure something blew up, or a final *kaboom* happened. I think it was with V'Ger [a massive *Star Trek* life form]. Visually, we see this bright explosive thing, and at the same time Jerry is putting all his juice on that explosive moment. It was a train wreck as far as how much sonic space was going to be occupied by music and sound effects at the same time. In this case, sound effects lost. It became a musical moment.

Later on, I remember having that conversation with him [Goldsmith] and saying, "We can peacefully coexist by letting the sound effects go *boom* and then creating a piece of the music that goes right after the boom, that tells us how we are supposed to feel about what just blew up. Is it a good thing or a bad thing?" He kind of internalized that and later integrated that into how the music gets written. It was a good lesson for his side as well as ours to just talk about it.

So, yes, there is an exchange there with the composers sometimes, but often the music department will do their thing and the sound effects department will do their thing, and the only time you know what is coming at you is at the mix stage, when everyone is already expecting to have 100 percent of the soundtrack available for their material.

I remember an incident on *Poltergeist* [1982]; this is another film that both Jerry [Goldsmith] and I worked on. There was this scene where I had created a whole "ghost chorus" in full surround. If you remember, at one point there was a TV monitor, and we saw all these sort of druid-looking ghosts coming through the room. And I had made this very elaborate ghost chorus and quadrophonic sound-effects track.

When we were on the dub stage, everybody was loving it and it was cool. Then Spielberg shows up and they open up Jerry's score, and in this case, Jerry's score took an entirely different viewpoint than this scary "ghosty" thing. It was all about the relationship between the mother and the daughter; it was about love and about "Mommy, Mommy."

So they decided to dump all the stuff I had done. I didn't know what the music was going to do, and it turns out my stuff wasn't supporting that viewpoint. . . . In the world of sound effects, you have to be ready to have your stuff thrown out and just move on. It is ultimately the vision of the director and the creatives as to what is the story and how is it going to be told.

Now, there have been a couple movies where I was both sound designer and composer, and in those cases the jobs had to be staggered. I can't be both at the same time. So if there is a chance to be the composer, do the score, turn it in, or have it mostly completed and then jump over to being the sound effects guy, cool. But otherwise it is sort of a train wreck: One or the other is not going to be as good as can be, because you're trying to do two things at once.

As a sound effects specialist, you've worked on some pretty iconic horror films. *Poltergeist*, **which you just spoke a little bit about, is a perfect example. There are a lot of stories about the making of that film and the nature of director Tobe Hooper and writer-producer Steven Spielberg's collaborative process. Can you tell me a little bit more about working on that film?**

Sure. As a sound effects specialist, working with the sound supervisors, who were Stephen Flick and Richard Anderson, you come in during postproduction. The movie is already filmed. So Tobe Hooper has done his thing and is already gone. Now comes in Steven Spielberg, [producer] Frank Marshall, and [editor] Michael Kahn, who are the principle post [postproduction] guys figuring out what to do with this movie. There was a lot of exchange in the area of concepts, and then there was a lot of going to ILM [Industrial Light & Magic] and having them make the visual effects to help fill in the holes in the story and make things go.

One good story is, I'm sitting in what we call a spotting session, which is where we're planning for sound effects design, and we come to the discussion about what is the sound of the Carol Anne voice. If you remember the film, at one point the girl is missing—she's in another dimension. In this particular scene, we're going to have her come through the scene only as a sound. We're going to hear her voice from another dimension, and the family is going to react to it. So there is a character in the room that we don't see, we only hear.

That particular task fell on my desk. I'm sitting in a room with Spielberg, Frank Marshall, and Michael Kahn, and I say to Spielberg, "Okay, Steven, what are you thinking?" His direction to me, and it is just Spielberg being Spielberg, is, "Kind of like, Earth to Venus." Of course, it is Steven Spielberg. So I look at him, and go, "Oh, that's a great idea. Yeah, I got it."

I walk out of the spotting room and I'm in the hall and I'm starting to sweat—I have no idea what he's talking about. I don't know what I'm going to do. If I don't get this right, I am dead in this town. There's the heavy burden of, "You know you have to deliver on this one, kid. You'd better get it together."

So I went back to my studio, and for about ten days I fooled around with everything that was sort of the "normal" stuff. I didn't have a lot of digital processing at that point; I think an Eventide Harmonizer might've been the only digital processing I had. Everything else was tape or synthesizer processing. . . .

Although I had filters, and fooled with some of that, none of it was really coming together. And then one time I was riding from my house in Glendale back to Hollywood, and this old Led Zeppelin tune, "Whole Lotta Love," comes on the radio. If you remember, in the middle of that the music stops and it goes into a break with Robert Plant. And when he goes to sing, there is this little, quieter pre-delivery of the line. So it would be, "You need . . . YOU NEED! My love . . . MY LOVE!" And I went, "That's it—Earth to Venus! That's what he's talking about!" It's a pre-echo, something you hear coming from a distance and then arriving at our location. It is the opposite of an echo, it's a backwards echo. So that's the inspiration for what turned out to be reverse reverberation and pre-echo.

I took that inspiration and came back to the studio, took the Carol Anne lines, put them on my analog tape recorder (which was a Teac eight-track that I had modified so that I had a varying speed that went zero to thirty ips [inches per second] on it, so I could manually just go up and down on the speed of the tape). I played everything backwards into an old spring reverb, fooling around with the speed and stuff like that, making separate passes for the left and right channels, so that it was a little wonky and disjointed and there were pitch changes in it. Then I made another pass going forwards, so I had another "reverberage" on it. So I had forward and reverse reverb that I put onto her voice.

I played it for them, and that was it. They called it the Doppler Effect [referencing the pitch-change phenomenon one commonly experiences with the horn or siren on a passing train or ambulance]. It was the idea of the voice flying through the room.

It saved the day and saved my career. . . . You just don't know where it is going to come from. You're just floating around, looking for ideas. And then it made sense. That's what Steven was talking about: "Earth to Venus."

Had you not been in the car listening to the radio at that time, you might not have gotten it.

Exactly. There's no schedule for inspiration. You're feeding the dog or cutting the grass or driving in your car and listening and observing other things, and then it triggers a thought that goes, "Oh, that's the solution!" Sometimes that's where it comes from.

Sometimes you're sitting down and you're just trying to grind it out, and it's just not coming right then and there. Mark Isham [composer for *Point Break* (1991), *The Mist* (2007), and *The Crazies* (2010)] told me that one of his techniques when he's just stuck for a theme is, he sits at the keyboard and he turns the sound off and just plays the keyboard with no sound whatsoever, and records that. Then he plays it back to see what happened. It is just his way to stimulate a new idea. So there are all kinds of different techniques.

What was it like working with filmmaker Don Coscarelli on *Phantasm II* [1988]?

I was a sound effects specialist, I wasn't involved on the entire soundtrack. I came in on *Phantasm II* as the guy who tried to make some effects for the silver ball thing: You want to make that ball deadly and nasty. You couldn't get rid of that thing. So when it was flying around, what noise did it make? Those were the effects I was doing.

Equipmentwise, that was still fairly early on, so there were a lot of analog things. I think my only digital sampler was an Emulator 1 at the time, which had a total of four seconds of eight-bit sampling. Don came by for one or two sessions and gave me some direction. I made some stuff for him. There was one sound that he said, "Hey, that was really cool. Can you give me a little more of this or that?"

It turned out that I had a personal connection to Don through my brother-in-law, who went to high school with him in Long Beach. So there was a little affinity there that was, like, "Hey, you know my brother-in-law," and stuff like that. Actually, I saw Don recently on this last movie that he did, *John Dies at the End* [2012]. We just said "hi." He's a man of passion. He has the same challenges as anyone who has had a long career: Every new thing is held up against the standard of everything you've done before that. You can't really mess around. The reviewers are merciless, they'll nail you, so you have to top yourself every time. And if you're not up to the challenge or you get slammed, then it is very frustrating.

I once interviewed Bruce Campbell about his role as a producer on the *Evil Dead* films, and he revealed to me that he really liked to be involved in the postproduction and the sound design of those films. Did you find that to be the case when you worked on *Army of Darkness*?

Oh yeah, Bruce was with me the whole time. He had a lot of input.

As the sound designer and sound supervisor for that show, I was involved in creating the effects and then also going through the mechanics of getting them all built. It was a bit of a protracted schedule, but I remember especially in the beginning, when I was creating effects, Bruce would come over. We were doing what we call temp dubs, or temporary sound effects tracks for screening purposes, etc.

Bruce was really involved with me in creating all of that stuff. We made a library of effects that would later be put back into the final movie. . . . He'd come over and hang and have a lot of input. We'd open a microphone and he'd be making noises with his mouth—breathing and grunts and groans. He even had his own collection of taped sound effects from the original *Evil Dead* [1981] that he brought to show certain creaks and rope pulls and impact sounds that were actually done on a Foley stage. He'd say, "Hey, give me something like this." So they were used as indicators for communication, to say, "Let's go in this direction."

He was a lot of fun, and he just wouldn't let it go. Even at the final mix, we're trying to finish the movie and all of a sudden he's going, "Oh no, open up a microphone; I have one more breathing to put on that one spot there," or one more grunt. And you'd kind of look at him, like, "Bruce, man!" He was very involved and it shows. He enjoyed it.

I think *Army of Darkness*, even though it was really "*Evil Dead 3*," unfortunately hit a bump in the road when it was time to come out. It got caught up in a dispute between Universal and Dino De Laurentiis over a *Silence of the Lambs* [1991] sequel. So the movie didn't come out until the *Silence of the Lambs* issue was resolved. We finished it and then, like, a year later, it came out. So a lot of the momentum that we all felt for it just kind of all died by the time it came out. Which was a drag, but things like that happen.

So, during a lot of that time that you and Bruce Campbell were working on the sound, was Sam Raimi working on the picture edit?

Yeah, Sam was involved with the editing, whereas Bruce was handling the sound pretty much. They split up the duties.

Your collaboration with Carpenter was unique, in that you were making film scores with the films' director. When you're working with other directors, do you find it difficult to create music to help fulfill someone else's artistic vision?

Sometimes directors are also musicians or have musical direction or talent. One of the directors I've worked with a lot, Anthony C. Ferrante, just got his launch with *Sharknado* [2013]. I worked with him for years before that. Anthony is enough of a musician that he'd come into the studio and he'd really get pretty involved, and occasionally want to push down the black-and-white notes because he had an idea for something that he wanted to try.

Also, and this isn't happening to me currently, but prior to this, I would sometimes get something that would have what we call a temp dub on it. They had already cut in music from other films for the purposes of screening, and they kind of really like what they've got. So now there's at least a template as to where they want to go. Now you have an artistic choice: "Well, I'll just give them what they want," or, "I now have to top that and give them something that they can't even imagine existed."

It's on a case-by-case basis. If I agree that the temp music is working, I don't want to be unoriginal about it, but there's a direction where there's a certain tempo or it has a lot of this or that orchestration or whatever it is doing that is kind of working. So you use that as a model or a sketch. But now, being more senior and farther down the line in my career, I have earned the privilege of being myself. People come to have me do *me*—and that's what I do the best, and that's the most fun.

Have you ever run into a filmmaker who is so in love with the temp score that you almost can't please him or her with something original?

It's a political move. Can you throw something at them that tops what they've got, or do you just acquiesce and do something that is like what the temp is? I haven't been in a situation where someone just *insists* on using the temp track that there's no way I can come close or anything like that. That's never happened to me. I've always found a way to satisfy the people.

What was it like working with filmmaker Brian Yuzna on the scores for *The Dentist* [1996] and *The Dentist 2* [1998]?

Brian was good. He let me do my thing, but he came in and literally sat with me, much like Carpenter, through the final scoring process and had a lot of input. He'd say, "Put something here," or, "Put something there. I need something on that look. Give me something here."

So the musical storytelling was really finally defined by Brian and what he wanted those particular scenes to do. I would get eighty to ninety percent of the way there, but then that last ten percent was where Brian really had a lot of input as to what happened here and what happened there: "How do we cut here?" "How do we treat that?" "Do we play against what we're seeing, or is it in concert with what we're seeing?"

He was very much a collaborator in the final stages, and I have to say that it helped. I can't be angry with that. That was the director guiding me as the composer to make the best score for his movie.

When you've scored a film and you really feel like you've gotten to a good place, do you sometimes get frustrated when a director comes in at the end and pushes you for more?

I am sure those moments happen. "I thought we were done, and why are you asking for more?" But they teach filmmakers that in school—to push more. Just when you think you're there, "What else you got?"

Do you have a particular favorite session? Not necessarily your favorite score or use of sound effects, but a session where there

was something about the process that made that session or film your favorite.

In the Carpenter world, I would have to say *Big Trouble in Little China*. It was the most elaborate, it had the most time, it had rock 'n' roll. We had feedback from the studio. They got to listen to stuff and wanted to put more layers into it. It had the most scope in it.

As far as sound effects, because I did six *Star Trek*s, there were several episodes in the world of *Star Trek* that I enjoyed a lot. One was on *Star Trek II* [*The Wrath of Khan*]: I actually got to go to both NASA and Lockheed Skunk Works [official moniker of Lockheed Martin's Advanced Development Program] to record sound effects from all this top-secret stuff. So that was really a behind-the-curtains moment. Sometimes I'd get into areas where I wasn't allowed to see what was there, but the guy that was working with me would let me be out in the hallway and he'd take the microphone in and set it down right next to something that was top-secret or classified. It was okay to record the sound of it, but I wasn't allowed to see what it was.

There were wind tunnels, compression devices. There were all kinds of really neat space simulation stuff. I remember one sound effect that I used a million times after I got it: They had what they called the "Space Vacuum Chamber." It was this big, hydraulically controlled air-pressure "space door." The thing must've been about ten feet across, and it had a mechanically connected door that would go, like [*makes a shhhh sound, followed by a big crash*]. It would seal and suck all the air out to create a vacuum [*makes a suction sound*] for things to be simulated that they were in space. This was all in the test world. And then there was the Mars Rover yard out back, with all these cool things. That was really a bridge between movies and the real future—that was way fun.

For *The Hunt for Red October* we needed a lot of underwater sound, because we had to deal with these submarines and propellers and stuff like that. There were several recording sessions that we did, trying to record things underwater.

We got into this whole study of hydrophones and hydrospheres. The Navy has a top-secret thing called a hydrosphere that is on a submarine. Think of it as thirty-two microphones that all point in a particular direction. So when you see the guy in the movie with the headphones on in the submarine, that's actually a real situation—they use the headphones and they have direction underwater. They're super-elaborate, with EQ and whatnot, to make it sound like you're in air. It doesn't sound like you're underwater, which gives him crystal clear sonic direction.

My brother-in-law had a small boat. So we went out into Long Beach harbor and I was taking, actually, condoms and putting condoms over my studio microphones to make them waterproof and dropping them into the water to record tankers going by and various little things underwater that would happen, just for effects and ambience—water on rocks from underwater, etc.

Also, right around that same time I had a swimming pool at the house that had one of these covers that would actually seal the pool up. (We had little kids and we didn't want them to fall into the pool.) So I had a way to use the swimming pool as a sound effect: I put a speaker up on top of the plastic cover, pointing down into the pool, and I dropped a couple of microphones down into the pool, down onto the bottom. In the studio you have something called a reverb chamber, but in this case this was my "pool effect." I could process sound effects by playing them into the pool and rerecording them through the water. So those odd experiments that you can set up to get some sound effects, all that was a lot of fun. I really enjoyed that.

One of the things I find very interesting about horror movie music is that, perhaps more so than other kinds of film music, it has a very loyal and passionate fan base. In recent year's you've been playing some of the compositions you did with Carpenter live for audiences, and the latest horror fad is collecting special edition reissues of classic horror film scores on vinyl. What do you think it is about horror film music that transcends the films for so many fans?

It's pretty unexpected that these scores from the 1980s that I did with Carpenter, or on my own, would still have a fan base and somebody would care. So that's pretty neat. I was invited to the *Halloween* 30th Anniversary Convention six years ago or so just to speak, and it was my idea to say, "Well, rather than speak, why don't I just play?" They said, "What? You can play?" And I said, "Yeah! I'll bring my MIDI keyboard and my laptop, and I'll play for everybody." They were like, "You'd do that? That's cool!"

So, kind of unannounced, I showed up, and when it was time for me to do my talk, I set up the thing and I played. They loved it! In fact, what happened was, I did it on a Friday and they said, "Wow that was really cool! Can you do it again tomorrow?" So that really launched it, and with that some people put some stuff up on YouTube, and then I actually got a call from an organization in Poland called the Unsound Music Festival.

In that season (I think it was 2010), the theme for their music festival was "Horror Movie Music: The Thrill of a Good Scare." They invited me to come do it again out there. So I went and I performed in Europe. They were super-appreciative and really warm and friendly. Actually, we hooked up with a band over there called Zombie Zombie, out of Paris, that had done covers of Carpenter music, and we've done several shows since then in Europe.

So instead of just playing as a solo artist, I picked up a drummer and a keyboard player—and they already know everything—and we improvise on the themes. That's a lot of fun. I never would've thought I'd be out doing this at this time, but it's a lot of fun and I enjoy it, and I look forward to doing it again.

To answer the other part of your question, the fan base and why horror music has one, I think it is because it tells the story very well, and horror movies, especially, have a lot of music that is kind of hanging all by itself. You've got a scene where somebody is walking around in an empty room or on a dark street, not much is going on, and the music is what says this is a horrible thing or something scary is happening. And people can relate to that.

Myself, ever since I was little, I was always a big fan of Halloween as a holiday, and it has really grown commercially in the last two decades. It is the other big holiday now—you start with Halloween, then Thanksgiving and Christmas. It is that whole festival season stuff and it is just fun to get dressed up and be goofy.

Most of the people that are in the horror movie community are really nice people. They're not cloaked serial murderers. They're people having fun, and there are a lot of people doing it. When I go to these festivals, the fans just come forward and tell stories about this and that and how when the music played etc., etc. They've integrated it into . . . it's sort of a soundtrack element to their own lives. And to meet the people that made it is really a thrill for them. That's cool.

Do you have any plans or a desire to officially tour?

Yeah, that would be great! I would love to do that. I'd love to mount a bigger tour, because right now it is sort of impromptu: I just show up with my suitcase and my laptop and a MIDI keyboard and I play. I've added a lady named Jade Boyd [a video, installation, and sound artist] as a VJ, so rather than just me sitting there playing, I have somebody that does abstract video work behind me, using the scenes from the movies, but not just running the movies. . . . I like that, that's very artsy. A more elaborate, planned-out version of that would be fun, but it takes someone that wants to organize it and get a series of venues together.

Last year I did play more than ever. I played in Atlanta, Ashville at the Mountain Oasis Festival, I played in Brooklyn, and the year before I was in Toronto and Switzerland and also I played in Paris and St. Petersburg and London. So it is spotty, but to mount a tour and go do a whole national thing, that would be fun, especially in the last two weeks of October. That would be the way to do it.

When you perform music live, there is instant gratification from the audience. But making a film is an extremely long process that can take over a year before it plays for an audience. Do you ever see the films you work on with an audience? If so, is it just as gratifying to finally get to see when something you did, months or sometimes a year beforehand, actually works and elicits the response you were hoping for?

Absolutely! There are two moments in every movie: One is the first time you watch it, before you've worked on it at all. You're in the audience trying to think about what's the arc of the movie. Where is this going? Where does my attention need to go once I stop enjoying this and get busy working on it?

Then the other side is, you've done all this work and it finally goes to a theater, and you're just anonymous. Nobody knows whether you've worked on this movie or not, and you get audience reaction to what is up on the screen, and if they laugh or they get scared, or if the reactions that you planned for are the ones that happen. It is really cool. Every now and then you get a situation where you thought it was cheesy and they really bought into it, or you thought it was cool and they thought it was cheesy. It can go both ways.

You never know, but certainly never discount the intelligence of the audience. You can't really bullshit people. They've seen enough, they've heard enough. If what you're doing is too much like other things, then it is not original anymore. Even though you thought it was original, the audience can be, like, "This is just like the last thing I saw. So what?" The idea is to give them a unique experience while watching the movie—to laugh, to be scared, to feel love, to get excited, to be on the edge of their seats because there is some tension. That is what we enjoy in movies.

When you think about movies, it is really the greatest art form in this time, because it involves storytelling, it involves acting, it involves photography, it has to do with sound and music. And at the same time it is all delivered in a real-time fashion. Somebody sits and experiences this story in a compressed way. It takes ninety minutes, whereas to read the book takes you days. Everything is really calculated. There is a whole lot of thought that goes behind it.

One of the other things is the use of music in movies. Carpenter expressed this and I always go back to this. He said, "If there is really good acting taking place, let the actors act. Don't get in the way. Just shut up and let them act and then put music in later on, after all that has taken place." As opposed to having that "too much" factor, where everything is happening all the time throughout the entire show and you just get numb to it, you kind of tune it out. So you have to make good choices throughout the entire process.

Do you have any words of wisdom for people considering going into film music composition or postproduction sound work?

I only get to be in the audience for a particular project once. So the first time I watch it, I forget what my role is; I just actually watch the movie to get kind of what it is and what it is going to be. The next time I do it, I am now on the job, I'm picking it apart. So the only time I really get to enjoy it is on that first pass. I try to savor that and capture those feelings and use them, to replicate them when moving forward, because that's a fleeting moment. You only get one first pass on these things, but that is where it starts, that's the seed. That's when the beginnings of whatever it is going to be happen. So, to anyone else doing this, savor that first pass. Don't let it pass you without some sort of "retainment."

The other thing I've found out, and this is just for me and this comes from the old days of rock 'n' roll: I just record everything and figure it out later. It is not like you're going to sit down and this is going to be the moment of creation. It is back to what we were talking about before. Where does the inspiration, where do the good ideas, come from? You just don't know. You can't plan for a good idea. I think that's the take-away. Just always be open to that it can happen now. Capture everything and be your own editor later.

HARRY MANFREDINI

*"On some level all movies are the same. I always make the joke,
'A horror movie is just a cartoon with knives.' It is just a cartoon
with axes and machetes and more blood, but it is still a cartoon."*

WHEN I TOLD HARRY MANFREDINI that I would like to interview him for an hour, his response was, "Oh, I will talk longer
than that!"

Manfredini, the man who brought us *Friday the 13th*'s "ki ki ki, ma
ma ma," was the first person I interviewed for this project, and I am
thankful that he was. In addition to being one of the most outgoing
people I have ever interviewed, he is also funny and well educated and
is, in the best sense of the term, an open book—full of information and
anecdotes. The ease, enjoyment, and content of my initial interview with
him were extremely encouraging. That interview was one of the things
that fueled my drive to continue moving forward with this book when
the project was still just in its infancy,

In addition to being an industry veteran with over 100 credits to his name, Manfredini is a seasoned jazz saxophonist and a teacher of workshops designed to educate and assist aspiring composers. The intention of the three-plus hours I spent talking to him may have been to gain insight into a professional artist's past works, but the end result was much closer to an invaluable crash course in the creative process, business, logistics, and history of creating music for film.

Coincidentally, the last interview I did for this project was a follow-up with Mr. Manfredini. It brought my journey as this book's interviewer-author full circle.

SELECTED FILMOGRAPHY

1980	*Friday the 13th*
	The Children
1981	*Friday the 13th Part 2*
1982	*Swamp Thing*
	Friday the 13th Part 3
1984	*Friday the 13th: The Final Chapter*
	The Hills Have Eyes Part II
1985	*Friday the 13th: A New Beginning*
1986	*House*
	Jason Lives: Friday the 13th Part VI
	Slaughter High
1987	*House II: The Second Story*
1988	*Friday the 13th Part VII: The New Blood*
1989	*DeepStar Six*
	The Horror Show (aka House III)
1992	*House IV*
1993	*Jason Goes to Hell: The Final Chapter*
1995	*Timemaster*
1997	*Wishmaster*
2001	*Jason X*
2006	*Going to Pieces: The Rise and Fall of the Slasher Film* (Documentary)
2011	*Beg*

One of the things I find most interesting about your story is that you've wanted to score films your entire life. Would you talk a bit about what led to you wanting to do it at a very young age?

Well, it is interesting and it is really funny. It never occurred to me until somebody asked me a similar question and I really started to think about it. I can tell you this: Obviously I am Italian, and I grew up playing the accordion and stuff like that. I used to watch a lot of films with my mom, and for some reason the music always spoke to me. In these cases we're talking about the masters, like Miklós Rózsa, Alfred Newman, Max Steiner, and of course Bernard Herrmann—composers of that stature.

At the same time, I was learning music, and I just found that the drama of it was always appealing to me. Now, I think some of that came from my father, who was a huge Italian opera fan. He listened to a lot of Puccini, and you can't get more dramatic than that. It just had incredible melody, and even though I didn't understand all the Italian, I just felt the passion of the music. My brother, who is about fifteen years older than I am, was really into Stan Kenton and progressive jazz—that was the third influence. So you get those three things and you mix them together, and that's musically where things started to happen for me.

The really strange thing about it is that I remember thinking, "God, I wish I could write music like that." And I used to have this recurring dream/fantasy where I was in this room with a magic piano and the film would be playing in front of me on the wall. This magic piano literally could sound like any instrument that I wanted it to. So if I wanted it be a trumpet, it would sound like a trumpet, not like a piano. . . . Then, one day many years later, I was sitting in my room working and I realized, "Oh my God, this is exactly what I was dreaming." The movie is being projected up in front of me and I'm sitting at a keyboard that can literally make any sound that I want. I went, "Wow, that's kind of scary." So be careful what you wish for, because it can happen [laughs].

I learned to play saxophone and made my living playing the saxophone when I was younger. When I went to DePaul University in Chicago, that is when my head really exploded. Up until then, I just thought Stan Kenton was the end of music, there was nothing more advanced or crazier than that. (This would be, like, the early Sixties.) And then I had friends that would say, Hey, you have to listen to this or listen to that. All at once I heard Stravinky and Bartók and Webern and Pierre

Boulez, and I just went, "Oh my God! I've got a lot of catching up to do [*laughs*]." So then I just immersed myself in all that kind of music and started learning about that.

Then I gave up being a composer for a while, because it just seemed like it was way too hard. I wanted to become a teacher, because I was very much interested in theory and stuff. So I got a master's degree at Western Illinois [University], I got a master's in music theory.

I also learned to conduct at DePaul, very well. One of my teachers hated the way I played the saxophone [*laughs*]. I was a "jazzer," and everyone there was very serious—my sound didn't quite fit in. So he said, "Why don't you conduct?" So I learned to conduct and became pretty good at it. I taught for a few years at Western Illinois and in Chicago, then I got a graduate assistantship at Columbia University in New York as a conducting major. I was going to get my doctorate there.

And that's when film and jingles and everything opened up. I was working as a composer and musician in New York, and I never finished my doctorate. I did all the course work, I did the orals and everything, I just never wrote the dissertation. And then off I went into the land of scoring music.

That was a simple question with a long answer [*laughs*].

At what point during the making of a film do you come aboard, and how much time are you typically given to finish a score?

In some cases I get hired even before the film is shot, in some cases it is almost done. That varies. I've done films where the film was done. It was scored and they were throwing out that score, and they had a release date and it was, like, "Harry, we know you can do this. You only have two weeks. We need seventy minutes of music, and I know you can do it." In other cases somebody will just say, "Hey, we want you to do our film. We haven't shot it yet." And I'll say, "Great! I'll do it."

That varies almost all the time. More often than not, though, it is a picture that is at least in a rough-cut situation. It may not be completely done, but it is in some sort of form.

As far as the time I have to get it done, two weeks is very fast; it is usually three to four weeks. Sometimes you get more. Sometimes, when it is too much time [*laughs*], I have to go slower just to get the pressure up. When you get the juices going, you can really write. Sometimes when they just give you too much time, you go, "Oh, I think I'll watch the Lakers, or go play my saxophone for an hour." There's a certain amount of time that's just about right, and that is usually about four weeks.

Can you talk a bit about your writing process?

I am probably different than most. Well, at least I think I am different. Everyone has his or her own rituals or approach to doing it. You want to know specifically about horror?

I do want to know about horror, but I am also just interested in general in your process.

A horror film is an interesting animal unto itself. Although I've always said, "A movie is a movie. There are only twelve notes, and you can make it funny or you can make it scary or you can make people cry. You can do a lot of things with those twelve notes."

On some level all movies are the same. I always make the joke, "A horror movie is just a cartoon with knives [*laughs*]." It is just a cartoon with axes and machetes and more blood, but it is still a cartoon. I don't like to read the script on a horror film. I want to see the picture for the first time straight through, just like the audience will. It is important for me to see where the jumps are, where the scares are, to see what is really spooky, what is really scary to me, what really makes me leap, how the actual mechanisms of the film are really going to work.

Because you only get to see a film the first time once—by the time you've scored it, you've seen it a hundred times. If you know there is somebody lurking in the closet or behind a tree, the scare is not the same as if you don't know it. So you want to get the visceral feel the very first time, because it is the only time you're going to get it. If you've read the script, it completely pulls the carpet out from under that feeling. The way I would write might be determined by how I react to that. If it really, really scared me, I don't have to worry too much about what I'm going to write, because that is really working. You also have your red herrings. Actually, I try to work harder on the red herrings than I do when something is actually going to happen.

I try to find elements of the script to guide me. If it is a good script, there are signposts along the way. The writer tries to, for the lack of a better term, drop pieces of cheese, or I always say, "It is like corn in front of a chicken": The chicken will just follow the corn as long as you're dropping it.

There are certain parts of the script that are really important, certain thematic things. It might be a magic dagger or, like in *Swamp Thing* [1982], it might be the secret formula that turns you into whatever it turns you into. So there are those elements. I try to find as many of those as I can. Sometimes I find things that even the director doesn't notice. I did a "movie of the week" once where there were all these wheels going around and spinning. It was actually about a guy from prison that was fixated on this woman that wrote children's books. It had to do with Rumpelstiltskin and spinning the wheel. There was a windmill and there were all these things spinning around, and I said, "Wow, you sure have a lot of wheels in this story."

The director was, like, "What do you mean?" I said, "Look, you've got this one and this one and that one. There's all this stuff going around in a circle." So I wrote this underlying ostinato [a repeating musical phrase or motif] of triplets [*hums the phrase*]. There was a melody sitting on top, but there was always this unraveling and spinning thing that drove the story forward, and it matched what you were seeing.

So I try to find all those elements, and I create those—for the lack of a better term—bricks. Even in *Friday the 13th* [1980], I created what some people call a chord—I prefer to call it a sonority—that was the sound of *Friday the 13th*, and it is everywhere. If I told you that there were only two chords in *Friday the 13th* you probably wouldn't believe me, but that is all there are. Everything comes from those sonorities. I think it is one of the reasons why that score is so effective. It is very unique and myopic. It is only about one thing, which is another aspect of that score.

We made the music be a character. I can give you an example: In *Friday the 13th* there's this scene where the girl is setting up the archery equipment, and this goofy guy, the clown, shoots an arrow into the bull's-eye while she's standing there. In any other movie there would've been a huge chord or a scare, and we just let it go with nothing. We made a decision that the music was only going to be for the killer, and that's it. There are really only two places in that whole film where there is music and it is not for the killer.

There's another scene early on in the movie—this would be another place where it is such an obvious place to put a music cue—that we just let go by: The guy that is running the camp is . . . looking at some pictures that Adrienne King (her name is Alice in the movie) had drawn. One of them is of him. He says, "Do I look like this?" She goes, "Well, you did last night." And he just sort of caresses her cheek as she walks away, basically saying that there is a relationship there. And again it would've been an obvious place for a piece of music, on that caress, but no, because we decided on no music unless it was for the killer. Those are decisions that you make. That was specific to that picture.

Was this something that you and filmmaker Sean Cunningham came up with together?

Yes. It was really my idea. . . . To me it was obvious, because you didn't see the killer until Reel Nine, and I needed to get the killer into this movie in Reel One. I told him that was what we should do.

Then of course you have all these POV shots of just the camera moving around and looking. I thought we needed to make it clear to the audience that it was just not the cameraman going nuts—it's the killer, it's the prowler. It was my job to create something that said, "This is not just strange photography, this is the killer." Whenever the killer was present, the music was there and it became associated with the killer. I think it was one of the things that made that picture work.

It is like John Williams's music in *Jaws* [1975].

It's like *Jaws*. In the old days, in the days of [composer Hector] Berlioz, they called it *idée fixe*, the fixed idea of that sound—that particular theme represents that character. [Composer Richard] Wagner had a term for it as well: *Leitmotif*. It's the theme for that character. It's in every opera.

You've talked about the vocal aspects of the *Friday the 13th* score many times. At this point I think every horror fan knows that you took the echoing sounds "ki ki ki, ma ma ma" that we're all so familiar with from the line of dialogue at the end of the film . . .

"Kill her, Mommy."

Can you talk about the process that brought you to that decision?

It was a very early picture in my scoring career. It was probably, like, the fourth or fifth picture I ever scored. As Sean [Cunningham] says, "We found lightning in a bottle." He hit makeup artist and actor Tom Savini on the upswing, he hit me on the upswing, we all hit at the same time. It was magic. We had conversations about this and that, and obviously there was no money for a music budget or anything. It was thirteen players in a basement in New Jersey.

At the time, I was studying a piece by [Krzysztof] Penderecki. I don't even remember what it was now, but it was for a huge orchestra. (I can't emphasize enough that you should listen to this guy's music. It is incredibly dramatic and incredibly powerful.) He had a huge chorus that was singing in Polish, and the one thing that really stood out to me was that at the end of certain words he would have them really emphasize the consonants. With a K or J, it would be, like, *Ka! Ja!* He would emphasize the consonants even more than sometimes singing the vowel, because you can't sing a consonant, you can only pronounce a consonant. It was really quite dramatic.

Then Sean one day says, "Can we get a chorus?" So of course I started laughing. I said, "Sean, we're lucky we can get some players, and you want a chorus in here?"

So, two things: One, I found a gizmo called an Orchestron [the Vako Orchestron, like its more popular competitor, the Mellotron, was a keyboard instrument that played back a library of prerecorded instrument sounds], which is that chorus thing, "awwww." It just sounded horrible, but it was a recorded chorus. I used that, but I knew that that Penderecki thing was incredibly dramatic, the pronunciation of a consonant right up close, as if it is right in front of you. . . .

Once again, the problem was to get the killer into the movie so everybody knew immediately it was the killer. It couldn't just be low, ominous notes; it had to have some kind of immediate effect, just like *Jaws*. It really is just [*hums the theme from* Jaws]—that's all you needed to know. With only two notes you knew it was the shark. We had the same problem, only if I go [*hums the* Jaws *theme again*], everybody is going to laugh. It's not a shark. What has happened is that it has become a cliché, it has become comedy. How many times have you heard *Jaws* in a movie now and everybody laughs?

The thing is, at the time, I'm thinking, "If I do something like that, that would be an immediate sound that grabbed you." So I'm watching the film [*Friday the 13th*] and thinking, "What sound am I going to make?" And that's when I came to the final scene, where Betsy Palmer's mouth is going, "Kill her, Mommy." And it was his voice and then her voice and back and forth, and I thought, "She hears voices! She hears the voice of her son in her head. There it is."

So I took the "ki" sound from the word "kill" and the "ma" sound from the word "Mommy." I said them into a microphone and we ran it through a gizmo, and it was spooky as hell and it worked. Necessity is the mother of invention.

When you look at many of horror's most memorable themes—for example, the themes from *Jaws* or the shower scene from *Psycho* or the 5/4 melody in *Halloween* or your "ki ki ki, ma ma ma" in *Friday the 13th*—they are all fairly simple musical ideas. Why are they so memorable?

They are memorable because a simple musical idea sometimes says it all. What's funny about them is, in a way, they are all ostinatos. An ostinato is a repetitive, motor kind of figure. . . . Think of somebody who is obstinate [*laughs*], they just keep doing the same thing over and over and over again. They're obstinate, and an ostinato will catch you and just not release. [*Sings the theme from* Halloween] It's that figure which is very similar to *Tubular Bells* [a popular Mike Oldfield piece from 1973 that was used in the film *The Exorcist*]. And the theme from *Jaws* is that two-note [*sings the* Jaws *theme*].

It's a machine, it's like a train. It's a thing that just drives forward. It's the same thing with the shower scene from *Psycho* [*sings the shower scene music from* Psycho]. It's the sound of a stab. In *Friday the 13th* it is somebody saying, "Kill her, Mommy." It's a very short thing. It's like a laser that just focuses in on one thing, and it gets into you and it says it in a very short amount of time.

In film you have to have time to say something. If I sang you the love theme from *Vertigo* [1958], it's [*sings the melody*], and then it is just that same rhythm over and over again. It may be different notes, it may be different harmony, but that rhythm is always there. . . .

Rhythm is the lowest element of music; it's the basic thing, like the drum, the first sound. It is like your heartbeat, it's inside of you. So something that is rhythmic usually gets to you much quicker, and in music, especially in film, you have to score your points while you can [*laughs*] or somebody is liable to cut it out [*laughs*].

The film *Halloween* [1978] had been very successful and set a trend that *Friday the 13th* followed. Was there ever any discussion about you doing a somewhat minimalistic score, in the style of John Carpenter, for *Friday the 13th*?

No. I hadn't seen *Halloween*. Here's the real secret: I am not a big horror film fan [*laughs*]. I just happened to be good at it. I think it is because they scare the hell out of me, so I don't go out of my way to see a horror film. But of course now I've seen too many. Now I look at them and I go, "Oh, yeah, this character is not going to make it to the end of the reel; they are only there to be killed." And then, sure enough, *boom*, they're gone.

If I think about what influenced me more . . . This always cracks me up, because people go, "It sounds like *Psycho* [1960] a little." And yeah, it does sound like *Psycho*, because, first of all, that's a good thing. [*Laughs*] If you're going to sound like Bernard Herrmann, you're probably on your way to doing a good thing.

What I'm saying is, there are certain intervals [the distance between two pitches, e.g., an octave is a common interval], if I played you that interval in the shower scene, that high C and a D-flat underneath it, it is [the interval known as] a major seventh—one of the most dissonant and angular sounds there is. . . . So you incorporate that into your own work and people say it sounds like *Psycho*.

Well, yeah, I took elements of what *Psycho* did, but at the same time I took elements of Penderecki, because I used a whole bunch of aleatoric [indeterminate or left to chance] stuff where I didn't even write notes, I just wrote X's and stuff and I told all the players, "Everybody go for a high note, but don't all go for the same note." I just wanted a screech. There aren't any notes there. I gave them six notes to pick from, and I'd say, "Okay . . . you can pick any note you want." So it is aleatoric in that sense.

At the same time, there was a Jerry Goldsmith score not too far removed from that for a film called *Coma* [1978]. It is a great movie; I really enjoyed the movie a lot, and I like that score a lot. So a lot of the ideas and things that I got, I got also from listening to *Coma*. It is a combination of a whole bunch of things, it's not just one thing. You steal from a lot of places, but you make it something unto yourself.

"Bernard Herrmann" is a name that comes up a lot when talking about horror film music. Can you tell me a little bit more about why his music is so influential?

It works. He wrote music that works. . . . He incorporated techniques that come from [Béla] Bartók, that come from the masters. He was a real composer. He was famous as a film composer and he was obviously incredibly talented as a film composer, but he was a studied master. He knew the techniques and the styles of all the great composers.

You can't go wrong with Bartók, you can learn a lot from Bartók. You watch *The Shining* [1980], and it is pretty much scored with Bartók. And you go, "Wow! That music really works." Well, I can guarantee you that Bartók wasn't thinking about *The Shining* when he wrote it, but it damn well worked!

It is the same with Herrmann. No matter what movie you see, the music works. Again, if you take the love theme from *Vertigo*, the orchestration is brilliant. You can learn a lot from just watching two movies that Bernard Herrmann scored, just seeing and listening to what he did: what sonorities he used, the orchestration, the manipulation of thematic material. It's all there. I don't think you can score a film without having something in there that is borrowed from Herrmann. [*Laughs*] If it wasn't Bernard Herrmann, it was something that you got from somebody that got it from Bernard Herrmann. He was at the top of his game.

Going back to *Friday the 13th*, toward the beginning of the film, when the characters are in the truck . . .

The banjo thing?

Yes, the banjo thing.

I had a banjo player come in, he played pedal steel and banjo. I wrote out some changes [musical chords] and said *Go!* and he played. It was supposed to be on the radio in the truck. I don't know why they played it where they did; I guess they didn't have any sound effects for the truck or something. You hear this music as you're coming down the road, and then all of a sudden they cut into the truck and it is louder than the damn dialogue, for Christ's sake. It is supposed to be on the radio! They could've at least given it an effect, play with the EQ so it sounds like it's on the radio. I don't know. By the time I heard it, it was too late. I heard it in the theater and I'm going, "What the hell?"

You went on to score most of the *Friday the 13th* sequels. Did having the original's groundwork already laid down make them easier or harder to do?

Each one had its own story. The second film [*Friday the 13th Part 2* (1981)] was easier, because I had already figured out everything that I wanted to do. It had happened rather quickly, subsequent to the first—they wanted to cash in on that baby.

I always characterize them by whatever new piece of gear I used for that particular film's score. For example, I didn't need the stupid voices that I had in the original, because finally somebody came out with a reasonable-sounding vocal thing. There was also a Korg synthesizer that had a feature called "sample and hold," which is a really cool feature. You could hold on a chord and it would randomly arpeggiate that chord [play the chord's notes one at a time in sequence], up and down, around itself. If you remember in *Part 2* when the girl is in what we called Chez Jason, where the mom's head was, with all the candles, and she's dressed up as the mom, there's a lot of that random thing [arpeggiating] with the chord going on there. That worked, and I liked that psychological thing.

But what happened subsequently, when Jason became the killer, the movies changed. . . . Basically, it became tension-chase-kill, tension-chase-kill. The first one was really a murder mystery. It was more of a thriller than it was a horror film, as opposed to the other ones, where Jason was the shark. You were doing something wrong and Jason took care of you. . . . But each one of them had its own character to it and, also, like I said, there was always some new piece of gear that I worked into it. So that sort of made it fun for me.

Part V [*A New Beginning*, 1985] was very difficult because *Part V*, of course, was the one where there wasn't any Jason. It was the ambulance driver. That was really hard, because . . . there was a situation where I knew it wasn't Jason. I'm trying to write these cues as if it is Jason, but I know it's not. [*Laughs*] It's funny: The characters in the movie, to me, become like real people. I go to a cast party and I'm always amazed that everybody is still alive, because I've killed them all. And I'm going, "What are you doing here?"

I liked *Part VI* [1986] a lot, because of its humor. The characters were more "characters" than in some of the other films, and I loved working with [writer-director] Tom McLoughlin. He is an incredibly talented guy—really, really good. Plus, I had a bigger orchestra. Oh, thank God, I had an actual percussion section, which was really great. [*Laughs*] Oh my God, live players! Great!

I didn't do *Friday the 13th Part VII* [*The New Blood* (1988)] and *Friday the 13th Part VIII* [*Jason Takes Manhattan* (1989)], because I was working on other movies at the time, and I'm not one to try and do two at the same time. Then I did part nine [*Jason Goes to Hell: The Final Friday* (1993)] and [*Jason*] *X* [2001].

Shortly after the first *Friday the 13th* you worked on Wes Craven's *Swamp Thing*. How did that come about?

I got a call from Wes, or maybe it was a letter. He was doing *Swamp Thing*, and he was so enamored with *Friday the 13th*, he asked, "Would you do the score for *Swamp Thing*?" I said, "Of course." Then he told me that he didn't have a lot of money, blahblahblah. And I said, "Wes, don't even worry about it."

He and Sean [Cunningham] worked together a long time ago and I really liked him. He's an incredibly talented guy. So that's how I got that picture. It is how you get a lot of pictures: You do something for somebody, and then someone else that knows him hires you. Word of mouth is a huge thing in this business.

In that picture there is thematic stuff. That's where we had the two-note theme for the formula, the glowing green stuff.

Sadly, Craven passed away recently. Can you talk a little bit about what he was like?

Wes was a very bright guy. . . . When I first met him, I was still new to the business. *Swamp Thing* may have only been my sixth or seventh picture. I was, like, "Oh my God, this is Wes Craven. Yikes! I better watch my Ps and Qs."

So I was just listening to what he said and going with what we talked about. But the one thing that I noticed about Wes was that, first of all, he really was knowledgeable, not only about filmmaking, but he was knowledgeable about art and culture, music, and things like that. He was a much deeper person than what you might think. Obviously, he made very successful films, but he was a pretty deep guy, a very serious guy, and a very bright guy. He could've easily taught a humanities arts class.

He was that well versed in so many arts and understood theater and drama and painting—everything.

That was one thing, and the other thing was that he was really funny. He had a great sense of humor, and even when things were not going well, he had the ability to laugh. He eventually ended up doing those *Scream* movies, which were poking fun at the genre. I am really glad he was able to do those, because I actually said to him a couple of times, "Wes, you are really funny. You see things in a funny way and you react in a funny way to things. You don't just scare people."

I didn't know how ill he was; I think that really snuck up on a lot of people. The thing I liked about him, more than anything, was that I respected his mind.

You also worked with Wes Craven on *The Hills Have Eyes Part II* [1984], which was a sequel. When you worked on it, did you have to familiarize yourself with the music from the original, or did you just take your own approach to it?

I took my own approach. If I recall correctly, that was a picture that he wasn't crazy about doing. I'm not sure how that worked out. Wes got reborn many times: He would do something, go down in popularity, and then all at once be reborn again. *The Hills Have Eyes Part II* was a movie that I think he just made because the producers said, "Hey, let's make another one."

That movie was pretty strange, because it had all kinds of flashbacks to the original movie. [*Laughs*] It was like, "How many flashbacks are you going to have?" It was, like, half the movie went back to the original! I remember when the *dog* had a flashback—I just completely cracked up, and Wes was, like, "Oh my God, I can't believe I'm doing this." I said, "They're going to take away your director's card." and he responded, "Well, maybe I can get a learner's permit."

[*Laughs*] He had a hard time with that movie. But at that time, he had just written the script to *A Nightmare on Elm Street* [1984], which I got to read. I told him, "Oh my God, Wes, this is great, this is going to be a huge thing." He said, "Really? You think so?" I went, "Yeah, I really think so."

Were you bummed that you didn't get to work on *A Nightmare on Elm Street*?

I was really bummed about that, yes. That would've been crazy, doing both *Friday the 13th* and *A Nightmare on Elm Street*. I would've been exhausted, even more than I am now.

I actually almost did one of them. I think it was part five [*A Nightmare on Elm Street 5: The Dream Child* (1989)]. They offered me that, and I think I was doing *DeepStar Six* [1989] at the time. I told them that I couldn't do two separate movies at the same time. I *actually* do the writing—I *do* it! And they were, like, "Oh, don't you have something in a drawer that you can use?" I said, "I don't have anything in a drawer! What are you talking about?" So I ended up not doing it. You can't do them all. You do what you can.

What was the process when working with a guy like Wes Craven?

Both he and [Cunningham] were pretty loose with it. There have been a few occasions, after I've written something, Sean has said to me, "You went for this and I wanted that." And then I say, "Oh, I see. You wanted it that way. Yeah, I can fix that." For the most part, they were both fairly open with letting me come up with my idea.

There's this thing called the infamous temp track, which some composers don't like. Temp tracks don't bother me that much. I actually kind of like them, especially if it is a good temp track. Sometimes it is a double-edged sword, though. Often a director cannot communicate musically, they don't have the vocabulary. But, at the same time, I have a way of listening to the temp track and saying, "I see what you like about this piece. You like this and that." They go, "Yeah, yeah," and I'll say, " . . . because it is doing this." And they'll go, "Yes! That's right. That's what I like about it." And then that's what I'll give them. So it can work really well.

On the other hand, sometimes it doesn't work well. Out here we call it "temp love," where the director is in love with the temp track, and if you deviate even the slightest bit from it they go, "Oh, no, no, no, that's not right." Well, do they want a lawsuit [*laughs*]? We're about three notes away from a lawyer calling here—it is almost dead-on! It happens more in TV than in films.

Why do you think that is?

TV is just rushed, it's faster. And when they use temp music, they've heard it so much that they can't get it out of their heads. It is very frustrating sometimes as a composer, because you have to write what they have *without* writing what they have. That's kind of tough. The other problem is that when it is really "temp love," there's nothing you can do. About a year ago I had to just walk away from a movie, because the guy was so locked into what he had that anything that I did, that I thought was creative or that I thought would help, was just not acceptable. I don't care if I'm wrong, but the director and I were just not seeing the picture in the same way. I've had that happen a couple of times.

I had a situation on a picture—it wasn't a horror film, it was a comedy—where I had written about five or six cues, and the director came over with the editor and we were playing one of the scenes for him, and he was laughing like crazy. He just thought it was so funny. It was really great. His only direction to me was, "Push the envelope—push it as hard as you want."

So I wrote this thing, and I just thought it was brilliant. [*Laughs*] At least I *thought* it was brilliant! And the director is sitting there watching it and he's laughing and laughing, and I'm thinking to myself, "Wow, this is really cool." The next day he calls me and he says, "Harry, I don't think this is working." I'm, like, "What do you mean it isn't working? You were laughing like crazy." He goes, "Yeah, but I don't think it is working. I don't like the approach you're taking."

It was as if somebody else called, like it was another person. In the end I just said, "Look, I think you and I have a different view of this picture," and I walked away. I told him, "Don't worry about it. I'll keep the five pieces I wrote and you can finish your movie. You can get somebody else. It's okay, it happens."

When you've written music for a film and you either walk away or they throw it out, what happens to that music? Do you use it for something else?

No, because sometimes you get paid—they own it and it is just gone. There was a picture I did a while back and, unfortunately, it was just not a good movie. I did the score for this picture, and for one reason or another the movie was just not working. When the studio tested it, it was getting, like, forty-threes and forty-fives—it is bad when you get, like, a sixty-four! [Although audience tests are not all the same and audience testing is not an exact science, generally speaking, numbers in the high seventies are average, and numbers in the nineties are considered excellent.—Ed.] So you can get a sense of how bad this one was.

The first thing they always do is throw out the score. They put in a completely different score. So they got these two rock 'n' roll guys to write a rock score, and it was still getting forty-fives. Then the producer, who had worked with [composer] Lalo Schifrin on another picture, brought in Lalo to do the score. Lalo is just sitting there with the music editor, and she's playing the movie for him with my score on it, and he's going, like, "What's wrong with this score [*laughs*]?" She goes, "Well, they threw it out. We can't use it."

So I get this call out of the blue from Lalo, saying, "Harry, is it okay if I use a couple of these ideas that you came up with here?" I said, "Sure! It is an honor to even talk to you. You don't remember this, but years and years ago, when you played with Dizzy Gillespie in Chicago, you came to my table. I was just a teenager, and you and Dizzy sat down and we all talked jazz."

He said, "Really? I remember playing that place in Chicago, but don't remember that." And then he said to me, "Let me give you my congratulations, because you have not arrived until you've had a score thrown out. Some of the best guys have had scores thrown out, so don't let it bother you."

I tried not to let it bother me, but it did bother me a lot.

You've scored all kinds of movies, but you're best known for doing horror, and horror films are known for being real hit-or-miss. Is it a bit spirit-breaking when you watch a film you're working on for the first time and it is just not good, and you know that you still have to work on it and give it your best?

Yes and no. I'm trying to make it the best version of the picture that it can be. Like I said earlier, I'm not a big fan of horror films. What bothers me is that, in my opinion, some horror directors don't seem to understand that sometimes less is more. Sometimes when you *don't* show it, it is more powerful than if you *do* show it.

One of the things I've learned about scoring in general, and I learned it along with Sean [Cunningham] and people like that . . . Sean calls it "mustache twirling [*laughs*]." Remember in the old silent movies, when they'd cut to the bad guy and he'd be twirling his mustache and he'd be, like [*laughs a villainous laugh*]? And it was, like, "Oh, he's scary." Sometimes these directors are, like, "We want music. We want music. Can you put music *here*? Can you put music *there*?"

At some point the music is going to lose its power, because it is just playing all the time. It is going to be more effective if I can stop and then come in at just the right spot or go out at the right spot. Let the sound effects work or, God forbid, you've got acting and dialogue [*laughs*]. Or develop some characters or something. And that's where you just need to be constantly pushing and pushing.

Look, I've seen it in many movies where composers far better than me have done the same thing. I keep thinking of an action film Jerry Goldsmith scored. I can't remember exactly what it was now, but the movie just lay there on the screen. It just lay there, and the only thing I was getting from the music was [*in an overexcited voice*], "Come on, everybody, come on! Oh, man, this is so good! Come on!"

But I'm just sitting there thinking, "Oh, my God." And it can't do it, because it is just not there in the movie itself. Someone always says, "This dialogue scene is so slow; can you play some music and make it faster [*laughs*]?" And I have to tell them, "If it is one minute long, I'm going to have to write one minute of music, and whether you like it or not it is still going to be one minute long." It can be one minute long with fast music—you could play [Khachaturian's] "Sabre Dance" behind something—but it isn't going to make the scene go any faster. How about cutting out some of it?

[*Laughs*] They don't like to hear that. What I love is when the director also wrote the script, because then, often, every word is sacred and they just can't cut it down.

As someone who is not particularly a fan of the horror genre, are you content with the fact that it is what you're known for?

There's a saying, "You have to grow where you're planted." And I've learned a lot about scoring as a result of the genre. . . . It's tough, because sometimes you'd kill to do something else—and I have done other things. But I learned a lot about scoring, because it is about the drama, and there is plenty of drama in a horror film and there is plenty of drama in regular dramas and even comedies. The techniques are transferable. It's not really that different.

Not that I'm comparing myself to this person, but take somebody like Elmer Bernstein, who was "the epic guy," then he became "the jazz guy," then he became "the comedy guy," then he became "the quirky movie guy," and then he became "the sensitive guy." [*Laughs*] They're all the same guy! It isn't, like, "Oh, I know you can do epics, but can you do *To Kill a Mockingbird* [1962]?" "Of *course* I can do *To Kill a Mockingbird*, and I can also do a jazz score."

Sure, but with the nature of the business, sometimes other people don't realize that.

Yes, of course, people don't realize that. But like I said, there are techniques and there are elements to scoring a comedy and elements to scoring a horror film that are really not that diverse from each other. You're going for a laugh or you're going for a scare—it's just what you're trying to induce in the audience. The mechanics of doing it are quite often the same. But when I do get offered a film that's not a horror film, I take it no matter what. I don't care, because that's a chance to do something a little bit different.

Obviously it differs from picture to picture, but, on average, how many minutes of music do you have to record for a film?

It is really funny. Horror films, in general, tend to have more music, just because there is always a lot of creeping around. Not that it is always great music, but there is music. I would say that the average horror film probably has sixty to seventy minutes, sometimes more. I just finished one that had eighty. Like I said earlier, *Friday the 13th* is an exception because of our choice to only have music for the killer. There's really only, like, forty-three or forty-five minutes in the first *Friday the 13th*. . . . The average film probably has fifty to sixty.

Having done so many horror films, does it get difficult to write new music? How many different jump-scare stings or violin shrieks can you do? Has it gotten difficult yet?

[*Laughs*] It's not difficult. One of the things   and this is a rewind all the way back to your first question . . . When I was a kid I would be out playing with my friends or playing baseball, etc., and I would always score what I was doing in my head—I heard music in my head. Even though I didn't know how to write it or anything like that at the time, in my mind I scored things. I always can hear music. I look at a movie and I can hear music.

So that brings us back to this question. I do a lot of lectures at colleges where I talk about scoring. I try to help young composers. I do a three-hour lecture about scoring. I then usually have another day where I take kids, one-on-one, and sit and work on whatever they're doing and try to help them. It is a lot of fun.

One of the things in my lecture is called "The Anatomy of a Hit." I don't mean a hit song; I mean a "hit," what you're calling a "sting." At the beginning of the lecture I explain that there's a difference between being a composer and a film composer. The film is the most important thing. As a film composer, half of your job is being a dramatist. Your job is to tell the story. Your job is to find the emotions to create what the director is trying to say, to create what the writer was trying to say, to manipulate the audience in the way that the filmmakers want them to react.

It doesn't matter if it is a horror film or a comedy or a drama. Whatever it happens to be, you have to sonically create those emotions. That's your job. You can show me that you know harmony better than anybody and you can write counterpoint and you can write fugues and you're the world's greatest orchestrator and you can play more notes on a saxophone than anybody else, but that is all irrelevant. When it comes to film scoring, no one cares about that stuff.

I talk to these kids, most of which are trying to score films, and I tell them, "The people that you are writing for don't care what chord you're playing. They don't care what it is called. They don't want to know, they don't care. The question is, Did that chord evoke in them the correct dramatic feeling for that particular scene? That's the only thing they care about." So I tell them to stop worrying about what chord they are playing and instead worry about what emotion they're playing.

I ask them, "What does this say? What does that do? How does it make you feel?" I play them a little melody on the piano, and I change the chords. I give them a sentence, "Jack loves Jill." I play F Maj/A, F Maj, G7, C [sings], "IV, V, I . . . Jack loves Jill." Then I say, "That is a declarative sentence. That is a musical declarative sentence. Now watch."

Then I play F, G7, C+ not C. Then I ask, "What does that say? It says 'Jack loves Jill?' No one in the room cares if that is C+ [the plus sign indicates an augmented or sharped fifth in the chord] or not. Because we are musicians, we know it is C+, but the person that doesn't know anything about harmony got the feeling, the '?' that it said."

That is what you're doing when you score pictures: You're sonically saying emotions. You've got to find those things that say what you need to be said.

So now, going back to "The Anatomy of a Hit." And by a *hit* I don't necessarily mean that somebody is stabbing somebody or a punch. It could be an explosion, it could be somebody starting to cry, it could be the camera starting to move, it could be a realization on the face of a character. A hit is something that is specific in the movie that is important to the story, important to the emotion. It is like Paul Newman in *The Verdict* [1982], where he sees that woman in the hospital. He's a drunk and he's a lawyer, and he sees what happened to her and all at once you just look at him and you see "I'm gonna get those sons of bitches." You know what I mean? It is there.

A hit can be taken care of in a lot of different ways. You can be right on it: Literally when that knife goes in, you can have your shrieking chord. But what if it is an explosion? If you write the note right on the explosion, guess what is going to happen? No one is going to hear your note. They're going to hear the explosion—the sound effects guy is going to win that one.

So what do you do? You can write your crescendo like, "Holy shit, holy shit, HOLY SHIT! *BAM!* ***KABOOM!***" or, "Holy shit, holy shit, HOLY SHIT! ***KABOOM! BAM!***" You need to figure out dramatically what works best for that scene. What happens after that explosion? Maybe you don't even want to crescendo to it. Maybe what you want to do is big crescendo, drop out, let the explosion happen, and *then* come in. There are dramatic ways of dealing with things.

Sometimes, if it is a sad thing, you don't want to be dead-on when it happens. Maybe you want it to happen and then hit when the audience reacts. Feel when you think the audience will react, and then start the music. The next time you watch *Friday the 13th,* watch how often the music goes out. I take the music out just before a big scare, because you're often going to get a bigger scare if the music is out.

There's a great scene in *Friday the 13th* that I show to the students during my lecture. I tell them, "The actor will show you where to take the music out." There's a scene with Adrienne [King], where she's in the kitchen being chased by Mrs. Voorhees, and I think she's got a baseball bat and a big grilling fork in her hands. She's scared shitless and she's in the kitchen and the camera is right on her. Then, all of a sudden, you just see her stop, and she sighs like she feels like she is okay.

I tell them, "Look! There it is, right there." That is where the music goes out. She is okay. Right when she sighs, the music just goes right down to nothing, and we sit there and it is quiet and we're in the kitchen and everybody relaxes, because she's relaxed . . . and then KABAM! The body comes flying through the window, and the chase is on again.

I tell them, "Look at the drama." You can see the drama. There's a reason to start the music and there's a reason to stop the music, but it is always either a dramatic or a visual thing. It could be the camera panning. It could be lots of things, but you're looking for the drama. You're a dramatist, you're not a composer.

So when you asked the question about how I deal with the same kinds of things over and over again, as opposed to thinking of it as a hit, I really try to find those dramatic elements. The score itself offers you ways and the ability to find different and creative ways of doing it, even though it is just another hit. There's always something. If you're a good orchestrator, it helps to listen to a lot of orchestral music. It will give you a lot of new sonic ideas for things.

Do you ever collaborate with the sound designer and sound editor?

That's an excellent question. More often than not I am not working with the finished picture. Let's say there's a special murder weapon or there's a bomb or there's a sound of a machine that's running. I will call the sound designers and ask them, "What is that going to sound like?" If he says it is going to be a real high sound, like fingernails on a blackboard, then I will go low so that we can live together in the [audible sound] spectrum.

I do that all the time: If there is something that I see and know that it is going to have a specific sound, I want to find out what it will end up sounding like. [*Laughs*] In *DeepStar Six* there's a scene where they open up a door, and in actuality it was a door in a swimming pool. The characters are in this room, and she opens up this door and 50,000 gallons of water just come flying through the door. So I'm sitting there, like, "What do you write under the sound of 50,000 gallons of water coming through a door?" And the answer, of course, is, you don't write anything [*laughs*]! There is no way anybody is going to hear it, so you just get the hell out of the way.

How did you get the job on the film *House* [1986]? And how did you choose the musical palette that you used?

What was interesting about that film was that Steve Miner was the director, and he was one of the editors of *Friday the 13th* and a very good friend of Sean [Cunningham]. So I had known him a long time.

That was a really fun movie to do, because it's a horror film, but at the same time it is a comedy. There was a whole second layer of things that were cool to do. Steve said to me, "I think we should have a cello at the beginning." And I said, "Yeah, that's interesting. That's a really good idea, but before I do that, I want you to tell me what a cello is." [*Laughs*] I only asked because sometimes directors aren't that musically astute.

So I asked, "What's a cello?" And he replied, "Oh that's the thing that the girl holds between her legs and she bows it back and forth. It's like a big violin." I said, "That's exactly right! Okay, you're getting a cello, because it is a great idea and that's a perfectly great sound. But I just wanted to make sure when I put a cello in, that's what you were looking for [*laughs*]."

It was a great picture. It offered a chance to really stretch out musically and not just be scary. Then the second one [*House II: The Second Story* (1987)] was even more fun, because there were baby pterodactyls and all kinds of stuff. For instance, what does a baby pterodactyl sound like musically? I ended up using a bassoon and an ocarina . . . kind of a wheezy bassoon sound. To me, that is what a baby pterodactyl sounds like.

There were a lot of cool things. There were Aztec Indians and [*laughs*] all kinds of things in there. So that's really fun. You go, "Oh, man, look at all this cool stuff I get to do!" In a *Friday the 13th* movie, you have stalk, scare, kill, *boom*, stalk, scare, kill, *boom*! It's the same thing over and over. Here you get to turn and musically change styles and do all kinds of things. They were really fun movies.

Did you find straddling the line between horror and comedy at all challenging on those films?

You have to understand that . . . horror and comedy are actually very close to each other. And you can step too far in either direction. When I do lectures at colleges, I always give this example. I say, "Imagine the face of a clock. As you go clockwise from twelve down to six, let's say that is horror. It's scary at twelve, and as you get closer to six it get's a little more scary and a little more scary. Then, once you pass six, it's just over-the-top scary—and it is starting to get funny.

I always think of *The Carol Burnett Show* [TV variety series, 1967–1978]. She would do these skits and the music would come in—*bum-bum-bum* [*mimicking dramatic music*]—and then you'd see her face [*laughs*]. It was just way over the top! The same thing happens with comedy: It's funny, it's funny, it's funny, and then it stops being funny. How many times have you heard in a movie, "Hey, you guys, this isn't funny anymore." You're funnier and funnier, and then all at once it's scary.

The other example I can give you—and I'm going to go back to *The Carol Burnett Show*—is where something is funny or scary based on expectations. For example, if you're sitting sixteen feet from your front door and if you got up and walked to that door, there would be an expectation of time. In other words, it is going to take me three seconds to walk to that front door. On *The Carol Burnett Show* Tim Conway would do this thing where he would walk real slow [*laughs*] and it would just take forever.

Let's say it took forty seconds for me to get to the door. Well, you'd start laughing, because there's an expectation of three seconds. But if it took me a fourth of a second to get to the door, that could be scary, because there's a certain expectation. One side of it is scary, the other side of it is funny.

So, musically, you always have to think about that. It can be funny or it can be scary. It all depends on what is there visually, what the audience is getting as an expectation, and what the director wants. If he's trying to make it funny, then you may have to "Mickey Mouse" it or cartoon it [in scoring parlance, "Mickey Mouse music" refers to music that directly underscores or highlights on-screen actions, often in a slapstick way, rather than playing a scene's subtext or underlying emotions], whereas if he were trying to make it scary you would do something else.

Horror relies heavily on suspense and timing, and those things are also crucial to comedy. For both a scare and a joke, there's the tension of the buildup, but then there's the release or the punch line.

Right, it is timing and the expectation of timing. And when does the joke really hit and what do you do? Do you hit it? In some cases you'd rather hit it after the audience sees it, in some cases you might hit it before. It goes back to what I was saying about "The Anatomy of a Hit": Musically you have to try it different ways and see which way it is funnier or which way it is scarier. You're absolutely right. It is all about timing.

Maybe more so than any other genre of film music, right now horror film music is extremely popular and has its own devoted fan base. Do you think there is something about this type of music that transcends the films for the listener in a way that perhaps other genres don't?

I would say yes. I agree with you. But there are other films that are like that. You could take *Raiders of the Lost* Ark [1981] or *E.T.* [1982]. Of course, then we're dealing with John Williams, which is a whole different thing; he has a wonderful way of telling a story. *Star Wars* [1977] is probably the most famous sci-fi movie score ever written, and there is not one synthesizer in the whole thing. That goes to show you how good the score is. What I am saying is, they tend to have a life of their own.

But the horror . . . score tends to be more evocative of the story, and I think sometimes it is simpler and it literally brings back the movie and the feeling of the movie. Whether it is the scare or the uneasiness, the creepiness, for a person that is really into it, they can relive the film by listening to the music. It tends to be more in tune with the drama as opposed to just sitting there. A horror score has a connection to the picture that other ones don't necessarily have. It tends to marry itself to the film more. Does that make sense?

Yes. Of course, there will always be examples of that kind of fan connection to scores from other kinds of films also. Bill Conti's score for *Rocky* [1976] is another great example.

It is a great score. But what I'm saying is that it is evocative of being a champion and stuff like that, but it is never going to make you feel like you did when you watched the movie. For example, the creepiness of some scene that is just much simpler, that if you've seen the movie, there's something about the music that is more dramatic. Although *Rocky* is dramatic, it is just different.

Maybe it is because fear is such a primal feeling.

Oh, yeah! You may have hit on it there. Fear and the feeling that you get from a really good horror film goes a little bit deeper—and the music is part of the injection [*laughs*].

I also find it interesting that the latest fad, for both cinephiles and audiophiles, is special edition reissues of classic horror film scores on vinyl.

They're doing that right now with *Friday the 13th* and *Friday the 13th Part 2*.

It is a big thing. Obviously there is an audience for it, and these scores from these smaller horror films from thirty years ago are doing something that even John Williams's score for *Star Wars*, as brilliant as it is, probably couldn't do.

Other genres of film scores don't go as deep as, I think, a really good horror score can. Just look at Bernard Herrmann.

Horror, in general, is a place where an artist and/or a composer can be slightly more experimental and push the envelope.

That's one of my favorite things about it: All bets are off. You can do whatever you want. When I'm writing the music for a TV movie, or a "movie of the week" or something like that, you're dealing with a tune ([*laughs*] I call them tunes). You've got a little tune that you have to deal with. You're locked into a chord progression. You're locked into certain harmonies that have got to function properly and work out properly.

On a horror film, everything—your choice of instruments, your choice of color, your choice of harmony, whatever it is—literally, the cupboard is open. Pick anything you like. That's what is fun about horror films. They are where you really are allowed to get more creative in many ways.

Is there anything unique about your process that people might find interesting?

One thing is, I never studied film composition; I don't even know what they teach. I hear what other people do and I just don't do that, I don't do it that way. Sometimes it comes out like that, but I don't do it that way.

I tend to see the cue (a cue is a piece of music in a film) . . . as a piece unto itself. I also try to see the *whole* score, all those little pieces put together, as one whole thing as well—I don't like to write from point to point. I've seen composers that write from here to there and then they write from there to there. Let's say it is a minute-and-thirty-seconds piece and at twenty-six seconds something happens. They will write twenty-six seconds and then stop. And then they'll write from there until the next thing and then to the next thing. They write it that way.

I tend to not start writing until I understand the whole piece myself. Until I can hear the whole piece in my head, I don't start. (Not that I'm going to end up writing exactly what I hear.) I want to know that I'm going to go from there to there and, in the process, those things are going to happen, but I'm going to have an overall sound of that whole cue before I start. So I don't write four bars at a time, and then another four bars. . . . There are a lot of people that write in groups of four bars. I feel like they teach that, but I don't know. I hear it in a lot of music.

You don't necessarily sit and write specifically to the image? You write and then apply it to the film?

Yeah. I'm walking around, I'm watching the picture. I watch it, and then I might walk around for a while and just keep listening in my head—like I said earlier, I always hear it in my head. I get an idea of what I want to do, and then I will start. . . . Sometimes I actually just draw a picture. I may have staffs of music there, but I don't write any notes. I just say, I hear this and then I hear this and then I hear that. It really almost looks like some sort of drawing.

Do you draw lines that rise up and down? What do your drawings look like?

Lines that wiggle. Lines that run up and down. Maybe there is something low going on and I want to start something here. I want to do that and then it turns left. It is just sort of a drawing of it as reference for myself.

Someday, during one of my lectures, I'd like to take a piece of music, maybe a Mozart piece or something, and have them listen to the music and then go backwards, have them draw a picture of that music. If you were going to write that piece, what would it look like in one of these goofy little drawings?

Then I'd say, "Now forget the Mozart piece, and just write what you've drawn as music." And they can write it in any style they want, and maybe they would take that same drawing and write several different pieces in different styles—as a twelve-tone piece or as a hip-hop tune, as a groove, as jazz—but they write them all from that same picture and see what happens, see what kind of music comes out. Then you just have a picture and four or five different pieces that might be totally different-sounding, all coming from the same picture. I think it is an interesting way to write. I don't know if it is "my" way or not, but it is something I tend to do. Like I said, the only training I ever had in film scoring was just watching films and listening to scores.

Do you get writer's block? Is there a way to work around it?

You can get writer's block. Invariably, I at least have some idea; I may not have the whole idea, but I may have something. And what I might do is, if you remember earlier when we were talking about signposts in a script, I will look for those. *This* happened here on page twenty-three [of the script]. It is going to come back on page forty-seven, then on page fifty-three it is going to mean something completely different. Then, on page ninety-seven, it is actually *ah-hah!*—a realization.

So I may have an idea for that, and sometimes what I'll do is write those four pieces, completely out of order, forgetting about the rest of the film. Just lay down those, and then, invariably, as you create one thing the other ideas will come. If I don't have an idea for one part, I will start someplace else.

You always have some idea. [*Laughs*] If you have no idea, wow, then it is time to go out for a sandwich or go for a walk or something. . . . When you have the picture, it might have a temp score. At least you can have conversations with the director: "What kind of scores do you like?" or, "What were you thinking of when you did this?" There's always something. It is not like it is always a blank sheet of paper, but I've had it too—believe me, I've had it where I sit there and I go, "I just don't know what to do here."

But I think the process that I use works well for me. I start out creating little blocks of things. It might just be a chord progression or a sonority, or it might be a specific instrument. I have a whole bunch of these little blocks in front of me, and that is where I'm going to build the score from and that's where I start. I don't just go, "I'm going to write this cue now." I don't do that. I may not use them all or they may change in the process, but at least I have a place to start.

Are certain notes scarier than others?

No, I don't really think in keys anymore.

Well, not so much like you would consciously decide that you're going to sit down and write in a certain key. But maybe you've found, after the fact, that you write horror music more often in one key than another.

There's always some guy that says to me, "Why are all your low notes either E or C#?" Well, the string bass can only go down to C—and that's an open string—and some string basses only go down to E. So those are the lowest notes they play, so those are the notes I use [*laughs*]. Sometimes there is a real simple answer for what seems like a real complicated question.

Do you have a particular recording session or other experience while creating a score that stands out in your memory as your favorite?

I don't think so. Each one of them has something that is memorable; I wouldn't say there is one in particular that I like better than the others. What is really fun, though, is when the orchestra likes the music. I have had experiences, like on *DeepStar Six* and other bigger pictures where I used a full orchestra, where the players really liked the music. There is a movie I did called *Timemaster* [1995], and I remember there were a couple of cues where the orchestra actually clapped. [*Laughs*] You know, they just play stuff all the time and it is hard to get through to them, but they were, like, "Aw, that was really cool!" That kind of stuff is always a nice feeling. It's happened a couple of times on bigger tracks, where the orchestra just really enjoyed playing it.

Is seeing the films you've worked on with an audience a gratifying experience?

Oh, for sure—that's when you know you've done your job. When we made the first *Friday the 13th*, we tested it with an audience, and Sean

[Cunningham] and I would go and sit in the front row—which is way too close to enjoy the movie—but we'd sit in the front row, and then when something scary was going to happen on screen, we would slide down in our seats, so that we could actually turn around without anybody noticing it. And then we would watch the audience react to the picture. We knew what was going on in the movie, so we'd watch them. What cracked me up was how excited Sean would get: "I got 'em!" Popcorn would be flying and people would be jumping out of their seats. It was really cool to watch. That's how you know it's working.

I was at a test screening for *Jason Lives: Friday the 13th Part VI.* This was a screening at Paramount Pictures, where they select audiences. There were a lot of huge *Friday the 13th* fans there, like 300 or 400 people, and there weren't enough kills—there just were *not enough kills* in the picture [*laughs*]. The audience had a chance to fill out a card and say what they thought—what they liked and what they didn't like, etc.— and something like ninety percent of the comments said there weren't enough kills [*laughs*]. But you learn a lot from those things, and usually the audience is right.

So they had to go back and shoot more footage and kill off a few more people. Talk about cardboard characters! They were just there to be killed. They had nothing to do with the plot. . . .

Many horror films are made on a very tight budget. Do you find that a lower budget fuels creativity?

Of course! Take *Friday the 13th,* for example. Yes, it does fuel creativity. It is frustrating, but at the same time it is kind of fun in a wacky sort of way.

There is a new project that you're working on right now that, even though it is not a movie, is very exciting. I think we should talk about it. How did *Friday the 13th: The Game* come about, and how did you become involved?

Originally, the video game was called *Summer Camp*, it wasn't *Friday the 13th: The Game.* This guy called me out of the blue; Wes Keltner is his name, and he is with Gun Media. They were doing this game called *Summer Camp.* He was trying to get myself, Tom Savini, and Kane Hodder to get involved with the game. Savini was going to design the various effects, and Kane was going to do the motion capture [recording human movements to be used in creating animated digital characters] for the killer.

At the same time, the people over at *Friday the 13th* were trying to develop a game . . . I think the *Friday the 13th* guys were going, "You know, we should develop a game." [*Laughs*] But they had never made one, and they didn't know what it entailed. So, eventually, the *Friday the 13th* people saw the advertising for *Summer Camp* and saw that I was involved and that Tom was involved and so was Kane, and they just called up Wes Keltner and said, "Hey, why don't we do this together? Instead of it just being some generic summer camp, we will license you *Friday the 13th* and Jason." That's how *Friday the 13th: The Game* got started.

Once the *Friday the 13th* folks came on board, the game just became a way bigger idea. . . . He [Keltner] has the brand now; he has Jason and the name.

What exactly is your involvement? Are you scoring it, or are they just using cues that you wrote for the films?

No, I am actually scoring it. I am not a game guy, so I don't know much about games myself, but it is not what they call a single-player or first-person shooter. It is not that kind of a game. It is a multiplayer game, which you log into online. I think they call it "nonlinear." My understanding is that the game is sort of like when you're playing poker online. You're virtually sitting at a table with seven other people, and each of you have options to do whatever you want to do, call or fold, raise or whatever . . .

So you're playing with other people who are online as well.

Right, you're playing a virtual game with seven other people, and one of the people is Jason. So one of the players is actually the killer and the other six players are camp counselors. And the object of the game is to survive [*laughs*] and not get killed by Jason. Supposedly, from what I understand, once you play as Jason, I think you have to play at least seven more games before you can be Jason again—you can't constantly just be Jason.

Right now, they only have very small demo versions that are only being played by the guys that are designing the game. No one is playing the full game yet. It is nowhere near ready to go yet. But they were saying that it is actually more fun to be a counselor, because you got to try different things. In other words, every time you play the game, you might want to try something else, because you can defeat Jason. You can escape and you can win. They think it is more fun to play that way than to just be Jason and try to kill people all the time. It is not going to be easy to win, but you can win.

Musically, what is interesting about it is, I am not writing music like you would in a first-person shooter or a game where, basically, "Oh, I am at Level One! Now I am at Level Two," where basically you write a bunch of music that is just a bunch of loopy stuff that just lies there. What I am writing is different, because the player constantly has options. You may be walking through the campgrounds and see a cabin. Well, you can go to the cabin or not go to the cabin. Or you may find something on the ground in the woods and you can look at it or not look at it. . . .. Or you might encounter another live counselor. If you do go to the cabin, do you decide to go in or not? Then you see what you see when you're in there. So it is a whole series of choices made by the player that are completely random every time you play.

What happens is, in a way, the player actually scores what he is doing. The music will change based on what the player decides, not what I decide the score should be. So what I am writing is not so much what you would think of as a regular piece of film music, where the film is going to be the same every time and there's going to be a hit here or it's going to get louder or faster or slower or whatever, because a film is a locked thing. Here I am basically writing a ton of modular pieces that can work with each other and will be able to change. One piece can follow another piece and transition into another piece at the whim of the player.

So I am really not writing a "score." That's why you can't just use a piece that is already written [*laughs*]: No one knows what's going to fit. It's kind of weird and it is quite a challenge for me. The other challenge is—and to be honest with you, I haven't been able to figure it out yet—is that I've never written music for Jason. Let's say that the player is Jason. I have no idea what music Jason hears [*laughs*]. Obviously, it is not the most pleasant music, but I haven't quite figured out what that is yet.

In the movies, though, they often took the perspective of Jason.

The music became Jason. In a movie, even though it is Jason, you're still scoring the audience, you're trying to manipulate the audience. But if you in fact *are* Jason, sonically you're going to have a different perspective of what's going on. And the Jason character has a whole bunch of things that he can do in the game himself.

I will be honest with you: I haven't seen any of the game. I've pretty much seen what you've seen, some pictures and the trailer and things like that. I haven't seen the game in action yet.

For what you've written so far, did they just give you a list of locations and scenarios?

Yes, exactly. At some points you will have things like your generic "woods music." But because it is generic, it can be one minute long or it could be three minutes long—it depends on what the player does. So what becomes the intricate part is a whole bunch of connective things that can connect the various pieces of music. For instance, let's say the person is in the woods and this piece [of music] is running out, but they're still going [in the woods]. So then there's what I'm calling "the box of various connective things"—a bunch of these little pieces of music that will allow them to transition into another piece. . . .

Or let's say he decides to move and go to a cabin. Then there will be a transitional element that will lead to a "going to the cabin" cue or an "opening the door" cue. They may discover something like a car that they can start and escape with, or a boat (I think there's a boat that you can use to escape [*laughs*]). I don't know, but what I am saying is that all these things are possible, and then you also gain strength the longer you last. If you happen to encounter Jason, you can run. So obviously there's a chase, and that needs music. Then Jason can grab you and, supposedly, you might be able to escape Jason, or he might kill you.

So there needs to be music for each one of those things. For every possible scenario, I am probably writing ten different choices. So that every time you play the game, your musical experience will actually be different.

I know you haven't finished working on it yet . . .

Oh my God no! I'm not even close.

When all is said and done, how much more music do you think you're going to have to write for this than you do for a standard film?

I would say it is going to be about three movies' worth. It could be somewhere between 120 and 160 minutes of music. Maybe 180. [*Laughs*]

I don't know the answer yet. I am going to write a bunch of music and just keep doing that. As the game becomes clearer, they are going to say, "We need this," or, "We need more of that," or, "Can you write us another one of those?" Or they may say, "We don't have anything at all for this." For example, what happens if you actually win the game? I don't know what that will be yet. Or if you're safe out in the boat and Jason can't get you? Those are things that remain to be seen until the game gets a little more fleshed out.

I know that this month [December 2015], they've been shooting a lot of the motion capture stuff with Kane. He's not only using motion capture for himself as Jason, but he's actually using real stunt people as well. Kane isn't one to pull any punches. He really wants to do things with actual people that can do the stunt. Even during the murders, it's not animated or anything like that; it's going to be very visual and seem fairly accurate.

So, basically, what you're saying is that you're creating puzzle pieces that will be interchangeable.

[*Laughs*] I am writing a giant musical puzzle that has all sorts of modular twists and turns that are applicable, depending on what the player decides to do. And then what I am also writing is the transitional glue. That can be short, little things, but they will allow the music to go from one place to another in a musical way.

As a matter of fact, we [Manfredini and Gun Media] were talking about this the other day, because one of the rewards on the Kickstarter campaign was a CD or an album of the music. But what is weird about it is that nobody wants 180 minutes of modular music. "Here's a whole bunch of music that actually goes nowhere [*laughs*]!" It has no musical value whatsoever. It is just forty seconds of this followed by twenty seconds of that, etc.

So what I'm thinking of doing is creating scenarios. So I may start out a piece walking through the woods, and then something happens. Literally take possible scenarios that might occur when you play, so that I end up making a full musical statement out of it. There might be a chase and a kill or an escape. So, once I get everything done, that is something I am going to do so that the album, or the CD, whatever it happens to be, is musically interesting to listen to. I don't know how interesting it is, but at least it will be a linear thing—it won't just be a bunch of puzzle pieces.

Being someone who is accustomed to writing music to picture, aside from the sheer amount of music, is it difficult to just blindly write music?

Yes, it's horrible [*laughs*]. It's really strange, because I have no point of reference. When you write to picture, you go, "Oh, okay, we go to *there* and then we go to *there* and then we go to *that*." So it is really strange, writing this way.

It reminds me of a class I took, way back a thousand years ago, back in college when I was just studying composition, not ever thinking that I would be scoring films or anything like that. I remember, one day, the professor [*laughs*] gave me an assignment. He said, "In music, you have to be able to connect sections of a piece. So I want each of you to write five transitional pieces." [*Laughs*] And I'm going, "What the hell is a transitional piece?" It goes from one thing to another, but you don't know where you are to start with—and you don't know where you're going to end up! How can you just write the part in the middle? [*Laughs*] That's pretty funny, and I laughed at it then, but now I'm, like, "Whoops! Here it is!"

This is what I'm doing now: I'm writing a piece that doesn't end. It just sort of starts, and then I'm writing another piece that also starts and doesn't end, and then I'm writing a piece that will connect those two [*laughs*]. And theoretically, no matter what the next piece is, it has to be able to connect. So it is a little bit weird.

Will you be recording the end product yourself, or are there plans to hire outside musicians to perform the music?

At least at this point, with the budget I have to work with and the time, etc., I think it is just going to be me in the studio, unless things change. Maybe they will want a special piece. For example, maybe if somebody actually wins the game, we may want to do a big piece. That's up to them, it's not really up to me. I will do whatever they'd like.

So far, as I've said, they have some demo games that they've played, and they were saying that the music *really* makes a difference. It is just so much cooler. You're doing what you're doing, but when you add the musical layer to it, that is *Friday the 13th*; they're saying that it really changes the whole experience. So that's cool to hear.

Did you start writing stuff before it officially became a *Friday the 13th* game?

No. This has been around for a while, because, as I said earlier, it was originally *Summer Camp*. I think I spoke to Wes before the people from *Friday the 13th* got involved, but I never wrote anything at that point. I said, "What are you going to do?" And he said, "Well, we just need some music that is *Friday the 13th*-ish, just so we can see if it works on the demo." So I told them, "Why don't you just use some actual *Friday the 13th* music?" I sent them a CD. "Here, just use this. You're not selling it, all you're doing is testing it." So they just used that.

So, no, I hadn't started writing anything yet, but once the *Friday the 13th* people started to show some interest, everything got rethought.

Do you have any advice that you might be able to give to aspiring composers about this business?

I would say that orthodontia is a good thing to go into [*laughs*]. No. The advice now is that the technology is extremely important. Depending on what instrument you play, you definitely have to understand the technology. But you still need to learn from the masters, and you see how they approached things. Also, listen to as many different kinds of music as you can. The reason why *Friday the 13th* sounds like what it sounds like is because I was listening to Penderecki in addition to Jerry Goldsmith and Bernard Herrmann. I listened to a lot of really difficult and complex classical music, and you can learn a lot there.

Also, I do a thing in my lectures that I call, "What does this music say?" Stop analyzing the music technically, and try to think about things emotionally and dramatically. Because that is going to be your job. Try to find out what causes something to feel a certain way—certain sonorities, rhythms—and try to feel that with the picture too.

A lot of times you see something that the director is visually doing and you . . . don't want to disturb that. So you go with something very subtle, underneath the layers of things that are going on. There are a whole bunch of things that you have to do. But there are a lot of things that you're not going to learn until you actually do it.

One of the other things—this is something that I learned early, and I actually learned it by watching rather than having the experience myself. When I first moved to California, I got invited to a recording session for a little television show. It turned out to be for one of my favorite composers, Allyn Ferguson. He did a lot of TV shows and things. He was the composer for this session, and the music was really cool, it was really great. I was enjoying it.

And then the producer walked in, and everybody went, "Oh no, here he comes. He's never happy." He's one of those guys that just always has something to say.

And there's this cue that they play, and the producer says to Ferguson, "Allyn, you said it was going to be funny. It's not funny, the music is not funny. You see, right there? That's not funny." Allyn stops and says, "Okay, we will take a break and I will fix it." In the case of this piece, it was two French horns, and he changed it to be two bassoons.

They came back from the break. They played the same piece of music—no French horns. Two bassoons played the same thing that the French horns played in the first take, and the producer goes, "Yeah! Now that is funny." [Laughs] And I said to myself, "He's right!" It *was* funnier.

So what I learned was that somebody doesn't get a job producing a TV show, or some guy isn't a director of a movie, for no reason whatsoever. He has some talent, he has an ear, he has an idea of what he wants. He may not be able to express it to you right away—[laughs] he may not express it until you're right there in a recording session. But he was right! People don't just get to where they are with no ability whatsoever. You can't just disregard what somebody says to you.

This goes back to what I was saying about temp music. A lot of times the director will use temp music, and I try to figure out what it is that they really like about that piece of temp music. Because quite often they can't say it, they don't even know why they like it. All they know is that they like it.

It is like in *Timemaster*. Jim Glickenhaus was the director and the writer, and he put a piece of Morricone in as a temp piece at the very beginning. I listened to it, and I said, "Wow, this really works well." And he replied, "Yes, I really love this piece. I like the way it works here." I kept listening to it, and I said, "Oh, I've got it! I know what it is." And he goes, "What do you mean?" And I replied, "You love that trumpet that is 'offstage.'" It was what we call an *offstage* trumpet, meaning that the trumpet player is not really on the mic. So it sounds like he's coming from far away.

I said, "That trumpet sounds like it's a call from the past, doesn't it?" He goes, "Yeah, that's what it is! It is like the past is calling you." And this movie was all about going forward and backwards in time.

So I recorded this piece that had a trumpet that was off mic, and Jim goes, "That's exactly it." Then I told him that I wanted to put in some reverse sounds, so that some things sound like they're going forward and some things sound like they're going backwards. And he loved that idea.

So you really have to learn to listen to what these people are saying to you. Often they can't say it to you in musical terms. People don't get to where they are without having some talent and ability. Quite often they have a lot of talent. So you have to be aware of that. Don't just think, "Oh, I know music and he doesn't know anything." It's not true.

CLAUDIO SIMONETTI

"When we [Goblin] wrote the score for Suspiria, *we wanted to write songs that could stand on their own, without the film. I always think that way. When I record music for a film, I try to imagine that it could live without the visuals; I want you to be able to listen to it like a record."*

OTHER THAN JOHN CARPENTER, NO single person is more respon-sible for my pursuing this project than Claudio Simonetti. My passion for his (and also his former band, Goblin's) music began while I was at film school, when I discovered and fell in love with the works of Dario Argento.

In the early 2000s, my love for horror film music began to grow, and it was in no small part due to three specific albums. In 2000, Goblin briefly reunited to do the score for Argento's film *Non ho sonno*, aka *Sleepless* (2001). The soundtrack album of that score was a welcome addition to the band's catalog and featured the signature Goblin sensi-bilities filtered through the sounds of modern musical technology.

That year also saw the release of the retrospective two-CD set *The Fantastic Journey in The Best of Goblin, Vol. 1*, which featured a disc of previously unreleased live Goblin material from the late 1970s.

Lastly, when the short-lived Goblin reunion ended, Claudio Simonetti formed a band called Daemonia, which released a debut album titled *Dario Argento Tribute*, which was a hard-edged prog-rock tour de force that featured modern reinterpretations of the most quintessential musical themes from Argento's filmography.

These three albums quite literally changed my life and are partially why this book exists today. The music Simonetti made with Goblin is some of the most internationally iconic in horror film history, and his post-Goblin years have found him adapting to the times and latest technologies, while breaking himself out of the Goblin mold with a fruitful working relationship with Dario Argento that is still active today.

Simonetti agreed almost immediately to do this interview, yet his busy touring and recording schedules made pinning down an exact time another thing entirely. Thankfully, we managed to make it work and, despite a minor language barrier, what you are about to read is likely one of his most in-depth English-language interviews to date.

Selected Filmography

1975   *Deep Red* (aka *Profondo rosso*, aka *The Hatchet Murders*;
        as a member of Goblin)

1977   *Suspiria* (as a member of Goblin)

1978   *Dawn of the Dead* (aka *Zombi*; as a member of Goblin)

1979   *Amo non amo* (aka *Together?*; as a member of Goblin)
        Squadra antigangsters (as a member of Goblin)

1982   *Tenebre* (aka *Unsane*; as Simonetti-Morante-Pignatelli)

1983   *Conquest*
        The New Barbarians (aka *Warriors of the Wasteland*)

1985   *Demons* (aka *Dèmoni*)
        Phenomena (aka *Creepers*; cues were written both solo
        and as a member of Goblin)

1986   *Midnight Killer* (aka *Morirai a mezzanotte*, aka *You'll Die
        at Midnight*)

1987   *Opera* (aka *Terror at the Opera*)

1988   *Primal Rage*

1989   *Nightmare Beach*

2001   *Sleepless* (aka *Non ho sonno*; as a member of Goblin)

2004   *The Card Player* (aka *Il cartaio*)

2005   "Jenifer" (*Masters of Horror* TV series)

2006   "Pelts" (*Masters of Horror* TV series)

2007   *Mother of Tears* (aka *La terza madre*)

2012   *Dracula 3D*

2014   *The Editor*

I'd like to begin by talking a bit about your musical influences. For example, I know your father was a musician.

I was born in Brazil. My father was working there as a musician and was quite famous, because he did a TV show. So I grew up getting to see behind the scenes of TV shows, and I learned a lot by just watching him. I started playing piano when I was eight years old. Then, when I was almost twelve, we moved back to Italy and I started playing guitar with bands, because of the Beatles and the Rolling Stones. I loved that kind of music.

I grew up with the 1960s and 1970s music. When I started to play guitar in bands, I told my father I wanted to be a musician like him. He said, "Yes! You can do this, but you have to study—you can't just have fun playing guitar in bands." So, when I was fourteen years old, I started studying in a music conservatory in Rome. I studied music composition and piano, but during that time, I continued to play with bands.

How did you meet guitarist Massimo Morante and bassist Fabio Pignatelli?

I had a band called Il Ritratto di Dorian Gray, which means "the picture of Dorian Gray," from the book by Oscar Wilde. (I love that book.) I met Massimo in 1970. At that time we had never played music together, he was just a friend. Then, when I finished playing with Il Ritratto di Dorian Gray, I served in the military. That was in 1972, and because I was doing my military service in Rome, I recorded a lot of demos with Massimo.

Then, after I finished my military service in 1973, we formed a band to play these original songs. And we decided to go to London, because our music was inspired by bands like Yes; Genesis; King Crimson; Gentle Giant; Emerson, Lake & Palmer; and Deep Purple. We had a dream to go to the UK and play there, and we lived there for almost one year while we recorded other demos.

When we came back to Italy, my father, Enrico, who was also popular and famous in Italy as an entertainer, introduced me to Cinevox Records; that was the same label he was on. And it was the people at this label that introduced us to Dario Argento, who was looking for a band to record music for his new film *Deep Red* [aka *Profondo rosso* (1975)]. That was in 1974.

The band was originally called Oliver, correct?

Oliver, yes. "Oliver" is also the name of one of the songs included on the album named *Cherry Five*, which was released later in 1975. I don't know who chose the name Cherry Five; it was not our choice. Someone at Cinevox named the album that. Because we were starting a new project with Dario, we changed the [band's] name to Goblin. We also changed the drummer: Walter Martino replaced the Oliver drummer. . . . So we had these two projects that we were working on, the Oliver/Cherry Five project and *Deep Red*. We used two different names, because we wanted to keep them separate.

How did you guys come up with the name "Goblin"?

The name "Goblin" was actually chosen by the record label during the recording of the music for *Deep Red*. We loved it, so we approved the name and kept it.

Was your love for British rock the reason why you recorded the album *Cherry Five* in English?

We preferred to sing in English, and in London we met an American singer, Clive Haynes, and he recorded all the demos with us. He also came with us back to Italy, but he then had family problems and had to go back to England. (Now he lives in the States.)

Then we chose a different Italian singer, Tony Tartarini, from another band, and he sang on the Oliver album [*Cherry Five*]. And it's funny, because if you see the LP for *Deep Red* there is a picture that is a mix between Oliver and Goblin. You can see myself, Massimo Morante, Fabio Pignatelli, and Walter Martino and also Tony Tartarini. He [Tartarini] never worked on *Deep Red*, but they had this picture. So he's included on that album, even though he never played on it [*laughs*].

So it was through the record label that you met Dario Argento?

Yes, thanks to Carlo Bixio; he was the producer that introduced us to Dario. Dario told him he wanted a band. Dario wanted Deep Purple or Emerson, Lake & Palmer or Pink Floyd. Carlo Bixio said, "No. Before you go pick a famous English band, listen to this Roman band. Maybe you will like them." Dario listened to us, and because the Oliver album [*Cherry Five*] had some gothic sounds, he ended up loving our music. He was very brave for deciding to allow us to record the music. We were very young. Initially we were hired to just record the music [jazz pianist and composer] Giorgio Gaslini had written.

Originally, Gaslini was hired to compose the score.

Yes. Before us, he started writing the music for the film. He wrote some orchestral parts, including the lullaby ["School at Night"], and then we recorded some of his music. But we were very lucky, because during the recording Giorgio Gaslini had problems with Dario. They argued and he left the film, and Dario came to us and said, "We don't have any more music from Gaslini. You have to write the main themes, because we don't have them yet." Then we recorded "Profondo rosso," "Mad Puppet," and "Death Dies," those three songs. They made up the A-side of the album. The B-side of the album is Giorgio Gaslini's compositions with the orchestra stuff, with Goblin's arrangements.

Were you familiar with Dario Argento's work before you met him?

Oh, yes! Dario Argento was a superstar [*laughs*]. *Deep Red* was his fifth film, and I was a big fan of his. At the time, I never would've imagined I would one day work with Dario. I saw his first film [*The Bird with Crystal Plumage*] in 1970, when I was eighteen years old, and I also saw the others later. It is incredible, because, when we were recording the Oliver album [*Cherry Five*] and he came into the studio, it would be as if a small American band had Steven Spielberg show up—[*laughs*] it is the same thing! Dario was very big in the Seventies. We were young kids, but he made a good choice. Ten months after the release of the album, we sold one million copies, just in Italy.

Can you talk a bit about Goblin's creative process while scoring *Deep Red*?

Deep Red was our first film and our first important work. At the time, we never realized we were doing something so important, and we just wrote the music. Now when I compose the music for a film, I watch the film; I have the computer, and I can write directly to the film and write for specific scenes. Every scene has its own music. But at the time of *Profondo rosso* and, later, *Suspiria* [1977], we never did that. We just recorded a few songs. We recorded the main theme to *Deep Red* without watching the film. We were inspired by the film, but . . .

So you had seen a rough cut of the film, but you weren't writing directly to it?

Yes, of course, we saw the film, but we didn't have the computer at home to watch the film again. The music was not synchronized. We just imagined what music could be right for this film. So we recorded the music, and then the editor, Dario, and us would cut the music into the film and apply it to the scenes.

Goblin was a band, and therefore there was an aspect of collaboration that doesn't exist for a lone composer. Can you talk about the band dynamic and writing music as a group?

Normally, like many other bands, everyone has small ideas and we put them together. I would say, "Try to do this," or, "Try to do that"; the others would say, "Try to do that." Because this is progressive music, it is not a typical "song." So we would try to do arrangements. Most of the compositions are made by the arrangements. . . .

Sometimes, even with very big hit songs, the arrangement is more important than the song itself. One of the best songs ever written in popular music is "A Whiter Shade of Pale" [1967, by British band Procol Harum]. That song has the arrangement with the organ at the beginning. It is a part just by itself, and they had many issues at the time because the organist that did that arrangement [Matthew Fisher] wanted to share writing credit with Gary Brooker [the song's composer]. They fought in court over it, and Matthew Fisher ended up winning, because he was able to demonstrate that the arrangement was important to the song. They now share credit on the song.

It is not the same with "Profondo rosso," but if I played one arpeggio and Fabio played bass and everyone puts their own idea in, that's what creates the song. We don't have lyrics, we just have chords and arpeggios. That is Goblin's music.

How long did it take you to do the score for *Deep Red*?

It was a very short time. I remember they called and told us that we had to finish the score very soon, because the film was going to be released within the next two months. We had ten days, maybe fifteen days, but no more than that. That's why we recorded just three songs. That wasn't the case with *Suspiria*, though. With *Suspiria* we stayed in the studio for almost three months.

What was Dario Argento's method of working with you guys back then?

Dario loves rock music, he is a fan of music. If you see *Four Flies on Grey Velvet* [1971], it is the story of a drummer. *Opera* [1987] is the story of a singer. There are always musicians in his films. Dario tells you the kind of music he wants. He comes to the studio and listens. He is not a musician, so he can't tell you exactly what to do, but he is able to give you the right information. We listened to a lot of music and records together to try and find the best sound for the film.

Do you recall what kinds of things you listened to for *Deep Red*?

We listened to a lot of stuff. Of course we listened to Pink Floyd and Deep Purple, Genesis and Yes, these kinds of things, and, of course, Mike Oldfield's *Tubular Bells*. Dario asked for something like that; he wanted an arpeggio that felt similar to that, just like what John Carpenter eventually did with the "Halloween Theme." Dario always had good ideas and he gave us suggestions. Now there is much less of that kind of thing. I've now done fourteen films for Dario. So now we talk about it, and then he just trusts me to do what I want. And I am glad for that.

It is not a film score, but let's talk about the album *Roller*.

After *Profondo rosso*, we decided to do something that was more like a prog [progressive rock] band, not film music. Also after *Profondo rosso*, we decided to change drummers. Agostino Marangolo replaced Walter Martino; he had a different style. And Maurizio Guarini played keyboards on *Roller*, because I briefly left the band after *Profondo rosso* and they called Maurizio Guarini to replace me. When I came back to the band, we both played keyboards. Then, after *Roller*, Guarini stopped playing with us. Guarini is more of a jazz keyboard player and I am more into rock. So that's why *Roller* is a sort of jazz-rock fusion. There are many different styles on the album, and it is one of the best things we ever did.

I find *Roller* interesting because it is only the second thing you guys did under the "Goblin" name and it is one of only a few of the things that you did that wasn't for a movie, but when you listen to it now, it is instantly recognizable as Goblin.

Oh, yes, it is very characteristic of Goblin, maybe even more so than *Deep Red*, but I think that the real Goblin sound is *Suspiria* . . . but *Roller* too. *Roller* is very much in the Goblin style, and I think it is very imitated throughout the world by other bands.

When we released *Roller*, all the people that knew *Profondo rosso* were, like, "What is this?" They thought we were doing another *Profondo rosso* album, but actually it was very different . . . except for the title song, "Roller." It is the only song that you can compare to "Profondo rosso," with the church organ, with the arpeggios, and a similar style of music.

You followed up *Roller* with the score to *Suspiria*. It has always been rumored that Goblin recorded some music before Argento began filming, and that he would play it on the set while shooting. Is that true?

Yes, that is true. We read the script and we recorded some music based on that, and he used it on the set to inspire the actors. But actually, when the film was finished and we watched it, that music was not right for the film. So we started over and wrote the music again, and the first music disappeared. We don't have any recordings of that, I don't know why. I don't know what happened to it. I remember it, but I don't have the tapes.

The *Suspiria* score is unique, even when compared to the other music in the Goblin catalogue. Can you talk a bit about how it was written and why you chose the instruments you used?

Dario asked us to write music that would always make the audience feel like the witches were there, even when there is nothing happening. The witch in *Suspiria* is Greek; her name is Markos. So we used the Greek bouzouki [a string instrument somewhat similar to a mandolin]. We also used the Indian tabla [a drum played with the hands]. I used the celesta and the Mellotron with choir. We also used the big Moog synthesizer, the same Moog that Keith Emerson always used. That was 1977, and that Moog was the first one to have a sequencer—not with a computer, but analog. We also needed a technician to help us use it, because I didn't know how to use it. We told him what kind of sounds we needed, and he did it. For the first time, we did the arpeggios with a sequencer, except for the main theme—that was played by hand.

The main theme is very powerful. Even without the picture, the music manages to be very ominous and eerie all on its own. What inspired that piece?

When we wrote the score for *Suspiria*, we wanted to write songs that could stand on their own, without the film. I always think that way. When I record music for a film, I try to imagine that it could live without the visuals; I want you to be able to listen to it like a record. With *Suspiria*, the witches in the film inspired us. When I did the lullaby with the celesta, I said, "Why not add a voice?" So I did, [*whispers*] "La, la, la." I did this horrific voice, with a sweet instrument underneath it.

I think that the score for *Suspiria* is one of our most modern-sounding scores. Even if you listen to it now, it sounds very modern; you could use that music now. I think we were a bit ahead of our time in the late Seventies.

Some of the other parts of the score, in a way, surpass what we usually think of as "film music." It is very percussive and comes off almost more like sound effects than music. For example, the tracks "Witch" and "Sighs."

Yes, because we used the big Moog with the sequencer and a lot of percussion, timpani, and our voices. I think there is something mystic in witch's music, and that's why we used these kinds of things.

You mentioned earlier that you worked on the score for almost three months.

Yes, almost, maybe two and half months. We had a lot of time to work on the music. After the success of the music for *Deep Red*, the record label decided to just let us work. There was no problem with money for the studio or for anything, because they wanted us to do something new and even better than *Profondo rosso*. We did *Profondo rosso* very quickly, so they gave us more time for *Suspiria*.

It has been a long time, but do you remember what you thought of the film, the first time you saw it completed with the music and everything?

Oh, yes. It is always incredible to go to the cinema and see the film with your music. Obviously, I was there when it was being mixed, so I got to see it with the music before it came out. But when you are in the cinema with the audience, it is a completely different mood.

Is it gratifying to see how the audience reacts to the films you work on?

Yeah, of course! That's why I like to go to the cinema. If you see it at home, even if you have the biggest screen and the best sound system, it is not the same.

With George Romero's *Dawn of the Dead* [1978] you recorded music for Dario Argento's European cut of the film. Is that correct?

Yes. The film was released in America before Argento asked us to write new music for it. Romero used music libraries to score the film. [Music libraries license the use of their "stock music" or "library music" to film, TV, and radio projects. This material, whose composer is generally anonymous, is not written with any specific project in mind and is therefore often rather generic-sounding.] When Dario brought the film to Europe, he cut out thirty minutes or so and decided to change the music, because he didn't like the library music. Later it was released again in America, with our score. I remember that I went to see the film while I was in New York in 1978, and the credits said the music was by "The Goblins."

So Romero had nothing to do with that music? You worked specifically with Argento?

Yes. I never met Romero, I've never met him in my life. If I walked past him on the street, I would never recognize him.

So the process in doing that score was similar to your previous scores, because Argento was the one who directed you guys.

Yes, he asked us to do new music for the film. But it is completely different than our previous scores, because here we played more rock, more heavy metal. It is "zombie music." I love that score, we had a lot of fun recording it. Can you imagine being in the studio watching the film and having to writing music for all those zombies? We had a lot of laughs recording that music.

The main theme is very dark and full of dread.

I think that when the zombies arrive, the music has to be very dark. Like [*imitating the music*] *dum, dum!*. That's why we used a lot of marimba and percussion—we thought that would go best with zombies. We also used Caribbean instruments mixed with the hard rock in a few parts.

The track "Zombi" has a very strong Caribbean feel. What was your inspiration for bringing in those Caribbean flavors?

The marimba was used for that track. It is a kind of rock mixed with the marimba and percussion, and a dark choir that sings over the [sings the bass line]. It had a very Caribbean mood to it, like something from Haiti.

So you were playing off of the original Haitian zombie lore?

More or less, yes. I was born in Brazil, so I know the *macumba* [an Afro-Brazilian religious practice] and the South American music very well. Of course, all this music comes from Africa.

There's also a rock track called "Zaratozom." What does that mean? Is there a translation for that word?

"Zaratozom." I don't know [*laughs*]—it is just a name we invented.

With *Dawn of the Dead*, were you scoring directly to the film at that point, or was it still separate?

No. Of course we were inspired by the scenes, but, for instance, "Zaratozom" is a song. Okay, so the bikers arrive, they are violent; so we wrote that song as a theme for them, but we never played while watching the film. We weren't synchronized with the film for the scenes.

The first time I started writing directly to the scenes was maybe for *Opera* [1987]. Even with *Phenomena* [aka *Creepers* (1985)], I just wrote the song and they edited it into the film.

Around the time of *Dawn of the Dead*, Goblin did another non-soundtrack album called *Il fantastico viaggio del "bagarozzo" Mark* [*The Fantastic Voyage of Beetle Mark*].

Yes, this was our last work with all of the original members of Goblin. It was sort of a concept album. We started recording the new songs for the album, and some of the songs reminded us of insects. That is why we called it "Beetle Mark," and then we started to write lyrics about this world made by insects. It is like the book *Animal Farm*. In the book, the characters are like people but they are animals. We did the same thing with insects. It is a human story, but the characters are insects, including a beetle named Mark that travels around the bad world.

This album didn't have much success. The band even started to split up before its promotion. It was not a lucky album, although I like it very much.

I also like that album a lot. But it has lyrics, and because I don't speak Italian, I always wondered what it was about.

[*Laughs*] Oh, yes. But actually my favorite parts on the album are the instrumental parts. I don't like the parts with lyrics and singing as much. A song like "E suono rock" is beautiful; that is a song that I still play live from that album.

You did a couple more scores with Goblin after *Il fantastico viaggio del "bagarozzo" Mark*, but then you left the band.

Yes, Massimo Morante and I left the band. Actually, Morante left the band before me. I did two more films without Massimo, *Amo non amo* [aka *Together?* (1979)] and *Squadra antigangsters* [1979]. Then I left the band and they did *Patrick* [1979], *Contamination* [1980], and *Buio Omega* [aka *Beyond the Darkness* (1979)] without Massimo and me.

Did you leave with the intention of doing a solo project?

When I left the band in 1978, I met a record producer and we started doing dance music, Italian dance music. I did a lot of dance music until 1984. I did that for five or six years, except for [Argento's film] *Tenebre* [1982]. That was a reunion of three of us, but not with the name Goblin. I decided to use the vocoder [a voice analysis/synthesis device that has been used in electronic and pop music for voice altering and voice-triggered and voice-controlled effects] and the dance sound on that score, because I was working on that kind of music.

So the familiar theme from *Tenebre* comes from your experience working in the dance music scene.

Yes, because I had a successful song in Italy named "Baby I Love You" from the band Easy Going, and I used the vocoder on that. And then, when I recorded the music for *Tenebre*, I said, "Why don't I use the vocoder again for *Tenebre*?" That's why I start the track with the vocoder singing the word *paura*. *Paura* in Italian means *fear*. A *film di paura* is a "film of fear."

Did reuniting with Massimo Morante and Fabio Pignatelli for
Tenebre **feel like the old days? Was the process the same?**

No, it was completely different, because we didn't have a drummer. We just used the LinnDrum [a drum machine], and we called in Walter Martino, the original drummer for the *Profondo rosso* score, to do some percussion. He actually only came in as a session musician, though. The music was composed by Pignatelli, Morante, and myself. We didn't have a drummer, and the sound was quite different than the "Goblin sound." After that we didn't play again until *Non ho sonno* [aka *Sleepless*] in 2000, and that was just a short reunion.

You went on to score many films on your own. You did a film for Lucio Fulci called *Conquest* **[1983]. Can you talk a little bit about working with him?**

Actually, Fulci is another director that I never met. Because when they called me to do the music, Fulci had problems with the production and he had left the film. The producer called me, and he is the one that asked me to work on it. So I worked with the editor and the producer. I know Fulci's daughter Antonella very well, but I never met Lucio Fulci. There were four directors I "worked with" but I never met: George Romero, Fulci, Menahem Golan, and Umberto Lenzi. I worked on Golan's film *The Versace Murder* [1998], and I did two TV movies for Lenzi but I never met him.

Can we talk about the music for Dario Argento's *Phenomena***?**

Dario Argento called me to write the main theme for *Phenomena*, and I decided, for the first time, to use a soprano vocal mixed with rock music. I remember when I gave my demo to Dario he loved it, even though at that time the vocal was just recorded with the keyboard. I told him, "I will use a soprano voice for this part." So that theme was the first time I used a soprano vocal. The second time was with *Opera*.

In the Eighties, starting with *Demons* [1985], then *Phemonena*, *Opera*, etc., Dario used compilations of songs in addition to the main themes. For example, in *Demons* you have a lot of dance music and popular music, like Billy Idol and stuff like that. With *Phenomena*, he asked me to do the main theme and he asked Fabio [Pignatelli], Bill Wyman, and Brian Eno to do some of the other themes. But he also used a compilation of music from many other bands.

Argento produced *Demons*, but Lamberto Bava directed it. Did you work primarily with Argento, or did you also work with Bava?

I worked a little bit with Bava, but when I started to record the music, Bava was involved with postproduction. So I worked mainly with Dario. I just wrote a few themes for *Demons*; and then they cut them up and put them in the film with the other music. They decided to use a compilation of different bands and songs, but they do that in America too. A film like *Scream* [1996] used a compilation of many different artists for the soundtrack.

Your main theme for *Demons* has become one of your most popular songs. Can you recall what your main inspirations were when you wrote it?

Like with *Tenebre*, I was influenced by the dance music I was doing at the time. I used the same sequencer, with electronic bass. It was completely electronic, except for the guitar and I used an African voice. It was a real singer and he sang the background vocals: [*sings*] "Demon, demon." If you listen to the soundtrack, it is the typical sound of the 1980s, with the Yamaha DX7 [synthesizer] and other keyboards like that. When you listen to it now you can recognize that it was written in the Eighties, because the sound is typical of that time.

After *Demons* and *Phenomena* you worked with Argento on *Opera*.

Yes. *Opera* was similar to *Phenomena*. I wrote the main theme and maybe one or two other songs.

That film's setting lends itself to a more classical score.

Yes, the music in *Opera* is very classical. It is a sweeter sound. The theme for *Phenomena* has the vocal, but it is hard rock. *Opera* is more sophisticated.

Did you work with other musicians and more classical instruments, or is it still a synthesizer?

I used a concert piano and the soprano voice, but the rest is all [electronic] keyboards. I never used an orchestra.

How did the reunion of Goblin for *Non ho sonno* come about?

I met Dario at a festival in 1999, and he said he would like to have me do the music for *Non ho sonno*, because it was a return to the *giallo* style [the slasher genre in Italian literature and film], and I thought, "Why don't we try to get Goblin together again?" He shot the film in Torino [Turin], the same city where he shot *Profondo rosso*. He used a lot of the same locations, and he even used one of the actors from *Profondo rosso*. So I decided to call the guys from Goblin to do the score.

That score was pretty well received by Goblin fans, including myself. Do you like it?

Yeah, I like it, even though we had [*laughs*] a lot of trouble. When I called them they came, and when they arrived we had the same problems that we had twenty years earlier. It's like if you go back to your ex-wife, the problems are still the same. During the recording of that score, there was a lot of discussion. Massimo and I like rock more, and Agostino and Fabio like funk and jazz more. So we decided to split up: I worked with Morante in one studio, and Agostino and Fabio worked in another studio. It is more of a hybrid score than a true collaboration. I like it, but it reminds me of a bad period. That's why the band is finished forever.

It is interesting to hear the band with a more modern sound.

Yes, of course. We used modern keyboards and sequencers. For example, when we recorded *Tenebre*, I used a real church organ, with the pipes, but I didn't do that for *Non ho sonno*. The church organ is one of the main instruments in that score, but it was a sample.

Are you into the technology aspect of composing and making music?

Yes, of course. Now we have the best keyboards and the best plug-ins [computer software components]—now you can do anything. For example, if I am working on a score that needs a big orchestra, but I don't have a big budget, I can record with a small orchestra and then play over it with the orchestral plug-ins. There is no difference in the sound. Now it is easier and cheaper. I can record an entire soundtrack in my house; I could never have done that in the Seventies. It was very expensive back then, because the label had to pay for the studio by the hour.

What is the most difficult part of composing a score?

The most difficult moment for me, when I compose, is the beginning, because I don't know what to do. I watch the film, and then I have to figure out what the best mood will be, what music will best character-ize the film. . . . I try something and I don't like it, I try something else, and I don't like that either. But when I find the right mood, then the score goes quickly. If you can find the right direction, it is then easy to continue going down that path.

Many of the other composers I've spoken to have told me that they always have music playing in their heads, and when they watch the rough cut of a film, they can hear the music. Then they just need to sit down and work it out.

[*Laughs*] Not me. The first thing I do when I watch the film is sit down at the piano. Then I try and write something on the piano. After that, I then open up the plug-ins and the keyboards and I try several different sounds. Maybe one sound can inspire me—maybe a new sound can inspire a few more notes than the piano did.

So I work with a lot of the technology. I record one instrument and then another one. An instrument can inspire what notes I write. Sometimes it is more technical, compared to the way we did it in the past, but I like it. Sometimes I use guitar, sometimes I use piano or drums or bass. I like to play all those instruments, and I know how to write music in different styles as well. I can even work with a big orchestra, because I've studied music and have learned how to do arrangements and orchestrations. I actually use an orchestra more these days than I ever did before.

Why is that?

Now, for example, when I wrote the music for *Mother of Tears* [2007] and for *Dracula 3D* [2012], especially for *Dracula*, I said, "Wow, this film has the same mood as the Hammer films." [Hammer Films is a British production company known for its gothic horror films from the 1950s through 1970s.] I could've used something very cheap, like the synthesizers, but I felt it would sound even better with a choir and the orchestra. So that's why I did that. But not for *The Card Player* [2004]— *The Card Player* was completely done in the computer.

Every film has its own mood. If I did the same thing for every film, I wouldn't like it. [*Laughs*] I know many musicians that do the same kinds of things every time. I don't like that. I prefer to invent something new, even if it sometimes feels too different than the other things I've done.

I'd like to get your thoughts about one of your contemporaries, Fabio Frizzi.

I actually just met with Fabio Frizzi two days ago. I was at an Italian horror festival with Fabio. We have been very good friends since we were kids. He did a concert, it was the first time I got to see his show. He wrote a lot of music for horror films, but he has his own sound. His music is a bit of a mix of Morricone and Goblin; he is more orchestral and more pop. My style is different. I know Frizzi very well. He is not as involved with Moogs and computers. He did this concert with an orchestra and violins and keyboards, but he doesn't use as many synthesizers as I do. He is more traditional.

Another contemporary of yours is John Carpenter. Do you remember the first time you heard his theme for *Halloween* [1978]?

Yes. When I heard that theme I thought it was similar to "Profondo rosso." And I know that he is a fan of Goblin and Dario Argento.

I have a good story. Two years ago I met John Carpenter in Los Angeles. And when we were introduced to each other, he said, "Oh, I know you very well! I stole all your music." [*Laughs*] It was incredible, and I told him, "You did it very well." I also know his son Cody. Cody told me that he loved prog rock, and he is also a musician. He sent me his demos and his album. He is a good guy.

But I love John Carpenter. The atmospheres he creates are incredible. Sometimes he plays only two notes, and you know it is John Carpenter and the mood is great, better than the London Symphony Orchestra. With the theme from *Halloween*, you can just listen for a few notes and you feel scared. That is the power of good music, when you can scare people with hardly doing anything.

I've heard that you sometimes play live along with the film *Nosferatu* [1922]. Is that true?

Yeah. That started because I was invited to come to Paris for a festival. The organizers told me that they had asked several musicians to come and play their own score along with screenings of silent movies, and they asked me to write something for *Nosferatu*. I told them I could do it, but I didn't have time to write music for the entire film (it is one hour and forty minutes). But I told them I could score some excerpts from the film. So, for the first time, I played my music for *Nosferatu*—it was something like twenty minutes. . . . That was the first time, then the second time was at a festival in Mount Pelée, and for that I wrote a score for the entire film. I also did it a third time in Bolzano in Italy.

Have you ever considered releasing a CD of the music or a DVD of the film with your music?

I would like to. I am trying to get the rights to use the movie, so that I can release it on DVD. The copyright is free, because the film is very old and [director F. W.] Murnau has been dead for almost 100 years [he died in 1931], but the restoration of the image is not free. I need to find a copy that has its own copyright on it. There are several different versions of the film, even in color. I love *Nosferatu*. It is a beautiful film. It is a masterpiece of horror.

Among your scores, do you have any favorites?

Yeah, of course. I love *Profondo rosso* and I love *Phenomena*, but I also love *Dracula*. I am very proud of the music in *Dracula*, even though the film was not a big success. I like my interpretation of the Hammer music, mixed with my sound; it is one of my favorites. I also like the music for "Jenifer" [2005], the episode of *Masters of Horror*. That is one of my favorites, but not just the music, also the film. Dario did a great job on that.

When you began working on Argento's *Dracula*, did you go into the project with the intention of paying homage to the Hammer films, or was that something that came naturally as you began to write?

I was there when Dario shot the film. I was on the set many times, and when I saw the mood, the vampires, the wardrobe, the castles, I thought about the Hammer movies and their music. I love that kind of mood in music, particularly in the Hammer films. James Bernard [a composer who scored many Hammer films] had his own style, even though many people do not remember his work.

I think the first horror film where you can remember the music is probably *Psycho* [1960], by Bernard Herrmann, because of the shower scene and the knife. He was an incredible and amazing composer, one of the best. I love Bernard Herrmann, because he always changed his music, like *The Day the Earth Stood Still* [1951] with the Theremin [an

early electronic music instrument known for its eerie vocal-like quality].
Bernard Herrmann is one of the biggest and best composers ever.

The Hammer films, though, have music that is more in the background, but this background music helps give the film the right mood.
With Dario's *Dracula* I wanted to use music like they did in the Hammer
films, but give it more identity and use more themes. [*Laughs*] At least
that is what I *tried* to do—I don't know if I succeeded.

**You just mentioned Bernard Herrmann. Are there other compos-
ers who influenced you and your work?**

Actually, I was more influenced by rock music, the progressive rock
music, like Emerson, Lake & Palmer and many others. But if I listen
to film music, of course I like John Williams and Jerry Goldsmith.
These are the most famous, but they are two of the best. I think
that, together, Spielberg and John Williams manage to reach perfec-
tion with the marriage of movies and music. I think that in the future
John Williams's music will be played like Mozart and Beethoven are.
He is that great.

**You've been touring and playing the themes from Argento's films
since 2000, first with the band Daemonia, then with New Goblin,
and now with Claudio Simonetti's Goblin. When you began, did
you have any idea just how popular the music would become over
the years?**

No, never. We were never supposed to have this story with the film
scores. We [Goblin] were born in the 1970s, where many bands played
progressive music, and it was not very popular or commercial. So we
never imagined that one song like "Profondo rosso" could be a hit, even
after forty years. But during this forty years, even after the splitting of
Goblin, I've played this music with new arrangements many times by
myself and with bands. At the end of the 1990s I decided to start a band
and to present this music with new arrangements, not with the old style.
It was a newer sound, so I decided to call the band Daemonia, and we
played heavier—more rock, more hard rock.

**Just last year you toured the US with New Goblin—a hybrid of
members from both Daemonia and Goblin—and you sold out**

shows. I saw you in New York City, and it was crazy: You guys had genuine "rock star" fame here. Was that surprising?

Yes, I am still surprised. I saw a lot of young people and middle-aged people and people that were in their sixties. And now that we are playing the music live along with the films, it is incredible. We played in Rome two days ago with my band Simonetti's Goblin. I played the music of *Profondo rosso* live during a screening of the film, with 2000 people in the audience. Dario Argento was there. It was an incredible concert, and I've now done this many times, all over the world, with *Profondo rosso*, *Suspiria*, and *Dawn of the Dead*.

And it is exciting, because a lot of the young people know the music well but they never had a chance to see the films in the theater. They've only seen them on DVD or on VHS, and for the first time we are presenting the scores live with the films playing on the big screen. And I am really surprised that after forty years people still love these films so much. It is incredible and unbelievable.

CHRISTOPHER YOUNG

"The wonderful thing about horror music that separates it from any other genre is that you can't pussyfoot around. You need to be ultra-dramatic, focused, and extraverted."

B ESIDES BEING ONE OF THE first composers I put on my wish list when I started this book, Christopher Young also happened to be one of the most asked-about composers of the lot: Everyone from friends and fellow fans to publishers and even some of the other composers featured in this book wanted to know, "Are you going to talk to Chris Young?" And if you're reading this now, you know the answer to that question is a resounding "YES!"

A lifelong horror, sci-fi, and fantasy fan, Young has referred to himself as the "Bela Lugosi of film music." He has worked with many of horror's most celebrated filmmakers, including Clive Barker, Tobe Hooper,

Sam Raimi, and George A. Romero. And though he is best known for his work in these genres, he has a surprisingly eclectic résumé, with well over 100 film credits to his name.

While researching and preparing for what turned out to be a series of fascinating and informative conversations with Christopher Young, it rapidly became clear to me that he is an extremely generous and passionate artist and person. He teaches film scoring at USC and has lent his time and efforts to numerous projects. His most gracious contribution to the film and music communities, though, is the low-cost housing program Tilden House Residency, which is designed to aid aspiring film composers and musicians looking to establish themselves in Hollywood. (For more information, visit Tildenhouseresidency.com.)

Young's generosity and passion were definitely confirmed when we spoke. We had an instant rapport, and I quickly found myself in awe of his knowledge, excitement, honesty, and sensitivity. He is a true artist, complete with the vulnerability that plagues the creatively gifted, and I found his openness and honesty absolutely inspiring—and even endearing. He may be a man with decades of professional experience, but he still talks about music and his favorite composers with such great enthusiasm that you would think they were amazing treasures that he discovered just yesterday.

In this interview, he tells a story about the exact vinyl LP that made him want to pursue film scoring. I recommend that you do as I did: Find that record and, while you listen to it, see if you can imagine the scene he describes. In your mind, be a fly on the wall as a teenage kid in New Jersey named Chris sits in his bedroom, places the record player needle on a piece of vinyl, and has his life changed forever.

SELECTED FILMOGRAPHY

1982	*The Dorm That Dripped Blood* (aka *Pranks*, aka *Death Dorm*)
1985	*Def-Con 4*
	A Nightmare on Elm Street 2: Freddy's Revenge
1986	"Monsters!" (*The Twilight Zone* TV series)
	"A Small Talent for War" (*The Twilight Zone* TV series)
	"A Matter of Minutes" (*The Twilight Zone* TV series)
	Invaders from Mars
	Trick or Treat
1987	*Hellraiser*
1988	*Hellbound: Hellraiser II*
1989	*The Fly II*
	Hider in the House
1992	*The Vagrant*
	Jennifer 8
1993	*The Dark Half*
1995	*Tales from the Hood*
	Species
	Virtuosity
1998	*Urban Legend*
2000	*The Gift*
2004	*The Grudge*
2005	*The Exorcism of Emily Rose*
2006	*The Grudge 2*
2007	*Ghost Rider*
	Spider-Man 3
2009	*The Uninvited*
	Drag Me to Hell
2011	*Priest*
2012	*Sinister*
	Scary or Die

The reason I decided to pursue this project is because I am a huge horror fan, film fan, and film music fan. But I am also not the only one. It seems that horror film music attracts a very big fan base in a way that other genres don't.

Oh, definitely. Horror films themselves also have a fan base that is unlike other genres. As you know, every year in the United States alone, there are approximately nine conventions that happen in one state or another that celebrate horror movies, and the fans are hard-core devotees. But you won't find comedy or drama conventions anywhere. They may have them, but I've never heard of them. There are conventions that celebrate a single film or series, like the *Star Trek* conventions, but above and beyond that, it seems as though the fans of horror are extremely devoted and loyal to the genre and are proud of it.

Horror films are a bit like the unwanted bastard stepchildren of Hollywood, and the people that love them, like myself, didn't quite "fit in" when we were kids. So what is nice about these conventions—and I've been to a lot of them as a fan myself—is that they are an opportunity for all of us to get together and realize that it is quite normal to adore these movies, these books, and these magazines. You know how it is, that "I know exactly where you're coming from" togetherness.

I'm going to tell you a bit of a side story. I got the Saturn Award for the score to the film *Hellbound: Hellraiser II* [1988]. The Saturn is an award given to the people working in genre films by an organization called the Academy of Science Fiction Fantasy and Horror Films. They have their awards around June, so they're after the Oscars, and it is for all those films that the Oscars wouldn't dream of giving awards out to, let alone a nomination. . . .

I remember when I got that award for *Hellbound*, I made note of the fact in my acceptance speech that, "The greatest reward here is that I am actually receiving an award from people that I don't have to explain myself to, that make me feel at home with all those qualities that made me an outcast when I was a kid. God, thank you so much for making me feel normal for the first time [*laughs*]."

I want to start by finding out how a jazz drummer finds his way to becoming a film score composer.

Indeed you are right, I was at one time aspiring to be a jazz drummer, and before that, a rock drummer. When I was a kid the first music that

I heard was either in the Episcopal church on Sundays—the wonderful choral music and the spectacular organ repertoire, etc.—or whatever happened to be on the AM radio . . . and that, of course, was rock 'n' roll, as well as vocal jazz stuff. But popular music was really all I knew, so my brain was wired to think that there was only rock and this Sinatra-like stuff around.

I picked up a pair of drumsticks when I was really young and headed down the path of committing myself to playing drums in rock groups. The Beatles appeared magically one night on *The Ed Sullivan Show*, and I was pissed off at God for not having made me Ringo Starr [*laughs*]. God kind of blew it by passing over me and giving the drumsticks to Richard Starkey [Ringo's original name], not me.

But, of course, I was too young. Then I graduated, as many of us did, into the world of jazz, and I was again pissed off at God for not having made me Buddy Rich. I went to Berklee School of Music [in Boston] for a summer session and studied with Alan Dawson, who was Dave Brubeck's second drummer. I was hoping that I was going to knock his socks off, but it didn't quite work out like that. I remember walking down Boylston Street after my last lesson with Alan had ended. I was in tears, thinking, "Oh my God, what the hell am I going to do? If I am not the drummer I thought I was going to be, where am I going to turn to?"

My head had started to think about things other than rhythms. As a drummer, the primary thought processes that we are attracted to are rhythmic—the tick-tock of a clock, for instance. Anything that sets off a rhythmic pattern is something that we use as a springboard to modify it. But my head started to think about pitches. Immediately I gravitated towards trying to write or arrange for the ensembles I had at hand, which were the jazz bands I was playing in or the various vocal groups I was singing in. So that's where I started: I segued into the idea of being a composer as I started to fade out my obsession with being a drummer.

Now, film scoring . . . that happened shortly after I redefined my musical thinking, and it was sort of by accident, when I went to the record store in my hometown, Red Bank, New Jersey. The store is still there and is called Jack's Music Shoppe. (Coincidentally, Kevin Smith's comic book store, Jay and Silent Bob's Secret Stash, is right across the street from it, and you can actually see Jack's in his movie *Chasing Amy*.) Well, that's the record store I used to go to as a kid to get the vinyl that stuffed my head with all these notes. That was really my musical class-room, because there weren't any music classes offered in my hometown. They just didn't exist.

My grammar school had a music appreciation class, but of course it was about the three Bs: Bach, Brahms, and Beethoven. We were immediately told how wonderful they were. I had no idea that there were living people still writing for the orchestra; I thought that music had evolved into the Beatles over time. How stupid was I?

But no one had been there to guide me, to tell me otherwise. I thought that orchestra music was a dead issue. If you didn't hear it on the AM radio, then it didn't exist. The only orchestral music I ever heard was probably the orchestral arrangements backing up Frank Sinatra, done by Nelson Riddle or Gordon Jenkins . . . and the music of Leroy Anderson, who had written some orchestral miniatures for the Boston Pops orchestra when it was under the baton of Arthur Fiedler. Anderson's most famous piece is probably "Sleigh Ride." I remember listening to that as a kid. I loved that music madly, and I actually went to school with his sons. My father was stationed in Iceland with him during World War II, so the first orchestral composer I ever met was Leroy Anderson, during the parents' weekend at the prep school I went to. God! I was shaking like a leaf, because I actually had quite a lot of his music branded in my brain and wanted so badly to impress him, but I was still drumming at the time.

So, anyway, one day I went into Jack's, and that's where my life changed. You would go in there with the amount of money that it would cost to buy the one or two records that you wanted to get, but you would always bring a little extra money in case you just happened to stumble into something unexpected. Well, the thing I stumbled into was in the section in the back corner of the store called Musicals and Soundtracks.

There happened to be a record there with a really cool cover, and I went, "Oh my God! What is this?" It was, like, "Wow! I want to hear what is on this record just based on the cover." It was called *The Fantasy Film World of Bernard Herrmann*. It was on the Phase 4 Stereo label, which was a subsidiary of Decca Records.

I flipped the record over, and there were short paragraphs written by the composer Bernard Herrmann, and it turned out that the pieces were selections or suites from four of his sci-fi/fantasy films: *Journey to the Center of the Earth* [1959], *The 7th Voyage of Sinbad* [1958], *The Day the Earth Stood Still* [1951], and *Fahrenheit 451* [1966].

I said, "Oh. Movies? Music? Hmmm, yeah, I remember the songs from the James Bond movies. Sure." I was totally into the James Bond films, and I remembered their songs because my head was still wired pretty exclusively for the vocal stuff. That's all that was on the radio in respect to film music, and though I did know there was the instrumental music accompanying films, I never really paid attention to it.

But, hey, this was music that had been written for science-fiction and fantasy films. And at the time, I was also extremely into science-fiction literature—guys like Arthur C. Clarke, A. E. van Vogt, Ray Bradbury, Isaac Asimov. . . . I was gobbling this stuff up. So I was very anxious to see what Herrmann had done for these films, and I will never forget it. I went back home, opened up that record, put it on the little stereo record player I had, and placed the needle on it. The first notes that I heard were the Mountain Top and Sunrise music from the suite to *Journey to the Center of the Earth*, and I went, "Holy Christ! What the hell is this?"

What little writing I had done up to that moment had been experimental, trying to find a sonority or a language that echoed or reflected my childhood interest in what I called "the invisible world"—the things that we can't see that are actually going on at night.

(We will talk in a moment about the eternal partnership that I have had, for as long as I can remember, with the horror genre—anything that dealt with this invisible world, things that couldn't be explained quite rationally, and all that illuminated what might be going on in the darkness, beyond what the eye was able to see at nighttime. All of this stuff always fascinated me.)

Now, I happened to have been born in a house in the middle of a street that, at the end of it, had a Quaker graveyard. God, I used to pass by it all the time on my way to catch the bus to school, and I used to hang out in it at nighttime. And with my own little dabblings in writing up to that moment, I had tried to figure out ways to capture that. But again, I was just a kid . . . I was around seventeen years old, and I was no Mozart.

My writing was nowhere, and then I hear this record called *The Fantasy Film World of Bernard Herrmann* and I immediately identified with the material. I thought, "This is the missing link! This guy is doing exactly what I've been alluding to in my own writing." His music is so loaded with this magnificent sense of mystery, and it seems to capture so well this place that I believed existed just around the corner, just over the horizon, those places we never could quite get to—this magical world that had to live just outside of our perception or that could only be described successfully to a composer or musician in notes. It worked perfectly for me.

Little did I know that when I put that needle on that track that it really was going to change my life. I had no idea at the time that I was going to become a film composer. I had no idea that I had the talent or inclination to do that—that that was going to be the stage on which I was going to be able to act in the world of music with the greatest ease.

If I could go back in time, I would love to witness myself in that moment. I talk about it as being a life changer. Every composer has that life-changing moment, that piece of music that they heard that all of a sudden added up. It is like the lost chord, the Holy Grail, the missing link in their life, and for me it was definitely that record. As I said, I wish I could go back in time and just look at myself at the age of seventeen and view that moment once again, knowing what I know now.

Bernard Herrmann has come up quite frequently while I've been interviewing composers. You've already touched on it a bit, but what is it about his music that seems to strike a chord with so many people that do what you do?

There are so many things about his music that I think so perfectly encapsulate everything that movie music, not just genre music, should aspire to be. What were his greatest contributions? Say what you will about the music—you may like it, you may not—but it is so strong and undeniable. His identity is immediately established by the fact that no one before him in the world of film music, nor really concert music for that matter, had set out to try to combine instruments that normally wouldn't have made good bed partners.

His obsession, apparently, was first and foremost about how to use instruments to create unique colors. So what he brought to movies was a way of thinking about what you could do orchestrally that had never been done before. The composers like Max Steiner, [Erich Wolfgang] Korngold,

[Dimitri] Tiomkin, [Miklós] Rózsa, [Alfred] Newman, who were already writing in Hollywood at the time, came to Los Angeles believing that the ensembles they needed to write for were the same romantic orchestras that were being used by concert composers, meaning that they were writing music that could be performed on a concert stage. They stayed within the convention of what was practically programmable music.

Herrmann comes along and says, "Well, the hell with this! Why should I care about whether or not the stuff is going to be concert friendly? I am in Los Angeles, where, if I want nine harps, if I want to write for a serpent [a rarely used, snake-shaped wind instrument traditionally made of wood, but considered a member of the low brass section because of its sound and trombone-like mouthpiece], if I want to write for sixteen French horns, if I want to write for a mammoth ensemble of low wood-winds, including clarinets, bass clarinets, contrabass clarinets, bassoons, contrabassoons—no matter what it is that I want to write for, I can find people here to play it. So I can pull together these ungodly ensembles and record them here in Hollywood, on a soundstage, have the best play-ers and realize this music without worrying if it is ever going to have a second life." So I think that shift in thinking is his major contribution.

That's the thing that I noticed immediately, his unusual use of instru-mental groups. Also, as you know, his music was pretty damn simple. For instance, he would take a progression of four chords and repeat them, but be constantly shifting the orchestration, and in so doing would keep your interest. Because he was such a great orchestrator, he knew exactly what ensembles he could use to best deliver something special, and modify them just enough along the course of the movie to keep your interest in what otherwise might've been less exciting material. If every single Herrmann score had been written for a string orchestra, like *Psycho* [1960] was, they wouldn't be as exciting as they were.

But at the end of the day, on top of that, I think the thing that struck me in particular and why I fell so in love with him and why so many composers identify with him, is because there is this inevitable sense of mystery in his music. It was his choice of chords, these minor-based chord progressions that he'd use; the way he orchestrated them, it made me immediately believe that he had some magic ability to see that invis-ible world and turn it into music in a way that I had never heard before and have really never heard since. . . . Everybody is influenced by him.

Another thing that he was great at was, he didn't pussyfoot around, he didn't tiptoe through the movies dramatically. He would lay it on hard. He would decide what it was he wanted to say and he'd go for it. He'd grab you by the throat. His music is extremely aggressive, and sometimes it may seem over-the-top because it is so strong, but it would never turn drama into melodrama. Even in some of the least effective movies, when he's hitting you hard over the head with his music, trying his best to invoke a response from you, it never comes off as corny. No, it is totally convincing. We're completely convinced, because he had an impeccable sense of drama and he knew how far he could go without crossing that line.

I don't think there is any composer that was able to get quite so far into pushing the limits of what you could do. Just look at the main title from *Vertigo* [1958] for Christ's sake! It immediately jumps out of the screen. The music is the first thing that you hear, and it goes "fuuuuck"! It immediately sucks you into the vortex and you just can't run away from it.

I have often said in my USC classes that in genre movies we, as the composer, have to play the role of a barker at a carnival: We have to think of ourselves as standing in front of a curtain, a curtain behind which there are all these dark and evil activities happening. If we had our wits about us, if we knew what was best for us, we would run as fast as we could in the opposite direction. But our job in genre films is to hook the audience with our music, to seduce them, saying, "Come behind the curtain with me. Let's take this trip together, even though you know in your heart it is not something you really should be doing. Come with me."

The temptation is overwhelming. It is the Pandora's box syndrome. A good movie score, a good main title in particular, has to insist that the audience step behind the curtain. And if they don't, you have failed.

Is it true that you learned the art of composing for films by recording the audio from movies and listening back to them?

Yes, that's very true. You probably know more about me than I do! You're absolutely right. As I just mentioned, my life-changing moment was hearing that record of Herrmann's, and I became obsessed with trying to get as many records of his music as possible. Back in those days, not many soundtracks were being issued, so if you were really interested you had to go to New York City. That was where there were these rare-record stores that had bootlegs and private pressings. I'd take trips there to get these hard-to-find pressings of every one of these Herrmann scores.

Of course, there were no [printed] scores. Printed music is still a problem. Ninety-nine-point-five percent of all movie music is not available to the public in its printed form. Songs? Yeah you can get lead sheets of songs, arrangements for piano and voice, but there is so little film music that you can go out and buy the full orchestral scores for. John Williams, of course, is the exception to the rule, but only some of his music. Even within our lifetimes, scores for a great like Jerry Goldsmith are not available. The only places you can get this printed music is by going to the music libraries at universities, where composers donated their music to, or to the film studio music libraries in Los Angeles, where hopefully there's at least one copy of their movie scores. But in both instances you can't check them out of those libraries.

So, to answer your question, yes, outside of vinyl, the only way you could familiarize yourself with the way the score was playing in the movie was to go to the theater itself with a cassette machine. This was before videos. If you wanted to learn about how the music worked, you either went to the movie theater and stayed and watched the movie over and over and over again, you recorded it like I did, or you watched a movie on television.

When I was a kid, there was this show on television called *The Million Dollar Movie* on Channel 9 [WWOR-TV], and all they did, as I recall (and I hope I'm not wrong about this), was show one single movie every night for a week. This meant you could watch it repeatedly at home. They would show old classic movies that had played in the theater for a limited release and then disappeared. So outside of Channel 9, where would you be able to see them? All you'd be left with, if you were lucky, was a memory of the film and a [vinyl] record of the score. Otherwise it was done, it was gone.

So I would go to the theater and record the entire sound onto a cassette. For old movies, you'd have to go to revival theaters in New York, and I went to a lot of those. Or if they were showing an old classic movie on television, like they did on *The Million Dollar Movie*, I would record the audio off of that. Then I would listen back to those tapes and study how the music was being used against the dialogue. The nice thing about *The Million Dollar Movie* was that I was able to remind myself what the images were by re-watching the movie on successive nights.

It's much the same way now: If you watch a DVD repeatedly, you get familiar with the images. Otherwise, I'd just listen to the audio and try and remember what was going on in the movie. So that was it.

As for books, at this time I wasn't aware of how many or how few had been written on film music. (I'm talking about the 1970s here. Now there are hundreds, but not back then.) But the one that became my bible was Tony Thomas's book called *Music for the Movies*. I got that in a store in New York somewhere, and I couldn't believe that there was actually a book devoted exclusively to movie music. Books on movie musicals had been around for a while, but not movie scores. Now, Thomas's book wasn't the first, but it was really the only one, for a period of time, that you could actually find in a bookstore.

So how did I learn about movie music? I only ever took one class on movie scoring, so I guess everything that I learned up to that moment was from those audio recordings of movies, Tony Thomas's book, and vinyl. I have a big collection of film music vinyl and classical vinyl. And I'm talking more about the contemporary classical stuff—you're not going to find much Beethoven here. But I do listen to the guys next to Beethoven, especially American-born, like Samuel Barber, [Leonard] Bernstein, Marc Blitzstein, Earle Brown, [John J.] Becker, and [Henry] Brant. You'll see lots of those other "B" guys in my collection; they are the guys that I do listen to in the classical world.

I got very familiar with the orchestral music of both the film world and the contemporary concert world, and that music was and is available in printed score form. So that was really it, until I moved out to Los Angeles. When I finally moved out here, I had never scored a movie or even written a single film music cue. I just knew that that was what I wanted to do and I had to be in Los Angeles. I knew the music, but didn't have anything to show for it, really. So the movie music thing really started for me when I moved out to Los Angeles.

I'd like to shift gears a bit and talk about your process. When you've been hired for a job and you're having that first meeting to talk about the film, are there certain things that you're looking for from the director?

I'm sure you've heard this over and over by now. The first thing that the composer has to contend with is the temp music, music that has been put in temporarily for test screenings and, more importantly, for the director to sell the producer on what they've done with their movie. I don't know if you've ever seen a horror film without music, but it is usually horrible and I don't mean that in the worst of ways. I hope I don't come off poorly by saying that.

Not at all. Music plays such a significant role in all films, but it seems to play a _very_ unique part in horror films. I think most people would agree that music is incredibly important in horror films.

Yes, it is incredibly important, and it is not surprising that is so important. The best compliments I've ever received from directors of horror films have been in situations where they feel that once my music was placed to the picture, it brought a level of dimension or depth that wasn't there before. It added something to the picture that the filmmakers wanted from the beginning, but couldn't quite achieve without the music.

So, when I am sitting down with a director, the first thing I always hope for is that he or she will enable me to first see the film without temp music, so that I can spend some time imagining what the score might be. I want to see the film in total silence and experience it without having been influenced by this temp music as a description of what they think it should be. (That very rarely happens, by the way, even with directors that I have worked with numerous times.)

When I sit down with them, I am hoping that they will have a strong concept of what the movie is and what the music can do. They usually have sounds in their heads: They go, "I see it sort of in this register," or, "I know it should be strings," or, "I know it shouldn't be strings." That I love. They've been carrying this film around in their heads for years, and then, when I join the team, I'm usually the first outsider that gets to see the film. The composer is typically the first person that is permitted to see the film—even before the director's spouse sees the film, the composer sees it. So they are really very eager to hear what we have to say, so we have to be very careful about what we do say [laughs].

As a general rule, I want to hear them be passionate and excited about the picture, about what they've done and what they want me to do. Then I will feel like I'm one of them, like I'm really one of the team and charged to the max!

After you've watched the film and you sit down to start writing, what is your first step? Some of the composers I've spoken to describe that they have a sort of radio playing in their head and it is just a matter of getting the music down on "tape" or paper. Other composers like to sit at a keyboard and improvise while they watch the film until they find it.

Well, that's not my thing, because I am an ex-drummer, and sitting behind the drum set is not going to do a lot of good [*laughs*]. Nor am I a keyboardist; in fact, I am a terrible keyboardist. I have a piano that I sit next to all the time, but I'm not a keyboardist. So, like you said, it's like a radio or whatever. I am a guy that has to work to get the music out of his head. I will watch the film, hopefully without temp music, and allow myself to digest the movie and carry it around in my head for a little bit.

Before we could record voice memos on our cell phones, there were digital cassettes; before digital cassettes there were the analog tape cassettes. I always had cassette machines with me, and thank the Lord that I did. I would carry them around so that I could record any idea that I had. I'd hum into these things. Once upon a time, before there were cassette machines, you had to jot these ideas down on manuscript paper.

I will watch the film once or twice and then stay away from it for a period of time, depending on what the schedule is. If I can, I give myself ten days when I don't look at the movie, I just let it seep into my body. And then I have a cassette machine at hand; I will immediately start to spit out whatever comes into my mind onto the cassette. It could be lots and lots of ideas—fifty, sixty, seventy or more different thematic ideas or sounds that I have going on in my head. I try to identify the personality of the film and how it can turn into something thematic. It is usually the themes and the sonority of those themes that I'm most interested in in the beginning.

As I said, I spend ten days at it, then I go back and review what I've come up with, watch the picture again, see if any of the stuff sticks. Usually fifty percent of it doesn't, and then I decide, "Maybe this one theme could be the main theme to the movie."

I will choose three to five of my favorite ideas as options for the opening sequence or the main title, and I will mock them up. I will do a synth mockup, usually with live instruments included, and I will then pull the director over and have him watch something. At that stage it is usually the main title, or one or more of the other important scenes. I will show him different takes of music on the same footage, so he can get a sense of the different directions the score can go in.

The main thing that has changed since I was doing films like *Hellraiser* [1987] is that, if the score is to be recorded by a live ensemble, you can mock these things up on a computer. Not only can you, but it is expected. You just can't have the director come over, like we used to do in the old days, and sit at the piano and play it for him. Now they come into the studio, you dim the lights, you push the button, and they want to hear it just the way it's going to be in the theater. That's what you're competing with—the expectation for it to sound really damn close to what they're going to get.

Can you talk a little bit more about the mockup process, and how technology in general has changed your way of working? Has it made it easier in all aspects, or has it, in some ways, made it more difficult?

That's a very good question. Technology has completely changed the outcome of the current state of music. I don't know when the synth thing and the need to mock-up music became a solidified way of life, but it was somewhere in the early Nineties. In the Eighties you would write the score directly onto paper. The only facility that you had to ensure that this thing was going to work with the instruments that you were writing it for was in your head, and if you didn't have it in your head you were in deep shit. What you had to do during those show-and-tells was sit at the piano with the director and do your best to communicate to him what it was going to sound like when you went to the scoring stage.

They were forced to use their imaginations, and some were better than others. I unfortunately was, and still am, a terrible pianist. That always got in the way of me being able to perform a cue from beginning to end without some sort of error. And, by the way, when you were performing that cue for the director, you were doing it to picture, but generally speaking you weren't doing it with a click. So he couldn't hear it done at exactly the right tempo to see exactly which cuts were going to be hit with the music. It was much more free, much more vague . . . it was more, "This is the style, these are the themes, these are the chords, this is the ostinato . . ."

And then I'd use my mouth, as a general rule, to sound out the instruments that I was using. One moment I was a brass instrument, the next moment I was the strings. Then I was percussion and then I'd pretend I was a flute or something from the wind section. But I had to plant that seed in their heads so that when they walked out they had a pretty damn good impression. Some of the best compliments I ever got were when I ultimately would walk on the scoring stage and turn to the director and say, "Hey, is this kind of what you thought it was going to sound like?" And they would say something like, "You know, based on the way you described it to me, it's exactly what I was expecting to hear." And I'd be, like, "Wow. Remarkable. Good." You definitely didn't want to hear the director say the opposite thing . . . "What the fuck is this?"

Those days are gone, though. What they've been replaced with are mocking-up your cues of the entire score. No more worrying about performing anything live with the director in the room. This means that you spend a hell of a lot of time trying to perfect the mockup. Most composers have given up the pencil-to-paper process and have gone directly to writing at the computer. So as they write, they are mocking it up, and it may never even be intended for live recording. When they finish completing the cue, there's nothing on the paper that represents it as of yet.

I'm still old-school, so I still write music in the sketch format. The synth programmers then input the sketches, and I go down and work with them to make them sound the best they possibly can. I would have to say that, because I do not write at the computer, because I do not write for what the samples do best, and because I'm adding more steps, it takes more time.

I don't like [writing directly into the computer], because it is time-consuming and you can get obsessed with the mockups. From my perspective, that's taking time away from the actual writing time. The advantage, of course, is they get to hear it—it's not vague anymore. You're doing most of your rewrites before you get on the scoring stage, and in some instances the directors are so excited about the mockups themselves that they don't even come to the recording sessions, because they go, "Well, give me what I hear on the mockup and we're fine." And so I've had directors not show up, because they're happy with the mockups and they don't have the time to be there.

I've tried not to allow computers and samples to influence my way of thinking. My music doesn't sound like it's written for the synthesizer. Most composers know what the synths do well and what they don't do well, so they will write to accommodate to its strengths—you know what I mean? That's why their music will work as a mockup really well.

When directors come in, they can hear something that is really exciting and it can be used as the final music for the movie. When they come to hear my mockups, I don't care how good they sound, since the music was conceived using an old-school orchestral thinking and they can't use those mockups for the movie. They have to wait until we get on the stage with the real thing doing it. However, I should say I've utilized synthesizers in my scores, but only to do what they do best, which is offer those special sonorities that you can't get anywhere else.

Do you have any thoughts as to where inspiration comes from?

I certainly have thought about this quite a bit, and I don't think anyone can say with certainty where it comes from, why it comes, why doesn't it come when it doesn't come, and where do we have to go to find it if it's not happening. However, I can say with certainty that in my case I've been extremely fortunate that I don't recall ever having writer's block.

Like so many others who spend years staring at an image on the screen, I am a well-seasoned film music composer. However, I'm much like a circus animal. This means that if I am just put in front of a piano with a blank sheet of music paper and instructed to come up with something right then and there, I would struggle. But show me some footage and something will start happening in my brain and I will begin to hear music.

I can't stop it. I'm not saying that it will be great; I'm not even saying it will be good, but it will happen. This is what distinguishes film composers: We're a cursed lot on one hand, because we have to serve the image, not the music. We're always playing second fiddle to the movie. But the upside of it is, for most of us anyway, if we're in a spot where we're not able to come up with music, all we have to do is return to the moving image and we are back on course.

There is also the brain to consider, and what role it plays in inspiration. What is the chemical activity that's going on in a part of my mind that means I'm able to hear music in my head? I've heard that this comes from an area of the brain close to the top of the right ear. Wherever it may come from, I do wonder, "Why does it come from that part of my brain?" or, "Why that specific collection of pitches?" Perhaps it comes from somewhere else? I'm not going to speculate on that one.

I do believe in God, though, and without wanting to sound too cracked here, in my best moments I hope I'm tapping into something that transcends the movie that I am composing for. There are usually certain themes that a film composer becomes identified with even more so than for the entire score—and it is those few themes that they are best remembered for. But it is the moment that they are created that I think they may be coming from some external source, like something is being whispered into that composer's ear.

Is it by God? Who knows. But in my classes I tell the students that if and when they are blessed with a really good theme, the best thing to do is to step out of the way and not let intellect spoil a damn special moment. I guess I'm old enough to know that if I'm getting a good idea, getting out of the way is the best thing to do.

How is music significant in horror films compared to other types of films?

The wonderful thing about horror films is that composers are being asked to participate in a much more active and visceral way. In horror films the music may be great or it may not necessarily be great, but the one thing for sure is that it has to be on solid ground when it comes to its dramatic intent. If you're faulty on that one, you're in trouble.

Horror film music needs to induce a very large and immediate emotional response from its listener. You've been in a theater . . . you know what I'm talking about. So, much of our task is to ensure that the audience is perplexed and overwhelmed at the right moments, on the edge of their seats at the right moments, that they are screaming at the right moments and literally jumping of their seats at the right moments, because they are affected by what's happening on the screen.

I've been to premieres with audiences that have been invited off the street, for both horror films and some dramas that I've worked on. There is nothing more rewarding than sitting next to a girl who is on a date, seeing a dramatic film that I've scored—but who doesn't know that I was the composer—in tears during a moment where there is a lot of pain and I know that the music is helping that happen.

To instill tears in a dramatic, romantic, or poignant moment in a movie is really rewarding, on one hand. But on the other hand [*laughs*], there's nothing cooler than sitting next to the same girl at a horror movie premiere when a stinger happens in the score for an unexpected scare, watching her jump out of her seat, screaming bloody murder, and knowing that it would not have happened without the music. That's amazing too.

So I'd have to say that the wonderful thing about horror music that separates it from any other genre is that you can't pussyfoot around. You need to be ultra-dramatic, focused, and extraverted. A kiss is a kiss, and music can enhance a kiss in a romantic film and make you a little more teary-eyed, but horror films really need the music to communicate those emotions—the music really needs to deliver the scares in places that, without it, that scare won't happen.

So it is fun, in that you don't need to apologize for being loud or furious in what you're trying to do. With dramas these days, as you know, it is not in vogue for music to be that involved. It has to whisper behind the image. I think the coolest thing about horror films is that they allow you to write in a language that is more in line with those ideas we hear in a lot of modern orchestral concert music or experimental electronic music. Where else can I spend time trying to figure out ways in which to capture the sounds I have in my head, even it means I would have to go to a building site where they're using a pile-driver to smash a hole in the ground, record it, and transpose it down, so that it is r-e-a-l-l-y s-l-o-w [*mimics a slow-motion effect*], and use that sound to communicate this feeling of intense horror? It's wonderful, because it really gives you the opportunity to explore music as pure dramatic sound, in a way that you can't in any other type of movie.

You talked about simplicity in Bernard Herrmann's music. How important is simplicity to music in horror films?

Often in horror films there are two different approaches used in manipulating the musical material. During the extremely aggressive moments in a horror film, where there is a lot happening and the music has to be very aggressive, it can get very complex and we [composers] can utilize that "sound mass" concept, where you use the orchestra as a non-tonal powerhouse, or sounds that you're modifying electronically, to create this dense and aggressive environment.

That's where my head was at in the beginning of my career. I remember when I started working in horror films, I thought that the special thing that I was going to bring to pictures was this interest in using masses of sound to completely control the audio text of the picture, excluding dialogue. And to that end, a lot of my early stuff is just big blocks of sound, extremely thick. As I look back on it, I now think it was often way too thick for its own good. I now call those moments "sonic vomit" [*laughs*]!

So there was room for this idea I was exploring when I started. But then, when I worked with Clive Barker on *Hellraiser*, I think the greatest lesson that he brought to my attention—which was something I should have known—is the fact that the key to a successful horror score is often something that is extraordinarily simple.

This is, of course, the second approach, and there are great examples of it. The most obvious in your and my lifetimes are things like the theme to *Jaws* [1975]. That is a classic example of a composer who realizes that the most effective thing he can do is just use an ascending half-step in the bass register. [*Sings the* Jaws *theme*] It is just two notes. He's boiling it down to the smallest basics imaginable. *King Kong* [1933] was the same concept, but it was *de*scending half-steps [*sings the* King Kong *theme*]. In the *Halloween* movies we have [*sings the* Halloween *theme*] something as simple as a treble ostinato.

Of course, the Herrmann shower sequence in *Psycho* is nothing more than a downward gesture, starting in violins and working its way down to the lower strings [*sings the* Psycho *shower scene music*]—you know, that screeching effect. In Harry Manfredini's wonderful score for *Friday the 13th* [1980] and the subsequent films, he's got the delayed syllables "ma ma, ki ki," and I think that is pretty damn genius. He's boiled it down to non-pitched gestures, and you can't get any simpler than that.

Now, that is what Clive was looking for in *Hellraiser*. The stuff I first sent him was like a big mass of dark, clustery craziness. I thought, "Hey, man, here's the guy that wrote the excessively dark stories in the *Books of Blood* series. Of course he's going to be into this big mass of stuff." But no. He said, "I need a simple tune, because there's nothing more haunting than being seduced by something simple." That shouldn't have surprised me.

Why is it that simple gestures are the most effective in horror films? If we can imagine ourselves at a time where the only night-light that was available was the light from the moon and the stars, and if it was overcast you were in trouble because it was pitch black, you can re-create this feeling of being in solitude. Turn the lights off in a room and just sit there for twenty minutes in total darkness, without any distractions. You'll find that it is the tiniest little gestures that are the ones that are most frightening—a sudden popping or crunching sound. Any unexpected sound introduced into the environment can scare the crap out of you.

You can imagine being these guys out in the forest and hearing sounds, or believing that they are hearing sounds, out there in the darkness and being terrified by the howl of the animals, the wind rustling the branches, or the simple little crunch of the leaf and not knowing what it was. That can be terrifying.

The same thing has been passed down throughout the centuries, even though we live in a world comforted by the knowledge that we never have to worry about being in total darkness. I guess that's why people are attracted to going to a movie theater and seeing a horror film, especially black-and-white horror films, because they are able to reconnect with the same primal sense of fear that the cavemen felt. It was H. P. Lovecraft who said so perfectly, "The oldest and strongest emotion of mankind is fear, and the oldest and strongest kind of fear is fear of the unknown."

Clearly you're a fan of the genre, but are you content with the fact that it is what you're primarily known for, even though horror really only makes up a small percentage of your catalogue of work?

That is the big question: How do I answer that question with this being a book about horror movie music?

I hope you will answer it honestly.

I am going to answer it honestly. As honestly as someone can who is confused right now about this whole thing. I'm no spring chicken. If I was in my twenties, as I was when I did *Hellraiser*, the words that would be coming out of my mouth then would be totally different than the words that are coming out of my mouth now . . . which is simply this: I have a love-hate relationship with horror. It apparently is a genre that I was meant to contribute to.

As a kid, I cannot deny the fact that the holiday that consumed me and that I looked forward to with such high expectations and such wonder was Halloween. It was an incredible evening. So to pretend otherwise would be to deny something that I apparently had no control over. It was there from the beginning.

I was never a gigantic movie lover. I was a music-maker. I was a drummer, and then, when I got into writing [music] I didn't know that movies were going to be the life that I was going to pursue. And, most importantly, I didn't know that my first movie was going to be a horror film. I didn't choose that; it came my way when I was a student at UCLA.

Should I have been surprised? Probably not. And now that I think about it, though I had no control over it, as a child I was attracted to all this darkness, this invisible stuff that I was referring to earlier—the anticipation, the idea of carving a pumpkin, lighting it, staring into the pumpkin on Halloween. To me it was the conduit to that invisible world. There was some connection that I made. No one can understand it.

I never could articulate it, but the music on that Herrmann record that I found, before I was a writer myself, managed to capture that thing that I saw, the thing that I imagined, the thing that I was experiencing when I was staring into all those hand-carved pumpkins that used to get placed on everyone's doorstep come Halloween. We're talking about a time before the plastic plug-in ones you get now . . . millions of hand-carved pumpkins on doorsteps across the country.

So my attachment to the invisible world was always there, but I didn't choose that first movie, *The Dorm That Dripped Blood* [1982]. I hustled to get it, because I wanted a credit. Even I was surprised at being able to pull it off. Had it been a drama, had it had been *Citizen Kane* [1941], things would've been different [*laughs*], as it was the case with Bernard Herrmann. But it wasn't. It was a horror film and, of course, due to the fact that I did okay on that one, the same people came back to me for their next movie, which was a science-fiction/fantasy thriller. Then that brought me to the attention of Roger Corman at New World Pictures and New Line Pictures, and before you knew it I am doing *A Nightmare on Elm Street 2* [1985] and I am doing all these horror films. I kept getting these calls.

I had the great fortune of working with some of the best horror directors of the 1980s and 1990s: Clive Barker, Tobe Hooper, George Romero, and now more recently Scott Derrickson—a lot of really top-flight directors who have made major contributions to that genre. I'm proud of the music that I have had the opportunity to write for those movies.

I listen to music that has clusters in it, that is basically working in this language of what is called "sound mass." It is that whole Polish thing . . . the kind of language that people like [Krzysztof] Penderecki, [Witold] Lutosławski, [Iannis] Xenakis, György Ligeti, and the whole lot of them in the 1960s and 1970s were pursuing and some still are. There is nothing unhealthy about dissonance.

For me, when I heard the first piece of music that utilized sound mass, which was a piece by Penderecki called *Utrenja, The Entombment of Christ*, it felt like I was hearing God. This is the magical language that I believed was the sound of the universe. It was the kind of music that you would hear if you had split the earth and were making trips into outer space. [*Laughs*] If you made it up to heaven, you weren't going to be hearing angels strumming harps. You'd be hearing something that was along the lines of the music that you heard in *2001: A Space Odyssey* [1968], like *Requiem* and *Atmosphères* and *Lux Aeterna*—these Ligeti pieces they used.

That was the world that I really tuned in to, and the music that you can write in horror films. You get away with it because it is accompanying pictures that the audience chooses to go watch. If you took the same music and put it on the concert stage, without the benefit of having the connecting pictures, an audience might run out of the room with their fingers in their ears. But I stand by the music that I wrote for those movies.

Unfortunately, at the end of the day, it seems like horror films are the idiot bastard sons of Hollywood. They've always been there, they will always be there. In the history of Hollywood, they have saved companies from going out of business numerous times. They pay the bills, but come award season it is the first genre that Hollywood seems to want to pretend like they had nothing to do with, because it doesn't make them look like an artistic community or like people that are interested in art, not just commerce.

As you know, horror is the first genre to get kicked out. Sci-fi? For special effects, you've got a chance of getting a nomination, but for music, as a general rule, they are excluded. Comedies, of course, are the other genre of movies that seem to be excluded from the party.

So here's the thing . . . horror films are not the kinds of movies that the majority of the world are interested in returning to regularly. The majority of viewers would rather sit around the television and watch *Gone with the Wind* [1939], not "the great horror movie," whatever that might be.

I'm not sure I agree with that.

First of all, I'm talking about the majority of the world. The majority of the world will talk rhapsodically about how wonderful *Gone with the Wind* is. I'm talking about films that an entire family could sit down and watch. Very rarely will you be able to get an entire family to sit down and watch a horror film.

As a matter of fact, here's an interesting personal observation: I'm single, and when I go out and date, I've learned that when they ask, "What do you do?" I say, "I write music for movies." I've learned that whatever you do, don't tell them that you work on horror films—they don't want to hear that. If I tell them that I worked on *Hellraiser*, they'll go "Hell-what?!? Oh the one with the guy with the pins? Oh, no, I don't know your music. I would never watch something like that. Those kinds of films terrify me. I don't want to have nightmares."

There is a contingent of people who are devoted to it. There's that percentage of the world that eats these movies up, and there's enough of them that these movies can make a lot of money. But at the end of the day, it usually appeals to a teenage audience who are going to go to them on a Saturday night, with their boy- or girlfriends. They go through a period where they are interested and then they move on.

Now, you can disagree with me, but it's my perspective. You're asking me, as a guy who has done other movies, what do I feel about my involvement in horror films. In the final analysis, I feel that it has prohibited me. You get typecast, you get attached to a genre. It is inevitable, everyone does here. It so happens that it keeps coming up because I am thought of as the guy that did *Hellraiser* . . . and *then* maybe the guy that did *The Shipping News* [2001].

Those are two of maybe 125-plus movies that I've done, but they are probably the most visible ones. The horror films were often the most successful at the box office, and that's usually what you're identified with.

I am not thrilled that at this stage of my life, as I am getting older, my epitaph might read, "By the way, in case you don't know who this guy is, he's the one that did the score for *Hellraiser*." That part, I'm not thrilled with at all—nobody wants to be solely known for one thing that they did thirty years ago.

This is the unfortunate thing about film music, and I truly believe this: The value of the score ultimately seems to be thoroughly bound up in the perception of the movie for which it was written. If the movie is a hit, people will be inclined to want to be interested in the score. If they love the movie, they will probably like the score no matter how good or bad it is. If the film sinks, everyone goes down with the ship.

That is something that I have been struggling with as of late. It is what I call the *Titanic* principle. I have written all this music, and now I'm wondering if I made a mistake contributing all these years of my life to movies. Because at the end of the day, you and I both know that the American public seems to be most interested in songs! They want to hear someone singing to them with a lyric, and it has to be approximately three minutes long, with verses and choruses and someone playing a drum set or a drum machine. That is just the name of the game. So if you're trying to communicate in a language that people will ultimately remember, I think it is songs.

Most people don't remember horror scores. They can remember horror motifs or gestures, like the ones I mentioned earlier. If you walk down the street and sing the *Jaws* theme to anyone, they'll go, "*Jaws!*" That's all you need to do. That's a horror film for whom the music immediately communicates something to people—and that's fear! It is not like hearing the motif inspires that listener to want to kiss their partner.

Anyway, I don't want to sound negative here. That's not my intention.

Well, the reason why I asked the question is because I can imagine that it is something that you and many of the other composers I've talked to think about. Nobody likes to be typecast, especially professionally. But, at the same time, you may be identified most closely with horror because horror fans, in general, are more fanatical about the music in their favorite films than fans of other genres.

No, you're absolutely right. The horror film music fans are great. I don't know what age group they are; I'm guessing they are between seventeen and forty and primarily male. How many would you guess there are at any given time?

Oh, I don't know, but it is a very tight-knit and loyal community.

Ten thousand? Twenty thousand? It's not a million people. There are not a million people out there that love horror movie music.

You're right. Maybe it is not a huge audience compared with pop music, but when it comes to film music—and I could be completely off base—I think that the bulk of the people that love film music and collect it,are probably very interested in horror music and also the music of the science-fiction and fantasy genres. Goblin is a relatively obscure Italian band, but they can come to America and sell out shows.

I was there. Were you there for those?

Yes. I saw them twice here on the East Coast.

I know Claudio [Simonetti] pretty well, and he was kind enough, when they came to town, to introduce me to the audience. I just came by to watch them. But remember, Goblin is a rock band at the end of the day, it is not an orchestra—it is a band playing live. You know what I mean? That bridges the worlds; that fulfills the need of most concertgoing Americans. I can't speak for Europeans, but most Americans will put out their bucks to see a live rock band before they will a live orchestra. So Goblin is the best of both worlds. But you're right, when I saw them, it was packed. It was sold out. And for good reason: Their music is both fantastic and original. Theirs was a new way of approaching how music worked in genre films when they started emerging in the Seventies.

I'm sorry if I've put a damper on the conversation.

No, no, no. You said you wanted me to talk about it honestly.

I thank my lucky stars, on one hand, that I got that call from Clive Barker. How lucky I was that he did not go with the group Coil, who would've done a great job for it. But he got talked into hiring me.

Working on *Hellraiser* changed my life. All of a sudden Chris Young had an identity as a composer. And I'm thrilled that I did that movie. Don't misunderstand me: Of all the films that I have worked on, this film has more of a devoted following than anything I've done since. It was around my tenth movie score, and it keeps coming back to me even though I've done so many since. Maybe there is something among those others that is as good, and I believe there is, but those films didn't get the same kind of attention. And I'm talking about even in the horror genre! Personally, I think there are horror scores I've done that are more exciting, for my money, than the *Hellraiser* score.

Look, I am blessed. It is just that as I'm looking back on things, as one does when you get older, I think, "Gee, I never did connect with that one big fantastic Oscar-type dramatic director." I never found my Steven Spielberg or my Robert Zemeckis or Tim Burton or the Coen Brothers, or David Lynch. I never got that one director. I did get to work with some great directors, though, Clive and Sam Raimi, and many, many others.

You have worked with some of horror's most celebrated film-makers. I'd love to get your thoughts on working with them. For example, what can you tell me about working with Tobe Hooper?

Yes, Tobe Hooper. Well, again, the thing I learned from Clive was sim-plicity. He was the one that made me come to realize that the best way to succeed in enticing the audience into taking the step behind that curtain into a dark movie is by offering up something pretty simple.

The *Hellraiser* theme is pretty simple. In terms of Tobe Hooper, that was an extremely exciting experience for me. I was scared shitless, of course. . . . I came in on the second of a three-picture deal that he had with Cannon Films. The first one was a film called *Lifeforce* [1985], which was scored by Henry Mancini. It is a great movie with a great score. The one I was scoring was the second one, a remake of [the 1953] *Invaders from Mars* [1986], and the third was *The Texas Chainsaw Massacre 2* [1986].

I remember that by the time I started on the film, Tobe was already in preproduction on the *Texas Chainsaw Massacre* sequel, and he had to move on to start shooting. I don't even think I got through the whole spotting session with him, or he was available one day but not the second day. One thing that is for sure is, essentially, after whatever time we spent spotting that movie that was the last contact I had with him, because he was too busy getting ready for the next movie.

I asked him, "What kind of music do you want?" He had just finished *Poltergeist* [1982], but he said, "I want something that is more like what I used in *The Texas Chainsaw Massacre* [1974]—more 'sound' stuff." So

I thought, "Oh, wow! This is great. He's giving me permission to do exactly what I want to do here, what I've always dreamed of doing." I am very much into *musique concrète* [compositions made by manipulating, juxtaposing, and layering recorded sounds]; that was my big thing, recording sounds, be they from the natural world, mechanical world, or the acoustic world of instruments, and manipulating them somehow. That was my big thing!

So I went off and did this kooky score, which ultimately got thrown out. It was the first thrown-out score that I had ever written. I was devastated. But it was just too weird. In retrospect, I'm really proud of it and it's even been released; I reworked it for a CD years later, and in many ways it is my favorite score. That's one of a handful of scores I am proudest of, because if you ever hear the suite that I did that's on the CD, it is not quite like anything you've heard before [*laughs*] in movie music.

But unfortunately it got pitched, and I don't blame him [Hooper]. I don't think he was around. The people that were running the postproduction felt it was too weird, and I can't blame them, either. I think it may have been too much for the movie, and as I've humorously said, "What they were looking for was music *about* Mars, not *from* Mars."

Oh God, it was heartbreaking, and then I had to do the orchestral portion of the score. There wasn't much orchestra stuff in that film. It was mostly electronic, and the orchestra stuff was entirely different. It was definitely a situation where, "You just had your electronic stuff thrown out, make the orchestra sound like Jerry Goldsmith." I was, like, "Oh, I can try to do that!"

So the orchestra stuff stayed in the movie and the rest of my electronic score got thrown out. They got someone else to do the electronic elements. He did a great job. But here's the thing: Time has passed and I've had the good fortune to run into Tobe and talk to him about it, and he was ultimately not upset with me.

I had put that score in the basement and treated it like it was a mutant child that I had given birth to and never wanted to see again. I locked it away and tried to pretend it didn't happen. But it was through a gentleman named Thomas Karban that I went back to listen to it again. Thomas worked for Enigma Records and had gained the rights to release all of the Canon Films scores. He called me up and told me he wanted to release this so bad, and I said, "You've got to be kidding me."

Each score I write is like giving birth to a kid. Every one of these scores is a child, of sorts, and that happened to have been the first mutant one, the one that was thrown out, that I had to pretend didn't happen. Ultimately, as I said, I am proud of the version that got released on CD.

What was it like working with George Romero on *The Dark Half* **[1993]?**

I was absolutely thrilled to be working with George Romero. I mean, *fuck*! I was still pretty young; I was in my twenties or early thirties and thinking, "I'm working with George Romero!" It was another shit-kicker. I knew that George's movies, up to that point, had been mostly scored with library music or electronic music by the very talented composer-director John Harrison. I got pulled in, and I wanted to bring an orchestral approach to it. I was so worried that he wasn't going to be happy with it and, unfortunately, during the postproduction of that movie, something went terribly wrong with one of his ears. I can't remember if it was his left ear or right ear, but he lost his hearing when we were working.

So he wasn't able to fly to Munich, where we recorded the score, because of that ear problem. He heard it for the first time after the score was completed on the dub stage. Oh my God! I was, like, "What happens if he doesn't like it?" . . . That film ended up sitting on the shelf for a long time before it actually got released, but ultimately he liked it. I ran into him at one of these conventions a few years ago and I reintroduced myself to him. I hadn't seen him for years, and I was just terrified that he was going to say, "You son of a bitch . . . you ruined my movie." But actually he was extremely gracious and said that, in retrospect, he was very happy with the score.

How did he convey to you what he was looking for?

That's interesting that you should ask that question. I remember going to the first viewing of that movie, and there was temp music in it. And I remember when the lights came up, I thought, "Oh my God. Why the hell did they hire me? I'm not going to do this."

Now, I had sent him a demo. I remember that I put together some music and called it "The Dark Half Suite." (This is back in the days of the cassette. If you were trying to get a job, you gave it your best shot and you put it on audiocassette, and whomever you sent it to listened to it in their car or something.) So I did something called "The Dark Half Suite," which was orchestral music. I put together some cues that I had already written, and then I did some other things and put together a continuous piece of music. He really liked it. That's how I got the job.

I actually remember hearing that his first choice was Henry Mancini. He wanted Henry Mancini to score that movie, but the studio wouldn't let him. They said, "No, no. We need some guy that has done some horror movies before." I think the studio believed that, by doing an orchestral score, it was going to increase the production value of the movie.

Unfortunately, I really can't remember how he communicated to me what he was looking for. I think he just communicated to me dramatically what he was hoping for, and then I translated that into what I thought was the best thing for the movie, accommodating his vision, but using an orchestra. I do have memories of the studio being very eager for me to use an orchestra, but I think he was okay with that.

I may be wrong on this, but I think I read that after that movie, he decided that he didn't want to do any Hollywood movies anymore. I remember he wasn't happy about the way things were going with the financial aspects of the film. Even when I was scoring it, he was telling me, "The finale is just temporary; we're going to reshoot this." And they never did reshoot it.

I'm sorry that the experience for him wasn't as positive as it should've been. I adore the movie, and to have had the opportunity to work with him was a remarkable gift. Hopefully, I wrote a score that he can go back to and, watching the film all these years later, he can say, "Chris didn't ruin my film [*laughs*]."

Please tell me about working with Sam Raimi. I love your *Drag Me to Hell* [2009] score.

Thank you. Working with Sam Raimi has been absolutely spectacular in so many ways. First and foremost, I wanted to work with Sam after I saw *The Evil Dead* [1980]. I said, "Oh God, oh my God! I sure-as-shit wished I'd scored that one! I damn well want to work with this guy!"

I thought that the two of us would be perfect bedfellows, I really did. I thought, "I understand the world that he is living in. I understand the vision that he has." And I could see the two of us meeting at some point. At the time, during *The Evil Dead*, he was using a composer from his hometown that he knew, Joseph LoDuca, who is a fantastic composer; he did a great job on *The Evil Dead* movies. Sam later connected with Danny [Elfman] for some of his bigger movies.

It was on a film called *The Gift* [2000], where Danny was not available, and the picture editor, Bob Murawski, who is a fantastic picture editor (he won an Academy Award with his wife, Chris Innis, for editing *The Hurt Locker*), has always been a big fan of mine, and he said, "You know what, Sam? You better check out this Chris guy."

Sam and I got along immediately. I went in for the interview, and we were both smokers at the time. We started talking, and I saw the cigarette pack bulge in his pocket and he saw the one in mine and we both decided, "Why don't we finish this interview while having a cigarette outside." So we went out for a smoke and we got along extremely well. I love his sense of humor. We were both able to laugh about similar things.

I record all of my dialogues with directors. Whenever I'm in a room with a director, I will get permission and then I will record everything they say. The thing that is remarkable about Sam is that he knows exactly what he's looking for. You talk about a director giving the composer such precise instructions, without saying, "And by the way, you better put a trombone on that line or I'm going to shoot you." He's not that specific. But dramatically, he's very focused about what he's looking for.

Figuring out how to translate the concepts that lurk in the brain of a director, that float around in the invisible world of quasi-notes that I imagine inhabit the mind of a non-composer, is one of the great challenges for film composers, and it's always a super-high for me when I finally manage to do it.

I've heard such positive things about the *Drag me to Hell* score. I didn't recognize it as being such an important score myself, until I started getting such positive reviews. The hook on that one is the idea of using the violin to depict the Devil. For movies or the concert world, or even popular music, the fiddle has always been considered the instrument of the Devil. The thing we tried to do, and it was something I promoted to Sam, was the idea that, whenever possible, rather than thinking of the violin as being performed by a normal human being, let's pretend he's playing the violin with ten fingers and he can use his tail to bow it. That way we can do things with a violin that one player can't do. There's moments where there is multitracking of the violin, and it gets to be able to do things that one violin can't do. And of course, the picture is so over-the-top that the music was allowed to be fun and loony. It was sort of tongue-in-cheek. It all worked out.

That movie has such a specific Raimi tone. I think that one of the reasons why people may like that score so much is because you managed to really capture that Raimi tone so perfectly.

Well, I am glad you feel that way. I remember for the first show-and-tell (I have that on tape, and sometimes I show it to my class), I wrote three thematic options for that main theme, which is first presented in the main title. I played him Option One, then Option Two, and then Option Three, and everyone—my music editor and my assistants at the time— were convinced that Option One was the best of the lot.

I'm never really good at knowing which is the best, because they are all like my children to me, they are all equally valuable. So I played Option One, and he was positive about it, but I knew it wasn't really clicking. Up comes Option Two, and he's enthusiastic, and Bob [Murawski] says, "Oh that's it, that's this movie. That's the one." And he said that what he liked best about it was that it reminded him of the old Universal [Studios] *Wolf Man* movies.

I played him the third one, but it was sort of a waste of time, because it was decided right then and there that Option Two was going to be the theme of that movie. And pretty much what you hear in the movie is almost exactly the translation of that mockup that I prepared.

You've worked on several sequels, including sequels to films that you originally scored—for example, *Hellraiser II*. Was that score easier than the first because you had already done it once, or was it more difficult because there was pressure for it to be bigger and better?

That was my first sequel to my own score. I would say, without a shadow of a doubt, that I was terrified. What you don't want to do, of course, is deliver a score that's worse than the first. And I thought there is no better way to demonstrate whether or not I, as a composer, had grown since the first film. So I was terrified.

Historically, in Hollywood there are examples of not only sequels but also trilogies where each score seems to get progressively better. In the world of horror, there is Jerry Goldsmith's music for the *Omen* trilogy, and in the world of fantasy there is the *Star Wars* trilogy and the *Indiana Jones* trilogy by John Williams, to name just a few. Those are the ones that I felt I was competing with. . . . "I need to outdo that one or I'm screwed." "Can I do it?" "Do I really have the talent?" "Can I make it better?"

Fortunately, I had a couple of things going in my favor. One, they had more money for the score on the second film. Again, I didn't really make much money off these movies—just a tiny bit, if any at all. It was more about making sure the score was bigger and better-sounding. So, right off the bat I knew I could get a bigger orchestra and I knew I wanted to use a choir. I could expand the size of the group, which was helpful. In the early days, I would sink as much money into the scores themselves as possible, because I saw them as an investment in my future.

The first film, as you know, is a sick love story that takes place in one location, basically inside a house. I wrote that music for a moderately large orchestra, but *Hellbound* [*Hellraiser II*] was a gothic story of death and destruction, which would allow me to get really fat and bombastic. So I was aspiring to have the size of the sound noticeably larger, trying to get more of that "wall of sound" that I was always hoping to accomplish in my early films scores—a sort of Phil-Spector-of-horror-film-scoring concept.

The second thing I had going in my favor was that my instructions on that were different. Tony Randel was the director, and he turned to me and said, "I want the score to be a celebration of horror. I want it to sound like it's the new and improved *Hellraiser*. I want it big, I want it ballsy. I want it to bash you in the face."

And so, right from the get-go, the main title sequence really allowed me to establish this new bigger sound. If you recall, *Hellbound* starts with a montage of scenes from the first *Hellraiser*, and the sound is mixed in mono with cues from the first film. Then, when that montage is finished and the first title appears, "New World Pictures," the new score hits in stereo to herald the new and improved *Hellraiser II*. That was the fun thing, because it was exclusively the music that gave the film that wider sound and bigger feeling than the first.

You've also worked on sequels where you didn't score the original film and you've had to fill the shoes of some pretty great scores

and composers. On *A Nightmare on Elm Street 2: Freddy's Revenge* [1985], for example, what was it like following Charles Bernstein's iconic score for the first film? What kind of direction did you get when you came into it? What were your goals in trying to bring some new musical life to the sequel of a successful horror film?

It's interesting you should mention that score, because I just spent the last couple of weeks reworking, revisiting, and remixing it, putting it into a sixteen-minute continuous piece. Some of it's old, some of it's new, but that's become my new thing: My new obsession is going back to old scores, rethinking them, and seeing if there's somehow a way I can reshape them into a listening experience that is not so attached to the films, something that is different than the way they were originally offered on CD. Which for me, today, generally means putting them into a suite format as opposed to a series of unconnected short tracks. I just did that with the *A Nightmare on Elm Street 2* score, and in fact I was never a fan of that score. It shows the eagerness of someone who's young.

I was thrilled to have been included on that movie. That was a big project for me. At the time, it was a hot series, and to have been given the invite was a special honor. They had very little money. I sunk everything into the score, and I remember that my instructions were, "Whatever you do, don't do anything like what Charles Bernstein did." And I was, like, "What do you mean by that?"

Well, they didn't want a synth score—they felt like they had been ripped off or something. It was one of the early home synth scores. They had given him money, and they figured, "Wait a second, he put this money in his pocket. If we're going to give the composer a certain amount of money, we want to see some bang for our buck." So, I made a promise to Bob Shaye, the owner of New Line Pictures at the time, that I could get him a certain number of musicians live in a room and he would get himself a full-blown orchestra score.

I remember we recorded that score at Mad Hatter, which was Chick Corea's studio. Now, of course that studio was never meant to record an orchestra—it was meant to record jazz combos—but I got it for a really good price. It was located far away from the center of Hollywood, so I didn't have to worry about the [musicians] union busting me. And I stuffed that place with more musicians than it ever had held before or ever had since. I think it may be closed now, but they kept on reminding me that I set a record. I mean, there were people sitting on top of each other almost.

And when Bob Shaye came in, I have a distinct memory of him going up to the glass window that separated the booth from the stage and actually counting the heads, to see if I came through with whatever number it was that I promised him. And I remember him turning around and smiling at me because I hadn't cheated him. I stuffed that room with whomever I could get. It was mostly UCLA students, because there was no money for it.

As for the score itself, first of all, they should have rehired Charles Bernstein. I believe that. He set the tone in the first score, and indeed it has become the identity of that series. Of all the horror movie series that came out in the Eighties, including *Halloween*, *Friday the 13th*, and *Hellraiser*, *A Nightmare on Elm Street* is the only one that doesn't have a real strong musical personality. I mean, it's constantly changing from film to film, as I recall. I could be wrong, but I don't think they ever used the same composer twice, and I don't think they ever asked Charles Bernstein back. They did ask me back, but I was unable to do it.

I feel sorry for Charles, because that series should have become his entirely. Ultimately, he has come up the victor on that one, because when people talk about the scores for the series, they will say, "Oh, gee, you know, Charles was probably the best of the lot."

But I must say that, now that I've gone back to that [*A Nightmare on Elm Street 2*] score and remixed it and put it into suite form, I feel a lot better about it now than I did years and years ago. I'm not saying I'm proud of that score, but I'm feeling a lot better about it now than I did. Unfortunately, it doesn't really have a theme that stands out. I don't think they really wanted me to write a theme for the *Nightmare* series. It was more like, "Set up the storyline." So I scored it as if it were a separate entity. At least, at a minimum, they should have forced me to use his theme.

Are you revisiting these things for a specific project, or just for yourself?

I revisited that one because Varèse Sarabande [a record label that specializes in film score recordings] is releasing a box set of all the scores. They approached me, and I said, "Listen guys, I'd like to go back and rethink this music and do something with it, if that's okay." And they were really excited about that. So, there you have it.

Since its release, *A Nightmare on Elm Street 2* has become a little bit notorious for being thought of as an allegory about a closeted gay teenage boy. Did you read any of that into it when you were doing the score?

You know what, not one bit. That shows you how naive I was. I wasn't thinking about that, I don't think anyone was thinking about that. I don't remember that coming up.

You also did the score for *The Fly II* [1989].

Right. I would have to say that was the same situation. The director of *The Fly II* was Chris Walas, who was the Academy Award–winning makeup artist and special effects artist on *The Fly* [1986]. He was offered the chance to direct the sequel and he really wanted me to do the score, and when I came on board it was the same thing: It was, like, "Don't worry about doing what Howard Shore did."

He hired me because he loved the score to *Hellbound* [*Hellraiser II*]. They were looking for something that was comparable to *Hellbound*, and that became sort of an ongoing request. For a while after *Hellbound* or *Hellraiser*, the guys that would hire me wanted that "sound." But I don't think the music in *The Fly II* is exactly like *Hellbound*, because the story is far from *Hellbound*.

I would say the nice thing about *The Fly II* was that it's a classic monster story, a good-guy-inside-of-a-monster's-body story, like Frankenstein. It is the classic horror-tragedy. In this case it's the son of the Fly—this kid turns into a fly even though, of course, he has no desire to.

You also worked with Chris Walas on *The Vagrant* [1992]. That is a really interesting score.

Thank you very much. I would have to say that's a very "different" score. It's not quite like anything else and certainly nothing like anything I had done before. There have been moments in some scores that I've done since that have been like it, but it's a stand-alone score in my output and it's one that, I cannot tell a lie, I'm proud of . . . but only because I was in a situation where Chris was at a loss about what the score should be for that movie.

It's a black comedy, and they just had no success in trying to find the right score to temp it. Horror scores were too over-the-top and took the humor out of it. The comedy scores, of course, took the horror out of it. And I think they even tried some synth drone scores, which took *everything* out of it.

So I was left on my own, and I said, "How much would you like me to try to do something different here?" And they were really supportive of me trying to do something different. I think one of the best compliments I ever got was from Mel Brooks himself, who said, "Before your music was added to this movie, I wasn't exactly sure what kind of a movie it was, but this music helped define the film."

Black comedies are tough films to make and certainly tough films to score, because their solutions are not quite as obvious as horror films or comedy films. They're somewhere in between, and the language of the music needs to reflect that. Even Jerry Goldsmith, who was not one to give out compliments very often, complimented that score. And God, of course, I was dumbfounded when he told me that he liked that score.

It is very unique. Do you remember how you came up that sound palette?

I do remember that I started with the main title. This is almost always the case: When I'm working on a movie, I focus on the bookends—the main title and the end title. Of course end titles now, for the most part, are nothing more than an edited suite of cues from the movie that are put together by the music editor, which I find extremely dissatisfying. Back in the old days, a composer would round up the movie with a meaningful end credit. John Williams still insists on preserving that school of thought, and I'm assuming that every film he's done has had an end credit that he's written. I still hold on to that. It's not very popular, but I still do it.

And of course, when I deliver that cue or when the cue is put up, they're, like, "Why do you want to record an end title? We'll just let the music editor take care of it." I will say, "Let me just try it. I just wrote it. Can we just run through it?" They go, "Jesus! Well, okay." Then of course I play it and they go, "Incredible. Why did you only make it two minutes?" I said, "Well, I thought you didn't want it." "We need four minutes of it man. It's great."

In the case of *The Vagrant*, I definitely started with the main title, which was a series of percussion patterns. They're like building blocks, and I worked out the instrumentation for each one of those blocks as an experiment for what I thought the sound of the movie might be. I guess, when I finished creating these building blocks—this collection of maybe eight or nine different ideas—I thought, "Well, you know, I'll just string these together." That's what it was, stringing together building blocks. It's like creating a necklace of aural beads that you just shift around. And as I recall, the night before we recorded it, Chris called me up and said, "I got some bad news. We added, like, forty seconds of credits onto the main title." I said, "It's the first thing I'm recording tomorrow!" He goes, "Well, you know, I'm sorry." So, I just moved some of these blocks around to fit the new time.

All those rhythmic ideas were written on paper and then prerecorded. Being an ex-drummer, I figured out the logic of the rhythmic patterns and the sonorities of the instruments that were going to be used to create these rhythmic patterns, and then I added some pitched material on top of them. So most of the ostinato portions of the percussion were recorded earlier and then played back while recording the chamber group live. Once I solved the problem of the main title, everything else fell into place with the rest of the score.

I'd like to talk about *Sinister* [2012], because it is such a different kind of horror score than I think most people are used to hearing from you.

With *Sinister*, I was lucky—thanks to [the director] Scott Derrickson— to have the opportunity to do something which I'd wanted to do for years. *Sinister* is a reflection of the state of the art of electronics and electronic aesthetics that are relevant to what is going on today. I have always had an affinity for electronics. As I've said . . . my primary interest in the earliest days of my work in monster movies was this thing called *musique concrète*, where you use the microphone to record sounds and then modify them using various studio techniques. So it is a world that my brain has always been comfortable living in, and a world that I would've wanted to use more often had I been given the chance.

But really, after *Hellraiser* and the a suspense film that I did called *Jennifer 8* [1992], it sort of became understood that when you hire Chris, he's going to have to use strings. I remember trying to encourage the directors to give me the opportunity to let go of that string stuff. "Let me try to do an electronic score." "No, no, no. We're not coming to you for the electronic stuff. If we want electronic stuff we'll go get a guy that does that. We want you to do that *Hellraiser* stuff." And so I found that that was the recurring request: "Chris, bring those strings in. That's what we're looking for."

Look, I love writing for strings, and there are things that only they can do successfully. There are a lot of synth scores that try to accomplish a lot of those crazy contemporary techniques, extended techniques, ideas that strings can do so successfully. But ultimately, in *Sinister*, there wasn't the money to do anything with an orchestra, period. It was a financial consideration . . . it was never going to get recorded by a live orchestra—and, by the way, there's no point in the synths trying to act like a live orchestra. So screw it!

Scott said, "You've always wanted to work with electronic sounds? Here's your chance." It was right for the movie. I don't think that putting an orchestra score in that movie would've worked. Finally a situation came where I was able to accommodate something that I had been trying to do for years—really years. So it was refreshing to me, and to those like yourself, who were actually listening to it. I get comments like, "This score is one of the scariest things I've ever heard!" So that's pretty cool.

I've often humorously said, with *Jennifer 8*, after that became somewhat of a hit, I kept on getting asked to repeat that. So *Jennifer 8* quickly became Jennifer 9, which became Jennifer 10, which became Jennifer 11 . . . a series of movies right after that where I was being asked to continue to repeat that sound.

How did you discover your theme for *Jennifer 8*?

I was hired at the last minute to replace a score by an extremely gifted and famous film composer who had apparently written a score that no one was happy with. I find that in situations like that, where a score is being thrown out, it's usually because there is no communication going on between the composer and the director, and I think that's precisely what happened. I don't think that the director, Bruce Robinson, wanted him there to begin with; he wanted *me* there, but I wasn't a big enough star. It was a Paramount movie and they just weren't comfortable with hiring me, and I get it. That makes perfect sense.

But then I did get hired at the last minute. I go off and I write the main theme. This is before you did synth mockups, so I did a piano demo recording of this theme, but I made the mistake of overloading the demo with everything the orchestra was going to do. It was a multitracked piano. It was too dense.

And when I went to the meeting, I thought it was just going to be the director and me alone, but I get to the studio and there are six or seven people there. It turns out they were there temp-dubbing the movie. They stopped the dub and they put the cassette up (it's back in the days when we had audiocassettes, not CDs), they play it, and I knew right away—you can tell within 0.077777 seconds that you've missed it. I knew immediately that it just wasn't going over.

The thing finishes, and there's dead silence in the room. The director pulls me aside, whispers a few things in my ears along the lines of, "Come on, man, I know you can do this." He was really supportive: "I know you can do this, but this is not it." He gave me a list of things to think about, and he basically sent me on my merry way.

I'm sure he was probably left in a room full of executives and producers and saying, "Listen, don't worry about it, he'll come through on this one. I'm very confident this is going to work out." And as I was driving back home, I pulled up to the intersection of Santa Monica Boulevard and Wilshire, which is right by the Beverly Wilshire Hotel, and there's a large fountain right there at the intersection. I remember looking over my right shoulder at the fountain while being in a state of panic, and then *bam!*—the theme came into my head, and I thank the Lord I had my cassette machine with me, because I sang it into it.

I came back to my little dumpy room and within fifteen minutes had it worked out. I called the director, played it to him over the phone, and he said, "That's my theme, you got it! That's the one!" So a bad story had a happy ending.

You are one of the few composers that seem to take some time to name the tracks on your soundtrack albums. You've picked some interesting ones, like "Rat Slice Quartet." I was wondering if you

could talk a little bit about naming tracks. Why is that important to you?

It's interesting you should mention the "Rat Slice Quartet" title, because I remember getting a phone call from Clive himself telling me how much he loved that name and begging me not to change it under any circumstance!

I was raised in the world of rock and jazz. My entrance into the world of music was through what was being played on the radio, and the titles that songwriters and jazz composers would come up with had something about them that was not just entirely functional. So I just was never comfortable with offering up music from the movies I worked on and simply giving them the same titles that were on the cue sheets—which are generally extremely functional titles like "The Battle Part One" or "The Monster Pursues the Young Boy" or "Pete Makes Love," this kind of stuff. There have been examples of other film composers who would come up with catchy titles for their tunes or tracks, like Mancini. He didn't call his stuff simply "The Dog," "The Monster," "The House." He gave them witty titles.

With Mancini and with what was going on in the pop music world and the jazz world, titles were important. I didn't want to seem pompous about it, because most film composers put functional titles on their cues. And why wouldn't they? It describes the scene that the music was written for, for the fans that want to identify the track with that scene.

Forget that! I try to structure the music on the CD in the most appealing manner musically. I've always thought that a good CD of a score is like a guy who's doing a song and dance on the stage. The curtain opens up, you want to get on the stage with a bang, do your song and dance, and make sure you get off with a bang before they boo you off the stage. Don't overextend your welcome.

I find that a title that is more than just a functional title can bring more pleasure to the experience of listening to a piece of music. Most of the titles I use have very little to do with the movie, though sometimes they do. This sometimes confuses the directors, but ultimately they get on board with it. I still do this. I still try to make the titles interesting, whenever it is possible.

And of course the one thing that I do—and it started on my very first album, much like the way Alfred Hitchcock would do little hidden cameos in his movies—I like to stick little hidden cameos of other film composers' names whose music I have admired into my titles. In pretty much all the CDs, if it's appropriate, you will find the name of a film composer hidden somewhere. When it began it was done, really, in sort of a stupid manner, probably too blatantly—you know, like "Jerry's Gold Myth," or "Her Man Awaits." Come on now! I think some of the puns have gotten kind of tough as I've gotten further into it, and some composers have even appeared twice by accident.

There are only a handful of soundtracks that don't have those hidden cameos, because the nature of the titling of the music didn't allow for it. *Hard Rain* [1998] was an example of a score that was released on a label, and I presented my wacky titles to them and they said, "We're not going to accept these." I said, "What do you mean you're not going to accept them?" They said, "No—we want titles, we want real titles. We want real titles that correspond to the scenes in the movie, so that the fans will know what they're hearing." And I went, "You mean things like 'The Bridge,' like 'The Truck?'" And they said yes. So the titles on that CD are just awful. I went, "Well, fuck it! That's what they want, that's what they'll get." And so I didn't put a composer's name on that one.

But, yeah, that's sort of my thing with titles.

I was wondering if you have any wisdom or advice you could give readers who are looking to pursue film scoring as a profession.

Actually, outside of writing movie music and music in general, the thing I get so excited about doing is teaching and mentoring young composers that are aspiring to get into the movie scene. To that end, I actually have a housing facility that I've set up for composers who are moving to Los Angeles, who have nowhere else to go and stay at.

I teach at USC and I travel around the world and teach at other places, but most importantly I connect with composers and try to encourage them to pursue a career in film music if they think that is what they want to do. I try to advise them to trust their instincts and make the commitment to move to Los Angeles if they are serious, instead of going through life wishing that they might've made the move.

So, to all the composers out there reading this book and who are on the fence or contemplating whether or not they should make the commitment to come out here . . . do it. This really is the place you have to be. It is Los Angeles, which is the center of movie music . . . on this planet for sure. There might be some film scoring going on the planet Mars, but I don't know anything about that. So this is the place you have to be. . . . I wish my hand could emerge from the page and grab theirs and yank them out here to Los Angeles to try to make a go of it.

The wonderful thing about being a composer is that, unlike acting, you don't have to worry about being in big trouble if you haven't made your mark by the age of twenty-seven or thirty or thirty-five. We're on the other side of the screen. In the history of film music, there have been composers who have not made their mark or even started working in movies until they were well into their forties or even fifties. So it can happen at any time. Don't think that if you haven't scored a big movie by the time you're in your twenties that you're over the hill. That is preposterous. Ultimately, if the love is there, you should commit yourself to pursuing film music. Only you will know it, if the love is there, and if it is . . . do it!

ACKNOWLEDGMENTS

I'D LIKE TO ACKNOWLEDGE AND THANK all of the filmmakers, writers, artists, musicians, and composers who have inspired me throughout the years, especially the fourteen amazing composers who graciously contributed to the creation of this book. I express my deepest appreciation for their time, effort, support, enthusiasm, patience, and honesty. I'd also like to thank the representatives and assistants who helped make some of these interviews possible, including Sean Sobczak, Chanon Billington, Elias Kennedy, Murat Selcuk, Nick Kenworthy-Browne, and the good people at Soundtrack Music Associates, Rain Talent, and Beat Records Company Publishing Group.

I'd like to thank Jim Fox of Silman-James Press and my agent, Doug Grad, for believing in this project and me.

Special thanks also goes to my family and friends, without whose support this book would have never been completed: my mother, Rose, who during my teenage years patiently sat through more viewings of *The Texas Chainsaw Massacre* (1974), *The Thing* (1982), *The Fly* (1986), *Repulsion* (1965), and *The Evil Dead* (1981)—among many other films—than any mother should ever have to; Rob, the best stepfather ever; my best friend and pillar, Lynne; my father, Ron, who introduced me to the wonderful world of film music and the films of John Carpenter; my stepmother, Vicki; my brother, Mark, and his wife, Dawn Marie; my amazing nephew Dustin; Aaron Lenchner and Dion Baia, the two best creative partners and sounding boards a guy could ever want; Stephen Altobello, Adam Hirsch, and John Cribbs, who lent invaluable feedback regarding this book when I needed it; my musical hero and friend John Pizzarelli, who introduced me to my agent and is always willing to help out when he is able; and, lastly, the brothers Hastings, Dave and Steve, whose shared love for horror film music is only one of the many reasons I consider them my spiritual brothers.

About the Author

J. Blake Fichera has taught film studies at the State University of New York at Purchase and has contributed as a writer and interviewer to several noteworthy film and music-related publications and websites, including *Video Watchdog* magazine, Fangoria.com, Dreadcentral.com, Podwits.com, and *American Blues News*. He has been a professional film/television editor and producer since 2001 and cohosts the film-themed podcast *Saturday Night Movie Sleepovers*. He is also a gigging musician in the New York City area and a New York Blues Hall of Fame inductee. He lives in Manhattan.